Jenny Parsons

with Nick Witherick

speakout

Pre-intermediate
Teacher's Resource Book

TEACHER'S RESOURCE BOOK CONTENTS

STUDENTS' BOOK CONTENTS

LISTENING/DVD	SPEAKING	WRITING
listen to people talk about what makes them happy	talk about what makes you happy; ask and answer personal questions	
	talk about relationships; talk about past events	write about an important year in your life; improve your use of linking words
	start/end a conversation; sound natural	
BBC Blackpool: watch an extract from a drama	talk about important people in your life	write a competition entry about your best friend
listen to people talk about how companies motivate staff	talk about work/studies	write an email about work experience
	talk about dangerous jobs; talk about work routines	
listen to interviews about jobs	discuss likes/dislikes; respond and ask more questions to keep the conversation going	
BBC The Money Programme: Dream Commuters: watch an extract from a documentary about commuting	describe your work/life balance	write a web comment about work/life balance
listen to a radio programme about young people having fun	talk about your future plans	write an email invitation
	ask and answer questions for a culture survey	
listen to four phone calls	make and receive phone calls; learn to manage phone problems	
BBC Holiday 10 Best: Cities: watch an extract from a travel programme about visiting Barcelona	plan a perfect day out	write an email invitation
listen to two people describing their secret talents	talk about your talents	write a competition entry about talents; check your work and correct mistakes
	talk about what you did at school; talk about obligations	
listen to a radio programme giving advice about language learning	give and to respond to advice	
BBC Horizon: Battle Of The Brains: watch an extract from a documentary about brain power	discuss five top tips for tests	write advice for a problem page
	describe journeys	
listen to a radio programme about travel items	talk about travel	write an email describing a trip or weekend away; learn how to use sequencers
listen to a man describing a special place in a city; understand and follow directions in a city	ask for and give directions; learn to show/check understanding	
BBC Full Circle: watch an extract from a travel programme about a trip across the Andes	present ideas of a journey of a lifetime for an award	write an application for an award
	talk about your health	
listen to a radio interview with a food expert	discuss food preferences; make predictions for the future	write about food; improve your sentence structure
listen to conversations between a doctor and her patients; predict information	explain health problems	
BBC The Two Ronnies: watch an extract from a short comedy about squash	ask and answer questions about sports for a survey	write about a sporting memory

COMMUNICATION BANK page 160   AUDIO SCRIPTS page 168

STUDENTS' BOOK CONTENTS

LISTENING/DVD	SPEAKING	WRITING
listen to a radio programme about two women who changed their lives	talk about a life change	write about a decision which changed your life; learn to use paragraphs
	discuss when you might tell a lie	
understand short predictable conversations	find out and check information	
BBC My Family And Other Animals: watch an extract from the beginning of a film	talk about a new experience	write a blog/diary about a new experience
listen to a radio programme about great investments	talk about a product that people should invest in; how to describe objects, places, things	write a description of a product; add emphasis to your writing
listen to a discussion about salaries	talk about quantity; discuss which professions should earn the most money	
listen to conversations in shops	describe things	
BBC The Money Programme: The World According To Google: watch an extract from a documentary about the success of Google	present a business idea	write an idea for a business investment
listen to a radio programme about environmental issues	talk about the environment	write about your views on the environment; notice similar sounding words
	talk about nature	
listen to people discussing a quiz	make guesses about pictures; learn to give yourself time to think	
BBC Joanna Lumley In The Land Of The Northern Lights: watch an extract from a documentary about seeing the Northern Lights	talk about an amazing natural place	write a travel blog
listen to conversations about different cities	discuss qualities of different places; talk about where you live	write a letter about an issue; use formal expressions
	talk about crime and punishment; decide on the punishments to fit the crimes	
listen to people complaining	roleplay a complaint; learn to sound firm but polite	write an email of complaint
BBC Power To The People: The Zimmers Go To Hollywood: watch an extract from a documentary about the world's oldest rock band	talk about an important issue or problem	write a web comment about an issue
listen to people talk about how they keep in touch	talk about things you have done recently	write a travel blog entry; improve your use of pronouns
	discuss computer games; talk about your future	
listen to a discussion about the internet	give your opinion on different issues; learn to disagree politely	
BBC Panorama: Is TV Bad For My Kids? watch an extract from a documentary about children and television	talk about technology you couldn't live without	write a web comment about your opinion of technology
	report other people's speech; talk about your favourite film	
listen to people talking about being famous	talk about hypothetical situations	write a profile of someone famous; improve your use of paragraphs
listen to people making requests	make requests and offers; ask for more time	
BBC Lewis Hamilton: Billion Dollar Man: watch an extract from a documentary about Lewis Hamilton	talk about your dreams and ambitions	write a web comment about your childhood ambitions

COMMUNICATION BANK page 160　　　　AUDIO SCRIPTS page 168

Before we started writing *Speakout*, we did a lot of research to find out more about the issues that teachers and students face and how these can be addressed in a textbook for the 21st century. The issues that came up again and again were motivation, authentic content and the need for structured speaking and listening strategies.

As English teachers, we know how motivating it can be to bring the real world into the classroom by using authentic materials. We also know how time consuming and difficult it can be to find authentic content that is truly engaging, at the right level and appropriate for our students. With access to the entire archive of the BBC, we have selected some stunning video content to motivate and engage students. We have also created tasks that will encourage interaction with the materials while providing the right amount of scaffolding.

We realise that the real world is not just made up of actors, presenters and comedians, and 'real' English does not just consist of people reading from scripts. This is why *Speakout* brings real people into the classroom. The Video podcasts show people giving their opinions about the topics in the book and illustrate some of the strategies that will help our students become more effective communicators.

Speakout maximises opportunities for students to speak and systematically asks them to notice and employ strategies that will give them the confidence to communicate fluently and the competence to listen actively. While the main focus is on speaking and listening, we have also developed a systematic approach to reading and writing. For us, these skills are absolutely essential for language learners in the digital age.

To sum up, we have tried to write a course that teachers will really enjoy using; a course that is authentic but manageable, systematic but not repetitive – a course that not only brings the real world into the classroom, but also sends our students into the real world with the confidence to truly 'speak out'!

From left to right: Frances Eales, JJ Wilson, Antonia Clare and Steve Oakes

STUDENTS' BOOK

- Between 90 and 120 hours of teaching material
- Language Bank with reference material and extra practice
- Photo Bank to expand vocabulary
- Audioscripts of the class audio

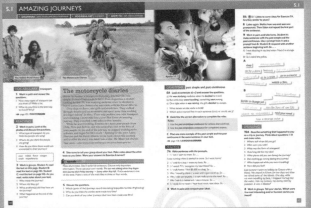

CLASS AUDIO CDs

- Audio material for use in class
- Test audio for the Mid-course and End of Course Tests

DVD & ACTIVE BOOK

- DVD content
- Digital Students' Book
- Audio, video and Video podcasts

WORKBOOK

- Grammar and vocabulary
- Functional language
- Speaking and listening strategies
- Reading, writing and listening
- Regular review and self-study tests

AUDIO CD

- Audio material including listening, pronunciation and functional practice

MYSPEAKOUTLAB

- Interactive Workbook with hints and tips
- Unit tests and Progress Tests
- Mid-course and End of Course Tests
- Video podcasts with interactive worksheets

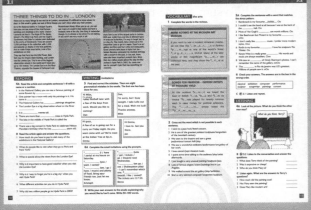

TEACHER'S RESOURCE BOOK

- Teaching notes
- Integrated key and audioscript
- Four photocopiable activities for every unit
- Mid-course and End of Course Test

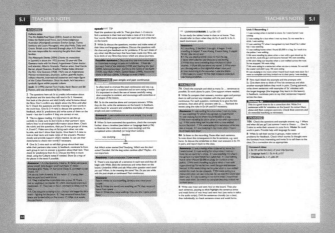
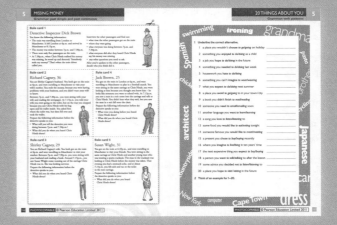

SPEAKOUT ACTIVE TEACH

- Integrated audio and video content
- Video podcasts
- Test master containing all course tests
- Answer reveal feature
- Grammar and vocabulary review games
- A host of useful tools
- Large extra resources section

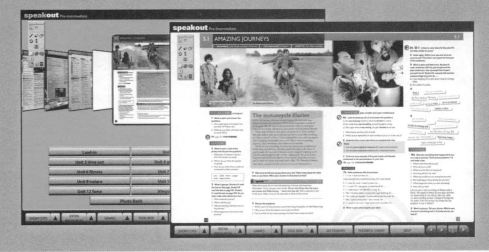

SPEAKOUT WEBSITE

- Information about the course
- Sample materials from the course
- Teaching tips
- Placement test
- A range of useful resources
- Video podcasts

A UNIT OF THE STUDENTS' BOOK

UNIT OVERVIEW

Every unit of Speakout starts with an Overview, which lists the topics covered. This is followed by two main input lessons which cover grammar, vocabulary and the four skills. Lesson three covers functional language and focuses on important speaking and listening strategies. Lesson four is built around a clip from a BBC programme and consolidates language and skills work. Each unit culminates with a Lookback page, which provides communicative practice of the key language.

INPUT LESSON 1

Lesson one introduces the topic of the unit and presents the key language needed to understand and talk about it. The lesson combines grammar and vocabulary with a focus on skills work.

The target language and the CEF objectives are listed to clearly show the objectives of the lesson.

Grammar and vocabulary sections often include a listening element to reinforce the new language.

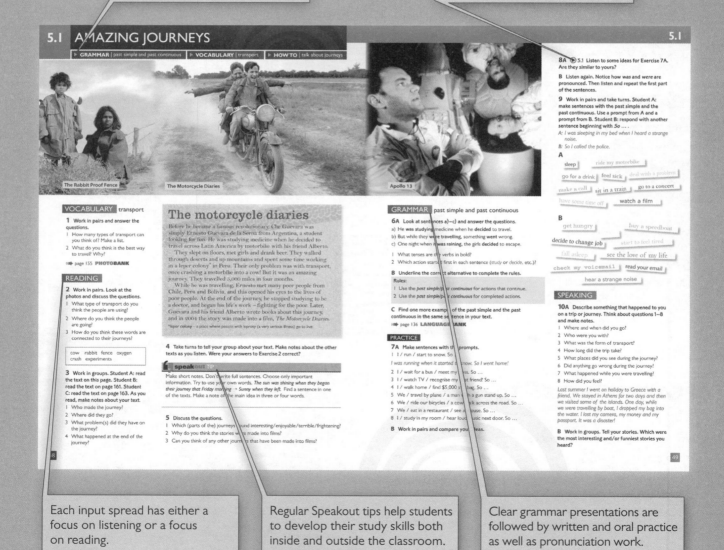

Each input spread has either a focus on listening or a focus on reading.

Regular Speakout tips help students to develop their study skills both inside and outside the classroom.

Clear grammar presentations are followed by written and oral practice as well as pronunciation work.

INPUT LESSON 2

Lesson two continues to focus on grammar and vocabulary while extending and expanding the topic area. By the end of the second lesson students will have worked on all four skill areas.

> Lexical sets are introduced in context. Practice of new words often includes pronunciation work.

> Every pair of input lessons includes at least one writing section with focus on a variety of different genres.

> Lexical sets are often expanded in the full colour Photo bank at the back of the Students' Book.

> Every grammar section includes a reference to the Language bank with explanations and further practice.

> All lessons include a focus on speaking where the emphasis is on communication and fluency building.

5.2 TRAVEL TIPS

GRAMMAR | verb patterns ▸ VOCABULARY | travel items ▸ HOW TO | talk about travel

VOCABULARY travel items

1 Work in pairs. Discuss the questions.
1 Do you travel light?
2 What do you usually pack when you go away for a short trip/long holiday?

2A Work in pairs. Look at the words in the box and choose two things for travellers 1–3 below.

suitcase notebook digital camera souvenirs waterproof clothes dictionary walking boots sunhat rucksack money belt binoculars map umbrella

1 a grandmother visiting her grandchildren in Australia
2 a student travelling around the world
3 a tourist visiting the sights in New York

B ▶ 5.2 Listen and repeat the words. Underline the stressed syllables.

C Work in pairs. Discuss. Which of the things in Exercise 2A do you own? Which do you take on holiday with you?
➡ page 155 PHOTOBANK

LISTENING

3A Read the introduction to a radio programme. Which of the items in Exercise 2A do you think the travellers will mention?

What do experienced travellers take on holiday?
The Holiday Show asks the experts to name one thing they always take on holiday.

B ▶ 5.3 Listen and check.

4A Work in pairs and complete the notes.
1 I try to learn ....
2 I love ....
3 I take a lot of ....
4 I usually spend my holidays in ....
5 I sometimes travel in .... places.
6 I don't carry too much ....
7 I write things down because I like to .... them.

B Listen again to check.

GRAMMAR verb patterns

5A Look at sentences 1–9 below and underline the verb + verb combinations.
1 We always expect to hear English.
2 I always want to talk to local people.
3 I love walking when I go on holiday.
4 I always seem to take hundreds and hundreds of photos.
5 I usually choose to go to a warm place.
6 I enjoy travelling in wild places.
7 If you decide to go walking, a rucksack is easier to carry.
8 It's best to avoid carrying too much money.
9 I need to write things down.

B Complete the table below with the verbs in the box.

expect want seem choose enjoy decide avoid need

verb + -ing	verb + infinitive with to
	expect

C Work in pairs. Add the verbs in the box below to the table above. Which two verbs can go in both columns?

hope finish imagine hate would like love

➡ page 136 LANGUAGEBANK

PRACTICE

6 Cross out the verb combination that is not possible in each sentence.
1 I hope/enjoy/expect to get a free plane ticket.
2 I want/would like/imagine to visit Australia.
3 She loves/avoids/needs travelling.
4 Where did you like/decide/choose to go on your next holiday?
5 They hate/want/love working with tourists.
6 He doesn't seem/need/enjoy to know this area well.
7 Do you like/expect/love going to different countries?
8 Why did you avoid/decide/hope to become a travel writer?

7A Complete the sentences and make them true for you. The next word must be either the infinitive with to or the -ing form of a verb.
1 When I travel:
  I always avoid ...
  I hate ...
  I love ...
2 On my last holiday:
  I chose ...
  I decided ...
  I enjoyed ...
3 For my next holiday:
  I want ...
  I hope ...
  I would like ...

B Work in pairs and compare your ideas.

SPEAKING

8 Work in pairs. Discuss the questions.
1 What type of holidays can you see in the photos? Which do you prefer? Why?
2 Is there anything that you really love doing when you are on holiday?
3 When you travel, do you try to learn about the place, its customs and its language? Why/Why not?
4 Do you enjoy visiting tourist areas, old cities, new cities, or none of these?

A: I really like sightseeing holidays. I love spending time looking at beautiful old buildings.
B: I love taking photos. I put these on my Facebook page when I get back.
A: Me, too!

WRITING using sequencers

9A Work in pairs. Read an email describing a trip and discuss. What were the good/bad things about the trip?

To: mmazuri@yahoo.com
From: Celine8@soutain.fr

Hi Mohamed,
I've just got back from my trip to Southern Africa. It was great. First we flew to Lesotho from Johannesburg. Then we took a boat down the river for two weeks. We saw lots of interesting animals and plants. After a while, it started raining heavily so I'm glad I had my waterproof clothes! After that, we went to Cape Town for a week to recover. Finally, we caught the plane back home. I loved the trip but I got tired of living out of a rucksack!
Speak soon.
Love,
Celine

B Underline five words/phrases that help us to understand the order of events. The first one has been done for you.

C Write an email to a friend about a trip or a weekend away. Use the words you underlined.

D Read other students' emails. Who had the most interesting trip?

FUNCTIONAL LESSON

The third lesson in each unit focuses on a particular function, situation or transaction as well as introducing important speaking and listening strategies.

The target language and the CEF objectives are listed to clearly show the objectives of the lesson.

Students learn a lexical set which is relevant to the function or situation.

Students learn important speaking and listening strategies which can be transferred to many situations.

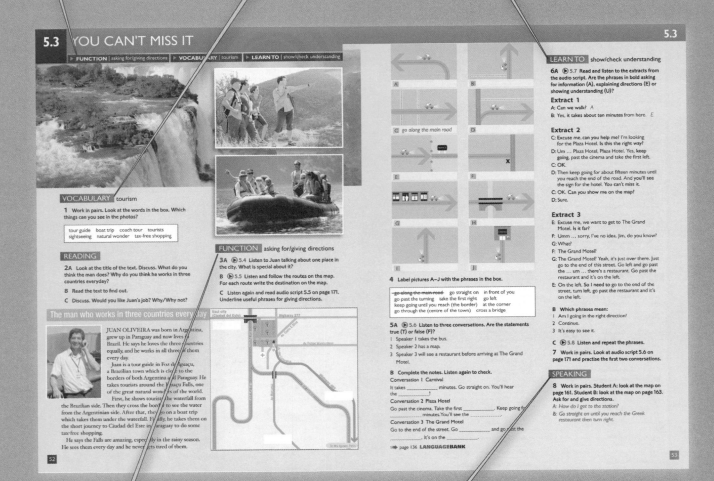

The functional language is learnt in context, often by listening to the language in use.

The lesson ends with a speaking activity which gives students the chance to practise the new language.

DVD LESSON

The fourth lesson in each unit is based around an extract from a real BBC programme. This acts as a springboard into freer communicative speaking and writing activities.

A preview section gets students thinking about the topic of the extract and introduces key language.

A series of different tasks helps students to understand and enjoy the programme.

The Speakout task builds on the topic of the extract and provides extended speaking practice.

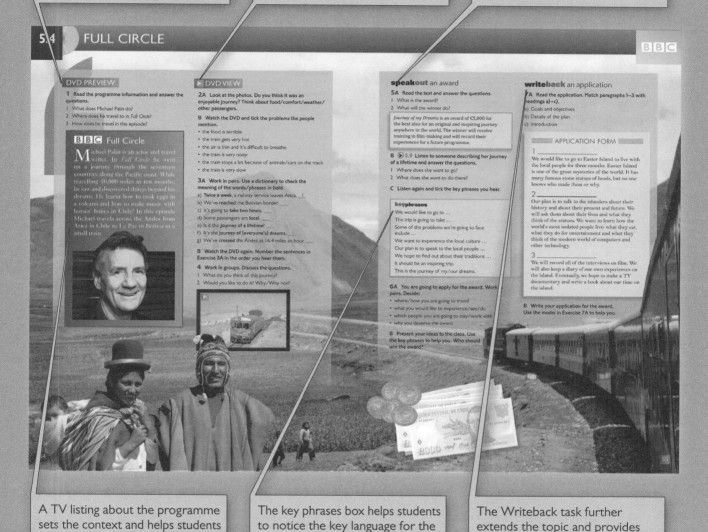

A TV listing about the programme sets the context and helps students prepare to watch the clip.

The key phrases box helps students to notice the key language for the speaking task and builds confidence.

The Writeback task further extends the topic and provides communicative writing practice.

LOOKBACK PAGE

Each unit ends with a Lookback page, which provides further practice and review of the key language covered in the unit. The review exercises are a mixture of communicative activities and games. Further practice and review exercises can be found in the Workbook. The Lookback page also introduces the Video podcast, which features a range of real people talking about one of the topics in the unit.

WORKBOOK

The Workbook contains a wide variety of practice and review exercises and covers all of the language areas studied in the unit. It also contains regular review sections as well as self-study tests to help students consolidate what they have learnt.

The Workbook features extensive practice of vocabulary, grammar, reading, writing and listening.

A variety of language practice activities consolidate the areas covered in the Students' Book.

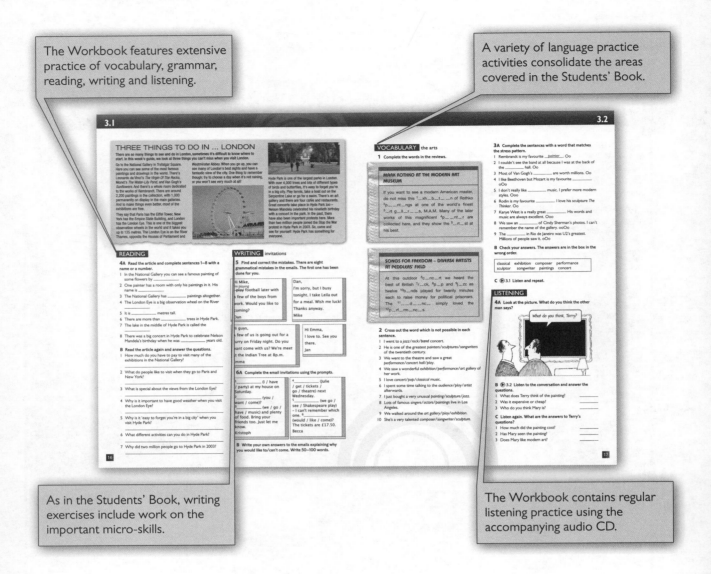

As in the Students' Book, writing exercises include work on the important micro-skills.

The Workbook contains regular listening practice using the accompanying audio CD.

MYSPEAKOUTLAB

MySpeakoutLab provides a fully blended and personalised learning environment that benefits both teachers and students. It offers:

• an interactive Workbook with hints, tips and automatic grade book.

• professionally written Unit Tests, Progress Tests, Mid-course and End of Course tests that can be assigned at the touch of a button.

• interactive Video podcast worksheets with an integrated video player so students can watch while they do the exercises.

ACTIVE TEACH

Speakout Active Teach contains everything you need to make the course come alive in your classroom. It includes integrated whiteboard software which enables you to add notes and embed files. It is also possible to save all of your work with the relevant page from the Students' Book.

Shortcuts to the relevant pages of the Language bank and the Photo bank make navigation easy.

An answer reveal function lets you show the answers to an exercise at the touch of a button.

All audio and video content is fully integrated and includes subtitles as well as printable scripts.

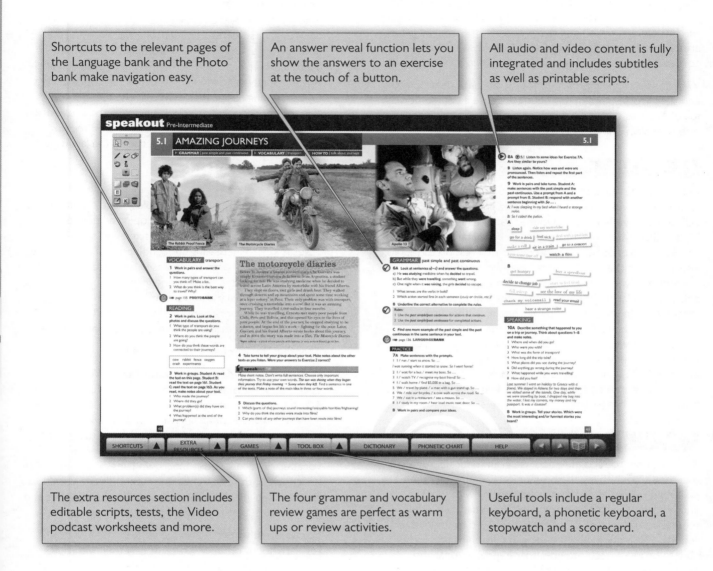

The extra resources section includes editable scripts, tests, the Video podcast worksheets and more.

The four grammar and vocabulary review games are perfect as warm ups or review activities.

Useful tools include a regular keyboard, a phonetic keyboard, a stopwatch and a scorecard.

WEBSITE

The Speakout website will offer information about the course as well as a bank of useful resources including:

• introductory videos by the authors of the course.
• sample materials.
• teaching tips.
• placement test.
• CEF mapping documents.
• Video podcasts for all published levels.

speakout is designed to satisfy both students and teachers on a number of different levels. It offers engaging topics with authentic BBC material to really bring them to life. At the same time it offers a robust and comprehensive focus on grammar, vocabulary, functions and pronunciation. As the name of the course might suggest, speaking activities are prominent, but that is not at the expense of the other core skills, which are developed systematically throughout.

With this balanced approach to topics, language development and skills work, our aim has been to create a course book full of 'lessons that really work' in practice. Below we will briefly explain our approach in each of these areas.

TOPICS AND CONTENT

In *Speakout* we have tried to choose topics that are relevant to students' lives. Where a topic area is covered in other ELT courses we have endeavoured to find a fresh angle on it. It is clear to us that authenticity is important to learners, and many texts come from the BBC's rich resources (audio, visual and print) as well as other real-world sources. At lower levels, we have sometimes adapted materials by adjusting the language to make it more manageable for students while trying to keep the tone as authentic as possible. We have also attempted to match the authentic feel of a text with an authentic interaction. Every unit contains a variety of rich and authentic input material including BBC Video podcasts (filmed on location in London, England) and DVD material, featuring some of the best the BBC has to offer.

GRAMMAR

Knowing how to recognise and use grammatical structures is central to our ability to communicate with each other. Although at first students can often get by with words and phrases, they increasingly need grammar to make themselves understood. Students also need to understand sentence formation when reading and listening and to be able to produce accurate grammar in professional and exam situations. We share students' belief that learning grammar is a core feature of learning a language and believe that a guided discovery approach, where students are challenged to notice new forms works best. At the same time learning is scaffolded so that students are supported at all times in a systematic way. Clear grammar presentations are followed by written and oral practice. There is also the chance to notice and practise pronunciation where appropriate.

In *Speakout* you will find:

- **Grammar in context** – We want to be sure that the grammar focus is clear and memorable for students. Grammar is almost always taken from the listening or reading texts, so that learners can see the language in action, and understand how and when it is used.

- **Noticing** – We involve students in the discovery of language patterns by asking them to identify aspects of meaning and form, and complete rules or tables.

- **Clear language reference** – As well as a summary of rules within the unit, there is also a Language bank which serves as a clear learning reference for the future

- **Focus on use** – We ensure that there is plenty of practice, both form and meaning-based, in the Language bank to give students confidence in manipulating the new language. On the main input page we include personalised practice, which is designed to be genuinely communicative and to offer students the opportunity to say something about themselves or the topic. There is also regular recycling of new language in the Lookback review pages, and again the focus here is on moving learners towards communicative use of the language.

VOCABULARY

Developing a wide range of vocabulary is key to increasing communicative effectiveness; developing a knowledge of high-frequency collocations and fixed and semi-fixed phrases is key to increasing spoken fluency. An extensive understanding of words and phrases helps learners become more confident when reading and listening, and developing a range of vocabulary is important for effective writing. Equally vital is learner-training, equipping students with the skills to record, memorise and recall vocabulary for use.

In *Speakout* this is reflected in:

- **A prominent focus on vocabulary** – We include vocabulary in almost all lessons whether in a lexical set linked to a particular topic, as preparation for a speaking activity or to aid comprehension of a DVD clip or a listening or reading text. Where we want students to use the language actively, we encourage them to use the vocabulary to talk about their own lives or opinions. At lower levels, the Photo bank also extends the vocabulary taught in the lessons, using memorable photographs and graphics to support students' understanding.

- **Focus on 'chunks'** – As well as lexical sets, we also regularly focus on how words fit together with other words, often getting students to notice how words are used in a text and to focus on high-frequency 'chunks' such as verb-noun collocations or whole phrases.

- **Focus on vocabulary systems** – We give regular attention to word-building skills, a valuable tool in expanding vocabulary. At higher levels, the Vocabulary plus sections deal with systems such as affixation, multi-word verbs and compound words in greater depth.

- **Recycling and learner training** – Practice exercises ensure that vocabulary is encountered on a number of occasions: within the lessons, on the Lookback page, in subsequent lessons and in the Photo bank/Vocabulary bank at the back of the book. One of the main focuses of the *Speakout* tips – which look at all areas of language learning – is to highlight vocabulary learning strategies, aiming to build good study skills that will enable students to gain and retain new language.

FUNCTIONAL LANGUAGE

One thing that both teachers and learners appreciate is the need to manage communication in a wide variety of encounters, and to know what's appropriate to say in given situations. These can be transactional exchanges, where the main focus is on getting something done (buying something in a shop or phoning to make an enquiry), or interactional exchanges, where the main focus is on socialising with others (talking about the weekend, or responding appropriately to good news). As one learner commented to us, 'Grammar rules aren't enough – I need to know what to say.' Although it is possible to categorise 'functions' under 'lexical phrases', we believe it is useful for learners to focus on functional phrases separately from vocabulary or grammar.

The third lesson in every unit of *Speakout* looks at one such situation, and focuses on the functional language needed. Learners hear or see the language used in context and then practise it in mini-situations, in both a written and a spoken context. Each of these lessons also includes a Learn to section, which highlights and practises a useful strategy for dealing with both transactional and interactional exchanges, for example asking for clarification, showing interest, etc. Learners will find themselves not just more confident users of the language, but also more active listeners.

SPEAKING

The dynamism of most lessons depends on the success of the speaking tasks, whether the task is a short oral practice of new language, a discussion comparing information or opinions, a personal response to a reading text or a presentation where a student might speak uninterrupted for a minute or more. Students develop fluency when they are motivated to speak. For this to happen, engaging topics and tasks are essential, as is the sequencing of stages and task design. For longer tasks, students often need to prepare their ideas and language in a structured way. This all-important rehearsal time leads to more motivation and confidence as well as greater accuracy, fluency and complexity. Also, where appropriate, students need to hear a model before they speak, in order to have a realistic goal.

There are several strands to speaking in *Speakout*:

- **Communicative practice** – After introducing any new language (vocabulary, grammar or function) there are many opportunities in *Speakout* for students to use it in a variety of activities which focus on communication as well as accuracy. These include personalised exchanges, dialogues, flow-charts and role-plays.

- **Focus on fluency** – In every unit of *Speakout* we include opportunities for students to respond spontaneously. They might be asked to respond to a series of questions, to a DVD, a Video podcast or a text, or to take part in conversations, discussions and role-plays. These activities involve a variety of interactional formations such as pairs and groups.

- **Speaking strategies and sub-skills** – In the third lesson of each unit, students are encouraged to notice in a systematic way features which will help them improve their speaking. These include, for example, ways to manage a phone conversation, the use of mirror questions to ask for clarification, sentence starters to introduce an opinion and intonation to correct mistakes.

- **Extended speaking tasks** – In the *Speakout* DVD lesson, as well as in other speaking tasks throughout the course, students are encouraged to attempt more adventurous and extended use of language in tasks such as problem solving, developing a project or telling a story. These tasks go beyond discussion; they include rehearsal time, useful language and a concrete outcome.

LISTENING

For most users of English (or any language, for that matter), listening is the most frequently used skill. A learner who can speak well but not understand at least as well is unlikely to be a competent communicator or user of the language. We feel that listening can be developed effectively through well-structured materials. As with speaking, the choice of interesting topics and texts works hand in hand with carefully considered sequencing and task design. At the same time, listening texts can act as a springboard to stimulate discussion in class.

There are several strands to listening in *Speakout*:

- **Focus on authentic recordings** – In *Speakout*, we believe that it is motivating for all levels of learner to try to access and cope with authentic material. Each unit includes a DVD extract from a BBC documentary, drama or light entertainment programme as well as a podcast filmed on location with real people giving their opinions. At the higher levels you will also find unscripted audio texts and BBC radio extracts. All are invaluable in the way they expose learners to real language in use as well as different varieties of English. Where recordings, particularly at lower levels, are scripted, they aim to reflect the patterns of natural speech.

- **Focus on sub-skills and strategies** – Tasks across the recordings in each unit are designed with a number of sub-skills and strategies in mind. These include: listening for global meaning and more detail; scanning for specific information; becoming sensitised to possible misunderstandings; and noticing nuances of intonation and expression. We also help learners to listen actively by using strategies such as asking for repetition and paraphrasing.

- **As a context for new language** – We see listening as a key mode of input and *Speakout* includes many listening texts which contain target grammar, vocabulary or functions in their natural contexts. Learners are encouraged to notice this new language and how and where it occurs, often by using the audio scripts as a resource.

- **As a model for speaking** – In the third and fourth lessons of each unit the recordings serve as models for speaking tasks. These models reveal the ways in which speakers use specific language to structure their discourse, for example with regard to turn-taking, hesitating and checking for understanding. These recordings also serve as a goal for the learners' speaking.

READING

Reading is a priority for many students, whether it's for study, work or pleasure, and can be practised alone, anywhere and at any time. Learners who read regularly tend to have a richer, more varied vocabulary, and are often better writers, which in turn supports their oral communication skills. Nowadays, the Internet has given students access to an extraordinary range of English language reading material, and the availability of English language newspapers, books and magazines is greater than ever before. The language learner who develops skill and confidence in reading in the classroom will be more motivated to read outside the classroom. Within the classroom reading texts can also introduce stimulating topics and act as springboards for class discussion.

There are several strands to reading in *Speakout*:

- **Focus on authentic texts** – As with *Speakout* listening materials, there is an emphasis on authenticity, and this is reflected in a number of ways. Many of the reading texts in *Speakout* are sourced from the BBC. Where texts have been adapted or graded, there is an attempt to maintain authenticity by remaining faithful to the text type in terms of content and style. We have chosen up-to-date, relevant texts to stimulate interest and motivate learners to read. The texts represent a variety of genres that correspond to the text types that learners will probably encounter in their everyday lives.

- **Focus on sub-skills and strategies** – In *Speakout* we strive to maintain authenticity in the way the readers interact with a text. We always give students a reason to read, and provide tasks which bring about or simulate authentic reading, including real-life tasks such as summarising, extracting specific information, reacting to an opinion or following an anecdote. We also focus on strategies for decoding texts, such as guessing the meaning of unknown vocabulary, understanding pronoun referencing and following discourse markers.

- **Noticing new language** – Noticing language in use is a key step towards the development of a rich vocabulary and greater all-round proficiency in a language, and this is most easily achieved through reading. In *Speakout*, reading texts often serve as valuable contexts for introducing grammar and vocabulary as well as discourse features.

- **As a model for writing** – In the writing sections, as well as the Writeback sections of the DVD spreads, the readings serve as models for students to refer to when they are writing, in terms of overall organisation as well as style and language content.

WRITING

In recent years the growth of email and the internet has led to a shift in the nature of the writing our students need to do. Email has also led to an increased informality in written English. However, many students need to develop their formal writing for professional and exam-taking purposes. It is therefore important to focus on a range of genres, from formal text types such as essays, letters and reports to informal genres such as blog entries and personal messages.

There are four strands to writing in *Speakout*:

- **Focus on genres** – In every unit at the four higher levels there is a section that focuses on a genre of writing, emails for example. We provide a model to show the conventions of the genre and, where appropriate, we highlight fixed phrases associated with it. We usually then ask the students to produce their own piece of writing. While there is always a written product, we also focus on the process of writing, including the relevant stages such as brainstorming, planning, and checking. At Starter and Elementary, we focus on more basic writing skills, including basic written sentence patterns, linking, punctuation and text organisation, in some cases linking this focus to a specific genre.

- **Focus on sub-skills and strategies** – While dealing with the genres, we include a section which focuses on a sub-skill or strategy that is generally applicable to all writing. Sub-skills include paragraphing, organising content and using linking words and pronouns, while strategies include activities like writing a first draft quickly, keeping your reader in mind and self-editing. We present the sub-skill by asking the students to notice the feature. We then provide an opportunity for the students to practise it.

- **Writeback** – At the end of every unit, following the DVD and final speaking task, we include a Writeback task. The idea is for students to develop fluency in their writing. While we always provide a model, the task is not tied to any particular grammatical structure. Instead the emphasis is on using writing to generate ideas and personal responses.

- **Writing as a classroom activity** – We believe that writing can be very usefully employed as an aid to speaking and as a reflective technique for responding to texts – akin to the practice of writing notes in the margins of books. It also provides a change of pace and focus in lessons. Activities such as short dictations, note-taking, brainstorming on paper and group story writing are all included in *Speakout*.

PRONUNCIATION

In recent years, attitudes towards pronunciation in many English language classrooms have moved towards a focus on intelligibility: if students' spoken language is understandable, then the pronunciation is good enough. We are aware, however, that many learners and teachers place great importance on developing pronunciation that is more than 'good enough', and that systematic attention to pronunciation in a lesson, however brief, can have a significant impact on developing learners' speech.

In *Speakout*, we have taken a practical, integrated approach to developing students' pronunciation, highlighting features that often cause problems in conjunction with a given area of grammar, particular vocabulary items and functional language. Where relevant to the level, a grammatical or functional language focus is followed by a focus on a feature of pronunciation, for example, the weak forms of auxiliary verbs or connected speech in certain functional exponents. Students are given the opportunity to listen to models of the pronunciation, notice the key feature and then practise it.

TEACHING PRE-INTERMEDIATE LEARNERS

Pre-intermediate students have usually not yet reached a plateau. This makes them potentially very rewarding to teach. While they have enough English to have a basic conversation, they will be able to see progress during the course in terms of the range, fluency and accuracy of output.

Pre-intermediate students still probably see the English language in terms of small, discrete pieces – verb tenses learned sequentially and basic lexical sets such as colours, jobs, hobbies, animals, etc. – which they have not yet 'put together'. One of the keys to teaching at this level is to provide students with deeper encounters with the language: setting more challenging tasks than at elementary, and sometimes asking students to deal with the complexities of authentic material – text and film – in order to develop strategies for coping with incomplete understanding. Strategy development, both metacognitive (learning habits such as keeping a vocabulary notebook, watching films etc.) and cognitive (ways to deal with tasks at hand, e.g. using phrases to ask for help, predicting content by reading a title etc.), as at other levels, are essential for students' progress.

Typically, pre-intermediate students are able to make themselves understood in a wider variety of situations than they could at elementary. They are also able to deal with short basic texts. However, they may have problems with extended discourse. This applies to all four skills: their spoken utterances will probably be short and their written compositions brief; they probably do little extensive reading, and they may have difficulty in sustaining concentration while listening to recordings or conversations that are longer than two minutes. One of the teacher's roles at this level is to gradually expose students to longer pieces of discourse while providing

both linguistic and motivational support. Teachers should do thorough, personalised pre-reading/pre-listening tasks, break long pieces into shorter sections, and use whole-class activities in order to foster students' confidence.

As regards the syllabus, it is very important for learners at this stage to encounter the same language again and again. Pre-intermediate students need a lot of review and recycling of grammar and vocabulary that they may have encountered but not yet mastered. Pre-intermediate is a key stage at which they begin to change passive knowledge (language they know) into active knowledge (language they can use).

Here are our Top Tips for teaching at this level:

- Recycle grammar and vocabulary. Although they will have covered many key points such as the past simple, they will not have mastered them.

- Introduce learning strategies – e.g. for recording vocabulary – by modelling them. By now the students are beyond 'survival English' and should be able to start 'collecting' vocabulary from the texts they encounter.

- Look at how words work together. At elementary students probably need to learn mainly one-word items in order to name things, but at pre-intermediate they are more able to work with phrases and chunks of language.

- Get students into the habit of reviewing language frequently. You could begin each class with a short review of grammar and vocabulary learnt in the previous lesson, perhaps by using a game or photocopiable activity.

- Do a lot of work on pronunciation through short drills. At this level, the students need to continue familiarizing themselves with the sounds of English, particularly the ways in which the sounds of words change in the context of connected speech.

- Get students to self-correct. At pre-intermediate level, many students start to develop awareness of correct and incorrect English. You could try having small signals on the board, for example, -s for third person 's', -ed for past tense endings. When the students make a mistake, you can just point to the board to remind them.

- Where possible, begin to use short authentic texts such as menus, brochures and newspaper articles.

- Use role-plays and structured speaking tasks to encourage students to extend their speaking skills.

- Encourage fluency by having conversations at the beginning or the end of the class. Use topics that students should all be able to talk about, like what they did at the weekend, or what their plans are for after the class.

Antonia Clare, Frances Eales, Steve Oakes and JJ Wilson

TEACHER'S NOTES INDEX

OVERVIEW

This video podcast extends discussion of the unit topic to friendship. It will also extend Ss' language on friendship, relationships and keeping in touch. Use this video podcast at the start or end of unit 1.

ARE YOU HAPPY?

Introduction

Ss revise/practise asking and answering questions with *be* and the auxiliary verb *do* in the context of talking about what makes them happy.

SUPPLEMENTARY MATERIALS

Resource bank p146

Ex 4/8: bring/download more pictures of people doing different activities and enjoying themselves.

Warm up

It's very important to build rapport with a new class. The activity here is designed to give Ss the opportunity to get to know each other, and help you to assess their language and speaking skills, in particular the use of question forms (reviewed later in the lesson). First tell Ss the aims of the activity and elicit the information they need to get to know each other, e.g. *name, age, home town, nationality/country, job/ occupation, hobbies/interests, reasons for learning English,* etc. Write the prompts on the board and elicit a suitable question for each one, e.g. *What's your name? How old are you? Where are you from?* Write the questions on the board if necessary. Ss then work in groups of 4–6 and take turns to ask/answer the questions. They should note down at least five facts about each person in their group for feedback.

Teaching tip

In feedback, nominate each student in each group to tell the class about one person in their group. The class listens and writes down another question to ask that person. This ensures that Ss pay attention and listen to each other. Ss then move around the class in an informal way, asking and answering the questions they wrote down.

Teaching tip

While Ss work through the activities, monitor and note down any particular strengths and weaknesses, including how well they use question forms: this will help you to decide how much support and input will be needed in the grammar section later.

VOCABULARY free time

1A Tell Ss to look at the photos and cover the exercises. Ask *What are the people doing? Where are they?* Elicit Ss' answers, e.g. *shopping, playing basketball, having a family barbecue, reading a book, on holiday,* but don't teach new language at this point. Ss then complete the phrases and compare answers. Monitor while they do the exercise and check/teach phrases Ss don't know in feedback, e.g. *have time off = don't go to work/have a holiday.*

Answers: 2 spend 3 eat 4 have 5 play

B Give Ss 3–4 mins to do the exercise together. Meanwhile, write the verbs from Ex 1A on the board. In feedback, nominate Ss to give their answers. Write the extra activities on the board under the correct verb, or invite Ss to write them.

> **Answers:** 1 go shopping A, go on holiday E, F 2 spend time with family, C spend money A, 3 eat with friends C 4 have time off A–F, have a barbecue C 5 play (a) sport B Possible extra activities: 1 go out/to the cinema/to work/running 2 spend £50/the morning in bed/a week in the mountains 3 eat a meal/a hamburger/a lot/at home/alone 4 have a party/friends round 5 play a game/football/tennis/in a team

LISTENING

2 First introduce the listening and check the rubric. (Don't tell them that the text of the listening is in Ex 3.)

> **Teaching tip**
>
> With *weaker classes*, play the recording for the first speaker as an example, and elicit the matching photo. Then play the complete recording: Ss listen and compare their answers. It is important to do this to build Ss' confidence with listening. If they don't agree about their answers, play the recording again for them to double-check: this gives them the chance to get the right answers.

Ss can compare answers again if necessary. In feedback, elicit reasons for Ss' answers, e.g. *photo C matches speaker 3 because he likes eating with friends and having a barbecue.*

> **Answers:** 1 A 2 E 3 C 4 D 5 B 6 F

3 Tell Ss that this is the recording from Ex 2. They shouldn't worry about unknown words but think of words that fit the context. Do an example with *weaker classes* if necessary. Give Ss 3–4 mins to read and complete the gaps before checking their answers in pairs. Play the recording again and check Ss' answers. Teach relevant new words/phrases if necessary, e.g. *spending time on my own.*

> **Answers:** 1 money 2 shopping 3 sun 4 beach 5 friends 6 music 7 book 8 sport 9 sea

4 Elicit examples of Ss' answers to the question, e.g. *Marie: I like going to the beach and swimming in a pool, too.* Then give them 2–3 mins to discuss and decide who they have most in common with. If you've brought some extra pictures (of people enjoying themselves), give them to *fast finishers*, who can talk about which activities they enjoy. In feedback, nominate Ss to tell the class about their partner's answers. If possible, find out what the most popular activities are in the class.

Unit 1 Recording 1
Speaker 1
The thing that makes me happy is money. I like it when I can go out and spend money on the things I really, really want. Yeah, going shopping makes me happy.
Speaker 2
I love being in the sun. Being on holiday and going to the beach. Swimming in a pool. That makes me really happy. You just forget all your problems and enjoy the sun.
Speaker 3
Being with friends and family. Eating a nice meal with your friends, or having a barbecue. Watching the children, you know, play around and have a good time.

Speaker 4
Having time off work, like I am now. Listening to music, or reading a good book. Just spending time on my own makes me really happy.
Speaker 5
I love playing sport. When my team wins a basketball game, for example. It doesn't always happen, but when it does, I'm so happy.
Speaker 6
Being somewhere beautiful makes me happy. Being near nature, by the sea, or in the mountains. Just walking somewhere beautiful.

SPEAKING

5A Read and check any new language in the questions, e.g. *right now.* Elicit an answer for each question from the class. Then give Ss time to prepare their answers: encourage them to make brief notes. Monitor and provide vocabulary Ss need, if necessary.

> **Possible answers:** 1 a cup of coffee in the morning, a phone call from a friend 2 the television, my partner, my dog 3 in the shower, on the beach, when I'm outside 4 the garden, my DVD collection 5 Yes – it's a sunny day./No – I'm tired. 6 Last night. A friend told me a very funny joke.

B Model and drill the questions. Ss then work in small groups and take turns to ask/answer them. Monitor and make notes on their performance, particularly with the accuracy of the tenses used. Check Ss' answers in open pairs across the class, i.e. nominate two students at a time to ask/answer a question.

GRAMMAR question forms

6A Ss look at the tables. Check the meaning of *auxiliary* and other meta-language (*infinitive*, etc.), if necessary. Ss should use the questions in Ex 5A to help them complete the tables.

> **Teaching tip**
>
> *Stronger classes* can work alone but *weaker ones* might need more support. In *mixed-ability classes*, strong Ss could work with weak ones. Done sensitively, this is a useful strategy for most classes: the need to help/explain language challenges *stronger Ss* and increases their language awareness.

While Ss complete the table, write the questions on the board with gaps. Elicit the answers and complete the gaps. Ask *Which are yes/no questions? Which are information (wh-) questions?* Then ask *What tense are the questions in? How do you know?* Elicit Ss' answers. Also elicit questions using a noun and verb + -ing, e.g. *Are you a teacher? Are you learning English now?*

> **Answers:** 1 do 2 When 3 Are 4 Where

B Ss read the rules of form and discuss their answers in pairs. In feedback, elicit and underline the auxiliary verbs and *be* in the questions on the board. Ss copy them into their notebooks.

> **Answers:** 1 before 2 before

▶ **LANGUAGEBANK** 1.1 p128–129

Stronger classes can study the tables and notes at home when they do the exercises. Otherwise, check the tables and notes with Ss, especially the difference between *which* and *what*. Elicit more examples using question words, e.g. *What are you doing? Why are you learning English? Which languages do you speak? Weaker Ss* could do Ex A–C in class. If you do Ex A in class, make Ex A and B into a competition. The first pair to finish with all the correct answers wins. If there are words/places they don't understand, tell them to use the answers in Ex B to work them out.

Answers:
A 1 How many 2 Who 3 What/Which 4 What
5 When 6 Where 7 Which 8 How
B 1 e) 2 b) 3 h) 4 f) 5 c) 6 d) 7 a) 8 g)
C 1 How much *does* this cost? 2 *Do* you have (and/or *Have you got*) any brothers or sisters? 3 What time *does* the film start? 4 How often do you *play* football?
5 Who *is* your new teacher? 6 Do *you* want to come and have a pizza? 7 Why don't you *like* grammar? 8 Where *did* you go on holiday last year?

PRACTICE

7A Check the rubric and do the first question as an example. Ss then work alone and write the questions in their notebooks. They then check their answers in pairs. Monitor and prompt Ss to self-correct, but don't do feedback yet. Ss check their answers in Ex B.

B Play the recording, pausing for a few seconds after each question for Ss to check/correct their answers.

Answers: 1 How many people are in your family? 2 How often do you see your parents? 3 Do you enjoy spending time with your family? 4 When was your last family celebration? 5 Who do you live with? 6 How often do you eat out with friends? 7 Where does your best friend live?

C Play the first question again and elicit the stressed words *How/people/family*. Ss then do the others alone/in pairs. Play the recording again for Ss to check before they repeat them.

Answers: 1 <u>How</u> many <u>people</u> are in your <u>family</u>? 2 How <u>often</u> do you <u>see</u> your <u>parents</u>? 3 Do you <u>enjoy</u> spending time with your <u>family</u>? 4 <u>When</u> was your <u>last</u> family <u>celebration</u>? 5 <u>Who</u> do you <u>live</u> with? 6 How <u>often</u> do you eat <u>out</u> with <u>friends</u>? 7 <u>Where</u> does your <u>best</u> friend <u>live</u>?

D Pair Ss who don't know each other well, especially in *monolingual classes*; this will create a wider information gap. They take it in turns to ask/answer the questions and make brief notes on their partner's answers. In feedback, nominate Ss to report back their own and their partner's answers to the class, e.g. *There are six people in my family, but there are ten in Diego's.*

Unit 1 Recording 2

1 How many people are in your family?
2 How often do you see your parents?
3 Do you enjoy spending time with your family?
4 When was your last family celebration?
5 Who do you live with?
6 How often do you eat out with friends?
7 Where does your best friend live?

SPEAKING

8A First ask *Where are the people in the photos? What are they doing?* Elicit Ss' answers, e.g. *playing chess, in Rome/the park.* Do an example, then give Ss 3–4 mins to finish the exercise in pairs. In feedback, elicit the questions and prompt Ss to self-correct any mistakes they make.

Suggested answers: 1 What do you do in your free time? 2 Do you have any hobbies? 3 When did you start this hobby? 4 Why do you enjoy it/this hobby? 5 Where do you usually go on holiday? 6 Do you usually go on holiday with friends or family? 7 How long do you usually stay/go on holiday for? 8 What do you usually do/like doing on holiday? 9 What do you usually do/like doing at the weekend? 10 Do you ever work or study at the weekend? 11 Where do you go out/like to go out? 12 What time do you usually get up at the weekend?

B In groups, Ss take it in turns to ask/answer the questions. They should make notes about one student in their group and prepare to tell the class about them in feedback. Monitor discreetly while Ss talk, and make notes of examples of good language and problems. In feedback, Ss tell the class about a student in their group, but they mustn't mention the name! The others listen and guess who it is. Finally, write some examples of Ss' errors and good language on the board. Ss discuss and correct them in pairs.

Optional extra activity
Instead of telling the class about the person they made notes about in Ex 8, they write a short paragraph about him/her, but don't mention his/her name, e.g. *X plays chess in his free time. He also paints pictures. He started when he was 16. He enjoys it because he likes art.* Ss then pass their texts round for other groups to read and guess who it is. Alternatively, put the texts on the classroom walls. Ss walk round and guess who the people are.

Homework ideas
- Ex 8: write three paragraphs about your answers to the questions here (or write about another person in your group).
- **Language bank** 1.1 Ex A–C, p129
- **Workbook** Ex 1–4, p5–6

TRUE LOVE

Introduction

Ss revise and practise the past simple in the context of reading and talking about relationships. They also practise using linking words in texts.

SUPPLEMENTARY MATERIALS

Resource bank p145 and p147

Warm up: prepare 12 verb prompts as described below.

Warm up

Review irregular past tenses with a pelmanism activity on the board. Before class, write six irregular verbs and their past simple forms, e.g. *become – became, fall – fell, meet – met, get – got, go – went, see – saw,* on A4 sheets of paper (one on each sheet). On the other side of each sheet, write a number from 1–12. In class, stick the sheets on the board with the numbers face up and do an example. Elicit any two numbers from Ss, e.g. 3 and 9, and turn over the corresponding sheets for them to see the words. If there's a verb and past simple form that match to make a pair, e.g. *go/went,* remove them from the board. If not, put them back in the same places. Ss should try to remember where they are so they can choose a matching pair of words later. Ss work in pairs/teams and take it in turns to choose two numbers. The pair/team with the most matching pairs wins. You could use this activity with any word game involving the matching of two items.

SPEAKING

1 Read and check the questions with Ss. Teach/check *love at first sight.* Then give them 3–4 mins to discuss the questions. In feedback, elicit their answers and have a brief class discussion.

Possible answers: 2 at work/college, in clubs/societies, playing sports, at parties or friends' houses, etc.
3 differences in age, culture, background, attitudes or interests

Culture notes
Bao Xishun says his height was normal until he was sixteen, but seven years later he was 1.70m tall. In October 2008, he and his wife had a son.

READING

2A Here Ss practise their prediction skills.

Teaching tip

We usually read a magazine or newspaper in our own language because the photos/headlines have aroused our interest in some way: they give us an idea of what the text is about. Ss need to practise and use this skill with texts in English too.

Tell Ss to cover the texts and look at the photos and headlines. Give them 3 mins to think/make notes about their answers and then discuss them in pairs. Do feedback after Ex B.

B Give Ss 2 mins to read the texts quickly and check their ideas. Ss discuss whether their ideas from Ex 2A were correct with the same partner. In feedback, check how close Ss' ideas were to the texts. Also check the meaning of *third time lucky.* Ask *How many times did they get married?* Three. *Do they want to get divorced again?* No, they got married for the third and final time. Do further comprehension after Ex 3.

Teaching tip

The aim of strict time limits is to encourage Ss to skim texts quickly and check the main ideas. Tell them not to worry about unknown vocabulary at the moment.

3 First Ss read the questions. Check vocabulary they need if necessary, e.g. *get on well, get divorced, argue, get back together.* Give Ss 3–4 mins to answer the questions and compare their answers. As with listening comprehension, build Ss' confidence by allowing them to read and check the answers they don't agree on. In feedback, elicit Ss' answers and ask them to correct the false answers.

Answers: 1 T 2 F 3 T (a month) 4 F 5 T 6 T

4 Ss discuss the question in small groups. Monitor and provide vocabulary Ss may need. Write any useful words/phrases on the board. In feedback, nominate Ss from each group to tell the class their opinions.

VOCABULARY   relationships

5A Check the meaning of *Whose?* in the rubric, if necessary. Give Ss 3 mins to read the sentences and match them to the correct text. In feedback, elicit more details of the stories where possible, e.g. *Why didn't he have a girlfriend? Because he was shy and he didn't go out much.*

Suggested answers: Tallest man finds love: 1, 2, 3, 4, 5, 9, 10. Third time lucky: 5, 6, 7, 8, 9, 10

B Ss match the definitions alone and check in pairs. In feedback, check/drill the pronunciation of the phrases if necessary.

Answers: a) 2 b) 6 c) 4 d) 3 e) 10 f) 7 g) 8

speakout TIP

Read the speakout tip with Ss and write the verbs *get* and *have* on the board. Give them 2 mins to write down phrases they remember in pairs. In feedback, elicit the phrases and write them on the board – or invite Ss to do it. They then copy the lists into their notebooks.

Teaching tip

It's important for Ss to record their vocabulary in a logical and accessible way so they can review it easily. Suggest that they either have a separate section in their English notebooks or a smaller notebook which they could carry around in their bag/pocket to refer to at suitable times.

GRAMMAR   past simple

6A Elicit the first two examples from the first text. Tell them to include negative forms and the verb *be.* Give 2–3 mins for Ss to underline the other examples, and compare their answers. In feedback, check answers and ask *Which are regular/irregular verbs?*

Answers:
Tallest man finds love: married, became, appeared, was, didn't go out, didn't have, worked, didn't make, started, decided, advertised, fell in love, got married
Third time lucky: married, liked, said, asked, accepted, started, argued, got divorced, remarried, divorced, got back together, did they get married, explained, fell, changed, decided

B Ss can refer to the love stories to help them complete the tables, before comparing their answers. Write the gapped sentences on the board. In feedback, elicit the regular and irregular past forms and the spelling of *-ed* endings, e.g. *marry – married*. Then nominate Ss to complete the gapped sentences on the board. Check the form of the past simple; Ss then copy down the three sentences.

> **Answers:**
> regular: started, decided, married
> irregular: became, fell, got, said
> negative: didn't
> question: Did
> short answer: didn't

> **Watch out!**
> The pronunciation of the *-ed* endings of regular verbs is a common problem for Ss. They over-generalise from the rule for verbs like *started, decided* and pronounce all *-ed* endings in the same way with /ɪd/. It's very important to highlight, drill and correct this mistake at all times to prevent fossilisation.

7A Ss now practise recognising the pronunciation of *-ed* endings. Write the phonemic symbols on the board and model/drill them.

> **Teaching tip**
> Teach Ss that /d/ is a voiced sound and /t/ is unvoiced. Illustrate this to Ss: tell them to touch their throat with their fingers. When they say /d/ they will feel a vibration in their throat, but with the /t/ sound, they won't. Then play the recording while Ss read the sentences.

B Check the examples and play the recording. Pause after each verb for Ss to write it in the correct column. Elict/check Ss' answers. To give practise of producing the regular verbs, Ss can listen and repeat again. Drill the verbs chorally (with the whole class) and then individually.

> **Teaching tip**
> With *stronger classes*, you could teach the rules of pronunciation for *-ed* endings: verbs end with the /d/ sound after vowels and voiced consonants except /d/, e.g. /b/ /v/ /z/ /g/ /m/ /n/ /l/. Verbs end with /t/ after unvoiced consonants except /t/, e.g. /p/ /f/ /s/ /k/. Verbs end in /ɪd/ after /d/ and /t/, e.g. *started, decided*.

> **Answers:**
> /d/ smiled, studied
> /t/ worked, stopped, walked, talked, helped
> /ɪd/ wanted, needed, decided

> ⇒ **LANGUAGEBANK** 1.2 p128–129
> Ss can refer to the notes on p128 when they do the exercises. *Weaker Ss* should do Ex A and B in class. Check new vocabulary before Ss do the exercise, or in feedback.
>
> **Answers:**
> A 2 saw 3 got 4 knew 5 emailed 6 fell 7 decided
> 8 asked 9 arrived 10 said 11 got
> B 1 taught 2 did (you) grow up 3 met 4 didn't get on
> 5 left, got 6 lived, didn't see 7 Did (you) enjoy 8 didn't
> have 9 finished 10 studied

PRACTICE

8A Do an example. Ss then write the verbs alone and check in pairs. In feedback, elicit answers and ask *Is it a regular or irregular verb?* It would also be useful to revise the time phrases in each sentence before Ss do Ex B and C. Elicit and write them on the board, e.g. *three months ago, last summer, all night*. Ss copy them down and add three more examples of each phrase, e.g. *two weeks/a year/five mins ago*. Check answers and write them on the board for Ss to copy if necessary.

> **Answers:** 1 saw 2 went 3 stayed 4 went 5 cooked
> 6 spent

B Check the example and give Ss 3–4 mins to write the questions in pairs. In feedback, elicit and drill the questions with the class, and then elicit possible answers with time phrases.

> **Suggested answers:** 1 When did you last see your best friend? 2 When did you last go to a wedding?
> 3 When did you last stay up all night? 4 When did you last go on holiday? 5 When did you last cook a meal for some friends/someone? 6 When did you last spend the day with your sister/brother/boyfriend, etc?

C Model/drill the example question and elicit personalised answers using time phrases. While Ss work in pairs, monitor and prompt them to self-correct errors with the past simple. Give feedback on persistent errors with the past simple.

SPEAKING

9A Give Ss 3–4 mins to write down five dates and make notes about them. Monitor closely to provide help with vocabulary, especially with *weaker Ss*. To provide a model for Ss, you could tell Ss about an important date for you.

B Check the example and point out that Ss can only use *yes/no* questions. Limit the number of questions to ten. In feedback, nominate Ss to tell the class about one of their partner's dates.

WRITING linking words

10A This should be revision for most Ss. So use the exercise to check. Check new words if necessary, e.g. *degree, flat-mate*.

> **Answers:** 1 c) and 2 d) because 3 b) so 4 a) but

B Ss look at the cartoon. Ask *What's the man doing?* Elicit/teach *internet chatroom*. Ss complete the text. In feedback, elicit answers and ask some comprehension questions.

> **Answers:** 1 because 2 and 3 but 4 so

C Give Ss time to think and make notes on an important year, using the linking words. It would be helpful for them to talk about it in pairs/small groups for 3–4 mins while you monitor and provide language they need. Give Ss 8–10 mins to write a paragraph. Encourage a collaborative approach to writing: Ss show each other their work and exchange advice/help. If time, Ss exchange texts with a different partner and answer questions about it. Otherwise, they can finish writing it at home.

> **Homework ideas**
> • Ex 9: write sentences about your/your partner's five important dates.
> • Ex 10C: write a final draft of your text.
> • Language bank 1.2 Ex A–B, p129
> • Workbook Ex 1–7, p7–8

NICE DAY, ISN'T IT?

Introduction

Ss learn and practise ways of making conversation when they first meet people. They also learn how to make their spoken English sound more natural.

> ### SUPPLEMENTARY MATERIALS
> Resource bank p148
> Warm up: prepare a short descriptive narrative like the example below (or use the one provided).

Warm up

Lead in to the lesson topic with a live listening. In a live listening, you tell the Ss a story/anecdote or give a description of an event which relates to/provides a model of a speaking activity that Ss will do in the lesson. You can ask comprehension questions about it, use target language that Ss will focus on later, or just allow Ss to listen – and practise hearing authentic English. Give Ss a short description – real or invented – based on the questions in Ex 1A.

Example text:

Last weekend, I went to stay with my friend James in Oxford and he took me to a local artisans' market on Sunday morning. It was fantastic. There was home-made bread and cakes, jewellery, clothes, cards and paintings – all sorts of things. It was great. James introduced me to a friend of his called Jane – she makes beautiful silver rings and necklaces and sells them in the market. I've recently started making necklaces too, so James thought we should meet. He was right. We got on really well and talked about our work for ages – I learnt lots of interesting new things and got some new ideas for my necklaces. And I'm thinking of making earrings now.

When you've finished, ask comprehension questions about your description. Include the questions in Ex 1A. Then move to Ex 1, where Ss will talk about their own experiences.

VOCABULARY   conversation topics

1A Lead in to the topic. Ask *Do you like going to parties/ meeting new people?* Elicit Ss' answers and have a brief class discussion. Then check the questions in Ex 1A. Give Ss 3–4 mins to discuss them in pairs. Elicit and discuss Ss' answers. Extend the discussion about question 3. Ask *Was it interesting/ boring? Why/Why not?*

B Ss read the words and phrases in the box and ask for clarification if necessary. Do the first two topics as examples. Ask *Why is/isn't it a good topic?* Answers, e.g. *Because most people watch/like/have an opinion about films.* In a *multilingual class*, Ss might have different opinions about which topics are suitable or not. Give Ss 1–2 mins to tick suitable topics alone, but don't check their ideas yet.

C Organise Ss into small groups. In *multilingual classes*, put Ss from similar parts of the world in different groups. Give them 4–5 mins to discuss and compare their answers. In feedback, nominate Ss from each group to report back to the class. Make a list on the board of topics which all Ss think are suitable for a conversation with people you don't know very well.

> **Suggested answers:** ✓ films, cars, sport, your last holiday, your family, the weather, your work/studies, your weekend

D Reorganise Ss into pairs with different partners. Elicit some sample questions about the topics in Ex B, e.g. *What sort of films do you like? What was the last film you saw? What was it like?* Give Ss 4–5 mins to choose three topics each to ask/ answer questions about. Nominate Ss to tell the class what they learnt about their partners.

READING

2A Lead in to the text. Check the meaning of *advice* and ask Ss to read the title and introduction to the article. They should cover the rest of it. Elicit Ss' ideas for improving conversation skills, or alternatively, give them 2 mins to discuss their ideas in pairs, followed by a class discussion. Write some of their ideas on the board. Ss then read the article and check how similar/different their ideas are. Check/teach new vocabulary, e.g. *recreation, social time, latest product.* In feedback, elicit Ss' answers and then discuss the questions in the rubric.

B Give Ss 3–4 mins to make a list of what they remember. They could then work with another pair to compare notes. In feedback, elicit the seven tips if possible, or give Ss 1 min to check their lists in the article by themselves.

FUNCTION   making conversation

3A Ss look at the situations in the pictures and cover Ex 3A. Tell them that all the people there are 'making conversation'. Look at the first picture and elicit examples of possible responses to the sentence in speech bubble 1, e.g. *Hi, nice to meet you./Hello, Rachel, I'm Judy.* Ss then work in pairs and do the same for responses 2–12. Monitor and check on the appropriacy of Ss' responses as well as problem areas you'll need to focus on in feedback later on. Ss then look at Ex 3A. With *weaker classes*, teach/check *architect, probably, keep in touch.* Otherwise, do this in feedback in Ex B. Give Ss 3–4 mins to match the responses alone. When they compare their answers, they should tick any that were the same/similar to their own responses earlier. Do feedback in Ex B.

B Play the recording. Ss listen, check and compare their answers. If they have any doubts, play the relevant conversations again. Check Ss' answers and teach new words/ phrases as necessary. It's important to highlight common fixed phrases for Ss wherever possible. The ones in this exercise are particularly useful in everyday contexts. Elicit two examples of fixed phrases and ask Ss to underline others, e.g. *Nice to meet you. How are you? Fine, thanks. See you soon. Would you like a ___? I'd love a ___. How do you know ___? Let's keep in touch. I'll probably see you on ___.* Elicit/drill complete sentences for those with gaps, e.g. *Would you like a sandwich/drink?* Finally, check Ss' own responses for situations 1–12 in Ex 3A. Ask *How many similar responses did you give? Which ones?*

> **Answers:** 1 g) 2 d) 3 a) 4 l) 5 j) 6 i) 7 f) 8 b) 9 c) 10 k) 11 h) 12 e)

Unit 1 Recording 5

W=Woman M=Man

Conversation 1

W1: This is my friend, Rachel.

W2: Hi. Nice to meet you.

Conversation 2

M1: Nice day, isn't it?

W3: Yes, it's lovely.

Conversation 3

M2: Would you like a drink?

W4: I'd love a coffee, thank you.

Conversation 4
M3: Where exactly do you come from?
W5: Woodbridge. It's a small town near Ipswich.

Conversation 5
M3: So, do you work here?
W5: No, I'm just visiting.

Conversation 6
M4: Did you have a good weekend?
W6: Yes, it was OK. I didn't do much.

Conversation 7
M4: Did you watch the match last night?
W6: Yes, it was terrible. We lost 3–0.

Conversation 8
M5: How do you know Hiro?
M6: Oh, we work together.

Conversation 9
M5: So, what do you do?
M6: I'm an architect.

Conversation 10
M7: It was nice to meet you.
M8: It was nice to meet you, too.

Conversation 11
M7: I hope we meet again soon.
M8: Yes, let's keep in touch.

Conversation 12
M9: See you soon.
W7: Yes, I'll probably see you on Wednesday.

4 Put Ss into A/B pairs and tell them to look at the relevant exercises on p160 or p162. Do question 1 as an example: elicit Student A's question (*Would you like a drink?*) and Student B's answer (*I'd love an orange juice, please.*) Tell Ss to face each other and not show their books. Monitor while Ss work and make notes of problems they have. With *mixed-ability* or *weaker classes*, provide more support for the preparation stage. Divide the classes into Student As and Student Bs. In pairs/small groups, Student As work together to prepare their questions and Student Bs do the same with their questions. Pair *stronger Ss* with *weaker ones* and monitor to provide extra help with accuracy where needed. In feedback, nominate Student As and Bs to ask/answer each question across the class. Then write problems Ss had on the board and ask them to correct the mistakes in pairs.

Answers:
Student A questions: 1 Would you like a drink? I'd love an orange juice, please. 2 Do you work here? No, I'm just visiting. 3 Did you watch the match last night? Yes, it was brilliant. 4 How do you know Sam? We work together. 5 It's a nice day, isn't it? Yes, it's lovely. 6 It was nice to meet you. It was nice to meet you, too.
Student B questions: 1 This is my friend, Pete. Hi, Pete. Nice to meet you. 2 Did you have a good weekend? Yes, thanks. I didn't do much. 3 What do you do? I work in an office. 4 Where exactly do you come from? I come from Madrid. 5 See you soon. I'll probably see you tomorrow. 6 I hope we meet again soon. Yes, let's keep in touch.

LANGUAGEBANK 1.3 p128–129
Ss can refer to the information in the tables to help them with Ex A and B.

Answers:
A 2 Hi. Nice to ~~know~~ *meet* you. 3 ~~Do~~ *Would* you like a drink? 4 It was nice *to* meet you. 5 Did you have *a* good weekend? 6 How *do* you know Pieter?
B 1 Let's keep in touch. 2 I'll probably see you on Saturday. 3 So, what do you do? 4 I hope we meet again soon. 5 Where exactly do you come from? 6 See you soon.

LEARN TO sound natural

5A Ss may already be aware of how words are linked in English, especially if they studied *Speakout Elementary*. Play the recording while Ss listen and read. Then ask *How/When do we link words in sentences in English?* Give Ss time to look at the sentences again and discuss their answers. Elicit the answer: when one word ends in a consonant and the following word begins with a vowel, e.g. *would_you*.

B Play the recording again for Ss to listen and repeat. Play it as many times as necessary until Ss are confident. Then do individual repetition and correction as needed. If Ss find the word linking difficult, drill the pairs of linked words in isolation, and then drill the whole phrase again.

speakout TIP
Read the speakout tip with Ss and check the examples. Ss then look at the questions in the speech bubbles in the pictures in Ex 3A, and find questions where they could add *so* in a natural way (7 and 8). It would also be useful to point out the use of *exactly* to ask for more detail. Elicit other examples: *Where exactly do you come from? What exactly do you do?*

SPEAKING

6A Check the rubric and example questions with Ss. Then give them 3–4 mins to prepare five different ones. They should also practise saying the questions to each other. Monitor to check the accuracy of their questions and help with pronunciation where needed.

B First check the flowchart and elicit an example for each stage. Ss then work in groups, or stand up and walk around the class, acting out the conversation with at least five other Ss. *Weaker classes* could first practise the conversation in pairs before moving on to the group activity. You can then monitor and provide support as necessary. During the activity, monitor discreetly, making notes of both good language and errors. In feedback, ask Ss what they learnt about their classmates. Then write 4–6 examples of the language you noted on the board. Ss correct the errors in pairs.

Alternative approach
Ss choose another identity to use in the conversation: an invented one or a famous person. Give them time to prepare facts about their new identity before they start the conversations.

Homework ideas
• Write two conversations from Ex 6B.
• Language bank 1.3 Ex A–B, p129
• Workbook Ex 1–4, p9

BLACKPOOL

Introduction

Ss watch an extract from the BBC drama *Blackpool,* in which a police detective tries to arrange a date with a woman he's recently met. Ss learn and practise how to talk about a special person in their lives, and write a competition entry about their best friend.

SUPPLEMENTARY MATERIALS

Warm up: bring/download a map of the UK to show where Blackpool is.

Culture notes

Blackpool is a very popular seaside town in north west England, near the large industrial cities of Liverpool and Manchester. It was one of the first British towns to have electric street lights and the annual Blackpool Illuminations (lights) in September are a huge tourist attraction. Blackpool's famous landmarks include Blackpool Tower, the promenade and pier and the Big Wheel (or Ferris Wheel).

Warm up

Lead in and create interest in the lesson. Tell Ss to cover the texts and look at the photos across the bottom of the pages. Ask *Where's Blackpool? What sort of place is it?* Elicit/Show where it is on the map of Britain, if you have one. Then give Ss 2–3 mins to describe the photos and discuss their impressions of Blackpool. Elicit and discuss Ss' answers, feeding in information about Blackpool from the **Culture notes**. Ask *Would you like to go there? Why/Why not?* Tell Ss they'll watch a DVD programme set in Blackpool.

DVD PREVIEW

1A Check the questions and elicit one or two initial answers. Then give Ss 3–4 mins to discuss the questions further and make notes of their answers. In feedback, nominate pairs to tell the class about their ideas. The other Ss can add extra ideas, and agree/disagree.

Culture notes

The BBC drama *Blackpool* was first screened in 2004. It's set in the town of Blackpool and is a mixture of musical, thriller and drama genres. It stars three well-known British actors: David Morrissey (Ripley Holden), David Tennant (Detective Inspector Peter Carlisle) and Sarah Parish (Ripley's wife, Natalie Holden). Ripley doesn't appear in the DVD here but he's a suspect in the murder investigation led by Peter Carlisle.

The **Samaritans** is a free service offered by trained volunteers to give 24-hour support to people with serious problems.

B Ss cover the programme information and look at the two photos. Ask prediction questions, e.g. *Who are the people? Where are they? What are they doing? Why is the man looking at the woman? Do they know each other?* Give Ss 1 min to read the programme information and check the answers to their questions. Ask *Were your guesses correct? What did you find out?* Ss then read the text again and answer questions 1–3. In feedback, check/teach the meaning of *investigate, murder episode, follow, ask (her) out.* Then discuss the last two questions. Ss now know that Peter is depressed and Natalie is a Samaritans counsellor. *Will he ask her out? Will she accept?* They'll find out in Ex 2A.

Answers: 1 He's a detective. 2 They first met when he visited the Samaritans to talk about his problems. 3 In a supermarket in Blackpool.

▶ DVD VIEW

2A Ss read the questions. Check/teach *pretends, go out (with).* Play the DVD.

Teaching tip

Tell Ss to focus on answering the question, and not worry about language they don't understand. They'll watch the DVD again in Ex 3.

Ss compare their answers. Play the DVD again if they don't agree. In feedback, elicit answers and check Ss' predictions from Ex 1B. (*Yes, he did ask her out and she did accept.*) Then invite some initial comments about the programme. Ask, e.g. *What are Peter/Natalie like? Does Natalie like Peter? Does he look like a detective?*

Alternative approach

Play the DVD without the sound first. Ss will be able to concentrate on what's happening and not be distracted by looking at their books. When Ss have compared their answers, play the DVD again with the sound so that they can check their answers.

Answers: 2 b) 3 d) 4 e) 5 c)

B Ss read and answer the questions. In feedback, check their answers and predictions for question 3.

Answers: 1 No, he doesn't. 2 Tofu is made from soy milk. Peter doesn't like it. He puts it in his basket because he is pretending to be shopping. 3 Ss' own answers. N.B. Ss won't see what happens next on the DVD, but Peter and Natalie do get together and eventually Natalie divorces her husband.

3 Ss read the sentences first. Elicit/teach a less formal and simpler way of saying *I wondered if you were doing anything tonight?* (*Are you doing anything tonight?*) With **stronger classes**, you could do this in feedback. Play the DVD. Ss watch, listen and compare their answers. If necessary, play the DVD again, and pause/rewind the sentences containing the answers (in bold in the DVD script). In feedback, ask *Does Natalie think it's a good idea to meet Peter? How do you know?* Because of her comments in questions 3 and 4. *Do you think she likes him?* Yes, because she agrees to meet him in a bar.

Answers: 1 P 2 P 3 N 4 N 5 N

DVD 1 Blackpool

P=Peter N=Natalie

P: Hello again.

N: Hello.

P: I came to see you in your other life. Er… Samaritans.

N: Yeah, yeah, I remember – 'The Questions Man'.

P: Yeah, that's me. **So, what are you doing?**

N: There you go again. Questions, questions, questions. Oh, I, I'm … just shopping.

P: Right.

N: I see you like tofu, then?

P: Yeah, I find it very adaptable.

N: Hmm.

P: And nutritious, and … ah, I don't like tofu, I just saw you in the supermarket and I came in and pretended to be shopping so that I had an excuse to contrive a second meeting with you.

N: Why would you want to do that?

P: Because **I wondered if you were doing anything tonight?**

N: It really, really wouldn't be a good idea.

P: You know what?

N: What?

P: I have lived all my life doing the right thing, and there's something about you that tells me that you have as well. Maybe just this once, you and me should do the wrong thing.

N: It's not going to happen.

P: OK. But, if it … if it was going to happen, where would we meet?

N: A bar called Funny Girls, 8.30.

speakout a special person

4A Ss now talk about people they know. Check the rubric and questions, and give Ss 3 mins to think about their answers. They should note down the names with reasons for their choice. Monitor and provide help if necessary.

B First elicit some answers before Ss work in pairs, making sure that Ss give reasons for their choices. Then monitor to ensure they are giving reasons. In feedback, nominate each student to tell the class about one of their choices.

5 Check the questions, especially question 2. Elicit examples of people who are important to your Ss, e.g. *family members, friends, teachers.* Give Ss time to think and note down their answers. They will be able to expand on these in Ex 6C after listening to the model text. Monitor and help where needed.

6A Check the rubric and questions. Ss then listen to the model and compare answers. Check these in feedback. Teach *grow up together* if necessary.

Answers: 1 They grew up together. 2 They know each other very well, have the same friends and enjoy the same things.

B First read/check the **key phrases** with Ss, then play the recording again. Ss tick the ones they hear and compare them. In feedback, play the recording and pause at each **key phrase** (in bold in the audio script). Elicit/drill the complete sentences and ask further comprehension questions, e.g. *Where did he and Bruno live? Did they go to the same school?*

Answers: I've known (name) for … , He is one of my best friends because … , We get on well because … , We both enjoy … , We keep in touch by …

Optional extra activity

Ss work in A/B pairs. A is the interviewer and B is the person on the recording. Ss A asks Ss B the questions from Ex 5, e.g. *1 Who is this person?* Bruno. Ss then listen to the recording again or read the audio script on SB p168 to check their answers.

Unit 1 Recording 7

I've **known Bruno for** as long as I can remember. **He's one of my best friends because** we grew up together. We lived in the same street and went to all the same schools. I think **we get on well because** we know each other so well. We have a lot of the same friends and we enjoy doing the same things. **We both enjoy** films, so we watch films together or we go out and have a good time. We don't live in the same town now, so we don't see each other very often. But **we keep in touch by** email. And when I go home, the first person I call is always Bruno.

C First give Ss time to check their notes from Ex 5 and add to or revise them using the **key phrases**. They can also use the audio script on SB p168 to help. Provide support to Ss who need it, or ask *stronger Ss* to help *weaker ones*. Ss then take turns to talk about their experiences in pairs. Remind them to ask questions from Ex 5 as often as possible to keep the conversation going. Monitor discreetly and note down the strengths and weaknesses of the language Ss use. In feedback, Ss tell the class about their own/their partner's special person. The class then decide which person was the most 'special' and why. Give feedback on Ss' strengths and weaknesses now, or in the next lesson.

writeback a competition entry

7A Ss first read a model of a competition entry about a best friend. Check the rubric and title of the competition. Ss then read the text and answer the question. In feedback, elicit Ss' answers and teach/check expressions in the text, e.g. *(be) there for me, help me through, sense of humour.*

Possible answers: 1 She is always there for me. 2 She has helped me through some difficult times. 3 We know everything there is to know about each other. 4 I can talk to Julie about anything. 5 She will be a friend forever.

B Give Ss time to think and make notes about who they'll write about. It might be the same person as in Ex 5, or a different one. They should use the **key phrases** and refer to the text in Ex 7A for help. Provide support where needed.

Teaching tip

Encourage a collaborative approach to writing, e.g. Ss show each other their drafts and give advice if possible.

Ss could add photos to their texts and/or put them on the class blog.

Homework ideas

- Ex 6C: write a description of your special person.
- Ex 7B: write a final draft of your competition entry

LOOKBACK

Introduction

The notes below provide ideas for exploiting the exercises and activities but your approach will depend on your aim, e.g. as a diagnostic test/assessment or for fluency practice/revision. For example, if you wanted to assess/test Ss' knowledge, then it would not be appropriate to monitor and help them.

FREE TIME

1A Ss complete the sentences alone and check their answers in pairs. In feedback, elicit and drill the questions to prepare Ss for Ex B.

Answers: 1 have 2 off 3 spend 4 on 5 eat 6 go

B While Ss ask/answer the questions, note down problems for feedback or assessment, if required. In feedback, write examples of correct/incorrect sentences on the board for Ss to correct alone/in pairs. Alternatively, write the sentences on an A4 sheet of paper after the lesson. Photocopy it for your Ss as a warm up for the next class (or use an OHP or IWB if available).

QUESTION FORMS

2 First give Ss time to read the application form and write the questions. Monitor and prompt Ss to self-correct errors they make if appropriate. Then put Ss into pairs, preferably with a partner they don't know very well so that there is a real information gap. Monitor and give feedback as needed.

Answers: How old are you? Where were you born? Are you married? Where do you live? What's your telephone number? Have you got a mobile phone number? What's your email address? What do you do? Do you have any hobbies?

3A Give Ss 3–4 mins to write questions about their chosen topics. In a *mixed-ability class* you could either put strong/weak Ss together, or put *weaker Ss* together and provide support.

Possible answers: love: Have you got a girlfriend or a boyfriend? When did you meet? home: Where do you live? family: How many people are there in your family? Have you got any children? work: Where do you work? Do you enjoy your job? food: Do you like cooking? Do you eat junk food? holidays: Where do you usually go on holiday?

B Ss take it in turns to ask their questions in groups, and make notes of the answers. Each student could then write a short summary of the answers. Monitor discreetly, making notes of Ss' performance for feedback/remedial work later. In feedback, nominate Ss to tell the class about their group.

RELATIONSHIPS

4A Give Ss 3–4 mins to work alone and note down their answers to the questions. Encourage them to give reasons and extra details about their answers. Monitor and provide language Ss need, if necessary

B While Ss compare and discuss their answers, note down problems for feedback or assessment, if required.

PAST SIMPLE

5A Give Ss 3–4 mins to write the questions. *Weaker classes* could work in pairs.

Answers: 1 Where did you go? 2 Why did you go there? 3 Did you stay in a hotel? 4 What did you do during the day? 5 Did you go out in the evenings? 6 Was the weather hot? 7 What language did you speak? 8 Did you make any new friends?

B While Ss ask/answer the questions, note down problems with the target language (past simple) for feedback or assessment, if required.

6A Depending on your aims, *weaker classes* could refer back to the verbs on p10–11 in their books.

B Ss could make a note of the number of incorrect answers their partners gave. The activity could also be done as a team game.

C Ss work alone to write questions for the verbs they chose in Ex 6A. Monitor and make notes of problems with the question forms for feedback.

D Give Ss 5–6 mins to ask and answer the questions and make notes. They could then work with another pair and tell them about their partners' answers.

Optional extra activity
Provide further practice of past simple forms. Draw a grid on the board with 12 squares numbered 1–12. Put Ss into teams and name them A, B, C, etc. Demonstrate the activity. Ask team A to choose a number from the grid. Give them the verb from the grid below, e.g. 1 *meet*. Ss must make a correct sentence in the past simple, e.g. *I met my husband in my English class*. Teams take turns to choose a number and select a student from their team to make a sentence. They get a point for each correct sentence. The team with the most points wins.

Your verb grid:

1 (meet)	2 (fall)	3 (go)
4 (cook)	5 (study)	6 (get)
7 (start)	8 (decide)	9 (say)
10 (have)	11 (stop)	12 (live)

MAKING CONVERSATION

7A Ss work alone to complete the conversations, though *weaker Ss* could work together. Ss should practise saying the conversations alone. Monitor and help them with pronunciation where needed.

Suggested answers: 1 Hi, *Marek*. How *are* you? Fine, *thanks*. 2 This is my *friend, Aiko*. Hi. *Nice* to meet you. 3 So, *do* you work here? No, I'm just *visiting*. 4 Where exactly do you *come* from? I come from *Athens*. 5 How do you know *Becky*? Oh, we *work* together. 6 It was nice to *meet* you. Nice to *meet* you, too. 7 I *hope* we meet again soon. Yes, let's *keep* in touch. 8 *See* you again. I'll probably see you later.

B While Ss practise the conversations, note down problems with pronunciation and do remedial work in feedback if appropriate. Ss could also choose one or two conversations and memorise/rehearse them to perform to the class.

OVERVIEW

THE COMPANY 4 U?

Introduction

Ss revise/practise the present simple and continuous in the context of work. They learn vocabulary to talk about their jobs/work, and how to start/end an email.

SUPPLEMENTARY MATERIALS

Resource bank p150

Ex 2A: Ss may need dictionaries.

Ex 9C: bring/download suitable job advertisements (similar to the one in Ex 9B) for the extra activity/homework.

Warm up

Tell Ss to think of a person they know well who has a job. Then ask them questions about the person, using the following questions, or your own: *1 Where is he/she now? 2 What's he/she doing at the moment? 3 Where does he/she work? 4 What time does he/she usually go to work? 5 When does he/she get home? 6 Does he/she work alone or with other people? 7 Does he/she work inside or outside?* Ss note down their answers. They then work in pairs, read each other's answers and guess the person's job.

VOCABULARY work

1 Give Ss 1 min to look at the photo and memorise the details. They then cover the photo and answer question 1 in pairs. Check answers and teach new vocabulary, e.g. *open-plan office, work on the computer.* Give Ss another 2–3 mins to discuss the other two questions.

2A Check the example and the meaning of *provide services.* Ss do the exercise and compare answers. In feedback, check/teach, e.g. *products, desks, manages,* if necessary. With **weaker classes,** you may want to check this language first. Alternatively, Ss could check it in their dictionaries.

Answers: 2 customer 3 salary 4 office 5 employee 6 task 7 boss 8 staff

B Ss listen and repeat the words. Elicit the main stress in each word. Play the recording as many times as necessary until Ss are confident. They copy the words and underline the stressed syllable.

LISTENING

3A Check the definition of *motivate* from the *Longman Wordwise Dictionary.* If Ss want advice about buying a monolingual dictionary, this is a good one to recommend for this level. Teach/check new language in the pictures, e.g. *have a massage.* Elicit Ss' ideas for the first picture: this is a prediction activity so encourage them to be imaginative. Give Ss 2–3 mins to discuss their ideas in pairs. In feedback, elicit and write their ideas on the board.

B Play the recording. Ss listen and check their ideas from the board, and make notes of other ideas they hear. In feedback, refer to the ideas on the board. Elicit/check those that were the same, and then discuss the other ideas that were mentioned (highlighted in bold in the audio script). Ss then discuss which ideas they think are the best.

Answers: A Yahoo employees have a free bus ride to work. B Yahoo employees watch films together once a month. C Google employees can have a cheap massage. D Google employees can bring their dogs to work. E Starbucks employees get free coffee. F A phone company has an office party on the last Friday of each month for their employees.
Other ideas: a dentist and hairdresser at the office, lunch is free, surprise holidays, employees can bring their children to work, fishing after work

Unit 2 Recording 2

M=Man W=Woman

M: These days many companies motivate their staff in new and different ways. Internet companies are a good example. At Yahoo there's a **free bus ride to work** for the employees. There's also **a dentist and a hairdresser** at the office. And one day a month **the staff watch films together**. These are all great ideas for motivating your workers.

W: Well, Google also has some interesting ways to motivate staff. **Lunch is free.** And after sitting at your desk for hours, you can **have a cheap massage** in the office.

M: Wow.

W: Another nice little bonus – you can **take your dog to work.**

M: Yahoo and Google are quite famous for this type of thing. But what benefits do other companies give their employees? Well, we found one company that **takes its employees on a surprise holiday every year**. The staff go to the airport but they don't know where they're flying to. In the past these trips included Amsterdam, Iceland and even the Caribbean.

W: At Starbucks employees get **free coffee,** of course, but they can also **bring their children to work.**

M: And there's a phone company that **has a party for the staff** on the last Friday of every month – with free drinks.

W: Finally, a very interesting idea: an insurance company keeps fish in a little river next to the office. The employees **go fishing after work** and they **take home all the fish that they catch.**

M: Fantastic.

W: Isn't that a great idea?

4A Check the meaning of the phrases in the box. Tell Ss to focus on the task and not worry about language they don't understand yet. Ss listen and compare their answers. In feedback, nominate Ss to answer (see answers in bold in the audio script). Elicit information about the companies mentioned: *Kinkos, etc.*

Answers: 1 choosing a CD 2 studying 3 checking emails

B Check *agreement* in question 1. Ss listen again and make notes. In feedback, check answers (in italics in the audio script) and replay the relevant sections if necessary: teach *flexible hours*. For further exploitation of the language/content of the recording, Ss listen again and read audio script 2.3 on SB p168 at the same time.

Answers: 1 The employees at the music shop get free coffee at Kinko's. The employees at Kinko's get one free CD a week from the music shop. 2 It pays for employees to do courses. 3 Because the company has flexible hours.

Unit 2 Recording 3

Conversation 1

I=Interviewer M=Man

M: Hi. I work at Kinko's coffee shop across the street. But, er, at the moment I'm having a break here in the music shop.

I: And what are you doing on your break?

M: **I'm choosing my free CD** for the week.

I: Free CD? Can you tell us a bit more? Why are you doing this?

M: Sure. Kinko's, the coffee shop, has an agreement with the music shop. *The employees at the music shop get free coffee at Kinko's.* They all come in during their break. *And we get one free CD a week from the music shop.*

I: Great!

M: We all know each other and it works really well.

Conversation 2

I=Interviewer W=Woman

W: So, this is the clothes shop. And this is the study area.

I: Right. So you have a study area?

W: Yeah. As you can see, David over there is studying. And these two are doing an online course.

I: And this is during company hours? Does the boss know about this?!

W: It's the boss' idea. *The company pays for employees to do courses.* So during our breaks or after seven when the shop closes, we can stay on and study.

I: That's excellent. And are you studying at the moment?

W: Yeah, but I'm not studying anything connected with fashion.

I: What are you studying?

W: **I'm studying history.**

I: And the company pays?

W: *The company pays. It pays for about six of us.* I think six of us are doing online courses.

I: Brilliant.

Conversation 3

I=Interviewer E=Employee

E: Hi there. I work for a software company.

I: And what are you doing now?

E: Well, **I'm checking my emails at the moment** because I need to see what work I have to do today.

I: At one o'clock?!

E: Well, *the company has flexible hours. You can arrive when you want and go home at any time.*

I: That sounds good.

E: It's great. We get a salary for good work, not for the time we spend in the office. So, really, the important thing is to do your job well. That's what the boss says, anyway!

GRAMMAR present simple and continuous

Watch out!

Ss may make mistakes with both the meaning and form of the two tenses, e.g. *I am not work in an office. He's coming from Japan.* Check the concepts carefully and monitor/correct at all stages of the practice.

5A Check *temporary* in question 2. Ss answer the questions alone and then compare answers. In feedback, elicit other examples of sentences in audio script 2.3 that use the present simple/continuous.

Answers: 1 a) 2 b) 3 a) 4 b)

B Follow the same procedures as in Ex 5A and elicit other examples of the two different concepts.

Answers: 1 a) and b) 2 c) and d)

➠ **LANGUAGEBANK** 2.1 p130–131

Stronger classes can study the tables and notes at home when they do the exercises. Otherwise, check the tables and notes with Ss, especially the use of state verbs. *Weaker Ss* should do Ex A–B in class.

Answers:
A 1 isn't 2 's working 3 'm playing 4 do (you) know
5 are you wearing 6 don't eat 7 'm waiting
B 1 ~~is going~~ goes 2 ~~'m not believing~~ don't believe 3 ✓
4 ~~isn't drinking~~ doesn't drink 5 ~~teaches~~ 's teaching 6 ✓
7 ✓ 8 ~~do you do~~ are you doing

PRACTICE

6 Check the examples. Ss then do the exercise alone and compare answers. Monitor and prompt them to self-correct (correct their own mistakes). Recheck the concept of the two tenses in feedback.

Answers: 2 I'm looking for a job at the moment. I look at my emails when I get to work. 3 I don't use English for my job. I'm not using the photocopier at the moment. 4 Do you watch the news on TV every day? Are you watching TV right now? 5 I'm not reading any good books at the moment. I don't read a newspaper every morning.
6 Are you having a good time at this party? Do you have a company car? 7 I'm selling my house. I sell IT products to companies in Asia.

7A Monitor while Ss write the questions. In *mixed-ability classes*, stronger and weaker Ss work together. Elicit/drill the questions in feedback to prepare Ss for Ex B.

Answers: 2 Do you speak any other languages?
3 Why are you learning English? 4 Are you studying for an exam now? 5 Are you working on a special project at the moment? 6 Do you have your own office? 7 Do you like your boss?

B Monitor and prompt Ss to correct errors they make with the accuracy of the target language (present simple/continuous).

SPEAKING

8A First check, e.g. *tasks, a chance, develop*. Elicit/discuss an example. Give Ss 4–5 mins to discuss and decide their answers.

B Ss work with another pair/in a group. Monitor discreetly while Ss work in groups, and make notes of examples of good language and problems. To make the task more challenging, *stronger classes* could discuss and agree on the top three items in order of importance. Write examples of Ss' errors and good language on the board. They discuss and correct them in pairs.

WRITING starting/ending an email

9A Check the example and elicit one or two more. Ss then work alone and compare answers before feedback. Check the meaning of new language, e.g. *Cheers, (Bye), Regarding*.

Answers:
formal: Dear Sir, Dear Dr Bryce, Regarding, Best wishes, I look forward to hearing from you, Best regards, Yours sincerely
informal: Hi, Hello, Dear All, Hi everyone, I'm writing about … , It's about … , See you soon, Bye for now, Speak soon, Take care, Cheers, Love

B Check *work experience* in the title and give Ss 1–2 mins to read the advertisement and answer the questions. Check new vocabulary, e.g. *high quality* in feedback.

Answers: 1 high quality clothes and shoes for successful professionals 2 people who want work experience in all areas

C Check the rubric/prompts and elicit sample answers. While Ss write their first draft, monitor and provide support. Also encourage them to show their work to a partner before they write a final draft. If you have a class blog, Ss could post their email on it, or send it to you.

Model answer:
Dear Mr Moore,
My name is Patricia Gonzalez. I'm from Venezuela, but I'm living in London at the moment.
I'm writing about your advertisement for work experience.
I'm twenty and I'm studying fashion design at the Royal College of Art in London.
Could you send me some information about your work experience programme?
I look forward to hearing from you.
Yours sincerely,
Patricia Gonzalez

Optional extra activity
If you've brought authentic job advertisements, Ss choose one and write another email in class or at home. Alternatively, Ss interview each other for the job in Ex 9B. Divide the class into pairs/groups of interviewers/applicants. Interviewers decide what qualities/qualifications they are looking for, while applicants decide what qualities/qualifications they need. Interviewers talk to at least three applicants and choose the best one.

Homework ideas
• Ex 9C: write a final draft of the email or another one using a different job advertisement.
• Language bank 2.1 Ex A–B, p131
• Workbook Ex 1–6, p10–11

A RISKY BUSINESS

Introduction

Ss revise and practise the use of adverbs of frequency in the context of reading and talking about work routines and dangerous jobs.

SUPPLEMENTARY MATERIALS

Resource bank p149 and p151

Photo bank p152: Ss may need dictionaries.

Ex 4: dictionaries should be available for Ex 4B and the extra activity.

Ex 7A: bring/download pictures of a variety of dangerous jobs as prompts, e.g. racing driver, police officer, soldier, jockey, circus performer, stunt man.

Warm up

Play the alphabet game to revise jobs. Say *A* and brainstorm all the jobs Ss can think of beginning with A, e.g. *artist, actor*. Do the same for each letter of the alphabet. This is a quick revision activity so keep the pace lively and move on if Ss can't think of jobs for certain letters (they will revise/learn job words in the **Photo bank** later).

VOCABULARY jobs

1A Ss first cover the words and describe/guess the jobs in the photos in pairs. They then match the job words. Elicit/check Ss' answers and the abbreviations *rep* and *IT* (representative, Information Technology).

Answers: A rescue worker B personal trainer C foreign correspondent D sales rep E IT consultant F motorcycle courier G fashion designer

B Check the example. Read the speakout tip with Ss before they listen and repeat the jobs. With *stronger classes*, you could point out that the main stress in noun + noun compounds is usually in the first word, but in adj + noun compounds, it's in the second word.

speakout TIP

Encourage Ss to use the speakout tip with Ex 1B and with other new vocabulary they come across.

Answers: The main stress is in underlined bold and secondary stress is underlined.

<u>sales</u> rep <u>fashion</u> de<u>sign</u>er <u>IT</u> con<u>sult</u>ant <u>foreign</u> corre<u>spond</u>ent <u>personal</u> <u>train</u>er <u>rescue</u> <u>work</u>er <u>mo</u>torcycle <u>cour</u>ier

C Check new language in the rubric, e.g. *opportunities, deal with, tasks*. Elicit answers for one job from Ex 1A and give Ss 4–5 mins to discuss/decide on the best/worst jobs in pairs. In feedback, ask Ss to vote on the best/worst job, and elicit their reasons.

Teaching tip

Use the finger highlighting technique to elicit stress. Hold up one hand and elicit/say each syllable of a word while touching your fingers with the thumb/first finger of your other hand, e.g. *accountant* has three syllables, so you touch three fingers: a-ccoun-tant. Then ask *Where's the stress?* Elicit *On the second syllable: ccount*. Then elicit/drill the word again: a**ccount**ant.

⟹ PHOTOBANK p152

1 Ss can check the job words in their dictionaries if they have difficulty matching them. In feedback, elicit the main stress in each job word.

Answers: 1 P 2 I 3 E 4 G 5 J 6 B 7 H 8 O 9 M 10 D 11 K 12 N 13 L 14 C 15 F 16 A

2 Check the meaning of *dangerous, enjoyable*. Give Ss 5 mins to discuss the questions, giving reasons for their choices. In feedback, Ss vote on each one.

2A Check *risk* in the word box and refer to the title of the lesson *A Risky Business*. Ss then complete the phrases in pairs. In feedback, check the meaning of each phrase by giving/ eliciting examples of jobs they could refer to, e.g. *Police officers risk their lives*. This will prepare them for Ex B.

Answers: 1 get 2 work 3 risk 4 deal with

B While Ss talk about the jobs, monitor and note down problems they have with the new phrases and give feedback afterwards.

Optional extra activity

Ss work in pairs/groups. They choose a job and describe it, using the phrases from Ex 2A and other language they know. Their partner(s) have to guess the job.

3A Ss practise the phrases further here. Give them 2–3 mins to complete and compare the sentences before checking their answers.

Answers: 1 get 2 under 3 holidays 4 risk 5 team 6 deal

B Discuss the first sentence as a class, eliciting reasons, e.g. *I agree because a good salary motivates people to work hard*. In feedback, nominate Ss to tell the class their opinions. Give feedback on language problems afterwards.

READING

4A Check the rubric and give Ss 3–4 mins to answer the questions. They can then compare answers with another pair and change their minds about their first opinions if they wish. In feedback, nominate Ss to give one opinion and reason each.

B Set up this jigsaw reading activity carefully.

Teaching tip

In a jigsaw reading, Ss read different texts about similar topics but have the same questions. They work on their own texts first and then exchange information with those who read the other texts.

Divide Ss into groups of three and name them A, B or C. Ss look at the title of their text. Teach *danger rating*. Then check the rubric and give Ss 3–4 mins to read their own texts and make notes of the answers. They can use their dictionaries to check new words, but tell them to only look up essential vocabulary they need to answer the questions (see also the Optional extra activity after Ex C).

C Ss take it in turns to read their notes and tell the others about their texts. They mustn't look at each others' books. Monitor to check that Ss do this correctly. In feedback, nominate Ss to tell the class about their text. Ask *Do you agree with the danger rating for each text?* Discuss their answers.

Answers:
Job: A motorbike courier B mountain rescue worker
C jockey
Country: A Brazil B Austria C France
People interviewed: A Luis Carlos de Gatto, a motorbike courier. B Emergency doctor Mathias Uhl, paramedic Andreas Würtl and helicopter pilot Martin Nussdorfer.
C Jockey Eric Legrix
Why the job is dangerous: A accidents and robberies
B weather conditions C broken bones and occasional deaths
Special memories/stories: A He was robbed twice and lost everything. B Two people on a ski tour got in an avalanche and broke every bone. A year later, one of the people brought some wine to say thank you. C He once fell off his horse and was knocked unconscious.

Optional extra activity
Ss check 3–4 new words/phrases (from the text they read in Ex B) in their dictionaries, e.g. Text A: *on average, robbery, insurance, respect, traffic laws*; Text B: *alarm, ring, jump into, fog, avalanche, broken bone*; Text C: *gun, gates, glory, generation, ribs, knock unconscious*.
Ss can then read the other two texts and 'teach' the new words/phrases to their partners from Ex C.

GRAMMAR adverbs of frequency

Watch out!

The position of adverbs or adverbial phrases in a sentence varies considerably, so Ss need to be made aware of this. Expose them to the language in natural contexts and provide sufficient controlled practice and feedback.

5A The sentences are from the texts in Ex 4. Ss work alone and then compare their answers. In feedback, draw the line on the board and invite Ss to write the adverbs in the correct place.

Answers: never, hardly ever, rarely, occasionally/once in a while, sometimes, often, usually, always

B Do an example from each text. Then give Ss 2–3 mins to underline the adverbs/expressions. *Fast finishers* can also read the other texts. In feedback, nominate Ss to read out the sentence containing the language, e.g. *The motoboys usually earn just $300 a month.* Elicit/check the position of each adverb in each sentence, e.g. *before/after the main verb* be, *at the beginning/end of the sentence.*

Answers:
Text A: usually earn, often work, never respect, Once in a while
Text B: usually we fly, is that often the people, sometimes get angry, these people always risk, occasionally they get, hardly ever say
Text C: it is sometimes easy, is rarely safe, it usually involves, Once in a while, he never worries

➧ **LANGUAGEBANK** 2.2 p130–131
Read/check the notes with your Ss. They can refer to them when they do the exercises. *Weaker Ss* should do Ex A and B in class. Check *waste money* in Ex A and *my boss is out* in Ex B.

Answers:
A 2 (Once in a while,) I go swimming (once in a while).
3 I never waste my money. 4 Najim doesn't often play tennis. 5 Akiko and Toshi usually stay at home in the evening. 6 Why are you always late? 7 I rarely work late on Fridays. 8 Mary hardly ever deals with customers.
9 (Occasionally) I (occasionally) work in a team (occasionally).
B 1 Usually 2 every day 3 sometimes 4 rarely 5 always
6 Once in a while 7 every year 8 occasionally

PRACTICE

6A Do an example. Ss then correct the sentences alone and check in pairs. In feedback, nominate Ss to write the answers on the board.

Answers: 1 I *always* work at night. 2 Once *in* a while I study at weekends. 3 I *hardly ever* study alone. 4 I work at home *occasionally*. 5 It is *sometimes* difficult to study and work at the same time. 6 I don't *usually* miss classes because of work.

B Check the example and give Ss 2–3 mins to write their sentences. Monitor and help Ss with language they need.

C Monitor and prompt Ss to self-correct errors with adverbs/ expressions. In feedback, invite Ss to tell the class about their partner's job.

SPEAKING

7A Check the rubric and questions. Then elicit ideas for suitable jobs. If you've brought pictures of dangerous jobs, use them as prompts, especially for *weaker classes*. Give Ss 5–6 mins to discuss the questions and decide on their three jobs. They can use the texts from Ex 4 as a model for question 3. Monitor closely to provide help with ideas and vocabulary where needed.

B Give Ss time to prepare their presentation to the other group. They should take it in turns to give their answers to each question in Ex 7A. While Ss talk, make notes on their use of the language they've studied in this lesson and do any remedial work needed later. In feedback, invite each group to tell the class what they thought of the other group's programme.

Optional extra activity
Ss 'present' their TV programme on a poster, using pictures and texts related to the questions in Ex 7A.

Homework ideas
• Ex 7: write a description of your TV programme or make a poster of it. Add pictures/texts.
• Language bank 2.2 Ex A–B, p131
• Workbook Ex 1–6, p12–13

I LIKE WORKING OUTSIDE

Introduction

Ss learn and practise ways of expressing likes/dislikes about work. They also learn how to respond to what people say, and ask more questions in order to sound interested.

SUPPLEMENTARY MATERIALS

Resource bank p152

Ex 3A: Ss need bilingual dictionaries here.

Ex 6C: use recording facilities to record Ss' pronunciation if available

Warm up

Lead in to the lesson via the photos. Ss work in pairs and describe the people, say what they're doing/wearing and guess the jobs, if possible. Monitor and provide useful vocabulary. Ss could also use bilingual dictionaries to look up words they need. In feedback, check Ss' answers using the following ideas. *Photo 1: A man is in the sea. He's wearing a mask and snorkel and he's writing. He's a marine biologist. Photo 2: The man's wearing a uniform and holding some keys/a mobile phone. He's a security guard. Photo 3: They wearing uniforms, helmets and gloves, and holding a water hose. They're putting out a fire. They're fire fighters. Photo 4: The man's sitting at a potter's wheel. He's making a vase/bowl. He's a potter. Photo 5: She's sitting at a computer. She looks very bored. She's a secretary/student.*

FUNCTION   expressing likes/dislikes

1A Check the rubric. Tell Ss to only focus on what he likes about his job. They listen and note down their answers, and then compare them. Play the recording again if necessary. In feedback, check answers and ask *Which photo is he in?*

Answers: He likes working outside, travelling, working alone, and learning new things.

B With *weaker classes*, pause the recording after each sentence in the exercise for Ss to write. Play the recording again and elicit Ss' answers after each question (see answers in bold in the audio script). Check the meaning of *can't stand, don't mind, be keen on.* Also check *get my hands dirty (do manual work), be my own boss (work for myself).* Ask *What do you notice about these verbs?* Elicit they all end in *-ing.* Teach the rule: verbs that follow the expressions/verbs in the exercise always end in *-ing.* Ss should write the new expressions in their notebooks.

Answers: 1 working 2 sitting 3 travelling 4 working 5 getting 6 learning 7 working 8 working

Unit 2 Recording 5

I'm a marine biologist. I work mainly in the sea and also in the lab. The good things about my job are … um … I like **working** outside. In fact, I can't stand **sitting** at a desk all day, so this job is perfect for me. What else? I absolutely love **travelling** and I travel a lot, particularly in South America and Australia. Also I don't like **working** in a team – I prefer working alone – and most of my time is spent alone or just me and nature. Um, what else? One thing that's very important: I don't mind **getting** my hands dirty. That's important in my work because it's a very practical job. You're working with animals and plant life the whole time. Also I'm keen on **learning** new things – and you do learn all the time in this job. So overall, it's the perfect job for me. I couldn't do an office job because I hate **working** under pressure. And I'm not very keen on **working** for a company. I want to be my own boss.

C Do questions 1 and 2 from Ex 1B as examples. Ss then work in pairs and discuss the others. In feedback, check Ss' answers. Then ask *Which sentences match the people in the photos?* Elicit answers, e.g. photo 1: *I like working outside*, photo 2: *I don't like working in a team*, photo 3: *I like working in a team*, photo 4: *I don't mind getting my hands dirty*, photo 5: *I can't stand working at a desk all day.* Finally, elicit examples of sentences that are true for Ss, e.g. *I like working in the garden. / I can't stand junk food;* to prepare them for the next exercise.

Answers: 1 positive 2 negative 3 positive 4 negative 5 not positive or negative 6 positive 7 negative 8 negative

2A Ss work alone and tick sentences that are true for them. They then rewrite the sentences that they didn't tick to make them true for them. Monitor and support Ss who need help.

B Demonstrate the activity. Ask *What do you love/like/hate?* Elicit an answer from Ss' sentences in Ex 2A for each question. Ss then do the same in pairs and make notes of their partner's answers. In feedback, nominate Ss to tell the class about their partner.

➠ LANGUAGEBANK 2.3 p130–131

Refer Ss to the note about *like* + infinitive and elicit more examples. Ss can refer to the information in the tables to help them with this exercise.

Answers:
A 1 listening 2 don't 3 on 4 doesn't 5 loves 6 stand

VOCABULARY   types of work

3A Check the types of work that Ss are not familiar with, e.g. *retail.* Ss could use bilingual dictionaries for words they need in their answers, or ask you. Tell them to write at least three answers to questions 3 and 4. In feedback, write Ss' answers to questions 3 and 4 on the board and check/teach and drill new words.

Suggested answers: 1 the food industry 2 the fashion industry 3 actor, singer, presenter, cameraman, make-up artist, researcher 4 designer, sales assistant, shop manager

B Elicit some examples and give Ss 3–4 mins to discuss their answers. Monitor to assess how well Ss are using the new language. Make notes of problems for feedback. Nominate Ss to tell the class about their own/their partner's answers. Find out which types of work are the most popular.

LISTENING

4A Check new language in the notes: *vocation, vacation* (US usage), *headquarters.* Elicit Ss' predictions to questions 1 and 2 and write them on the board.

B Ss listen and check their predictions. In feedback, check their predictions from Ex 4A and ask *Were you right?*

Answers: 1 You go on holiday with the company and try out a different job (your dream job). 2 The services are for people who can't stand their job and/or want to try a new job.

5A Check the questions. Ss listen and note down their answers, and then compare them. Monitor to check if they need to listen again. Play the recording again if Ss still have doubts. Otherwise, play only the sections of the recording they need to hear again. In feedback, check answers (in bold in the audio script) and teach/check new job words, e.g. *fisherman, magazine publisher, chocolate taster.*

Answers: 1 You spend one weekend working with an expert in the job, e.g. a cheese maker. 2 You can try over 75 jobs: how to make wine, be a TV producer, a fisherman, a magazine publisher, a marine biologist.

B Give Ss 2–3 mins to discuss their answers and report back to the class in feedback.

Unit 2 Recording 6

A: The company is called VocationVacations.

B: VocationVacations?

A: Yeah, and the idea is that you go on holiday with the company …

B: <u>Right.</u>

A: But during the holiday you try out a different job – your dream job.

B: <u>Oh, I see. That sounds interesting.</u>

A: So if you can't stand your job any more, you can try something new!

B: <u>Great. So how does it work?</u>

A: **The holiday is usually just one weekend. You work one-to-one with an expert who shows you how to do the job** …

B: <u>Right.</u>

A: Say, for example, you want to be a cheese maker. You spend the weekend with a real cheese maker who teaches you all about cheese.

B: <u>That's great. So how many jobs can you try?</u>

A: I looked on their website. There's a lot, actually. **You can try over seventy-five jobs.**

B: <u>Wow! Really? And what type of jobs?</u>

A: You can learn **how to make wine.** You can learn to be **a TV producer, a fisherman.**

B: A fisherman?!

A: Yep. **A magazine publisher** … um … **a marine biologist** … and lots of other jobs.

B: <u>Well, I absolutely love the idea.</u> Actually, I'm really keen on working as a chocolate taster.

A: What?

B: Do you think VocationVacations has a holiday for chocolate tasters? I don't mind getting up early …

LEARN TO respond and ask more questions

6A Play the extract. In feedback, ask Ss *What does the listener do when she responds?* Elicit/say that she responds to what the speaker says to show interest and/or asks another question to find out more information.

B Play the recording. Ss listen and repeat.

Teaching tip

Encourage them to copy the intonation and extend their voice range. For example, with the phrase *Oh, I see,* illustrate the rise/fall of the intonation on the words *Oh* and *see* with your arms and hands, as if you were conducting an orchestra. Play the recording for Ss to repeat as many times as necessary until they are confident. Then do individual repetition and correction as needed.

Unit 2 Recording 8

B: Oh, I see. That sounds interesting.

B: Great. So how does it work?

B: Right.

B: That's great. So how many jobs can you try?

C Ss now practise using the phrases. If you have recording facilities, Ss can record the phrases and compare their pronunciation with the recording.

Unit 2 Recording 9

A: But during the holiday you try out a different job – your dream job.

B: Oh, I see. That sounds interesting.

A: So if you can't stand your job any more, you can try something new!

B: Great. So how does it work?

A: The holiday is usually just one weekend. You work one-to-one with an expert who shows you how to do the job …

B: Right.

A: Say, for example, you want to be a cheese maker. You spend the weekend with a real cheese maker who teaches you all about cheese.

B: That's great. So how many jobs can you try?

A: I looked on their website. There's a lot, actually. You can try over seventy-five jobs.

D Give Ss 3–4 mins to underline the phrases and compare their answers. In feedback, elicit and drill the phrases (underlined in audio script 2.6). Play the recording again as a model, if necessary.

Answers:
comments: Right. Great. That's great. Wow! Well, I absolutely love the idea.
questions: So how many jobs can you try? Really? And what type of jobs?

7A Organise Ss into A/B pairs. Elicit an answer to question 1 as an example. Monitor while Ss complete their answers and prompt them to self-correct any errors.

B Check/drill the example dialogue. Ss should sound as interested as they can in their responses. Do feedback in open pairs across the class. (Nominate one student to ask another.) Have a class vote on the student(s) who sounded the most interested.

SPEAKING

8A Check the rubric and prompts with Ss. Then give them 5–6 mins to make notes in pairs. Monitor and support *weaker Ss* if necessary.

B Check the examples and give Ss time to prepare and rehearse how they will 'sell' their vacation. Provide help and support while they do this, especially with intonation. Ss can work in groups or walk around the classroom to find a 'buyer'. During the activity, monitor discreetly, making notes of both good language and errors. In feedback, 'buyers' tell the class what they bought and why.

Homework ideas
- Ex 3B: write about three types of jobs that are good for you, and why.
- Ex 8: write an advertisement for your vacation.
- Language bank 2.3 Ex A, p131
- Workbook Ex 1–4, p14

DREAM COMMUTERS

Introduction

Ss watch an extract from the BBC *The Money Programme: Dream Commuters* which explores the life of a man who decided to move abroad with his family and commute to work in the UK. Ss then learn and practise how to talk about the work/life balance and write a comment on a website.

SUPPLEMENTARY MATERIALS

Ex 3: bring/download maps of England (showing Reading and Gatwick airport) and France (showing Toulouse and the River Lot.

Warm up

Lead in and create interest in the lesson. Tell Ss to cover the texts and look at the photo across the bottom of the pages. Ask *What kind of place is this? Where is it, do you think? What's it like? Would you like to live there? Why/Why not?*

▶ DVD PREVIEW

1 Give Ss 2–3 mins to discuss the questions. In feedback, invite Ss to tell the class about their partner's journey to work. Ask *Who has a good/bad journey to work or school?* Ask for a show of hands to see which is most common.

2A Give Ss 1 min to read the programme information and answer the questions. In feedback, check Ss' answers, but don't teach new vocabulary yet: this is done in Ex B below.

Answers: 1 Because his journey to work took a long time. 2 He took his family to live in France.

B Read/check any problematic language in the definitions, and do the first question as an example. Tell Ss to look at the words in bold in the text and work out which one fits the definition. Ss then work alone and check their answers in pairs. In feedback, elicit/check and drill the words. Ask further checking questions, e.g. *What makes you feel fed up? Do you own a property?* Refer Ss to the photo. Ask *Who is the man? Where is he?* Ss can speculate, but will find out the answers in Ex 3.

Answers: 1 transformed 2 flights 3 commuters 4 traffic 5 commute 6 property 7 fed up with

▶ DVD VIEW

Culture notes

Budget flights are typically offered by airlines such as Easyjet and Ryanair in the UK. Flights are cheaper than normal scheduled flights: seats are not reserved, check-in baggage is restricted and free meals are not provided.

Reading is a large town about 40 miles west of London, on the border of **Hampshire** and **Berkshire**.

Gatwick is one of London's major airports, about 40 miles south of the city. **Toulouse** is in south west France.

The **River Lot** flows into the Garonne.

BT is British Telecom, a UK telecom company.

3 Check the questions and the meaning of *budget flights*. Tell Ss to focus on answering the question, and not worry about language they don't understand. They'll watch the DVD again in Ex 4. Play the DVD. Ss complete the task and compare their answers. Play the relevant sections of the DVD again if they still have doubts. In feedback, elicit answers (the words on the DVD are not exactly the same as in the exercise – see answers in bold in the DVD script). Check the difference between miles/kilometres (1mile = 1.6 km). Also check Ss' predictions from Ex 2. (The man in the photo is Justin Saunders. He is outside his new home in France.) If you've brought some maps, elicit/point out where Reading and Toulouse are and show them the River Lot, where Albas is situated.

Answers: 1 and commute to their jobs in the UK 2 cheaper houses in Europe and budget flights 3 £38 4 700 miles (1127 km)

4 Ss read the sentences. Check *available, terrace*. Ss watch the DVD and compare their answers. Play it again if necessary. Ask Ss to tell you to pause the DVD when they hear the answers (underlined in the DVD script).

Answers: 1 J 2 P 3 J 4 R 5 J

Optional extra activity

Play the DVD again, pausing at suitable points. Ask questions about what Ss can see, e.g. *What's he/she doing now? Where are they? What do you think of the plane/house/view/Albas?* You can do this kind of activity with any DVD. It involves Ss and gives them the opportunity to learn/focus on language and ideas in an authentic context.

DVD 2 The Money Programme: Dream Commuters

P=Presenter JS=Justin Saunders RS=Rebecca Saunders
W1=Woman W2=Woman 2

P: Tonight on *The Money Programme*. Are you fed up of travelling to work on packed commuter trains? Are you tired of being sat in endless traffic queues? Well, now there's an alternative. **More and more people are choosing to live abroad and commute to their jobs in Britain** like this. **It's cheap houses in Europe and budget flights that are changing the way we live.** We're following some of the lucky people who've moved across the channel but still earn their living here. They're Britain's dream commuters.

It's the end of the working week and Justin Saunders is heading home.

JS: Bye everybody. See you next week then.

W1: See ya.

P: He runs an online map company near Reading.

JS: I get fed up with the traffic. There's just so many cars on the road. It's been a tiring, tiring week but I'm glad to be going home.

P: But his home is a little further away than most. Justin's part of Britain's new breed of Euro commuters.

W2: Boarding starts at six o'clock and the gate number will be on the screens in Departures.

P: He flies from Gatwick to his house in south west France. And Justin's not alone. He's one of a group of commuters who take the same flight to Toulouse every week. There's a hotel operator, an IT worker, a charity manager and a BT consultant. Only this week they've got one more: me. It's straight off. No time for shopping with these guys. So why did you decide to make this move in the first place?

JS: We basically decided to move to France for the better quality of life. We thought we looked on the internet and we saw properties available much cheaper than in Britain. We were fed up with the commuting and the traffic.

P: But what's the cost of the commute?

JS: When I book the flights early enough, **I'm paying something like 38 pounds return.**

P: Justin's life is in a village in south west France, an hour's drive from Toulouse Airport and **over 700 miles from his Hampshire office.**

JW: Daddy's home.

JS: Where's Georgie?

RS: She's asleep.

JS: She's asleep.

RS: So how was the flight?

JS: Oh, not too bad. Nice to be back home, though.

P: It's morning in the French village of Albas, beside the River Lot and Justin Saunders seems pretty happy.

RS: That's the house down there. With the terrace.

P: The one just here with the river view.

RS: The river view, yeah.

JS: We're still pinching ourselves. Is this really real? We've just transformed our lifestyle.

P: Well, wouldn't you commute by plane for this?

5 Elicit an example of a benefit/problem of being a 'dream commuter'. Ss then discuss the questions and make a list. In feedback, elicit Ss' answers and write them in two columns, or ask Ss to write them. Then ask question 1. Ss vote *yes/no* and explain why.

speakout work/life balance

6 Ss now have the opportunity to talk about the work/life balance in their own countries. First teach *on average, percent (%)* for the text. Then check the questions and give Ss 4–5 mins to read and discuss them. In *multilingual classes*, Ss might want to work with others from the same part of the world. They should note down their answers. Monitor and provide help if necessary. Discuss Ss' answers in feedback.

7 First read and check the **key phrases** with Ss. They then listen and tick the answers, and compare them. In feedback, play the recording again, pausing at each **key phrase** (in bold in the audio script). Elicit/drill the complete sentences and ask further comprehension questions, e.g. *How long does Zeinab spend studying? How often does she have a holiday?*

Answers: Yes, she does.
Key phrases: How much time do you spend sleeping? Do you ever have a holiday? What about your weekends?

Unit 2 Recording 10

A=Alistair Z=Zeinab

A: Zeinab, can I ask you a few questions about your work/life balance?

Z: Of course.

A: OK. First question: **how much time do you spend sleeping?**

Z: Lots! Probably about eight or nine hours a night!

A: Really?!

Z: Yep.

A: OK. And what about studying?

Z: Well, I suppose usually about five or six hours a day, although it depends. I mean if I have an exam coming up or something, it's probably more.

A: **Do you ever have a holiday?**

Z: Oh yeah. Probably twice a year I try and go abroad and just completely relax.

A: OK. **What about your weekends?** Do you ever study at the weekend?

Z: Not usually, but once in a while I open a book!

A: Right. And do you think you have a good work/life balance?

Z: I think so, yeah. I'm not too stressed or anything.

A: Easy life being a student.

Z: Oh yeah!

8A First elicit more example questions, using the **key phrases**. Ss should then write at least one question for each topic. *Stronger Ss* could also refer to the audio script on SB p168 for ideas. Provide support to Ss who need it, or ask *stronger Ss* to work with *weaker ones*. Monitor closely to check the accuracy of Ss' questions.

B Ss then take turns to ask/answer their questions in groups. Monitor discreetly and note down the strengths and weaknesses of the language Ss use. In feedback, Ss talk about a person from their group with a similar work/life balance to theirs. Give feedback on Ss' performance, either now or at the beginning of the next class.

writeback a web comment

9A Check the questions. Give Ss 3 mins to read the text and answer the questions. They can compare them in small groups. In feedback, discuss Ss' answers and teach/check expressions in the text, e.g. *get stressed, partying*.

Possible answers: 1 Not really. The person has a good work/life balance, except for the commute every day.
2 Ss' own answers

B Give Ss time to think and make notes for their comment. They should use the **key phrases** and refer to the text in Ex 9A for help. Provide support where needed.

Homework ideas
- Ex 5: write about the benefits and problems of being a 'dream commuter'.
- Ex 9B: write another comment for the website/your class blog.

LOOKBACK

Introduction

Lookback activities are designed to provide revision and communicative practice in a motivating way. This helps the Ss and gives you the opportunity to assess their ability to use the language they've learnt in the unit. It's a good idea to monitor and assess individual Ss while they do the activities, and compare their performance with their results in more formal tests.

PRESENT SIMPLE AND CONTINUOUS

1 Ss first read the sentences. Check the meaning of *keep fit, published, divorced*. Ss should decide on the verbs they can use first and discuss them in pairs. They then complete the sentences alone and compare answers. In feedback, ask Ss to justify the tense they chose: present simple for routines or things that are generally true; present continuous for things happening now or around now.

> **Answers:** 2 a) 'm/am doing b) do 3 a) play b) 's playing
> 4 a) write b) 's writing 5 a) 's working b) works 6 a) makes
> b) 'm making 7 a) has b) 's having 8 a) 're getting b) get
> 9 a) reads b) 'm reading 10 a) 'm visiting b) visit

2A Elicit some examples to show Ss what to do, e.g. *I usually sing opera in the bath.* Give Ss 4–5 mins to write their sentences. Monitor and prompt them to self-correct where necessary.

B Check the example. Point out that Ss must use words from each box in Ex A in both their statements and responses, e.g. *rarely, work, at my desk* and *often, work, at home*. They can respond to their partner's sentences with a follow-up question or statement. Do more examples to illustrate this, if necessary. Ss then work in pairs and take turns to read out their sentences and respond to each other. They should try to extend the conversation for as long as possible, e.g. *A: I never drink tea at my desk. B: Do you usually drink coffee? A: No, I always drink water. B: Oh, I occasionally drink water, but I prefer coffee.* Monitor and note down problems Ss have with tense, word order or meaning/use of the adverbs for feedback (or use the information for assessment if required). In feedback, nominate Ss to act out one of their dialogues to the class. The pair with the longest string of follow-up questions and statements wins.

ADVERBS OF FREQUENCY

3A First check new language in the exercise, e.g. *go camping, wake (me) up*. Give Ss 3–4 mins for the exercise. They then compare answers and discuss the ones they don't agree on. Encourage them to justify/explain the answers they gave during this checking stage. In feedback, check answers and recheck the meaning of *once in a while/occasionally, hardly ever*. With *weaker classes*, drill the questions and answers chorally, and then in open pairs across the class. Correct pronunciation mistakes as required.

> **Answers:** 1 d) 2 a) 3 f) 4 e) 5 b) 6 g) 7 c)

B Give Ss time to rehearse the questions by saying them to themselves. Monitor and help them with their pronunciation where needed. Ss then take turns to ask/answer the questions. They should note down their partner's answers so that they can report back to the class in feedback. Monitor discreetly, making notes of individual student's performances. In feedback, Ss tell the class/group about their partner. Give feedback and do remedial work as required.

EXPRESSING LIKES/DISLIKES

4A First ask Ss to sit with a classmate they think they know well. They then read the statements. Elicit one or two example questions that Ss think they know how their partner will answer, e.g. *Do you like opera, Olga? No, I can't stand it.* Give Ss 3–4 mins to write a question for each answer. Monitor and prompt them to self-correct any errors they make. Try to check all Ss' work so that the questions they ask in Ex B are grammatically correct.

B Read/check the example dialogue. Tell Ss that they can give themselves 3 points for each question their partner answers as predicted, e.g. *Do you like Italian food? I absolutely love it.* They can also get one extra point for each follow-up question they ask. Tell them you will be assessing their use of follow-up questions while they work. In feedback, find out who had the most points. Then invite pairs to act out their conversations to the class. Tell the other Ss to listen and write down any other follow-up questions to ask once each pair has finished talking. Finally give feedback and do remedial work as needed.

WORK AND JOBS

5 Check the example and elicit another one to demonstrate the activity clearly, e.g. *a personal trainer doesn't have to risk his/her life.* First, give Ss 2–3 mins to think about which words/phrases can be used together to make sensible statements. Monitor and provide help, if needed. Then put Ss into pairs of similar ability. They take turns to go first. They should give each other a point for a correct answer. The one with the most points is the winner. Do feedback in open pairs across the class: one student says a word/phrase and the other must choose another and explain the connection between them. Prompt Ss to correct themselves/each other. Finally, do remedial work as needed.

OVERVIEW

LONDON FOR FREE

Introduction

Ss revise/practise the present continuous and *be going to* to talk about future plans and arrangements. They learn vocabulary to talk about going out in London, and how to write an invitation email.

SUPPLEMENTARY MATERIALS

Resource bank p154

Photo bank p153: Ss may need dictionaries.

Warm up: bring pictures of the famous London sights given in the warm up notes and make photocopies of words for the activity in the warm up.

Ex 2B: use the pictures of Trafalgar Square and Covent Garden from the warm up.

Warm up

Introduce some famous sights in London. Write the names of the places below on the board, or give Ss photocopies of the names if you have them. Leave gaps in the words, e.g. Tr _ f _l g _r Sq_ _re. In pairs/teams, Ss complete the names of the places. Elicit/check the names and discuss what Ss know about them. N.B. If you've brought pictures of the places, Ss can match them to the names.

Places: Trafalgar Square, The National Gallery, Covent Garden, Tate Modern, Tower Bridge, Piccadilly Circus, Oxford Street, Buckingham Palace, The British Museum.

VOCABULARY time out

1A Give Ss time to read the word webs. Check/teach and drill unknown words. Ss write their answers alone and check in pairs. In feedback, check answers. Ss then copy the word webs into their notebooks. Advise Ss to use a separate section in their notebooks for recording new vocabulary.

Answers: 1 go to 2 see 3 get 4 go 5 have

B Tell Ss to use at least one example from each word web in their questions. Monitor while Ss do the exercise and give feedback on problems you noticed.

⏵ PHOTOBANK p153

1 Ss can use their dictionaries to check words they don't know.

Answers: 1 E 2 O 3 L 4 B 5 D 6 C 7 N 8 A 9 K 10 F 11 M 12 G 13 H 14 J 15 I

2 *Stronger classes* may know how to use the present perfect with *ever/never*. However, to help *weaker classes*, write these prompts on the board for Ss to use in their answers: 1 *I've never collected/been to/seen/played/surfed/walked/cycled …* . 2 *I'd like to …* . Elicit some sentences using the prompts before Ss work in pairs.

LISTENING

2A First elicit what Ss know about the places in the photos before they discuss the questions. In feedback, nominate pairs to tell the class about their ideas.

> **Suggested answers:** What you can do: see Big Ben, go on the London Eye, walk around Theatreland and go to a play/musical, walk around or go shopping in Camden Market, walk through Green Park, visit the British Museum **Free activities:** Big Ben, the British Museum, Camden Market, Green Park. **Not free:** the theatre, shopping

> **Culture notes**
> Columbia Road flower market is a popular Sunday market in East London.

B Give Ss time to read the notes first. If you have pictures of the places mentioned (from the warm up), use them again here. Ss then listen and complete the notes.

C After comparing answers, play the recording again, if necessary. In feedback, check the answers (in bold in the audio script) and replay any sections Ss still have problems with.

> **Answers:** 1 museums and art galleries 2 sightseeing
> 3 parks 4 markets 5 comedy, concerts

Unit 3 Recording 1

P=Presenter K=Ken

P: Hi, this is George Thomas on *The London Show*. Now, London is one of the world's top five expensive cities to live in. But did you know that there are lots of things you can do in London for free? That's right. This morning we're talking to Ken Smith, a tourist guide from Going Out in London. So, Ken, what can we do in London for free?

P: Hi, George. Well, many people come to London to visit its famous museums and art galleries. **But did you know that many of London's museums and art galleries are free?** You can go to the British Museum or see paintings by Raphael and Picasso in The National Gallery. And you don't need lots of money in your pocket.

P: Free museums – that's good, because they can be very expensive.

K: That's right. And another thing. If you **go sightseeing, some of London's most famous sights: Big Ben, Tower Bridge, Piccadilly Circus and Trafalgar Square are all free. And the parks, too. If you want a really good view of London, you can walk through one of London's many parks.**

P: That's a good tip. Now what about shopping? People love to shop in London, but you can't do that for free?

K: No, you're right. But go to one of London's famous markets to experience the atmosphere of the city. **Try the busy markets in Camden, or Covent Garden. Or for something different, go to the flower market in Columbia Road.** It's beautiful.

P: OK. I love markets. They're a great place to meet people. You meet all kinds of people in a market, don't you?

K: Yes, you do.

P: Right. So, we've got culture, museums, sightseeing, parks, markets. Is there anything else? What about entertainment? Going out?

K: Well, yes. **Lots of comedy shows are free in the city, and many theatres offer free (or very cheap) seats, too.** You can find **free concerts with all kinds of music, from classical to jazz.** In Hyde Park in the summer, you can go to the **'Proms', a free classical music concert. And you find lots of free music in pubs, too.**

P: Thanks Ken. That sounds brilliant. I had no idea you could do so much for free in London. Now, you know what we're going to do next. We've got this week's £15 challenge. Here's the challenge …

> **Culture notes**
> The King's Head is a well-known pub in Islington in north London.
>
> Brick Lane is in the East End of London. There's a popular 'flea market' and lots of restaurants/shops.

3A Check the questions before Ss discuss them. N.B. Tell Ss what £15 is worth in euros, dollars or the local currency. In *multilingual classes*, put Ss of different nationalities together so there is a real information gap. In feedback, Ss tell the class about their partner's answers.

B After Ss have listened and compared answers, play the recording again, if necessary (answers in bold in the audio script).

> **Answers:** 1 free 2 Concert 3 dinner/a restaurant
> 4 Gallery 5 free 6 £8

C Elicit one or two answers to the questions to set up the activity. While Ss talk, monitor and make notes of remedial work to focus on in feedback.

Unit 3 Recording 2

P=Presenter D=Dominique R=Rob

P: … on this week's £15 challenge. We're going to send two people out for a night in London, and their challenge is to have a good night out, but not spend more than £15. So, is it possible? Well, we're going to find out. We've asked Dominique and Rob to spend an evening in London, and not spend more than £15. So, let's speak to Dominique first. Hi, Dominique.

D: Hi, George.

P: Tell us, Dominique, what are your plans?

D: Well, first of all **I'm going to see a free art exhibition at the Tate Modern.** I don't normally like modern art, so I hope it's OK. Then I'm meeting some friends and we're going to **a concert at a pub called The King's Head.** There's a free band playing and so I only need to pay for my drinks. Afterwards **we're having dinner in Brick Lane** where there are lots of Indian restaurants. They've told me that if you go to one of the restaurants there at 10p.m., **you can get a free meal.** I don't know if that's true, but I'm going to try anyway. Then I'm getting the bus home. A taxi is too expensive.

P: That sounds great. Have a good evening, and you can tell us all about it tomorrow.

D: I will.

P: Our second volunteer is Rob. Rob, can you tell us about your evening?

R: Yes. I'm starting the evening with a visit to a museum, too. I'm going to **the National Gallery** to see the paintings there. They stay open one night a week, and it's free. Then I'm going to **Covent Garden to watch the street entertainers.** Um … that's free, too. And after that, I'm going to watch some comedy. There's a really good comedy club just near Covent Garden. **It's £8 to get in.** I'm not having dinner. There isn't enough time.

P: Thanks, Rob. Enjoy your evening, and don't forget …

GRAMMAR present continuous/*be going to*

Watch out!

Ss are often confused when they learn that the present continuous is more commonly used for arrangements (plans which involve other people and a fixed time/place), and *be going to* is more commonly used for plans which don't involve other people, e.g. *I'm going to relax this weekend.* It's very important to check the differences carefully and correct/give feedback at all stages of the lesson.

4 Ss do the exercise alone and compare answers while you write sentences a)–d) on the board. In feedback, elicit/check Ss' answers using the sentences on the board. Elicit/underline the present continuous and *be going to*. Check the forms and drill the sentences. With **stronger classes**, add *at the club on Saturday/with John tonight* to sentences b) and d) respectively. Explain that it's more common to use the present continuous for arrangements with other people and at a fixed time/place, and also that *be going to* is more common for plans that don't involve other people, as in sentences a) and c). However, reassure them that both the present continuous and *be going to* can usually be used for future plans/arrangements.

Answers: 1 the future 2 No 3 present continuous
b) and d); *be going to* a) and c)

▷ **LANGUAGEBANK** 3.1 p132–133

Read and check the notes with *weaker classes*. Ss can do Ex A and B now, and Ex C after Ex 5A in the Students' Book, p29. In Ex B, remind Ss to try to mention other people, a time/place in their sentences. In Ex C, both tenses would be acceptable in 4, 5, 6, 9, 10.

Suggested answers:
A 1 C 2 B 3 D 4 A
B A I'm having a meeting with my boss next week. B I'm staying at home to watch TV with my wife this evening.
C John's playing football for his school team on Saturday.
D I'm going to the cinema with Jane next weekend.
C 1 are (you) doing 2 'm going to 3 're going to be
4 are (you) going to take 5 're going to bring
6 're not going to bring 7 is (he) going to have 8 's going to play 9 are (you) going to get 10 going to drive

PRACTICE

5A Do question 1 with Ss. Point out that when the main verb is *go*, it isn't necessary to use *going to go*. We can say *We're going to the cinema on Friday*. (The same applies to question 6.) After Ss have written and compared their answers, check them in feedback.

Answers: 1 We are going to the cinema on Friday.
2 Are you going to stay at home this evening? 3 She is not working this weekend. 4 What time are we meeting tomorrow? 5 I am going to watch a football match later.
6 They are going out for a pizza on Saturday.

B Elicit an example before Ss do the exercise. Monitor and check their work for accuracy.

C Ss compare their answers and find out if they have anything in common.

SPEAKING

6A Check the rubric and elicit examples of Ss' plans. Then give them 3 mins to complete the *you* column in the table.

B Drill the example question and answer chorally (with the whole class) and in open pairs across the class. Ss then do the exercise. To follow-up, they can work with a different partner/pair and exchange information about their plans. Monitor and make notes of Ss' problems for feedback.

WRITING invitations

7A Check the meaning of *invitations*. Ss then do the exercise alone. After they have compared answers, check them with the class.

Answers: 1, 3, 4, 2

B Elicit an example. Ss then underline the other answers. In feedback, elicit and drill the sentences.

Answers:
inviting: Would you like to come? Do you want to meet us for dinner?
responding: I'm sorry, but I'm busy. I'd love to.

C Do the first email with Ss. Then give them 4–5 mins to write the others alone/in pairs. Monitor closely and prompt Ss to correct any errors they make. In feedback, Ss write the emails on the board. Discuss and correct them with the class.

Answers:
Hi Matt,
What are you doing tonight? A few people are coming to watch the football at my house. Do you want to come?
Ali

Great to hear from you. I'd love to. What time is everyone coming?
Matt

Tilly,
What are you doing at the weekend? Would you like to go dancing on Saturday night?
Frank

I'm sorry, I'm busy on Saturday evening. Do you want to go to the cinema on Sunday?
T

That's a great idea. I'd love to. What do you want to see?
Frank

D Ss should work with the same partner as in Ex 6. Monitor and take notes of examples of good language and problems, and write them on the board. Ss discuss and correct them in pairs in feedback.

Homework ideas
• **Ex 6:** write two paragraphs about your/your partner's plans.
• **Ex 7D:** write a final draft of the email or a different one.
• **Language bank** 3.1 Ex A–C, p133
• **Workbook** Ex 1–6, p15–16

WEIRD OR WONDERFUL?

Introduction

Ss revise and practise the use of questions without auxiliary verbs in the context of reading and talking about the arts.

SUPPLEMENTARY MATERIALS

Resource bank p153 and 155

Warm up: download/bring pictures, advertisements or posters of contemporary/traditional art (paintings/sculptures/installations), exhibition info, concerts, etc.

Ex 2A: Ss may need dictionaries.

Ex 4C and 6A: bring pictures or music of the people, art works or songs in these exercises to show your Ss.

Warm up

Show Ss the pictures/realia you have brought and distribute them to pairs/groups of Ss if possible. Give Ss 3–4 mins to name and describe the items in as much detail as possible, e.g. *This is a picture of Damien Hirst's new sculpture in the exhibition in The National Gallery.* In feedback, elicit and discuss Ss' answers. Teach/check only essential vocabulary, e.g. *sculpture/sculptor* as Ss will learn more later in the lesson.

VOCABULARY the arts

1A Give Ss 2–3 mins to complete the text about themselves.

B Ss compare their answers. Invite them to tell the class about how similar/different their group's answers were.

2A Check the examples and ask Ss to copy the word webs into their notebooks. Give them 3–4 mins to complete them. Monitor and provide help, if necessary. Ss can also use dictionaries to check words they're not sure about. Check Ss' answers in feedback, but note that meaning and pronunciation are checked in Ex B and C.

Answers:
music: jazz, rock, audience, band, singer, concert hall, songwriter, artist, pop, classical, performance, composer, concert
art: art gallery, sculptor, painter, sculpture, artist, exhibition, (performance)
theatre: audience, actor, performance
Words that can go in more than one column: audience, artist, performance

B Elicit an example for each question. Ss then work in groups and answer them. Put *weaker Ss* together and provide them with more support if necessary. In feedback, write *people, places, photos* on the board. Invite Ss to write their answers under the correct heading. The class can agree/disagree and suggest alternatives.

Answers: 1 audience, band, actor, sculptor, singer, painter, songwriter, artist, composer 2 art gallery, concert hall
3 painting, exhibition, art gallery, play (n), actor, sculpture, sculptor, audience, theatre, concert hall, performance, singer, concert, painter, artist

C Check the example and elicit one or two more. Give Ss time to write 3–4 sentences to ensure greater accuracy and confidence before they work in pairs. Provide help where necessary. While Ss work in pairs, monitor and make notes on problem sentences for feedback later.

3A When you check the example, hold up two fingers and ask *Where's the stress?* Elicit *The first syllable.* Then drill the word. Use the same technique with problem words when you check Ss' answers in feedback.

Answers: painting, play, jazz, rock, art gallery, audience, band, actor, sculptor, singer, concert hall, painter, songwriter, sculpture, artist, pop, exhibition, classical, performance, composer, concert

B Ss should be able to repeat the words with more confidence. If not, use the finger highlighting technique again.

READING

4A Elicit some initial answers to the questions, ensuring that Ss give reasons for their answers. Give them 2–3 mins to discuss the questions in pairs and discuss them with the class in feedback.

Culture notes
Kanye West, born 1977, is an American singer/rapper. Jackson Pollock (1912–1956), an influential American painter in the abstract expressionist movement. Samuel Beckett (1906–1989), Irish writer and Nobel Prize winner, wrote *Waiting for Godot.*

B Introduce the *Culture Quiz.* If you have a *multicultural class*, some Ss might not be very familiar with western art and culture. Pair them with Ss who are – but at the same time tell Ss that this is a light-hearted activity. They should guess answers they're not sure of, and will be able to check them in Ex C. Before Ss start, pre-teach language they'll need, e.g. *drop, funeral, upside down, consists of.* Then give them 5 mins to do the quiz.

C Ss listen and check. If necessary, play the recording again before feedback.

Answers: 1 b) 2 c) 3 c) 4 a) 5 c) 6 b) 7 c) 8 c)

D Ss listen again and answer the questions. In feedback, find out how well Ss did in the quiz. Then discuss what they learnt/know about the people and things mentioned.

Answers: 1 Jackson Pollock 2 Number 7

Unit 3 Recording 4

W=Woman M1=1st man M2=2nd man

W: Who's got the answers then?
M1: I have.
W: What did you put for the first one?
M2: That one's easy. It's Michelangelo, isn't it?
M1: It's Michelangelo. He painted the Sistine Chapel.
W: What about the second one?
M2: Michael Jackson?
M1: Yep. It's Michael Jackson.
W: And number three?
M2: I don't know very much about art, but I'm guessing it's Pollock.
M1: It is Jackson Pollock.
M2: Thought so.
W: Is number four *Candle in the Wind*?
M1: 'A' is correct. *Candle in the Wind.*
W: What about number five?
M2: Well, it has to be 'C', doesn't it? If no one noticed for two months that it was upside down …
M1: Correct. Though I didn't know this story.
W: That's quite funny. Where was it, The Museum of Modern Art?
M1: Unbelievable, isn't it?
M2: What about the next one, number six?

W: Live 8.

M2: Live 8.

M1: Yep. It was Live 8.

W: Number seven, I have no idea. I guessed 'B', *Heavenly*.

M1: Nope.

M2: So is it *Scrambled Eggs*?

M1: The answer is 'C', *Scrambled Eggs*.

W: No way!

M1: Yep.

M2: So how about the last one? It isn't Shakespeare, I know that.

W: It's not Shaw either, is it? I guessed Samuel Beckett.

M2: Me too. What's the answer?

M1: Correct. The answer is 'C', Samuel Beckett.

M2: I got them all right.

W: Aren't you cultured?

M2: Not really.

GRAMMAR questions without auxiliaries

Watch out!

Ss usually find auxiliary verbs in English quite difficult to get used to as many languages don't use them. For this reason, they may not find questions without auxiliaries particularly strange. However, they will probably confuse the two forms initially. Clarify the difference carefully and provide sufficient controlled practice and feedback.

5 Some of the sentences are from the quiz in Ex 4. Ss should answer the questions alone and then compare their answers. In feedback, check Ss' answers and then illustrate the language further. Write the questions and answers below on the board (but without the boxes around the answers). Ask *Is question b) asking about the subject or object?* Elicit *The subject* and draw a box around *Michael Jackson*. Then ask the same question about question d). Elicit Ss' answer, *the object*, and draw a box around *when he was five*. Then ask *Which question doesn't use an auxiliary verb?* Question 1. Ss then copy the sentences into their notebooks.

b) Who became famous as a five-year old singer?

Michael Jackson became famous.

d) When did Michael Jackson become famous?

He became famous when he was five.

Ss find and underline more examples of subject/object questions in the quiz in Ex 4.

Answers: 1 a) and b) 2 c) and d) 3 Questions a) and b) do not use the auxiliary verb (*did*). They use the past simple form of the verb, not the infinitive without *to*.

➡ LANGUAGEBANK 3.2 p132–133

Read/check the table/notes with your Ss. In feedback for Ex B, check if Ss know the answers to the questions.

Answers:
A 1 ✓ 2 Who ~~does read~~ *reads* the most … ? 3 Who ~~be~~ *is/was* your … ? 4 ✓ 5 What ~~did be~~ *was* your favourite book … ? 6 Who ~~did write~~ *wrote* it? 7 How often *do* you read … ? 8 ✓
B 1 What colour was The Beatles' submarine? (yellow) 2 Who wrote *Stairway to Heaven*? (Jimmy Page from Led Zeppelin) 3 Whose home was Graceland? (Elvis Presley) 4 Which country did Diego Rivera come from? (Mexico) 5 Who painted the *Mona Lisa*? (Leonardo da Vinci) 6 Which painter invented Cubism? (Pablo Picasso/ Georges Braque)

PRACTICE

6A Check the example. Tell Ss to check the tense in each sentence carefully when they write the question. Ss then correct the sentences alone.

B Ss check their answers in pairs. Monitor to see what type of problems they're having. In feedback, nominate Ss to give their answers and check them carefully. If you've brought materials about the people/things mentioned here, use them to elicit what else Ss know about them.

Answers: 2 Where does the singer Bjork come from? 3 What type of music became popular in Brazil in the twentieth century? 4 What/Which is Shakespeare's longest play? 5 Who continued composing music after he became deaf? 6 Who/Which musician invented Afrobeat? 7 How many self-portraits did Frida Kahlo paint? 8 What is Fernando Botero's art famous for? 9 Why are Alberto Giacometti's sculptures famous?
Questions 2 and 7 use auxiliary verbs.

SPEAKING

7A Set up the activity in two stages carefully to ensure greater accuracy. Check the example and then elicit a suitable question to find out information for question 2, e.g. *How many CDs do you have/have you got?* Give Ss 4–5 mins to prepare the questions they need for the other topics, alone or in pairs. Monitor closely and provide support where needed. Check the questions with the class before they do the information-finding activity (see suggested questions below). To find out the information for questions 1–8, Ss can work in groups, or do it as a class mingling activity. They ask their questions and note down the answers. Alternatively, assign one of the questions to each student/pair: they ask the question and report their findings back to the class.

Suggested questions: 2 How many CDs do you have/ have you got? 3 Have you got/Do you have an iPod or MP3 player with you now? 4 How many classical composers do you know? 5 Have you been to the theatre or cinema in the last six months?/When did you last go to the theatre or cinema? 6 Have you been to an art exhibition in the last year? When did you last go to an art exhibition? 7 Do you go to art galleries and/or concerts regularly? 8 Have you ever bought a painting?

B Give Ss time to analyse their findings and decide who is the most/least interested in culture. They then report back to their group/the class. The other Ss are free to agree/disagree with the results!

Homework ideas
- Ex 4: write about the art forms you like best/least and say why.
- Language bank 3.2 Ex A–B, p133
- Workbook Ex 1–6 p17–18

CAN I TAKE A MESSAGE?

Introduction

Ss learn and practise making phone calls in both informal and formal situations. They also learn how to manage problems they might experience during phone calls.

SUPPLEMENTARY MATERIALS

Resource bank p156

Ex 8: use recording facilities if you have them.

Warm up

Lead in to the lesson with common collocations for using the phone. Write these verbs on the board for Ss to copy: *make, answer, call, switch on, leave, put.* Then dictate these phrases which collocate with the words on the board, but not in the same order: *a phone call, the phone, a wrong number, the answering machine, a message, down the phone.* Ss write them next to the correct word. Check their answers.

SPEAKING

1 Check the questions and do an example. Elicit answers about one person in the picture in question 1, e.g. *picture C: I think he's talking to an employee. He wants him to explain why he didn't come to work.* Give Ss 3–4 mins to discuss the questions. In feedback, nominate Ss to give their answers.

VOCABULARY collocations

2A First check the meaning of the collocations, e.g. *have a chat, cancel, talk business.* Ss then work alone and write *yes/no* next to each phrase.

B Model and drill the example dialogue. Elicit and drill questions using the phrases in Ex 2A, e.g. *Have you arranged to meet friends/booked a table?* Ss then ask/answer the questions in pairs, and make notes of their partner's answers. In feedback, nominate Ss to tell the class about their partner.

3A Check the rubric and play the recording. Ss write their answers and compare them. Play the recording again if Ss have doubts. Then do feedback.

> **Answers:** 1 He (Rodney) wants to book a table.
> 2 She (Judy) wants to change the date of a ticket booked for a show. 3 She (Wendy) has arranged to meet friends.
> 4 He (Andy) wants to cancel dinner/(his reservation).

B Give Ss time to read the notes. Check *original date.* **Stronger Ss** may be able to complete some of the answers before listening again. After listening, Ss compare answers. **Weaker Ss** may need to hear the recording again; pause after each answer and elicit it (see answers in bold in the audio script).

> **Answers:** 1 four, 10p.m. 2 Starr, June 5th, June 9th
> 3 8.30p.m., Saturday 4 dinner

Unit 3 Recording 5

Conversation 1

A: King's Restaurant.

B: Hello, I'd like to book a **table for four** on Friday night. Around eight-thirty, if possible.

A: Let me just have a look. Sorry, we're completely full on Friday. There's nothing at all.

B: Ah, what about Saturday?

A: Saturday, Saturday. Um … the best I can do is a table at ten o'clock.

B: Ten o'clock? You haven't got anything earlier?

A: Nothing at all, I'm afraid.

B: OK, let's go ahead. **Ten o'clock.**

A: Can I take your name, please?

B: The table is for Rodney Collins.

A: Rodney … Oh! Can you repeat that, please? Did you say Rodney Collins?

B: Yes.

A: OK, that's all booked. **Table for four, ten o'clock, Saturday.**

B: Great. Thank you.

A: Thank you.

Conversation 2

C: High Tower Productions, Paul speaking. How can I help you?

D: Hello, I was wondering if you could help me. **I've booked a ticket for the show on the fifth of June, but I'd like to change the date.**

C: OK, one moment. Can I just check? What's the name, please?

D: The tickets are booked in the name of **Judy Starr.**

C: Sorry, I didn't catch that. Did you say Starr?

D: Judy Starr. S-t-a-double r.

C: OK, yes. **Two tickets for June the fifth.** What date would you like to change to?

D: What dates do you still have seats for?

C: There's nothing on the sixth or seventh. There are two seats for the eighth, but they're separate. We have …

D: Sorry, can you slow down, please? Two seats for?

C: Sorry, two seats for the eighth, but they aren't together. We can do you two seats together on the ninth of June.

D: **Ninth of June. That's fine.**

C: OK. I'll just go ahead and book that.

Conversation 3

E: Hello?

F: Hello, it's Wendy here.

E: Oh hi, Wendy. How are you?

F: Very well, thanks. And you?

E: Yeah, fine.

F: Are you doing anything on Saturday? Because a few of us are going out for dinner.

E: Sorry, Wendy, can you speak up, please? I'm on Oxford Street and I can't hear a thing.

F: D'you want to go for dinner on Saturday?

E: Oh, that sounds nice.

F: There's going to be a few of us, Tom and Zoe, and Steve.

E: That sounds like fun.

F: Are you free?

E: I think so.

F: Alright. Eight-thirty, Saturday, Zanzibar's.

E: OK. **Zanzibar's on Saturday at eight-thirty.**

F: That's right. Brilliant. See you soon.

E: OK. Thanks for calling.

Conversation 4

G: Thomson and Co. Who's calling?

H: Hello, this is Andy. Andy Jones. Can I speak to Sarah Hobbs, please?

G: I'm afraid she's not here at the moment.

H: Ah, do you know when she'll be back? I've tried her mobile three or four times and left messages, but she hasn't called back.

G: She's visiting a customer. She should be back this evening. Can I take a message?

H: **It's about dinner tonight. I've had to cancel because of work.**

G: OK. I'll ask her to call you back.

H: Thanks.

G: Does she have your number?

H: It's 0988 45673.

G: Can you repeat that, please?

H: 0988 45673.

FUNCTION making a phone call

4 Check *caller/receiver* in the table headings. Ss read the information and check if they need clarification of language there. Ss then complete the sentences and compare answers. In feedback, elicit/check and drill the answers. Highlight the use of *It's Andy* as *I am Andy* is a common error. Ss then work in pairs and take it in turns to read out the part of the caller/receiver. Monitor and help Ss with their pronunciation.

> **Answers:** 1 it's 2 Can 3 leave 4 here 5 take 6 back 7 for

5A Ss first read the conversations. Check *managing director*. Do question 1 as an example, then Ss do the exercise alone and check in pairs, using the language in Ex 4 to help them. Elicit and drill the answers chorally and individually. Model the sentences first: beat the sentence stress and illustrate the intonation with your arms and hands, as if you were 'conducting'. This will prepare them for the next exercise.

> **Answers:**
> Conversation 1: 1 speaking 2 it's/this is 3 See
> Conversation 2: 1 speak 2 calling 3 isn't 4 message

B Ss should sit back-to-back and pretend to be talking on the phone. While they practise, monitor and help them with pronunciation.

⟶ LANGUAGEBANK 3.3 p132–133

Ss can refer to the information in the tables when they do the exercise.

> **Answers:**
> A: David speaking. B: Hello, it's Mark Johnson. A: How can I help you, Mr Johnson? B: I'd like to speak to Sara Torres, please. A: I'm afraid she's not here at the moment. B: Can I leave a message? A: Yes, of course. B: Can you ask her to call me back? A: No problem. A: My number is 0276 765356. A: Can you repeat that, please? B: 0276 765356. A: OK. Thanks for calling. B: Bye. A: Bye.

LEARN TO manage phone problems

6A The extracts are from recording 3.5 (see the underlined sentences there). Check problems a)–d) and do an example before Ss do the exercise. Don't check pronunciation in feedback, Ss do it in Ex B.

> **Answers:** b) 3 Sorry, can you slow down, please? c) 4 Can you speak up, please? d) 1 Can I just check?

B Ss listen and repeat the phrases. Play the recording as many times as necessary until Ss are confident. Do individual repetition and correction as needed.

Unit 3 Recording 6

1 Can I just check?
2 Sorry, I didn't catch that. Did you say Starr?
3 Sorry, can you slow down, please?
4 Can you speak up, please?
5 Can you repeat that, please?

7A Ss listen and write their responses. With *weaker classes*, Ss can just listen first, and then listen again to write their answers. Ss compare answers, but don't check them until Ex B.

Unit 3 Recording 7

Conversation 1
A: My phone number is 765 9876 2135. OK?
Conversation 2
A: My full address is the one I gave you last week, the New York address.
Conversation 3
A: My phone number is 245 9888.
Conversation 4
A: I'll be taking the 6.45 from Houston and changing at Miami, and I'll arrive at about 2.00.

B Ss check their answers and correct them if necessary.

> **Answers:** 1 Can you slow down, please? 2 Can you speak up, please? 3 Can you repeat that, please? 4 Can I just check?

Unit 3 Recording 8

Conversation 1
A: My phone number is 765 9876 2135. OK?
B: Sorry, can you slow down, please?
Conversation 2
A: My full address is the one I gave you last week, the New York address.
B: Sorry, can you speak up, please?
Conversation 3
A: My phone number is 245 9888.
B: Can you repeat that, please?
Conversation 4
A: I'll be taking the 6.45 from Houston and changing at Miami, and I'll arrive at about 2.00.
B: Can I just check? Did you say 2.00?

SPEAKING

8 Prepare Ss for the role-plays in two stages. First divide the class into Students A and B. Student A reads the situations on p160, and Student B on p162. Check that Ss know all the language in the tasks. Read the speakout tip with the class before doing the exercise. Ask *Why is this a good idea?* Because it gives you more confidence and helps you feel more prepared. Put Student As into pairs, and Student Bs into pairs. Give them 4–5 mins to prepare, using the speakout tip. Monitor and provide support where needed. Then put Ss into A/B pairs, sitting back-to-back with plastic phones if possible. They take turns to make a call and answer the phone. Monitor discreetly, making notes for feedback. Invite pairs to act out a conversation to the class. Record this if you have the facilities. Give feedback to Ss and do remedial work as necessary.

speakout TIP

Encourage Ss to use the speakout tip in Ex 8 and in real-life.

> **Homework ideas**
> • Ex 8: write a phone conversation for one of the situations on p160 and 162.
> • Language bank 3.3 Ex A, p133
> • Workbook Ex 1–6, p19

BARCELONA

Introduction

Ss watch an extract from a BBC travel programme about Barcelona. They then learn and practise how to talk about a perfect day out and write an invitation.

SUPPLEMENTARY MATERIALS

Ex 6A: bring/download pictures of Prague's main sights.

Ex 6C: bring pictures of other famous, popular cities to use as prompts for ideas.

Culture notes

The **Sagrada Familia**, Antoni Gaudí's unfinished masterpiece, is visited by millions of tourists every year and is Barcelona's most important landmark. When Gaudí died in 1926, he'd worked on it for over 40 years. His unique style was inspired mainly by nature. Work continues on the building, but is not expected to be completed until 2026.

Warm up

Lead in and create interest in the lesson. Ss look at the photo of the Sagrada Familia in Barcelona at the bottom of the pages. Ask, e.g. *What's the name of this building? Where is it? Who built/designed it? When? What's it like? Have you been there?/Would you like to go there? Why/Why not?* Ss discuss their answers in pairs/groups. In feedback, check Ss' answers and use information from the **Culture notes**, if necessary.

▷ DVD PREVIEW

1 Give Ss 2–3 mins to discuss the question. In feedback, discuss Ss' ideas with the class.

Culture notes

Barcelona is the capital of Catalonia and is Spain's second largest city with 2 million inhabitants. It's situated on the Mediterranean. Catalan and Spanish are the main languages.

2A Give Ss 2–3 mins to answer the questions. If possible, put Ss together with others who know Barcelona. In feedback, discuss the answers with the class.

B Ss read the information and should use the photos to help them make predictions in pairs. In feedback, elicit Ss' answers. They can check their predictions in the next exercise.

▷ DVD VIEW

Culture notes

Churros are long, curly doughnut-like cakes, usually eaten for breakfast. **Tapas** are delicious bar snacks made with fish, meat, vegetables and salads.

3 Check the questions and tell Ss they will find out what *churros* and *tapas* are in the DVD, if they don't know already. Play the DVD. Ss tick their answers and compare them. Play the DVD again if they don't agree about the answers. In the feedback, elicit and check answers (see answers in bold in the DVD script). Also check Ss' predictions from Ex 2.

Alternative approach

As the task is very visual, play the DVD with the sound turned off. Ss watch and tick their answers. Play it again with the sound for Ss to check their answers.

Answers: 11:00 a) 13:00 a) 16:00 b) 18:00 a) 22:00 b)

4A Ss read the sentences first. Check new language, e.g. *northern girl* (from the north of England), *approach*, *nibble*. Ss watch the DVD again and compare their answers.

B Ss watch the DVD and tell you when to stop at each answer (underlined in the DVD script). Replay each extract for Ss to read and listen to authentic English again.

Answers: 11:00 e) 13:00 f) 16:00 b) 18:00 a) 22:00 d)

Optional extra activity

Exploit the DVD for extra comprehension and attention to interesting detail. Pause it at suitable points and ask questions, e.g. *What's Ginny doing now? Where is she? Why is it her favourite city? What's the Sagrada Familia/the Ramblas like? What do you think about Barcelona?*

DVD 3 Holiday 10 Best: Cities

Holiday 10 Best takes a journey to the coolest, the hippest, the biggest and the most exciting cities around the world. We've got shopping, socialising, sightseeing, history, culture, and of course the odd beach or two.

So, what is it that makes a city truly great? Let's face it we spend most of our time trying to get away from them. They're busy, they're crowded, they aren't exactly relaxing. So, how does Barcelona manage to get it so right?

I love Barcelona. I've been here about a dozen times, and what keeps bringing me back? Well, it's the art, the great buildings, fantastic shopping, and just the general laid-back attitude to life. It's my favourite city and I'm going to show you my recipe for the perfect day here.

10:00

Now you don't want to start your day too early because it's going to be a long one, but when you do manage to drag yourself out of bed, the only way to kick things off here is with **a nice, big fat, creamy cup of hot chocolate, and some lovely sugary churros.**

11:00

First stop on my sightseeing tour: La Sagrada Familia.

Barcelona likes to think of itself as such an individual city and for me the Sagrada Familia really sums that up.

13.00

People always think that a siesta is about sleeping. Not true. In Barcelona, it means **a nice, long lunch, and that means it's time for tapas.** What I love about tapas is the way you can just try a little bit of this, a little bit of that, and if you really want to find out what it's all about, get Juan Carlos, who's the owner of the oldest tapas bar in Barcelona, just to serve you up a selection.

16.00

No city break is complete without a spot of **serious shopping.** Most first-timers will end up on the Ramblas, famous for its silly statues and being ridiculously crowded.

What can I say? I'm a northern girl and I love my markets, and this is the best one I've found anywhere in the world. Now, there's probably more tourists here than there are locals, but that's because of two reasons: this fantastic bar – Pinocchio's Bar, and the amazing array of things that you can buy here. Well worth a visit.

18.00

Now one thing that will probably surprise you about Barcelona is that it's got beaches. Five of them. Now they're not the best you're going to find on the Med, but it's one of the things that makes this place so special.

22:00

There are two things to remember when **you're heading out for the night here.** One: don't even think about coming out early. Nobody has dinner before nine. And two: pace yourself. It's going to be a long night.

The way to approach a night out in Barcelona is to take a drink here, a nibble of tapas there, and then repeat until you get tired, or the sun comes up. And that's exactly what I'm going to do.

5 Ss can refer to Ex 3 and 4 as a prompt for ideas. Give them 5 mins to discuss the questions. They should make a list of things they'd enjoy and note next to them when/where they last did them. Ss can then work with another partner and exchange information. Elicit Ss' answers in feedback and find out which things were most common.

speakout a perfect day

> **Culture notes**
> Prague is the capital of the Czech Republic in Central Europe and has a long and colourful history. The historic centre of the city is a UNESCO World Heritage Site and has made Prague one of the most popular tourist destinations in Europe.

6A Play the first sentence of the recording. Ask *Where's Dana?* Elicit what Ss know about Prague: where it is, its main sights, etc. If you have pictures of Prague, use them here. N.B. If Ss don't know anything, it doesn't matter as they'll find out in the recording. Ss listen and compare their answers. Play the DVD again for them to check. In feedback, elicit the names of famous sights/places they heard.

> **Answers:** 1 Dana is planning to visit Prague.
> 2 d), b), c), f), a), e)

B Ss read the information and then listen and complete the sentences. Play the recording again, pausing at each **key phrase** (in bold in the audio script) to elicit/check the answers. Drill the sentences and ask further comprehension questions, e.g. *What's the main square like? What can you see in the park?*

> **Answers:** 1 We're going to 2 It's going to be 3 We're starting the day 4 In the evening, we're planning to
> 5 Afterwards, we're

Unit 3 Recording 9

I'm going to tell you about my perfect day in Prague. First of all, **we're starting the day in the main square.** It's a beautiful place to have breakfast in one of the cafés. It's a little bit expensive, but we're going to sit outside so we can watch the clock tower. After breakfast, **we're going to walk through the old city,** and go to Charles Bridge. There are some interesting statues on the bridge, and there's a market where you can buy some souvenirs. From the bridge, we're walking up to the castle. And we're going to have lunch in a restaurant near there. In the afternoon, we're taking a tram around the city. It's a good way to see the sights because it's cheap and easy. **Afterwards, we're going to relax in the park** at Petrin Hill. There is a tall tower here, where you can see wonderful views of the city too. We're going to a coffee shop in the afternoon, in the Municipal House, where they do wonderful coffees. And then, **in the evening, we're planning to go to a classical music concert** in St Nicholas church. You can come here to listen to Bach, Mozart or Vivaldi, and the atmosphere is very special. When it's finished, we're having dinner at Kolkovna, in the old town, which serves traditional Czech food, and then we're going to spend the rest of the evening trying different bars in the old town, which serve very cheap, local beers. **It's going to be fantastic!**

C If you have pictures of famous cities, use them to prompt ideas/support *weaker Ss*. Group Ss who want to talk about the same city together. Remind them to use the **key phrases** and recording for ideas while they plan.

D Put Ss into pairs/groups with different Ss. They take turns to talk about their plans. Monitor and note down examples of good language and errors that need to be addressed in feedback later.

E Ss tell the class (or another group) about their plans. They listen and make notes about which plans are the best, and why. In feedback, discuss Ss' plans and have a class vote on the best one(s). Give feedback on Ss' strengths and weaknesses now, or at the beginning of the next class.

writeback an invitation

7 Ss use their ideas/notes from Ex 6 and the emails on p29 to write their invitations. Monitor and prompt Ss to self-correct any errors. They give their emails to other Ss who can then reply, also using ideas from p29.

> **Homework ideas**
> • Ex 5: write your answers to the questions in this exercise.
> • Ex 7: write an invitation to have a perfect day in your town/city. Put it on the class blog or send it to your teacher.

LOOKBACK

Introduction

As well as revising and practising the language in the unit, use the **Lookback** exercises to provide you with an informal assessment of your Ss' speaking skills. Fluency practice is usually given in Ex B or C in each section. When assessing speaking skills, take these four areas into account: accuracy of grammar, range of vocabulary, fluency and pronunciation.

TIME OUT

1 Ss complete the sentences alone and check their answers in pairs. In feedback, ask Ss to suggest verbs that collocate with the word/phrase that is not possible in each question, e.g. *go sightseeing, go to an art gallery*.

> **Answers:** 2 Do you want to get the bus/a snack/~~an art gallery~~? 3 They went to the art gallery/the museum/~~a snack~~. 4 She has gone ~~a pub~~/sightseeing/dancing. 5 Can we have ~~a club~~/dinner/a drink?

> **Optional extra activity**
> In pairs/teams, Ss write four similar sentences using the word webs on p28. They then give them to another pair/ team to cross out the wrong words.

PRESENT CONTINUOUS/*BE GOING TO* FOR FUTURE

2A Do the first sentence as an example to show Ss what to do. Give Ss 4–5 mins to write their sentences. Monitor and note down problems they're having with them in terms of word order. Give feedback and do remedial work if necessary, before Ss do Ex B. Model and drill the questions using contracted verb forms to prepare them for Ex B, e.g. *Who's cooking your dinner this evening?*

> **Answers:** 1 What are you doing tonight? 2 Are you doing anything special this weekend? 3 Who is cooking your dinner this evening? 4 When are you going on holiday? 5 Which city are you next going to visit? 6 What are you going to do after the lesson?

B Ss take turns to ask/answer the questions and note down their partner's answers. Ss then tell the class about their partner's plans/arrangements.

THE ARTS

3 Check the rubric and the examples. Elicit one or two sentences before Ss work in pairs. Give Ss 4–5 mins for the exercise. Monitor and prompt Ss to self-correct their errors. Ss then read out their clues. Other pairs should put up their hands to answer, and get a point for each correct one.

QUESTIONS WITHOUT AUXILIARIES

4A Check the example. Ss read the prompts first. Elicit/ check what Ss know about the people and things mentioned there. (The answers are included in the answer key for Ex 4C, but don't check them until Ss do Ex C.) Give them 4–5 mins to write the questions. Monitor and assess how accurate the questions are. Do remedial work in feedback and/or use the information for assessment if required.

> **Answers:** 2 Who was an actor before he became US President? 3 Which 1975 Queen album includes the song *Bohemian Rhapsody*? 4 Who was a fourth great Renaissance painter, besides Leonardo, Michelangelo and Titian? 5 Which 'John' won an Oscar for his song *Can you feel the love tonight?* from *The Lion King*? 6 Which Bob Marley song includes the words 'Let's get together and feel alright'? 7 Which watery Italian city has an international art exhibition every two years? 8 Which member of the Dion family sold 200 million records by 2007? 9 Whose hit songs include *I'm like a bird, Promiscuous* and *Maneater*?

B Tell Ss that the answers here are also answers to the questions in Ex A. Ss can do the quiz alone or in pairs.

C Ss check their answers and then match them to the questions in Ex A. (See Ex A answer key).

> **Answers:** 2 Reagan 3 A Night at the Opera 4 Raphael 5 Elton 6 One Love 7 Venice 8 Céline 9 Nelly Furtado

MAKING A PHONE CALL

5A Ss first read the conversation. Ask *What did you notice about it?* Elicit/Tell them that it's like a poem: the words at the end of each line rhyme with each other, e.g. *blue – you*. Ss then complete the phone call alone and check their answers in pairs. Do feedback and check the glossary for the meaning of the expression *get the sack*. Elicit more examples of rhyming words at the end of each line (*Chow – now, back – sack*), but don't practise reading out the 'poem' yet: this is done in Ex C.

> **Answers:** 1 it's 2 can 3 like 4 here 5 back

B Ss complete the gaps with words from the box and check their answers in pairs. In feedback, nominate Ss to give the answers. Also elicit examples of words that rhyme at the end of each line, e.g. *Paul – all, meeting – eating, game – name, soon – moon*. Check the glossary for the expression *pigs might fly*.

> **Answers:** 1 this 2 busy 3 leave 4 message 5 call

C Ss first practise reading the poems out loud as a class. Do this two or three times as it will give them more confidence with their pronunciation. The rhyming words at the end of each line will also help Ss to focus on the rhythm of the poems. They then work in pairs and practise saying the poems. *Stronger Ss* might like to memorise them. In feedback, invite Ss to read out or recite the poems to the class.

> **Homework ideas**
> • Workbook Review and Check 1, p20–21
> • Workbook Test 1, p22

OVERVIEW

4.1 SECRET TALENTS
GRAMMAR | present perfect + ever/never
VOCABULARY | make and do
HOW TO | talk about your talents

COMMON EUROPEAN FRAMEWORK
Ss can generally understand clear, standard speech on familiar matters; can write simple phrases and sentences about themselves (and imaginary people), where they live and what they do.

4.2 SCHOOLS OF THOUGHT
GRAMMAR | can, have to, must
VOCABULARY | education
HOW TO | talk about obligations

COMMON EUROPEAN FRAMEWORK
Ss can understand short, simple texts on familiar matters of a concrete type which consist of high frequency everyday or job-related language; can participate in short conversations in routine contexts on topics of interest, e.g. education/obligation.

4.3 WHAT SHOULD I DO?
FUNCTION | giving advice
VOCABULARY | language learning
LEARN TO | respond to advice

COMMON EUROPEAN FRAMEWORK
Ss can make and respond to suggestions.

4.4 THE INTELLIGENCE TEST
BBC DVD
speakout | tips for tests
writeback | a problem page

COMMON EUROPEAN FRAMEWORK
Ss can give a simple description or presentation of people, living or working conditions, daily routines, likes/dislikes, etc. as a series of short simple phrases and sentences linked into a list; can write about everyday aspects of their environments, e.g. people, places, a job or study experience in linked sentences.

4.5 LOOKBACK
Communicative revision activities

BBC VIDEO PODCAST
Are you learning anything at the moment?

In this video podcast, people describe what they are learning at the moment and the most difficult things they've ever learnt. It also extends Ss' vocabulary of education and learning, and exemplifies real usage of the present perfect + ever. Use this video podcast at the start or end of unit 4.

SECRET TALENTS

Introduction
Ss revise/practise the present perfect simple with ever/never in the context of talking about their own and other people's talents. They learn collocations with make/do and practise how to correct mistakes in their written work.

SUPPLEMENTARY MATERIALS
Resource bank p158

Ex 1A: dictionaries should be available for Ss to check the verb phrases.

Warm up
Ask Ss What were you good/bad at when you were a child? What did you want to do when you grew up? Did you have any secret ambitions? Ss discuss the questions in pairs/small groups, and then as a class. Some Ss might have been good at, e.g. singing/football and had ambitions to be famous when they were young. If not, it doesn't matter as the questions lead in to the topic of the lesson.

VOCABULARY make and do

1A Ss should be familiar with most of the vocabulary in the questionnaire except do business. First do an example: elicit the meaning of make a speech, using the pictures. Then elicit a definition, e.g. talk in public. Give Ss 4–5 mins to do the same with the other verb phrases, using the pictures/their own definitions. They can use dictionaries if necessary. Monitor to check Ss' progress. Check Ss' answers in feedback. They should then copy the list of verbs with make/do into their notebooks.

Answers: make a speech, make friends, do something interesting with a group of friends, do a dangerous sport

B Illustrate/check the instructions for this exercise carefully. Read the rubric with Ss and check the meaning of None/A few of us … . Then model/drill the first question and elicit a Yes/No answer from each student. Write the number of yes answers on the board. Then elicit the correct summary sentence using the appropriate prompt, e.g. None of us/Two of us have made a speech. Ss then work in groups and take turns to ask all the Ss in their group one of the questions; they then note down the number of yes answers. After asking all the questions, Ss each write their sentence(s) using the appropriate prompt, e.g. All of us have done well in an exam. Monitor closely during this activity to check the accuracy of their sentences. Prompt them to self-correct any errors if possible.

C Do this exercise with the whole class. Number each group 1, 2, 3, etc. Elicit each group's answers to each question in Ex B. Write the number of the group which has done/made the most things on the board, e.g. Group 3: 4 Ss made a speech. Ss then work out which group has made or done the most things overall.

GRAMMAR present perfect + *ever/never*

Watch out!

Ss make mistakes with both the meaning and form of the present perfect. This is because Ss may have the same form in their L1 but it's used in a different way, e.g. *I've seen it last week*, and they may also confuse the form with the past simple, e.g. *Did you have seen that film?* Check the form and concept of the two tenses thoroughly and give Ss as much contextualised practice as possible.

2A First check the meaning of *conference*. Ss then do the exercise and compare answers. Elicit Ss' answers in feedback.

Answers: present perfect and past simple (plus some examples of the present simple)

B Check the concept of *general experience* in question 1, using an example, e.g. *I've made a terrible mistake.* Ask Ss *Is this sentence in the past or present?* The past. *Do we know exactly when it happened?* No. Ss then answer questions 1–3 and check in pairs before feedback. After checking their answers, write the first three lines of the conversation on the board. Draw Ss' attention to the abbreviated spoken form of *No, never. Have you?* (Instead of *No, I haven't. Have you ever made a speech … ?*)

Answers: 1 Have you ever made a speech in public? Have you ever made friends with someone from another country? *Have* you (*ever*) + past participle 2 (I made a speech) At a conference last year. He met a woman from Chile in 2006. In fact, they got married a week ago! Verb tense: past simple 3 No, never. Yes, I have. No, I haven't.

C Tell Ss to listen to the pronunciation of *have/haven't* carefully. In feedback, refer back to the sentences on the board in Ex B. Elicit/underline the main stress in each sentence, *Have you ever made a speech in public? No, never. Have you? Yes, I have.* Elicit/tell Ss that *have* is stressed in short answers and pronounced /hæv/, but isn't stressed in questions, where it's /həv/. Ss can then listen and repeat the conversation, paying attention to the sentence stress and weak (unstressed) forms.

Unit 4 Recording 1

A: Have you ever made a speech in public?
B: No, never. Have you?
A: Yes, I have. I made a speech at work.
B: Really? When did you do that?
A: Um … at a conference last year. I was really nervous.
B: I'm not surprised. OK, have you ever made friends with someone from another country?
A: No, I haven't but my brother has. He met a woman from Chile in 2006. In fact, they got married a week ago!

⏩ LANGUAGEBANK 4.1 p134–135

Stronger classes can study the tables and notes at home when they do the exercises. Check the notes in class with *weaker Ss*, who then do Ex A–B.

Answers:
A 1 Have you ever ~~saw~~ *seen* the film *Titanic?* 2 Two days ago she~~'s been~~ *went* to a museum. 3 Unfortunately, we have ~~ever~~ *never* won the lottery. 4 Has *she ever* visited you? 5 I haven't ~~meet~~ *met* your brother. 6 In 2006 they~~'ve~~ travelled to Geneva. 7 ~~Have you seen~~ *Did you see* that TV programme last Wednesday? 8 He *has never* played a musical instrument.
B 1 Have you ever done 2 's worked 3 visited 4 Has he made 5 haven't heard 6 ate

PRACTICE

3A Check *snails/project* and do an example. Ss do the exercise alone and compare answers. In feedback, recheck the concept of the two tenses: ask *Do we know when? Is it important?*

Answers: 1 was 2 Have you ever written 3 I've never eaten 4 finished 5 Have you ever been 6 finished

B Elicit examples for question 1 that are true for Ss, using phrases with *make/do*. Monitor Ss' accuracy while they write their sentences. In *mixed-ability classes*, stronger and weaker Ss could work together, or pair *weaker Ss* and give them extra support.

C Ss find out if they have anything in common. In feedback, invite Ss to give their own/their partner's answers to the class. Correct as appropriate.

4A Give Ss 2 mins to write and check their answers on p127. Advise them to try to memorise 3–4 past participles a day, e.g. before they go to sleep/on the bus.

Answers: keep – kept, make – made, drive – driven, do – done, fly – flown, come – come, cross – crossed, give – given, swim – swum, sleep – slept, lose – lost, win – won, pay – paid, grow – grew

B Check/drill the example and write the phonemic symbol on the board. It's very useful to have a phonemic chart available nearby, on a wall or notice board. You can then refer to it easily to help Ss with their pronunciation. In feedback, check/drill the participles. Ss could write them down with the phoneme for each pair of sounds. (See phonemes in the key below.)

Answers: kept – slept /e/, made – paid /eɪ/, driven – given /ɪ/, done – won /ʌ/, flown – grown /əʊ/, come – swum /ʌ/, crossed – lost /ɒ/

C Check the words in the box and elicit one or two examples. Ss write their questions while you monitor and prompt them to self-correct any mistakes.

D Check/drill the examples. Point out that with *yes* answers Ss should add an extra piece of information. This time, monitor and make notes of problems Ss have with tenses for feedback.

LISTENING

5 Ss do the exercise and compare answers. In feedback, teach/check new language, e.g. *secret talent,*

Answers: 1 A talent show is an entertainment show where people can show what they are good at. 2 six people

6A Check the questions and play the recording.

B After Ss have listened and compared answers, play the recording again. With **weaker classes**, pause after each answer for Ss to check/complete their notes (in bold in the audio script). In feedback, teach/check *caricature, backwards, visualise.*

Answers: 1 Ralph can draw cartoons of people (caricatures) in about fifteen seconds. Carly can say sentences backwards. 2 Ralph: Yes, but he doesn't usually tell people. Carly: Yes, at parties and with friends.
3 Ralph: No. Carly: Yes, she visualises the words in her head.
4 Ralph: Yes. Carly: No.

Unit 4 Recording 3
Conversation 1
I=Interviewer R=Ralph

I: So Ralph, can you tell us a bit about your secret talent?
R: Um, well, I started drawing people when I was very young.
I: OK. What sorts of drawings do you do? Mostly cartoons?
R: What I do is I draw cartoons of people when I'm sitting in cafés or when I'm on the train. And I can do a face in about fifteen seconds.
I: So they're like caricatures?
R: Exactly. They are caricatures.
I: Has anyone ever asked what you were doing or caught you drawing them?
R: It's happened a few times …
I: But usually you do them in secret?
R: Usually. And occasionally I tell the person that I've drawn them.
I: Oh really?
R: Yeah. Actually, while sitting here I've drawn you!
I: No way!
R: Yep. It's right here.
I: That's brilliant! Definitely a secret talent. So tell me, how do you do it? Is there a special way to do it?
R: No, I just love drawing and I practise.

Conversation 2
I= Interviewer C=Carly

I: What's your secret talent?
C: I can say sentences backwards.
I: Backwards? That's amazing. How fast can you say them?
C: Well, I can say them at normal speed, but backwards.
I: Can you give me an example?
C: What, my last sentence?
I: Yes.
C: Backwards but speed normal at them say can I.
I: Wow! Can you give me another example?
C: Yes, I'll say your sentence. Example another me give you can.
I: Can you do it again?
C: Sure. Example another me give you can.
I: How do you do it?
C: I don't know. I think I visualise the sentence, I see the words in my head, and it just appears to me.
I: Amazing. Have you ever done it in public?
C: Yeah, I've done it at parties and with friends. They all think I'm very strange.

SPEAKING

7A Elicit other talents Ss could talk about and write them on the board. Prompt Ss to use ideas from the lesson or suggest other ideas, e.g. *writing stories/poems, remember names, speak in different accents, read people's hands/handwriting, make friends easily.* Give Ss 2–3 mins to make notes alone/in pairs. Monitor and support Ss with vocabulary/accuracy.

B Monitor discreetly while Ss work in groups, and make notes of examples of good language and problems. In feedback, invite members of each group to tell the class who should enter the competition and why. Write examples of Ss' errors and good language on the board. Ss discuss and correct them in pairs.

WRITING correcting mistakes

8A Check the rubric and give examples for each of the symbols. Ss then work alone and compare answers before feedback.

Answers: 1 I can ~~to~~ (gr) speak like Lenny Henry. 2–3 I first discovered this ~~abillity~~ ability (sp) when I was [a] (gr) child. 4 I often watched cartoons and then 'did' the voices myself [.] (p) 5 They always think it's ~~funy~~ funny. (sp) 6–8 There is no magic secret [; or .] (p) I just listen ~~carefuly~~ carefully (sp) and ~~am practising~~ practise (gr).

B Ss write their own entry, but reassure them that it doesn't have to be true. They must not write more than 75 words.

C Before Ss do the exercise, read the speakout tip together. They then check and correct each others' entries, using a different colour for corrections.

speakout TIP
Encourage Ss to use this tip and to get into the habit of always checking their work before they give it to you for checking.

Homework ideas
• Ex 8C: write another competition entry for yourself/another person.
• Language bank 4.1 Ex A–B, p135
• Workbook Ex 1–5, p23–24

SCHOOLS OF THOUGHT

Introduction

Ss revise and practise the use of *can, have to, must* for obligation in the context of reading and talking about education.

SUPPLEMENTARY MATERIALS

Resource bank p157 and 159

Photo bank p154

Ex 3B and 5A: Ss may need dictionaries for unknown vocabulary in the text.

Ex 6A and 7B: optional extra activity: provide sheets of A4 paper for Ss to make posters of their ideas.

Warm up

Lead in to the lesson. Ask *Where did you go to school? Did you like it? Why/Why not?* Ss discuss the questions in pairs/groups. Elicit their answers and discuss the topic briefly with the class. Lead on to Ex 1.

VOCABULARY education

1 Check the meaning of the subjects in the box (use the **Photo bank** on p154 if necessary). Ss do the exercise and compare answers with another pair before reporting back to the class about what they have in common, e.g. *We were all bad at maths, but were interested in IT.*

Culture notes

In England, education is compulsory until the age of 16. Those who want to study for advanced school-level qualifications (A-levels) either stay on at a **secondary school** with a **sixth form**, transfer to a local **sixth form college**, or go to a **Further Education (FE) College**.

⮕ PHOTOBANK p154

Check the subjects in the photos and drill the pronunciation. Ss underline the stressed syllable in each word/phrase. Look at the diagram of State Education in England and check the meaning of *FE College, Sixth form*. Ss then discuss the questions in pairs. In *multilingual classes*, Ss might like to draw diagrams of their educational systems at home and share them with the class.

2A Ss complete the phrases and compare answers. Elicit/ check their answers.

Answers: 1 study 2 play 3 make 4 do/take 5 give 6 wear

B Check the rubric and elicit examples before Ss do the exercise.

C Do an example. Elicit sentences based on Ex 2B, e.g. *I enjoyed art, but I didn't enjoy French. I've never studied online.* Ss then make sentences about their answers in Ex 2B and compare them in the same way.

READING

Culture notes

Cheryl Heron introduced **24-hour teaching** into her school in 2006. She'd taken over as head teacher in 2001 when the school failed its inspection. The Department of Education monitored the new timetable to assess how well it worked. **Rudolph Steiner**, Austrian scientist, philosopher and educator, wrote *The Education of the Child* in 1907. The first school based on its educational philosophy opened in 1919 in Germany. It emphasised the role of the imagination and creative thinking in helping children develop their individuality, and used eurhythmy, meaning 'harmonious movement', as one way to achieve this. The **Suzuki method** is an educational philosophy created in the mid-20th century by Shin'ichi Suzuki, a violinist who wanted to bring beauty to the lives of children in Japan after World War II. Although originally used with the violin, it has been adapted for other instruments, the flute, piano, etc.

3A Elicit alternative ways of learning that Ss know, e.g. *distance learning, studying online, self-study, with a private teacher.* Give them 3–4 mins to discuss whether alternative ways are better than conventional education in schools. In feedback, nominate Ss to give their opinion and reasons. Then have a class vote on the question: yes or no.

B Check the rubric and give Ss 1 min to read the text quickly and match the topics. In feedback, check their answers and teach/check new vocabulary in the texts for the next exercise, e.g. *creativity, free thinking.* Ss could also use dictionaries.

Answers: a) paragraph 3 b) paragraph 1 c) paragraph 2

C First elicit one idea Ss think is 'good' and discuss why. Then give Ss 4–5 mins to read the text more carefully and underline what they think is the best/worst idea. Ss compare answers and discuss their reasons for their choices. In feedback, elicit and discuss Ss' ideas and check if there is a consensus.

GRAMMAR can, have to, must

Watch out!

Due to both L1 and L2 (English) interference, Ss may confuse both the meaning and form of modal verbs *can/ must* with *have to*, e.g. *I can't to go./You don't can smoke here.* Highlight and check the meaning/form of the verbs carefully, and provide thorough contextualised practice.

4 The sentences are from the texts in Ex 3. Check the table headings and the example: ask *Is it possible for children to decide when they go to school?* Yes. *Is it allowed?* Yes. Ss then do the exercise alone and compare answers. Monitor while Ss work to check how familiar they are with the language and any specific problems you'll need to focus on in feedback. Draw the table on the board and invite Ss to write the verbs in the correct places. The class discuss if the answers are correct. During this process, check meaning and form. Ask concept questions for each sentence/verb, e.g. *Is it necessary/possible/ allowed?* Double-check the meaning of *don't have to*, e.g. *You don't have to do any tests – but you can if you want to.* Elicit more examples if necessary. N.B. Ss might ask about the verb form in question 6. With *weak classes*, don't explain that *must be involved* is the passive. Just say it's the same as *You have to involve the parents, too.*

Answers:
not possible/not allowed: can't, mustn't; **necessary:** have to, must; **not necessary:** don't have to

Optional extra activity 1
Ss underline all the examples of *can/can't, have/don't have to, must/mustn't* in the texts in Ex 3 and match them to the categories in the table in Ex 4.

Optional extra activity 2
Ss work in pairs/groups and write 4–6 questions about the texts in Ex 3 to ask the class or other pairs/groups.

⟹ LANGUAGEBANK 4.2 p134–135

Ss can refer to the notes when they do the exercises. *Weaker Ss* should do Ex A and B in class. In Ex A, check *Hang it up!* In Ex B, check *log in, illegal.* In Ex B, there may be more than one answer.

Answers:
A 1 have to 2 can 3 can't 4 have to 5 can 6 mustn't
7 can't 8 don't have to
B 1 can 2 don't have to 3 must/have to 4 can 5 doesn't have to 6 can't/mustn't 7 has to/must 8 can't/mustn't

PRACTICE

5A Check the title of the text. Give Ss 1 min to read it quickly for general understanding (gist) first. Check/teach *advantages, home-schooled, qualifications* if necessary or Ss can check in their dictionaries. Do question 1 as an example. Ss then complete the text and check in pairs.

B Play the first sentence of the recording (extracts from the text in Ex 5A) for Ss to notice the pronunciation of *have to* /hæftə/. Then play the whole recording. Ss check their answers and compare them. In feedback, nominate Ss to answer. Recheck the concepts where needed, as well as the pronunciation of *have to.*

Answers: 1 don't have to 2 don't have to 3 can
4 have to/must 5 can 6 have to/must 7 mustn't/can't
8 mustn't/can't 9 can't 10 can

C Ss listen and repeat the sentences.

Teaching tip
While they are doing so, beat the sentence stress and intonation with your hands/arms, as if you were 'conducting' them. Pay particular attention to the pronunciation of *have to* /hæftə/ and the unstressed forms of *can/must* where appropriate.

Unit 4 Recording 4
1   They don't have to wear a uniform.
2   They don't have to wait for the school bus.
3   You can choose which subjects you want to study.
4   You have to work hard. You must work hard.
5   But you can choose to work when you feel like it.
6   You have to be at school at 8.30a.m. You must be at school at 8.30a.m.
7   You mustn't wear trainers. You can't wear trainers.
8   You mustn't use your mobile phone in class. You can't use your mobile phone in class.
9   Some people think that children who study at home can't go to the exams and get the same qualifications.
10 But they can, and they do.

6A Elicit some examples from the text in Ex 3. Then give Ss 3–4 mins to write a list of other ideas in pairs. Monitor closely to provide support with language if necessary. Ss then compare their lists with another pair and add to their own if possible. In feedback, invite Ss to write their ideas in lists on the board.

Suggested answers: They don't have to get up to go to school. They can study in their bedroom. They can have lunch at home. They don't have to study at the same time as school children, etc.

Optional extra activity
If appropriate to your Ss, provide them with A4 paper, if you have any. Ss write two lists of their ideas: one for *can/have to/must* and the other for *don't have to,* etc. They display their posters around the classroom – or pass them round – for other Ss to compare and discuss. Alternatively, use this idea for Ex 7B below.

B Use the ideas from Ex A as a starting point, e.g. *Pupils can go to school when they want.* Ask *Is it a good idea?* and elicit Ss' opinions. Ss then discuss the other points on their lists in pairs/groups. In feedback, invite Ss who think home-schooling is/isn't a good idea to give their opinions to the class.

Teaching tip
This could be organised as a debate: those in favour of home-schooling present their arguments to the class, and those against do the same. The class then votes for one or the other.

SPEAKING

7A First check/teach *national anthem, get in* from the statements. Give Ss 3–4 mins to decide if they are true or false in pairs. Check Ss' answers and ask *Which did you find surprising?*

Answers: Only 8 is false. Children in the UK don't have to eat a vegetarian lunch, but they can if they want to.

B Elicit some examples before Ss work in pairs to compare rules and customs in their own country. In *multilingual classes,* pair/group Ss of different nationalities/cultures so they can compare ideas and opinions. While Ss talk, make notes on their use of the language they've studied in this lesson and do any remedial work needed later. In feedback, invite each pair/group to present their comparisons and opinions to the class.

Homework ideas
- Ex 6B: write your opinion of home-schooling.
- Ex 7B: write about school rules/customs in your country and say which you think are good/bad ideas.
- Language bank 4.2 Ex A–B, p135
- Workbook Ex 1–6, p25–26

WHAT SHOULD I DO?

Introduction

Ss learn and practise ways of giving/responding to advice, particularly in the context of language learning.

SUPPLEMENTARY MATERIALS

Resource bank p160

Ex 2A: Ss may need dictionaries.

Ex 9: use audio/video recording facilities to record Ss role-plays, if available.

Warm up

Lead in to the lesson through the photos. First ask *What do you think is happening in the photos?* Ss discuss their answers in pairs and report back to the class. During/after the feedback stage, you could also ask other related questions, e.g. *Which of these activities have you done? When/Where? How old were you when you passed your driving test?* You could also write on the board *It's never too late to learn.* Ask *Do you agree? Why/Why not?*

SPEAKING

Culture notes

[What we have to learn to do,] we learn by doing is a quote from Aristotle.

The quote *A little learning (knowledge) is a dangerous thing* was first used by poet Alexander Pope in *An Essay on Criticism,* 1709. It means that a small amount of knowledge can make people think they are more expert than they really are.

The best way to learn is to teach is a quote from Frank Oppenheimer (1912–1985), an American physicist.

The quote *Anyone who stops learning is old, whether at twenty or eighty* is by Henry Ford (1863–1947), the founder of the Ford Motor Company.

1A Check the quotes with Ss and elicit which photos they match. Then ask *Do you have the same/similar sayings in your language?* Elicit examples. Discuss the first quote with Ss. Then give them 2–3 mins to make notes on the others.

B Ss compare their ideas in pairs/groups. In feedback, invite Ss from each pair/group to report back to the class. Find out what the majority opinion is.

VOCABULARY language learning

2A Ss should be familiar with most of the words in bold so allow them to match the definitions alone initially. They then compare answers and check new words in their dictionaries, if necessary. In feedback, check answers and elicit other sentences using the words in bold.

Answers: 1 b) 2 a) 3 e) 4 g) 5 c) 6 f) 7 d)

B Check the questions and give Ss 4–5 mins to discuss them. Monitor and notice Ss' answers, especially those for question 3. Nominate Ss to tell the class their own/their partner's answers. Discuss which Ss think are the most important/useful and elicit other ideas. This will give you important information about the language learning strategies your Ss are aware of

and/or use outside the classroom. They'll learn more about them in Ex 3–6.

FUNCTION giving advice

3A Give Ss 1–2 mins to read the message. Then ask comprehension questions, e.g. *Why did he write it? What does he need/want?* Discuss which areas of English Tomasz might most need to improve: spoken, written, vocabulary, reading/listening skills, etc. Then give Ss 2–3 mins to note down three pieces of advice. They can use ideas from Ex 2A if necessary.

B Ss compare their answers and decide on the three most useful ideas. In feedback, elicit their ideas and discuss which will help Tomasz the most.

4 First give Ss 1 min to read the replies quickly and check if any of their ideas from Ex 3 are mentioned. Elicit their answers. Then check the rubric. Ss read the replies again and discuss their answers in pairs. In feedback, elicit Ss' answers and write the three most useful ideas on the board.

5A Do an example and then give Ss 3–4 mins to write the replies in their notebooks. Monitor to check accuracy and invite Ss to write their answers on the board in feedback. Elicit/underline phrases for giving advice, e.g. *I think you should* … and drill the sentences.

Answers: 1 I *think you should study online.* 2 You should *get a good grammar book and do the exercises.*
3 You shouldn't *worry about grammar.* 4 Why *don't you watch films in English (without the subtitles!)?* 5 I (don't) think *it's a good idea to focus on listening.* 6 Find *someone who speaks English and talk to them.* Do *the exercises.* Read *news websites every day.* Look up *new words in a dictionary.*

B Ss discuss their answers in pairs. In feedback, refer to the sentences on the board from Ex 5A and elicit/check Ss' answers. Write positive (+) or negative (−) next to each sentence.

Answers:
positive: I think you should, You should, Why don't you …?, I think it's a good idea to
negative: You shouldn't, I don't think it's a good idea to …

6A Ss first read the information in the table: check *frightened, native speaker, podcast.* Ss then listen and complete the notes. With *weaker classes*, first play the recording up to *Have you got any advice for Andy?* and elicit the answer to question 1. After Ss have compared answers, play the relevant parts of the recording again if they don't agree. Check Ss' answers (in bold in the audio script). With *stronger classes*, play the recording again, pausing to ask more detailed comprehension questions, e.g. *Why is it a good idea to talk to yourself in English?*

Answers: 1 grammar 2 speak/talk 3 don't worry
4 can't understand 5 speak 6 practise 7 listen 8 read

B After Ss have discussed the questions, elicit their answers. They can then offer advice to their partner about his/her language learning problems.

Optional extra activity

Ss work in pairs and choose one or two new learning strategies each to try out. They should decide which areas of English they need to practise more and also which strategies would be the most suitable/achievable for them.

Unit 4 Recording 5

P=Presenter S=Sally

P: Hi. You're listening to *Ask the expert* and in today's programme we're talking about languages and how to learn a language. Our expert today is Sally Parker, who is a teacher. Hi, Sally.

S: Hello.

P: Sally, our first question today is from Andy. He says, 'I've just started learning English. **My problem is that I am too frightened to speak. My grammar is not very good** so I'm worried about saying the wrong thing.' Have you got any advice for Andy?

S: OK. Well, the first thing is **I think Andy should practise speaking to himself.**

P: Speaking to himself? <u>I'm not sure that's a good idea.</u>

S: I know it sounds silly, but talking to yourself in a foreign language is a really good way to practise. You don't have to feel embarrassed, because nobody can hear you. You can talk to yourself about anything you like – what you had for breakfast, where you're going for the weekend – anything. And the more you do it, the more you will get used to hearing your own voice and your pronunciation, so you won't feel so frightened in the classroom. Andy should try it.

P: <u>I suppose so.</u> Anything else? What about his grammar?

S: He has only just started learning English, so he is going to make lots of mistakes, but that's not a problem. That's how he'll learn. **Andy shouldn't worry about making mistakes.**

P: <u>You're right.</u> So Andy, try talking to yourself, and don't worry about making mistakes. Our next problem comes from Olivia in Brazil. She is worried about pronunciation. She says, '**The problem is I can't understand native speakers. They speak so fast and I can't understand their pronunciation.**' So Sally, any ideas for Olivia?

S: Well, first of all **it's a good idea for her to practise her listening skills.** She should listen to English as much as possible to get used to how it sounds. Listen to the news, listen to podcasts, watch English television.

P: OK – <u>that's a good idea.</u>

S: And **another thing she should do is to focus on listening and reading at the same time.** If you listen to something on the internet, you can often read the transcript. If you listen and read at the same time, it will help you see what the words sound like and how the words sound when a native speaker is talking.

P: Great. Thank you, Sally. I'm afraid that's all we have time for today, but …

LEARN TO respond to advice

7A Check the rubric and elicit Ss' answers.

Answers: 1 ✓ 2 ? 3 ✓ 4 ✗

B Play recording 4.5 again. Ss listen and write the response from Ex A in the correct place. In feedback, elicit/drill the advice and responses (underlined in the audio script) in open pairs across the class.

Answers: 1 I'm not sure that's a good idea. 2 I suppose so. 3 You're right. 4 that's a good idea.

Optional extra activity

Ss read and listen to the audio script on p170. Then ask *Did it help you to listen and read at the same time? How?* Elicit specific examples.

➡ LANGUAGEBANK 4.3 p134–135

Ss can refer to the information in the tables when they do Ex A and B.

Answers:
A a) That's a good idea. b) I think we should go out after the lesson. c) I'm not sure because I haven't got much money. d) Why don't we go out for a meal? e) OK, let's go to Butler's café for a coffee.
B b), a), d), c), e)

8A Ss cover the text and look at the pictures. Give them 1–2 mins to answer the question in pairs. They then check their answers with the text.

Suggested answers: A She eats unhealthy fast food, but he eats healthy salad and fish. B She works out on her exercise bike, but he plays computer games. C She's very fit and can run a lot, but he isn't fit and gets tired easily. D His clothes are old and unfashionable so he needs new ones.

B Ss can use language from Ex 5A and 7 to complete the conversations. Check their answers in feedback and drill the conversations. Ss then practise reading them out in pairs.

Answers: A you should eat, a good B shouldn't spend, You're C Why don't, I'm not sure that's D it's a good/it would be a good, suppose so

9 Organise Ss into groups of four and number them A, B, C, D. First read out one of the problems and elicit how to change it into their own problem using *I, my son,* etc. Ss then look at the relevant pages/texts. Give them 1 min to think about how to change them. Ss then take it in turns to explain their problem and get advice from their partners. Monitor and make notes of problems Ss have with the language of advice and give feedback afterwards. If you have recording facilities, record the role-plays. Ss watch them and then try to improve on their performance.

Homework ideas
- Ex 6B: write about two new learning strategies you want to try out. Say why you chose them and what you'll do.
- Ex 9: write advice for two of the problems.
- Language bank 4.3 Ex A–B, p135
- Workbook Ex 1–4, p27

THE INTELLIGENCE TEST

Introduction

Ss watch an extract from the BBC documentary programme *Horizon: Battle Of The Brains*. It explores test results achieved by the same group of people after a gap of seventy years. Ss then learn/practise giving advice about taking tests.

SUPPLEMENTARY MATERIALS

Warm up: select a short, simple test, e.g. from a test book, Lookback exercise, an online IQ test, a spelling test you prepare yourself.

Ex 2: Ss need dictionaries for this exercise.

Warm up

Lead in to the topic of the lesson by giving Ss a surprise test! The aim is to remind them, in a light-hearted way, how tests make them feel. Tell Ss to put their books away and not talk during the test. Hand out the test (see suggestions in the supplementary materials section above) and collect it after 10 mins. You can mark it later/at home. Tell Ss what your aim was. Ask, e.g. *How did you feel about the test – nervous, bored, angry, happy? What memories did it bring back of your school days? Are tests a 'good' thing?* Ss discuss the questions in pairs and then as a class. Follow on immediately with Ex 1.

Culture notes

The term **IQ (intelligence quotient)** was created by the German psychologist William Stern in 1912 as a method of scoring children's intelligence tests.

DVD PREVIEW

1 Give Ss 2–3 mins to discuss the questions. In feedback, invite Ss to tell the class about their partner's experiences. Ask *Who likes test? Why/Why not?*

2 If Ss don't have dictionaries, put *weaker/stronger Ss* together in pairs to work out the meaning of the phrases in bold. In feedback, check the meaning of each word. Ask, e.g. *If you're bright, you're not very intelligent – true or false?* Also model and drill the pronunciation.

Answers: 1 e) 2 d) 3 c) 4 a) 5 f) 6 b)

3A Give Ss 1 min to read the programme information and discuss their answer. They should write it in not more than 15 words, if possible. In feedback, nominate one or two Ss to read out their answer. Discuss it and check any unfamiliar words in the text, if necessary.

Answers: It's about elderly people who do the same intelligence test they did in 1932 (nearly seventy years before/when they were younger).

B Ss read the information again and compare their answers. In feedback, ask them to justify the answers.

Answers: 1 F: all 11-year-olds 2 T 3 F: the test results might tell us about the type of people who live the longest

DVD VIEW

4A Check the questions and the meaning of *score*. Ss could predict what they think the answers might be, based on the programme information in Ex 3. Elicit their predictions and write them on the board. Play the DVD. Ss note down their answers and compare. Play the last part again if they have doubts (see the underlined text in the DVD script). Elicit which predictions on the board were correct. Ss can add more information from the DVD if necessary.

Answers: 1 The second time. 2 People with more education, a more professional job, non-smokers.

B Check *rediscovered* and *basement* in question 1. Ss then work alone/in pairs, and underline the correct alternatives before watching the DVD again. Check Ss' answers (see the text in bold in the DVD script). Ask their opinions of the test results: *Were you surprised? Why/Why not?*

Answers: 1 The results of the 1932 test were 2 the same as they were in 1932 3 the exam they have done 4 well

Optional extra activity

Play the DVD again, pausing at suitable points. Ask questions about what Ss can see, e.g. *What's he/she doing now? Where are they? What did children do/wear/look like in 1932? How are things similar/different now? Do you agree that people with a high IQ live longer?*

DVD 4 Horizon: Battle Of The Brains

N=Narrator I=Ian Deary W1/2=Woman 1/2 M1/2/3=Man 1/2/3

N: Recent research into the history of IQ tests in Scotland suggests your IQ score might predict, to an extent at least, your health and even your life expectancy.

W1: You have forty-five mins to do the test, OK?

M1: OK.

N: Bill and Davina are seventy-nine years old. This is the second time they've done this test. The first time was in **1932, when every eleven-year-old in Scotland was put through an intelligence test.** It's the only time this kind of mass testing has ever been done in the UK. **The results were rediscovered recently in an Edinburgh basement.** If you want to know how our intelligence changes as we get older, these results are a potential goldmine.

I: We brought hundreds of people back and we got them to sit the exact same test that they had sat when they were aged eleven. Now these people are now seventy-nine or eighty years old. **We gave the same instructions. We gave the same test. And we gave the same time limit.**

M2: It was a little stickier than I thought it would be.

M3: I walked through it quite happily, quite honestly.

W2: I felt I must have been very bright at eleven if I sat that exam and passed.

N: There were some intriguing results. <u>Almost everyone had a better score at eighty than they did at eleven.</u> But some had gone from being just averagely intelligent to a much higher level.

I: Now that's what really drives our research. We're interested in: Why have those people who've gone from IQ 100 at age eleven up to a 110 or 120? What have they done right? What can be the recipe for successful ageing? <u>We're finding that the person with more education, even though they had the same IQ in childhood, is doing slightly better in old age, on average. The person who had a more professional job, in old age, is doing slightly better on average than the person who had a manual job, despite the fact that they started at the same level.</u> The people who smoked have got slightly less good mental ability than you would expect.

N: What's even more remarkable is that **the kids who had higher IQ scores at eleven are the very ones still alive today.** So it seems high IQ in childhood is good for survival.

5 Elicit examples, e.g. *I was good at maths at school, but I haven't studied it for 20 years. It would be more difficult now.* Give Ss 3–4 mins to discuss the questions. In feedback, elicit examples of specific tests they would find easier/more difficult now, with reasons.

speakout tips for tests

6 Discuss question 1 with Ss before they work in pairs. They should note down both their own and their partner's answers if they disagree. Nominate Ss to give their opinions/reasons in feedback.

7A Ss listen and write brief notes for their answers. After they've compared notes, play the recording again if they need to add more detail. Check key words, e.g. *concentrate/ concentration.* Elicit and discuss Ss' answers. Ask further comprehension questions, e.g. *Why does it help to study with friends? What helps you to concentrate?*

Answers: 1 studying with friends at the same time each day 2 not eating too much before an exam 3 going to bed early the night before an exam

B Ss read the **key phrases**, then listen and tick the ones they hear. In feedback, play the recording again, pausing after each **key phrase** (in bold in the audio script). Elicit/drill the sentences.

Answers: How about this one? In my opinion, this is a really good idea. I agree with this one. It depends. I'm not sure about this advice.

Unit 4 Recording 6

A: OK, so we need to think of the best ideas for taking tests.

B: Yep.

A: Well, **how about this one?** It's a good idea to study with friends at the same time each day.

B: **In my opinion, this is a really good idea.** You can make it a regular part of your daily life.

A: You mean like having breakfast at the same time, lunch at the same time, studying at the same time.

B: Yes. And also I think it helps when you study with friends.

A: Yeah, I think it's more motivating.

B: And you can actually talk to someone, not just look at books. I find that if I'm only reading my notes it's easy to lose concentration. I start thinking about other things. But when you are talking to someone, it really helps you concentrate. So, yes, **I agree with this one.**

A: OK. Another idea is not to eat too much before the exam.

B: Oh really?

A: When I eat a lot, I get sleepy.

B: Oh I see. I think **it depends.** Because if you don't eat enough, you start to feel hungry in the middle of the exam.

A: That's true.

B: And then you can't concentrate.

A: Yeah, that's true.

B: So, **I'm not sure about this advice,** for me. As I said, I think **it depends.** I always try to eat a good meal before an exam. I'm so nervous that I never get sleepy.

A: OK. What other ideas do you have?

B: Well, there's one thing I always do before an exam.

A: What's that?

B: I go to bed early the night before.

A: Right.

B: I always try to sleep for eight hours the night before the exam.

8A Ss can use the tips from Ex 6 and 7 and add their own. They should rank their five tips in order of importance, 1–5, if possible. Provide support to Ss who need it, or ask *stronger Ss* to work with *weaker ones*. Monitor and prompt Ss to correct errors of accuracy in their tips.

B In feedback, nominate Ss from each group to report back to the class. The rest of the class tick the tips that are the same, or make a note of those they disagree with. When all groups have reported back, Ss discuss the tips they disagree with.

writeback a problem page

9A Give Ss 2–3 mins to answer the questions and compare them. Nominate Ss to give their answers. Ask *How many problems does Barry have?*

Answers: 1 He's a language student. 2 He doesn't have a quiet, comfortable place to study for his exam and he can't concentrate.

B Ss work in pairs/groups and make a list of three/four pieces of advice for Barry. They then write a draft reply using advice language from lesson 4.3. Provide support where needed. Ss write a final draft in class or at home.

Homework ideas
- Ex 9B: write your reply and put it on your class blog.

LOOKBACK

Introduction

The notes below provide ideas for exploiting the exercises and activities but your approach will depend on your aim, e.g. as a diagnostic test/assessment or for fluency practice/revision. For example, if you wanted to assess/test Ss' knowledge, then it would not be appropriate to monitor and help them.

MAKE AND DO

1A Check the example and give Ss 2 mins for the exercise before they compare answers. Check their answers and drill the question, e.g. *Who in your family makes most of the meals?* Elicit Ss' answers in preparation for Ex B.

> **Answers:** 2 makes most of the meals 3 does a lot of homework 4 makes the most phone calls 5 does projects at work 6 makes speeches

B Give Ss time to prepare their answers before they work in pairs. Monitor while Ss ask/answer the questions and make notes of problems for remedial work in feedback/assessment purposes. To follow-up and provide extended speaking practice, Ss can tell another student about their partner's family, e.g. *Alicia's husband makes most of the meals, but her daughter makes the most phone calls.*

PAST SIMPLE OR PRESENT PERFECT + EVER/NEVER

2A You could do this exercise as a real test of Ss' understanding of these two tenses. Give them 3–4 mins to write the completed sentences on a piece of paper, with no help. In feedback, Ss swap papers and mark each other's sentences with a tick or cross as you give the answers. Ss write the result on their partner's papers, e.g. 4/6. Ss then correct their wrong answers. Recheck the answers before moving to Ex B.

> **Answers:** 1 Have you ever swum in the sea? 2 (Where) did you go on holiday last year? 3 I have (I've) never visited Africa. 4 I didn't go out last night. 5 I have (I've) lived in more than one country. 6 I ate in a restaurant last weekend.

B If possible, put Ss into pairs with someone they don't know very well. In feedback, check who guessed both answers correctly.

C Ss prepare the questions alone. Monitor while they do this and prompt them to correct their mistakes. Don't check the questions with the class but assess how well they use the two tenses while they ask/answer the questions. In feedback, invite pairs to ask/answer their questions in front of the class. Tell the class to listen and write down follow-up questions to ask, e.g. *Did you go out last night? Yes, I did.* Follow-up questions: *Where did you go? Who did you go with?* Give feedback on Ss' problems and do remedial work as needed.

EDUCATION

3A Check *particularly well* in question e). Give Ss 2–3 mins to match the questions. Check/drill them before Ex B.

> **Answers:** 1 e) 2 c) 3 g) 4 d) 5 b) 6 a) 7 f)

B If possible, pair Ss with a partner they don't know very well in order to make the questions more authentic. Ss should take turns to ask a question and make a note of the answers. They can then report back their partner's answers to the class in feedback.

CAN, HAVE TO, MUST

4A Ss could work in pairs and discuss what they think the answers are for questions 1, 2 and 5. Check Ss' answers and ask them to give reasons for their choice of verb.

> **Answers:** 1 must 2 can't 3 can't 4 don't have to 5 have to

B In a *mixed-ability class*, pair stronger/weaker Ss for this exercise. Alternatively, put weaker Ss together and help/prompt them with ideas. Try to check all Ss' work to check that their sentences are grammatically correct.

> **Suggested answers:** In my country, women can vote/you can't drive until you are 18. I have to go to the dentist next week. In an exam you mustn't look at other students' work. At the weekend I don't have to get up early. You must try to speak in the language as much as possible. You mustn't use a mobile phone while driving. I have to brush my teeth every day. You don't have to go to work when you are a child.

C Ss read each other's sentences and compare them. In feedback, Ss read out their sentences. The rest of the class note down any new ideas and add them to their own. Discuss any facts that surprised Ss or that they found particularly interesting. Do remedial work as required.

LANGUAGE LEARNING

5A Give Ss 1 min to complete the words before they compare answers. Check meaning and pronunciation in feedback.

> **Answers:** 1 reread 2 practise 3 subtitles 4 chatroom 5 memorise

B Ss take it in turns to ask/answer the questions. They should note down their partner's answers so that they can report back to the class in feedback. Monitor discreetly, making notes of Ss' performance. In feedback, Ss tell the class/group about their partner. Give feedback on Ss' problems if necessary.

GIVING ADVICE

6A Ss complete the tables and then check their answers on p43.

> **Answers:**
> giving advice: (I think) you should/you shouldn't …
> Why don't we/you … ? I (don't) think that's a good idea …
> Find/Try/Go …
> responding to advice: That's a good idea. I suppose so.
> You're right. I'm not sure that's a good idea.

B Give Ss 3–4 mins to complete the conversation. *Stronger Ss* can write more. Pairs read out their conversations to the class. Prompt Ss to correct them where necessary.

> **Suggested answers:** A: Why don't we *watch a DVD later?* B: That's a *good idea.* A: I think we should *watch one without subtitles.* B: OK. Let's *try the new James Bond film.*

C Ss rehearse their conversation and try to memorise it. Monitor and provide help with stress and intonation. Each pair acts out the conversation: the class votes for the best one.

OVERVIEW

AMAZING JOURNEYS

Introduction

Ss learn/practise the past simple and past continuous used to talk about interrupted past actions. They also learn vocabulary for transport and talk about journeys.

SUPPLEMENTARY MATERIALS

Resource bank p161 and 162

Photo bank p155: Ss should have dictionaries available for these exercises.

Ex 3: Ss may need dictionaries.

Ex 4: a map of the world to show the places mentioned in the texts: Chile, Bolivia, Peru, Australia, Houston.

Warm up

To lead in to the lesson, play a word game such as hangman to revise transport vocabulary, e.g. *bus, bike, coach, helicopter, lorry,* etc. (See the **Photo bank** on p155 for more words.)

Write a word in blanks on the board, e.g. _ _ _ _ _ (coach). Ss work in pairs/teams and take it in turns to guess a letter. If the letter is in the word, write it in the correct place(s) on the board. Also write it underneath to remind Ss it's already been used. If the letter isn't in the word, add a part of the body to the gallows (head, body, left arm, right arm, etc.). Ss continue guessing letters until they either guess the word, or all the body parts are completed. Pairs/teams get a point if they guess the word before the 'body' is completed. Play the game for 5–6 mins. Invite Ss to write the words (blanks) on the board themselves if appropriate.

VOCABULARY transport

1 Give Ss 2–3 mins to make a list of words from the warm up, and add others they know. They then check them in the **Photo bank**, Ex 1, p155. Check answers and elicit the stressed syllables in the words. Ss copy new transport words into their vocabulary notebooks and underline the stress. Then give Ss 3–4 mins to discuss question 2 in Ex 1, first in pairs, and then as a class.

> ▶ **PHOTOBANK** p155
>
> **1** Ss can use their dictionaries to check words they don't know.
>
> **Answers:** 1 F 2 M 3 K 4 L 5 N 6 G 7 H 8 B 9 E 10 J 11 I 12 D 13 C 14 A
>
> **2** Ss could discuss this question together with question 2 in Ex 1 above.

READING

Culture notes

The film *Rabbit-Proof Fence* (2002), based on the book *Follow the Rabbit-proof Fence*, stars three indigenous Australian (Aboriginal) actresses Everlyn Sampi, Tianna Sansbury and Laura Monaghan, who play Molly, Daisy and Gracie. British actor Kenneth Branagh plays A.O. Neville, the man responsible for removing the girls from their families.

The Motorcycle Diaries (2004) (*Diarios de motocicleta* in Spanish) is about the 1952 journey 23-year-old **Che Guevara** made with his friend, Argentinean-Cuban doctor and scientist, Alberto Granada. Mexican actor, Gael García Bernal, played Guevara. Brazilian Walter Salles directed the film. Che Guevara (1928–1967) was an Argentinean Marxist revolutionary, physician, author, guerrilla leader, military theorist, international statesman and major figure of the Cuban Revolution. Since his death, he's become a symbolic figure within popular culture.

Apollo 13 (1995) starred Tom Hanks, Kevin Bacon and Bill Paxton, and was directed by Ron Howard.

2 The questions here ask Ss to predict information about the photos and the texts they will read in Ex 3. However, first look at the photos and elicit briefly what Ss know about the films. Don't confirm any details about the films until after Ex 4. Check the questions and the meaning of new words in the word box. Give Ss 3–4 mins to discuss the questions. In feedback, elicit Ss' predictions and write some of them on the board – but don't confirm if they are correct or not.

3 This is a jigsaw reading. It's important to set this up carefully to make sure Ss don't look at their partners' texts before they've all exchanged information about them. Check the rubric and the questions, then put Ss into groups of three, A, B and C. Make sure they sit facing each other, not side-by-side, and don't show their books. Give them 4–5 mins to look at their texts and make notes of the answers. Monitor closely and provide support where needed. Ss can use their dictionaries to check new words if necessary.

4 Give Ss 2 mins each to tell their group about their text while their partners take notes. In feedback, nominate Ss from each group in turn to answer a question about their text. Then check Ss' predictions from Ex 2. Discuss the films in more detail, using the **Culture notes** if needed. Show Ss a map of the places in the texts if possible.

Answers: 1 A: Che Guevara, Alberto B: three astronauts: James Lovell, John Swigert and Fred Haise C: three Aborigine girls: Molly, 14, her sister Daisy, 8, and their cousin Gracie, 10
2 A: across Latin America B: the moon C: a camp, then they escaped and went home
3 A: They crashed the motorbike into a cow. B: There was an explosion on Apollo 13, which destroyed important equipment. C: They had no food, nowhere to sleep, and no map.
4 A: Che stopped studying to be a doctor and began his life's work – fighting for the poor. B: They returned home from space and landed safely in the ocean. C: After nine weeks they got home.

speakout TIP

Read the speakout tip with Ss. Then give them 1–2 mins to find a sentence in their text and make a note of it in three or four words. Elicit some examples for each text and write them on the board.

5 While Ss discuss the questions, monitor and make notes of their ideas and language problems. Discuss the questions with the class and give feedback on Ss' problems. If Ss can't think of any other real-life journeys that have been made into films, ask Ss to think of any films they know which are about journeys.

Possible answers: 2 Because they are true stories with an important message to pass on/celebrate. 3 Real-life journeys: *Scott of the Antarctic* (1948) and *Touching the Void* (2003); fictional journeys: *Journey to the Centre of the Earth* (1959), *Easy Rider* (1969), *Central Station* (1998), *Around the World in 80 days* (2004), *A Passage to India* (1984)

GRAMMAR   past simple and past continuous

Watch out!

Ss often tend to overuse the past continuous and say, e.g. *Last night we were in a restaurant and we were seeing a mouse.* It's important to check the use of tenses carefully using clear examples in context, and encourage self-correction at all stages of the lesson.

6A Ss do the exercise alone and compare answers. While they do this, write the sentences on the board. In feedback, elicit/check Ss' answers and underline examples of the past simple and past continuous.

Answers: 1 past continuous and past simple 2 a) study b) travel c) rain

B When Ss have answered the questions, check the concepts further: draw a timeline (see below or **Language bank** p136) to illustrate the continuous action (*was studying*) and the completed action (*decided*) (or long/short action).

Ask *Which action started first?* Studying. *Which was the short action?* Decided. *Did the long action continue after?* Maybe – it's not important.

Answers: 1 past continuous 2 past simple

C There's one example of a sentence in each text and they all begin with *While*. Elicit the sentences and write them on the board. Underline *While* and ask *What other question word could you use?* When. *Is the meaning the same?* Yes. *Do you use while with the past simple or continuous?* Past continuous.

Answers:
Text A: While he was travelling, Ernesto met many poor people …
Text B: While the world was watching on TV, they returned home from space …
Text C: While they were walking, they saw the 'rabbit-proof fence' …

▶ **LANGUAGE**BANK 5.1 p136–137

Ss can study the tables/notes in class or at home. They should refer to them when they do Ex A and B. In Ex A, teach *lawnmower*, *priest*.

> **Answers:**
> A 1 was living 2 decided 3 bought 4 began 5 was travelling 6 helped 7 was driving 8 were fixing 9 stayed 10 did (the story) end
> B 1 He was playing tennis when he hurt his leg.
> 2 Sarah didn't like the job because it was boring.
> 3 While they were travelling they met lots of other tourists. 4 How did you know my name? 5 Who were you dancing with in that nightclub when I saw you?
> 6 I was swimming in the sea when I saw the shark.
> 7 Did I pass my exam? 8 The thief broke in while Jack was having breakfast.

PRACTICE

7A Check the example and elicit as many *So …* sentences as possible. Ss work alone/in pairs. Give support where needed.

B While Ss compare their answers, monitor again and prompt them to self-correct any mistakes with the past simple/continuous. For each question, nominate Ss to give the first sentence, then elicit all Ss' answers with *So …* . Recheck the tenses using the rules in Ex 6A and B if necessary.

> **Answers:** 2 I was waiting for a bus when I met my boss.
> 3 I was watching TV when I recognised my best friend!
> 4 I was walking home when I found $5,000 in a bag.
> 5 We were travelling by plane when a man with a gun stood up. 6 We were riding our bicycles when a cow walked across the road. 7 We were eating in a restaurant when we saw a mouse. 8 I was studying in my room when I heard loud music next door.

8A Ss listen to the recording. Pause after each sentence. Ss note down the consequence in the *So* sentence, e.g. *went home*. Ss discuss the similarities to their own answers in Ex 7A in pairs, and report back to the class.

> **Answers:** 1 I was running when it started to snow. So I went home! 2 I was waiting for a bus when I met my boss. So we went for a drink. 3 I was watching TV when I recognised my best friend! So I called her. 4 I was walking home when I found $5,000 in a bag. So I took it to the police. 5 We were travelling by plane when a man with a gun stood up. So we hit him, took the gun and became heroes! 6 We were riding our bicycles when a cow walked across the road. So we stopped. 7 We were eating in a restaurant when we saw a mouse. So we told the waiter and didn't pay. 8 I was studying in my room when I heard loud music next door. So I went to complain and they invited me to their party.

B Write *was* /wəz/ and *were* /wə/ on the board. Then play each sentence, pausing to elicit/highlight the sentence stress and weak forms of *was* /wəz/ and *were* /wə/ (see verbs in italics in the audio script). Drill the sentences chorally (as a class), then individually, to check sentence stress and weak forms.

Unit 5 Recording 1

1 *I was running* when it started to snow. So I went home! *I was running*.

2 *I was waiting* for a bus when I met my boss. So we went for a drink. *I was waiting*.

3 *I was watching* TV when I recognised my best friend! So I called her. *I was watching*.

4 *I was walking* home when I found $5,000 in a bag. So I took it to the police. *I was walking*.

5 *We were travelling* by plane when a man with a gun stood up. So we hit him, took the gun and became heroes! *We were travelling*.

6 *We were riding* our bicycles when a cow walked across the road. So we stopped. *We were riding*.

7 *We were eating* in a restaurant when we saw a mouse. So we told the waiter and didn't pay. *We were eating*.

8 *I was studying* in my room when I heard loud music next door. So I went to complain and they invited me to their party. *I was studying*.

9 First read/check the example and the prompts with Ss. Give them time to think of five/six sentences and elicit another example before they work in pairs. During pairwork, write down sentences with examples of Ss' mistakes with the target language (the language they learnt in this lesson). In feedback, nominate pairs to say their sentences/respond across the class.

> **Teaching tip**
> This is a good time to do a correction slot. Write 5–6 sentences with Ss' mistakes on the board. Ss correct them alone and then compare answers. Check their answers and do remedial teaching as necessary.

SPEAKING

10A Check the questions and example answer, e.g. 1 *Where and when did you go? Last summer I went to Greece …* . Give Ss 5 mins to write their answers in note form. **Weaker Ss** could work in pairs. Provide help with language Ss need.

B While Ss tell their stories in groups, make notes of problems for feedback. Check which stories Ss thought were the funniest/most interesting and invite Ss to tell them to the class. Do a correction slot as appropriate.

> **Homework ideas**
> • Ex 10: write the story of your trip/journey.
> • Language bank 5.1 Ex A–B, p137
> • Workbook Ex 1–7, p28–29

TRAVEL TIPS

Introduction

Ss learn and practise the use of verb patterns and vocabulary for travel items in the context of describing journeys.

SUPPLEMENTARY MATERIALS

Resource bank p163

Photo bank p155

Warm up: download/bring pictures of people on different kinds of holiday, doing different activities, e.g. sightseeing, eating/drinking in outdoor cafés, relaxing/swimming on beach, walking, camping, skiing, water sports, extreme sports, yoga/meditation, painting/craft-making, horse riding, etc.

Ex 9C: download/copy advertisements with itineraries for weekend breaks/holidays to use as prompts for Ss' emails.

Warm up

Show Ss the pictures you've brought of different kinds of holidays/holiday activities. Ss work in pairs/groups and describe each type of holiday, and then choose two they like and don't like. In feedback, elicit and discuss the top three most/least popular types of holiday. If you haven't got any pictures, elicit ten different kinds of holiday first and write them on the board.

VOCABULARY travel items

1 Give Ss 2–3 mins to discuss their answers. *Stronger classes* could use the words in the box in Ex 2A.

2A Check the rubric and the words in the box. Ss should be familiar with all of them.

Teaching tip

If you have a *weaker class,* teach/check the words via the pictures in the **Photo bank**, Ex 1 p155. Give Ss 3–4 mins to do the exercise: they must give reasons for their answers. In feedback, discuss Ss' reasons for their choices and find out what the consensus is.

Suggested answers: 1 suitcase, digital camera, sunhat, souvenirs 2 notebook, waterproof clothes, walking boots, rucksack, money belt 3 suitcase, notebook, digital camera, map, binoculars

B Ss should listen to the words first. Ask *Where's the stress?* and elicit Ss' answers. They then listen/repeat the words and then underline the stress in each word.

Answers: <u>suit</u>case, <u>note</u>book, <u>di</u>gital <u>ca</u>mera, <u>sou</u>ve<u>nirs</u>, <u>water</u>proof <u>clo</u>thes, <u>dic</u>tionary, <u>wal</u>king boots, <u>sun</u>hat, <u>ruck</u>sack, <u>mo</u>ney belt, bi<u>no</u>culars, <u>map</u>, um<u>bre</u>lla

C Give Ss 3–4 mins to discuss the questions. While Ss work in pairs, monitor and make notes on their pronunciation for feedback. *Stronger classes* could do Ex 1 in the **Photo bank** first and incorporate the words there into this exercise.

▶ PHOTOBANK p155

1 Ss can use dictionaries to check words they don't know.

Answers: 1 1N 2O 3H 4K 5C 6P 7L 8I 9B 10J 11Q 12D 13A 14G 15R 16M 17F 18E

2 Do this exercise now or use it as revision in the next class.

LISTENING

3A Give Ss 2 mins to decide on eight items and write them down.

B Ss listen and tick the items they hear in the box in Ex 2A. They then compare their answers with their own predictions. Check how many of Ss' predictions were correct.

Answers: 1 a dictionary 2 walking boots 3 digital camera, binoculars 4 sunhat, waterproof clothes 5 suitcase, souvenirs, rucksack 6 money belt 7 notebook, pen

4A Elicit Ss' answers for question 1. If they can't remember the information, give them a tip. They can work out what kind of word they need, e.g. question 2: there will be a noun or verb + *-ing* after *love*. Give Ss 3–4 mins to complete the sentences.

B Ss listen and check their answers, and then compare them. Play the recording again if necessary. Nominate Ss to give their answers in feedback (see text in bold in the audio script).

Answers: 1 a few words of the language 2 walking 3 photos 4 a warm place 5 wild 6 money 7 remember

Unit 5 Recording 3

1 These days <u>we always expect to hear English</u> in tourist areas. Most people working in tourism speak it, but <u>I always want to talk to local people</u> and many of them don't speak English. **So I try to learn a few words of the language,** especially 'please' and 'thank you', and I always take a small dictionary.

2 <u>I love walking when I go on holiday</u> … 'cause I think … I think you see more, so I always take a really good pair of walking boots.

3 I think a good digital camera is important when you travel. <u>I always seem to take hundreds and hundreds of photos</u>. And I also take binoculars.

4 When I'm not travelling for work, <u>I usually choose to go to a warm place</u> for my holidays, so I always take a sunhat. But when I go somewhere during the winter or rainy season, I always take waterproof clothes.

5 I think it's a good idea to buy a really good suitcase. And when you pack, leave enough space for souvenirs. On the other hand, <u>I enjoy travelling in wild places,</u> so quite often I take a rucksack not a suitcase. <u>If you decide to go walking, a rucksack is much easier to carry.</u>

6 <u>It's best to avoid carrying too much money</u> because you don't want to look like a rich tourist! 'Cause of this, I always take a money belt on holiday.

7 <u>I need to write things down</u> to remember them so I take a notebook and pen.

GRAMMAR verb patterns

Watch out!

It takes time for Ss to acquire confidence with verb patterns. It's important to encourage Ss to notice them in all contexts: reading/listening texts, exercises and their own speaking and writing.

5A Check the examples. (The sentences are underlined in audio script 5.3.) Ss then work alone and compare their answers. In feedback, tell Ss there are no fixed rules for verb patterns: they will learn them as part of the learning process.

Answers: 4 I always <u>seem to take</u> hundreds and hundreds of photos. 5 I usually <u>choose to go</u> to a warm place. 6 I <u>enjoy travelling</u> in wild places. 7 If you <u>decide to go</u> walking, a rucksack is easier to carry. 8 It's best <u>to avoid carrying</u> too much money. 9 I <u>need to write</u> things down.

B Ss can refer to the sentences in Ex 5A when they do this exercise.

Answers:
verb + *-ing:* enjoy, avoid
verb + infinitive with *to:* want, seem, choose, decide, need

C In feedback, elicit examples of sentences with *love/hate* in both forms, e.g. *I love to play/playing tennis.*

Answers:
verb + *ing:* finish, imagine, hate, love
verb + infinitive with *to:* hope, hate, would like, love
verbs which can go in both columns: love, hate

➡ LANGUAGEBANK 5.2 p136–137

Check the table/notes with your Ss, paying special attention to the verbs *love/hate.* Ss can refer to the notes when they do the exercises. *Weaker Ss* should do Ex A and B in class.

Answers:
A 1 to visit 2 living 3 drinking 4 to play 5 to have
6 swimming 7 to finish 8 reading
B 1 Would you like ~~doing~~ *to do*… 2 … people who hate ~~spend~~ *spending* 3 If you enjoy ~~to travel~~ *travelling* 4 if you don't mind ~~to stay~~ *staying* 5 and want ~~knowing~~ *to know* 6 we promise ~~helping~~ *to help* you 7 If you choose ~~booking~~ *to book* 8 you can expect ~~living~~ *to live*

PRACTICE

6 Check the example. Ask *Is there a difference between* hope *and* expect? Ss discuss the question in pairs. Answer: *hope* means you want something to happen; *expect* means you think it is going to happen. Tell Ss to think about differences in the meaning of the verbs when they do the exercise. They work alone and then compare answers. *Weaker Ss* can refer to the table of verbs on p136. In feedback, check Ss' answers and any differences of meaning between the correct verbs. Then elicit sentences using the verbs that don't fit, e.g. *I I enjoy flying long distances on a plane.*

Answers: 2 imagine 3 needs 4 like 5 want 6 enjoy
7 expect 8 avoid

7A Elicit some examples for question 1. While Ss write, monitor and prompt them to self-correct their mistakes. They can compare their answers, but try to check all Ss' sentences before they do Ex B. Also note if Ss have remembered that *hate* and *love* can be followed by both forms.

B Ss should work with a different partner for this exercise. They compare notes to decide what they have or don't have in common and prepare to report back to the class in feedback.

SPEAKING

8 Ss look at the photos and read the rubrics and examples. Ask, e.g. *Do you like looking at beautiful buildings? Do you put your photos on Facebook?* Give Ss 4–5 mins to discuss the questions and encourage them to use the verbs they've practised in the lesson. They should make notes of their partner's answers for feedback/homework. Note down mistakes Ss make with verb patterns. Ss could then compare their answers with another pair to find out what they have in common, and report their findings back to the class. Do a correction slot if necessary.

WRITING   using sequencers

9A Use a map of Southern Africa if possible: elicit/show Ss where Lesotho, Johannesburg and Cape Town are. Give Ss 2 mins to read the email before they discuss their answers in pairs. Check Ss' answers and teach the expression *live out of a rucksack/suitcase.*

Answers:
Good things: took a boat down the river, saw lots of interesting animals/plants, relaxed for a week in Cape Town, great trip/experience
Bad things: heavy rain, living out of a rucksack

B Check the example *First.* Ss then underline the other four words/phrases and compare their answers. In feedback, check the meaning of *after a while* (after a period of time), and the use of commas after the last three sequencers. Ask *Which words can't change places?* First/Finally. Practise further: ask *What did you do this morning/yesterday/last Saturday?*

Answers: Then, After a while, After that, Finally

C First elicit brief details of Ss' recent holidays. If they haven't travelled recently, provide them with advertisements with itineraries of holidays from the newspapers/internet as prompts for the email. They could also use their ideas from Ex 10 p49. Give Ss 6–10 mins to write a draft of their emails, using the sequencers from Ex 9A. To build Ss' accuracy and confidence with their writing, encourage them to show each other their drafts, and exchange ideas/advice. They then write a corrected final draft.

D Ss exchange emails with as many classmates as possible. Alternatively, display them around the room on walls/tables so Ss can walk round and read them. In feedback, check which were the most interesting and why.

Homework ideas
• Ex 9C: write another email about last weekend or another trip. Send it to a classmate or your teacher or put it on the class blog.
• Language bank 5.2 Ex A–B, p137
• Workbook Ex 1–5, p30–31

YOU CAN'T MISS IT

Introduction

Ss learn and practise making phone calls in both informal and formal situations. They also learn how to manage problems they might experience during phone calls.

SUPPLEMENTARY MATERIALS

Resource bank p164

Warm up: download/bring a map of Brazil, Argentina, Paraguay to show where the Iguaçu Falls are.

Culture notes

The Iguaçu Falls are located on the border of Brazil and Argentina. There are 275 waterfalls and some of them are 82 metres high. The Devil's Throat is the most impressive: water falls over a U-shaped cliff, 150 metres wide and 700 metres long. The Falls were nominated as one of the world's New7Wonders of Nature. **Foz do Iguaçu** is a Brazilian town near the Falls.

Warm up

Use the photos to lead in to the lesson. Ss cover the texts and look at the photos. Ask *Do you know this place?* Don't elicit or tell them more than the name: *the Iguaçu Falls.* Then ask the questions below, and give the alternative answers. Ss discuss each answer in pairs and write it down (the correct answers are underlined). *1 The Iguaçu Falls are on the border of which countries? Brazil, Peru, Argentina? 2 How many falls are there – 275 or 157? 3 What's the highest fall – 64 or 82 metres? 4 Are they bigger or smaller than the Niagara Falls? Bigger.* Check Ss' answers and elicit anything else Ss know about the falls. Show them a map of the area if possible.

VOCABULARY tourism

1 Check/teach and drill new words in the box. Ss look at the photos and discuss the question in pairs. In feedback, nominate Ss to answer.

Answers: natural wonder, tourists, tour guide, sightseeing, boat trip

READING

2A Give Ss 1 min to make predictions. They should cover the text. Check/elicit their predictions and write them in note form on the board.

B Ss read the text and check their predictions against the information in the text. In feedback, ask *Were your predictions correct? Why/Why not?*

Answers: The man is a tour guide. He lives in Brazil, takes tourists to the Iguaçu Falls on both the Brazilian and Argentinian sides, and then takes them shopping in Paraguay.

C Give Ss 3–4 mins to discuss their answers. They make a list of three/four reasons why they'd like the job or not, and report back to the class in feedback. After they've done this, do a show of hands to find out how many Ss would like to do this job.

FUNCTION asking for/giving directions

3A Check the rubric and play the recording. Ss listen and then discuss the answer. Play the recording again if necessary. Check Ss' answers.

Answers: From a point in the centre of Foz do Iguaçu, it only takes half an hour to get to Paraguay and Argentina and see the falls, too.

Unit 5 Recording 4

There's one point in the centre of Foz do Iguaçu city where you can get to Paraguay and Argentina easily. From this point, it only takes half an hour to get to both countries. It's great because you can visit three countries in one hour. And of course you can see the falls!

B Give Ss time to study the map: the names of the streets, highways and rivers. Tell Ss to start where the man on the map is. After listening, Ss compare their answers. Play the recording again if necessary. In feedback, play it again, pausing after each answer to elicit it (see answers in bold in the audio script).

Answers: 1 Paraguay 2 Argentina 3 The Iguaçu Falls on the Brazilian side

C After Ss have listened to/read the audio script, elicit one or two examples. Then give them 5 mins to underline the phrases and compare answers. Check Ss' answers (underlined in the audio script). Illustrate the meaning using the map.

Suggested answers: go left, go along (the main road), past the turning, turn right, keep going until you reach (the highway), go left, (the bridge) is at the end (of the highway), cross the bridge, (you wait) at the corner, (it) takes you down (Avenue das Cataratas), (the bus) goes straight on for (about 25 mins), cross the bridge, turn right and just go straight on down (Highway 469), (the falls are) in front of you, you can't miss them

Unit 5 Recording 5

1 To get to **Paraguay**, you have to go left. You go along the main road, past the turning for the international hospital. Then you turn right and you're on the main street called Avenue Kubitschek. This goes through the centre of the town. From there you just keep going until you reach the highway, Highway 277. Go left and the bridge is at the end of the highway. You cross the bridge and **you are in Paraguay.**

2 To get to **Argentina**, you wait at the corner for the bus. It takes you down Avenue das Cataratas and right into Avenida Mercosul. The bus goes straight on for about 25 mins. Cross the bridge and **you're in Argentina.**

3 To see **the Iguaçu Falls on the Brazilian side**, you turn right and just go straight on down Highway 469 and **the falls are** in front of you. You can't miss them – they're the biggest in the world!

4 Give Ss time to study the diagrams carefully and check the example. Then they label the pictures and compare answers. Check/drill them in feedback. Alternatively, Ss check them in the **Language bank** 5.3, p136.

Answers: A go left B go past the turning C go along the main road D take the first right E keep going until you reach (the border) F at the corner G go through the (centre of town) H cross the bridge I go straight on J in front of you

5A Check the rubric. Play the recording twice if necessary before you check Ss' answers (underlined in the audio script below).

Answers: 1 F 2 T 3 T

B Ss complete the notes alone/in pairs. After they've checked their answers, do feedback (see answers in bold in the audio script)

Answers: 1 ten, music 2 left, fifteen, sign 3 left, restaurant, left

Unit 5 Recording 6
Conversation 1
A: Excuse me. We're trying to get to the carnival. Is this the right bus stop?

B: Yes, <u>but you don't need the bus. It's very close.</u>

A: Oh! Can we walk?

B: Yes, **it takes about ten minutes** from here. Just go straight on. You'll hear the music!

A: OK. Thank you very much.

Conversation 2
C: Excuse me, can you help me? I'm looking for the Plaza Hotel. Is this the right way?

D: Um … Plaza Hotel, Plaza Hotel. Yes, keep going, past the cinema and **take the first left.**

C: OK.

D: Then **keep going for about fifteen minutes** until you reach the end of the road. And **you'll see the sign for the hote**l. You can't miss it.

C: OK. <u>Can you show me on the map?</u>

A: Sure.

Conversation 3
E: Excuse me, we want to get to The Grand Motel. Is it far?

F: Um … sorry, I've no idea. Jim, do you know?

G: What?

E: The Grand Motel?

G: The Grand Motel? Yeah, it's just over there. Just **go to the end of this street. Go left and** go past the … um … <u>there's a restaurant.</u> <u>Go</u> <u>past the restaurant</u> **and it's on the left.**

E: On the left. So I need to go to the end of the street, turn left, go past the restaurant and it's on the left.

G: Yeah, that's it.

E: Thanks a lot.

> ⏵ **LANGUAGEBANK** 5.3 p136–137
>
> Ss can refer to the information in the diagrams/tables when they do the exercise.
>
> **Answers:**
> A 1 h) 2 e) 3 d) 4 g) 5 a) 6 j) 7 i) 8 b) 9 c) 10 f)
> B 1 along 2 reach 3 go 4 in 5 cross 6 take 7 through
> 8 corner

LEARN TO   show/check understanding

6A Ss listen to the extracts and then do the activity alone/in pairs. Nominate Ss to give the answers.

Answers:
asking for information: Excuse me, can you help me? Is this the right way? Can you show me on the map? Is it far?
explaining directions: keep going, you'll see,
You can't miss it.
showing understanding: OK, So I need to …

B Ss refer to the phrases in bold in the extracts above to find the answers to this exercise.

Answers: 1 Is this the right way? 2 Keep going. 3 You can't miss it.

C Ss now practise the pronunciation of language they've learnt in the lesson.

Teaching tip
Support the Ss while they listen and repeat: beat the sentence stress and highlight the intonation with your hands/arms as if you were conducting an orchestra. Ss should repeat the phrases chorally and then individually. Encourage them to correct themselves, and each other, when they do this.

Unit 5 Recording 8
Can we walk?
It takes about ten mins.
Excuse me, can you help me?
Is this the right way?
Keep going.
OK.
You'll see …
You can't miss it.
Can you show me on the map?
Is it far?
So I need to …

7 Monitor while Ss practise to check/help them with their pronunciation. *Stronger Ss* could try to memorise/rehearse one of the conversations and act it out to the class.

SPEAKING

8 Prepare Ss for the role-plays in two stages. First divide the class into As and Bs. Student As read the situations on p161, and Student Bs on p163. Check if they have any doubts about language in the tasks. Put Student As into pairs, and Student Bs into pairs. Give them 3–4 mins to study their maps and prepare the questions they need to ask to get directions. Monitor and provide support where needed, especially with the pronunciation of the names. Tell Ss that the town hall and florists are on both maps. Then put Ss into A/B pairs, facing each other. They take turns to ask for directions and write the places on their maps. Monitor discreetly, making notes for feedback. In feedback, invite Ss to ask for/give directions in open pairs across the class. Give feedback and do remedial work as necessary.

Homework ideas
- Ex 8: write a dialogue asking for/giving directions based on your map on p161 or 163.
- Language bank 5.3 Ex A–B, p133
- Workbook Ex 1–4, p32

FULL CIRCLE

Introduction

Ss watch an extract from the BBC documentary *Full Circle* presented by Michael Palin of Monty Python fame. The series was made in 1995 and broadcast in 1997. Ss then learn and practise how to apply for an award and write an application.

SUPPLEMENTARY MATERIALS

Warm up: download/bring a map of South America, and pictures of famous places there if possible, e.g. Rio de Janeiro, the Sugar Loaf, Machu Picchu, Lake Titicaca, Perito Moreno glacier, Angel Falls.

Ex 3A: Ss need dictionaries for this exercise.

Ex 5B: bring photos of Easter Island and its statues to illustrate the task.

Ex 6A: Ss can use computer facilities to research places, or bring pictures of suitable places for an inspiring journey, e.g. Machu Picchu, Angkor Wat, Petra.

Warm up

Lead in and create interest in the lesson. Show Ss a map of South America and elicit the countries/capital cities. Ask *What do you know about these countries? Have you visited any of them? What famous places can you visit there?* If you've brought pictures, use them as prompts. Ss discuss their answers in pairs/groups. In *multilingual classes*, pair Ss with others who come from/know South America. Elicit/discuss answers with the class.

DVD PREVIEW

Culture notes

Michael Palin, English comedian and actor, is well known as one of the Monty Python group. Since 1980, he's also become famous as a presenter of BBC travel documentaries, which are said to be responsible for the *Palin effect*: places he's visited have often become popular tourist attractions, e.g. Machu Picchu in Peru.

Arica, the most northern city in Chile, is situated on the Pacific coast, 20 km from Peru and 319 km from La Paz, Bolivia.

La Paz is located in the Andes at an altitude of 3,660 metres, the world's highest capital city. A small train takes passengers between the two cities.

1 Ss look at the photos. Ask *Do you know this man/the Andes?* Elicit Ss' answers but don't confirm details yet. Give Ss 2–3 mins to read the information and answer the questions. Elicit answers and give more information about Palin from the **Culture notes** if appropriate. Then ask further comprehension questions, e.g. *How far did Michael Palin travel? How long did it take? What did he learn? Where does he travel in this episode?* Elicit/discuss Ss' answers with the class.

Answers: 1 Michael Palin is an actor and travel writer. 2 The seventeen countries on the Pacific coast. 3 By train.

▶ DVD VIEW

2A Ss extend their discussion of the question in the warm up. Elicit an example answer and then give them 2–3 mins to discuss their predictions about the topics in pairs. In feedback, elicit Ss' predictions and write them in note form on the board under each topic: *food, comfort,* etc.

B Ss read the statements and then watch the DVD. After comparing answers, they watch it again if necessary. In feedback, check their answers and the predictions on the board. Ask *How many did you predict correctly?*

Alternative approach

Put Ss into pairs: one student facing the screen, and the other facing away from it. Play the DVD. Both Ss answer the questions and compare their answers. Ss then swap places. They watch the DVD again and compare their answers. Check them in feedback.

Answers: ✓ the air is thin and it's difficult to breathe, the train stops a lot because of animals/cars on the track, the train is very slow

3A Give Ss 3–4 mins to check the words/phrases they don't know in their dictionaries. They work alone/in pairs. Check their answers in feedback and drill the new language.

B Ss watch the DVD and number the sentences. Play it again to check/elicit Ss' answers (in bold in the DVD script). Then ask *Why was it the journey of a lifetime/the journey of everyone's dreams?* Give them 2–3 mins to discuss their answers in pairs or with the class.

Answers: 2 c) 3 d) 4 b) 5 e) 6 f) 7 g)

Optional extra activity

Exploit the DVD for extra comprehension and attention to interesting detail. Pause it at suitable points and ask questions, e.g. *Why is Michael Palin embarrassed? How many suitcases does he have? What was the rail bus built for? Where did they cook the food? Why is the air thin? How does the woman feel? Why did the train have to stop twice?*

4 Ss discuss the questions in pairs/groups and make a note of their partners' answers. In feedback, find out how many Ss would like to make this journey, and why.

DVD 5 Full Circle

MP=Michael Palin W=Woman

MP: **Twice a week, a railway service leaves Arica** for the Bolivian capital, La Paz.

This is going to take forever. Do you want a hand? Can I help? It's just … it's only two of you to do all this. **It's going to take two hours.** OK.

I've rarely felt quite as embarrassed at travelling with forty-five cases. **Some passengers are local**, some have come from countries far away. None have come quite as far as the train itself. We're to cross the Andes on a rail bus built for the branch lines of Munich thirty years ago. From the world's tiniest galley, two of our three-man Bolivian crew produce the first of several hot dinners.

Three and a half hours after leaving the Pacific, we're at 10,000 feet and still climbing.

Where air is thin and simple things suddenly become difficult.

MP: How are you feeling?

W: Terrible! Terrible!

MP: Is it the altitude?

W: It's the air, it gives you the headache … nausea … and er … it's hard to breathe. You start to wheeze.

MP: Six and a half hours and a few llamas after leaving Arica, **we've reached the Bolivian border.** We're entering the poorest country in South America. **Is it the journey of a lifetime?**

W: It's the journey of everyone's dreams.

MP: A few hours later, the lights of La Paz twinkle below us.

As you can see, we've got a right of way problem here. This is the railway line and this is the road. And er … our conductor is trying to get people to clear out of the way. That's it. They've cleared them out so we can go on. Getting to La Paz is not easy.

To our enormous relief the lights are still on at La Paz station, when our heroic vehicle finally pulls in. **We've crossed the Andes at 16.4 miles an hour.**

speakout an award

5A Ss read the text and answer the questions. In feedback, check *original, inspiring.*

> **Answers:** 1 €5,000 for the best idea for an original and inspiring journey anywhere in the world 2 receive training in film-making and record their experiences for a future programme

> **Culture notes**
> Easter Island, a Chilean territory, is in the South Pacific Ocean. It's a World Heritage Site due to the hundreds of monumental statues, called *moai,* built by the native Rapanui population between 400–1700AD. The population of the island is around 4,000 nowadays.

B Ss should make notes of their answers and compare them. Play the recording again if needed. In feedback, elicit Ss' answers. Find out what they know about Easter Island and show them pictures of it, if possible.

> **Answers:** 1 Easter Island 2 She wants to experience the local culture, their music, food, way of life; find out about their traditions and what they think about their history.

C Ss read the **key phrases** and tick the ones they hear. After they've compared their answers, play the recording again. Pause at each **key phrase** (in bold in the audio script) to elicit/check the answers. Drill the sentences and ask further comprehension questions, e.g. *What's Easter Island like? How are they getting there?*

> **Answers:** ✓ We would like to go to (Easter Island). The trip is going to take (three months). We want to experience the local culture … Our plan is to speak to the local people … We hope to find out about their traditions … This is the journey of our dreams.

Unit 5 Recording 9

OK, well, **we would like to go to Easter Island.** It is very isolated, very far from other places, and the nearest country is Chile, over two thousand miles away. We are going to travel there by plane and stay with different families and **the trip is going to take three months. We want to experience the local culture,** their music, food and way of life. So **our plan is to speak to the local people** about these things and to film them. **We hope to find out about their traditions** and to see what they think of their history. Well, finally, my husband and I always wanted to go to Easter Island. I read about it when I was a child and I saw pictures of these amazing stone heads on the island. So for us **this is the journey of our dreams.**

6A Brainstorm places Ss would like to visit if they won the award and write them on the board. If computer facilities are available, Ss could research things to see/do there. Otherwise, prompt ideas/support *weaker Ss* with pictures of suitable places for an inspiring journey. Give Ss the necessary amount of time to prepare and make notes. Provide help where needed. Remind them to use the **key phrases** or recording in their notes.

B Ss present their ideas to the class. The other Ss listen and note down ideas that are original/inspiring. At the same time, make your own notes with examples of good language and problems. In feedback, discuss Ss' presentations. The class votes for the winner of the award. Give feedback to Ss now, or at the beginning of the next lesson.

writeback an application

7A Ss read and answer the questions. In feedback, ask Ss to justify their answers with, e.g. examples of details, goals/objectives.

> **Answers:** 1 c) 2 a) 3 b)

B Ss work alone/with the same partner as in Ex 6. They write a draft of their application, using the model in Ex 7A and their ideas from Ex 6. Encourage a collaborative approach to the process of writing to build Ss' confidence. They can show their drafts to each other/you and ask for and give opinions and advice. Ss write a final draft of the application when they're ready and send it to you or other Ss for a reply, or put it on the class blog.

> **Homework ideas**
> • Ex 4: write your answers to the questions.
> • Ex 7B: write a final draft of the application form.

LOOKBACK

Introduction

As well as revising and practising the language in the unit, use the **Lookback** exercises to provide you with an informal assessment of your Ss' speaking skills. Fluency practice is usually given in Ex B or C in each section. When assessing speaking skills, take these four areas into account: accuracy of grammar, range of vocabulary, fluency and pronunciation.

SUPPLEMENTARY MATERIALS

Ex 6C: download/copy simple maps of your town/area for your Ss, especially with *multilingual classes*.

TRANSPORT

1A First elicit one or two examples, e.g. *minibus: This type of transport is bigger than a car. It has four wheels and usually carries 10–15 people.* Ss write their sentences alone and check their answers in pairs. Monitor and assess Ss' understanding of transport vocabulary, and the accuracy of their sentences. Provide extra support for *weaker Ss*, and allow them to check vocabulary in the **Photo bank** on p155 if necessary. *Fast finishers* should write more sentences. It's important that Ss' sentences are as accurate as possible for Ex B.

B Check the example and pair Ss with different partners from those in Ex A above. Monitor and make notes of errors with the meaning and pronunciation of transport vocabulary. In feedback, nominate different pairs to read their sentences/respond across the class. Do corrections and remedial teaching if necessary.

PAST SIMPLE AND PAST CONTINUOUS

2A Check the example and use of the two tenses. Also check new words from the unit, e.g. *oxygen, equipment*. Give Ss 2–3 mins to write full sentences. Monitor and note down problems they have with the two tenses for feedback. Check Ss' answers and ask *Why is the verb in the past simple/past continuous?*

Answers: 2 ran away, was raining 3 were travelling, met 4 was losing oxygen, fixed 5 was working, decided 6 were flying, stopped

B Give Ss 2–3 mins to answer the question, and try to remember as much detail as possible about the films. Check their answers or allow them to check in their books on p48, p161 and p163.

Answers: 1 and 2 *Rabbit-Proof Fence;* 3 and 5 *The Motorcycle Diaries;* 4 and 6 *Apollo 13*

3 Give Ss 1 min to note down what they were doing at the specific times yesterday. Drill the questions, e.g. *Where were you yesterday at 6 o'clock in the morning? What were you doing?* Highlight/remind Ss of the weak form (unstressed) of *were*. They then work in pairs and take it in turns to ask/answer the questions, noting down their partner's answers. Monitor and make notes for feedback or assessment purposes. In feedback, Ss tell the class about their partner.

TRAVEL ITEMS

4A Check the example. Ss can do the exercise alone or make it into a team game. The first pair team to finish with the correct spelling and pronunciation of the words wins.

Answers: 2 rucksack 3 waterproof clothes 4 walking boots 5 sun hat 6 souvenirs 7 binoculars 8 notebook 9 digital camera 10 money belt

B Check the example and elicit one or two more ideas. Give Ss 3 mins to make as many different sentences as possible. Stop the activity after 3 mins and invite Ss from each pair to give one answer each. The pair with the most sentences wins.

VERB PATTERNS

5A First do question 1 as an example. Give Ss 2–3 mins to write the answers and compare them before feedback.

Answers: 1 to go 2 to visit 3 to have 4 to travel 5 travelling 6 flying 7 going 8 to have

B Elicit Ss' answers to question 1, e.g. *I always/never/hardly ever/often choose to go somewhere on holiday because a friend recommends it. I prefer to choose it myself./I never know where to go.* Give Ss 2 mins to decide which sentences are true for them, and why/why not. Monitor and help Ss with vocabulary if necessary. Ss then exchange information in pairs/groups. Monitor and assess the accuracy/fluency of their language. Do remedial work in feedback and/or use the information for assessment.

ASKING FOR/GIVING DIRECTIONS

6A Ss read the conversations. Elicit a mistake as an example before Ss work alone. Check Ss' answers and drill the conversations.

Answers:
1 A: Is this *the* right way? B: It's ~~in~~ on the right.
2 A: Is *it* far? B: You can't miss *it*.
3 B: Keep going ~~long~~ along the main road. Then you'll see a sign and it's in front ~~to~~ of you.

B Monitor while Ss practise the conversations to assess and help them with their pronunciation. Invite pairs to read them to the class and do any remedial pronunciation work needed with sentence stress and intonation.

C If you haven't brought maps of your town/area in relation to the school or Ss' houses, they could draw simple ones to make the task clearer and provide authenticity. N.B. You can adapt the places mentioned in the instructions to your Ss' knowledge of the area around the school. Give Ss time to prepare for the role-play and monitor/support them as needed. During the activity (depending on your aim: revision or assessment), monitor and make notes on errors with the target language, or assess Ss' speaking skills.

OVERVIEW

BBC VIDEO PODCAST
What do you do to keep fit?

This video podcast extends discussion of keeping fit and extends Ss' vocabulary of health and fitness. This video podcast would work best at the end of lesson 6.1, or at the start or end of unit 6.

A LONG LIFE?

Introduction

Ss learn/practise the present perfect + *for/since* in the context of healthy lives. They learn health vocabulary and read/talk about other people's and their own health.

SUPPLEMENTARY MATERIALS

Resource bank p166

Ex 2B: Ss may need dictionaries.

Warm up

Introduce the topic of the lesson. Ask Ss to write three things that make them feel stressed and three things that help them feel relaxed. Elicit one or two examples for each category, e.g. *traffic jams/classical music.* Ss write their lists and compare them to see what they have in common. Then ask *Could you avoid things that make you feel stressed? Why/Why not?* Ss discuss their answers in pairs, and then as a class.

VOCABULARY health

1A Check unfamiliar words, e.g. *fizzy, caffeine,* and elicit examples of good/bad things. Then give Ss 1 min to do the exercise alone.

Suggested answers:
good: walking, lots of sleep, fresh fruit and vegetables, vitamins, exercise, oily fish
bad: junk food, fizzy drinks, working with computers, stress/worrying, city life, alcohol, missing breakfast, smoking, caffeine, frozen food, fatty foods

B Give Ss 4–5 mins to compare answers. They should think of at least three words/phrases that are good, and three that are bad. In feedback, elicit the good/bad things. Then invite Ss to write other words/phrases on the board. Correct/drill pronunciation problems as they arise.

C Check/drill the questions and elicit some sample answers. Give Ss 1 min to think about their answers before they work in pairs. In feedback, nominate Ss to ask/answer the questions in open pairs across the class. Give feedback/correct as needed.

READING

2A Ss cover the texts. Look at the photos and elicit an example, e.g. *in the first photo, the people are eating a meal of salads/fruit outside in the sunshine with their family.* Give Ss 2–3 mins to discuss the other photos and answer the questions. Elicit Ss' answers and write them in note form on the board. This will give Ss a reason to read the text in Ex B.

Teaching tip

In real-life, we never read anything without a reason or purpose: it helps us to focus on looking for specific details/information. It's also important to do this in the classroom.

B Give Ss 3–4 mins to read and underline things that help people to live longer. They compare answers and check them with the notes on the board. *How many things in the text did Ss talk about?* In feedback, elicit/check the things mentioned in the text/on the board. Teach/check new words and phrases, e.g. *surgeon, perform surgery.* Alternatively, put Ss into groups of four. They each look at one text each and check 3–4 words/phrases in their dictionaries. They then 'teach' the words to the others.

> **Answers:** working hard, being active, being a vegetarian, having a large family, having a healthy diet (fruit, soya, vegetables), not eating too much (eating until you are only 80% full – 'hara hachibu'), doing exercise, being religious, laughing every day

C Check the example. Give Ss 4–5 mins to find the answers. Alternatively, Ss work in groups of four. Each student finds the significance of the numbers in one text: the group then exchange information.

> **Answers:**
> 37: Dr Ellsworth Wareham has been a heart surgeon for 37 years
> 20%: people in Okinawa eat 20% less than people in the West
> 80%: people in Okinawa eat until they are 80% full
> 102: Marge Jetton is 102 years old
> 6: she rides 6 miles on a bicycle before breakfast
> 5–10: research has shown that people who are religious live for 5–10 years longer
> 7: some people say that laughing every day makes you live 7 years longer
> 1997: Dr Madan Kataria started Laughter Yoga in 1997
> 900: 900 people went to the Laughter Conference in Bangalore
> 3: the people at the laughter conference laughed for 3 days
> 3–4: the number of times Dr Wareham performs surgery a week

D Elicit some answers to question 1. Ss then work in pairs. Monitor to support Ss and provide language they need and write new words on the board. Ss can then compare their answers with another pair before having a class discussion. *How many Ss answered* Yes *to question 1?*

> **Optional extra activity**
> Revise words from the texts that go together (collocations/fixed phrases). Read out the texts, stopping at appropriate points: Ss must give you the next word/words, e.g. *He's a specialist in heart ___ . / ... he still performs _____* (Ss should say *surgery* in both cases). Other examples in text 1 are *working hard, being active, cut the grass, help with the housework, peace of mind.* You can use this activity with any text to revise collocations and fixed/semi-fixed phrases.

GRAMMAR   present perfect + *for/since*

Watch out!

> Ss may make mistakes with the use of *for/since*, e.g. *I've lived here since two years.* Check the difference in use carefully. Provide plenty of controlled practice and opportunities for self-/peer correction at all stages of the lesson.

3A Ss answer the questions alone and compare answers. Elicit Ss' answers in feedback.

> **Answers:** 1 in 1970   2 yes   3 for 37 years

B Elicit and check Ss' answers further. Draw a timeline as below using a <u>true</u> example about your Ss, e.g. *You've been in this class since September/for 6 months.* Point to and exploit the timeline while you ask these questions: *Are you in this class NOW?* Yes. *When did you start?* In September. *How long have you been in this class?* For 6 months/Since September. *Which word is used with a period of time?* For. *Which is used with a point in time?* Since.

Elicit other phrases that Ss could use, e.g. *since last year, for two weeks.*

> **Answers:** 1 in the past and continue until now   2 for, since

C Check the examples. Ss copy the table into their notebooks, complete it and compare their answers. In feedback, draw the table on the board and invite Ss to write answers in the correct column. They can then write 3–4 sentences about themselves (alone/in pairs) using *since/for* and the phrases in the table. Check/correct their answers.

> **Answers:**
> for: a long time, two weeks/months/years, an hour or two
> since: July, Saturday, I left university, 2p.m., last night, I was a child/teenager

> ⮕ **LANGUAGEBANK** 6.1 p138–139
> Ss can refer to the notes when they do the exercises. *Weaker classes* should do Ex A and B in class. In Ex A, check *retired* in question 3.
>
> **Answers:**
> A 1 haven't done, since   2 haven't been, since   3 was, for 4 haven't seen, for   5 left, since   6 didn't see, haven't seen, since   7 since   8 hasn't driven, since
> B 1 since, came   2 bought, have lived, for   3 have known, for, met   4 moved, have been, for   5 haven't been, since 6 hasn't seen, since   7 since, started   8 has had, for

PRACTICE

4A Elicit answers for question 1 that are true for your Ss. They then do the exercise alone. Monitor and prompt them to self-correct (correct their own mistakes).

B Ss compare their answers: they should check both the form of the present perfect, and the use of *since/for*. Again, monitor and prompt Ss to self-correct/correct each other. In feedback, elicit some answers and recheck the use of *since/for*.

> **Suggested answers:** 1 I've studied English for 2 years/since 2008.   2 I've had this phone for 8 months/since January.   3 I've known this teacher for 1 year/since last September.   4 I've lived in this town/city for 20 years/since I was a child.   5 I've wanted to buy a new jacket for a few months/since last winter.

5A Tell Ss there are eleven questions. Play the first two and check the example answers: then elicit other possible answers. Play the remaining questions. Ss listen and write their answers. With *weaker classes*, play the recording first for Ss to familiarise themselves with the questions. Ss may need to hear the questions again after they've written their answers.

B Ask the first question and elicit Ss' answers. They then work in pairs. If Ss can't remember the questions, they just compare their answers. In feedback, elicit/give Ss the questions and nominate Ss to answer. Correct/drill sentences as needed.

Unit 6 Recording 1

1 Do you live in a town or by the sea?
2 How long have you lived there?
3 How long have you lived in the house you live in now?
4 What is the name of your best friend?
5 How long have you known him/her?
6 Do you work or study?
7 How long have you worked or studied where you are now?
8 What hobby do you enjoy?
9 How long have you done it for?
10 Do you have a bicycle or a car?
11 How long have you had it?

6 Play the first question as an example. Write it on the board, elicit/underline the stressed words and drill it with the class. Ss then listen and write the other questions. They compare them and then listen again to underline the stressed words. In feedback, elicit the questions and drill them chorally and individually. Beat the stress and highlight the intonation with your hands/arms.

Answers: 1 How <u>long</u> have you <u>lived</u> there? 2 How <u>long</u> have you <u>known</u> him? 3 How <u>long</u> have you <u>had</u> it? 4 How <u>long</u> have you <u>studied</u>? 5 How <u>long</u> have you <u>worked</u> there?

Unit 6 Recording 2

1 How long have you lived there?
2 How long have you known him?
3 How long have you had it?
4 How long have you studied?
5 How long have you worked there?

SPEAKING

7A Check the topics/pictures first. Then check the example questions and elicit alternative ideas, e.g. *Do you live in a flat or a house? Do you do yoga/extreme sports? Do you study in the evenings/work in a large company?* Ss then write their own questions. Monitor and prompt them to self-correct and write accurate questions to use in Ex B.

Suggested answers:
possessions:
Do you have a watch?
How long have you had it?
hobbies/sport:
Do you do Tai Chi?
How long have you done it?
work/study/school:
Do you go to university?
How long have you been there?

B First check/drill the example conversation. Ss then ask/answer their questions. Monitor and encourage them to find out as much information as possible and note it down. At the same time, make notes of problems Ss have with the present perfect and *since/for*.

C Give Ss time to prepare the information about their group, then nominate Ss to tell the class. Give feedback on Ss' performance as necessary.

Homework ideas
- Ex 7: write about your group using your notes.
- Language bank 6.1 Ex A–B, p139
- Workbook Ex 1–6, p33–34

THE FUTURE OF FOOD

Introduction

Ss learn and practise the use of *may, might, will* to talk about future possibilities/predictions in the context of listening to and talking about food.

SUPPLEMENTARY MATERIALS

Resource bank p167

Photo bank p156

Ex 6A: bring/download a map of Sri Lanka and pictures of its food (curries, fish, rice).

Warm up

Lead in to the topic. Ss think of items of food/drink in as many different colours as possible, e.g. *yellow: pepper, banana; green: apple, peas; white: milk.* Give them 3 mins to make a list in pairs. Elicit/write the colours Ss thought of on the board. Then elicit the names of food/drink to write next to the correct colour. Alternatively, Ss take turns to write the words on the board. Elicit the word stress and drill the pronunciation.

VOCABULARY food

1A Ss use the food from the warm up exercise and put it into the four categories, e.g. *fruit: apple.* Give them 3 mins to write their new lists and add other words they think of.

B Ss compare their lists and then check them in the **Photo bank** on p156. They should add the names of food they didn't have to their lists.

➠ PHOTOBANK p159

Elicit/drill the names of food/drink that were new for Ss. They then discuss the questions in Ex 1 and 2 of the **Photo bank**. In feedback, find out which food Ss eat a lot of, and which they think are good for you.

C Check the food in the photos. Ask *Where do these dishes come from?* Spain, Japan, Mexico, Egypt. *What's in them?* Fish, seafood, rice, chicken; raw fish, rice; minced meat, beans, chilli, tortilla; fried onions, chickpeas or beans, spices. Ss then discuss the questions and make notes of their partner's answers for feedback. Check what Ss' favourite foods are and how often they eat food from other countries.

LISTENING

2A Elicit the items in the pictures. Ss then read and answer the questions, giving reasons if possible. In feedback, elicit Ss' answers and reasons. Then move on to Ex B.

B Ss listen and check their answers from Ex 2A (in bold in the audio script).

Answers: 1 F 2 F 3 T

C Read the speakout tip with Ss and use it with Ex 2C. First do an example. Ss look at question 1 and work out what type of word it is, e.g. noun, adjective, verb. The answer is noun. Then ask about the meaning: *Is it a positive/negative word?* Positive. Finally, elicit/give Ss the word *vitamins.* Ss then do the exercise alone/in pairs, using the tip if they're not sure of the words. Ss listen to the recording again and check their answers. In feedback, elicit/check the meaning and pronunciation of each answer (underlined and key words in italics in the audio script). In *stronger classes,* ask further comprehension questions related to each answer.

speakout TIP

Encourage Ss to use this speakout tip with Ex 2C and any time they come across words they don't know.

Answers: 1 vitamins 2 day 3 space 4 popular 5 different 6 common

---

Unit 6 Recording 3

I=Interviewer W=Woman

I: Can you tell us a little about superfoods?

W: Well, superfoods include tomatoes, broccoli and spinach.

I: Mmm.

W: These have lots of *vitamins,* and they are really good for you.

I: Right.

W: Anyway, **they may improve our health, but I don't think superfoods will be the answer to our eating problems in the future.**

I: Can you tell us why not?

W: Well, the most important thing is to eat healthy food every *day.*

I: Right.

W: And this is more important than the idea of superfoods. Eating an apple a day is better for you than eating a kilo of spinach one day a week.

I: I see. So what you're saying is …

I: There's been a lot of talk about food pills.

W: Yes.

I: Are they healthier than other types of food? Could they be the food of the future?

W: Well, in the past, astronauts ate a type of food pill when they were in *space.* It was dried food and they added water to it.

I: Right.

W: But **I don't think food pills will replace normal food.**

I: Right. Why's that? For health reasons or social reasons?

W: Well, cooking and eating together is an important part of family life and it always will be. You sit down together at a table and you eat and talk. It's a very old tradition, and eating pills isn't the same.

I: So we won't eat only food pills?

W: Food pills might become more *popular,* but no, we won't eat only food pills in the future.

I: Well, that's interesting because I was reading about …

W: In the future we may have special food that can change its flavour.

I: Can you give an example?

W: For example, imagine you like chocolate ice cream, but your friend likes strawberry. You eat the same ice cream but it will taste *different* for both of you.

I: The same food that tastes different for different people …

W: You'll think it's chocolate ice cream and your friend will say it's strawberry. It might happen with drinks, too. You take a bottle of liquid out of the fridge. You press the button which says 'coffee' or 'lemonade' or 'hot chocolate'. You put the bottle in the microwave and the liquid becomes the drink that you choose.

I: So it starts off as the same food or drink, but then we change its flavour by pushing a button.

W: That's right. Just by pushing a button.

I: So how does it work?

W: Well, this is possible because of nanotechnology. The technology might not replace normal drinks and food but it may become *common* in the future.

I: And nanotechnology is something that's used in different …

GRAMMAR *may, might, will*

Watch out!

Ss often use *will* to talk about future plans/arrangements instead of *be going to* or the present continuous, e.g. **I'll have dinner with Sue and Dave tomorrow night*, not *I'm having dinner …* . Here *will* is presented with *may/might*, which helps to avoid this problem in the practice exercises. However, it's important to be aware of this problem and clarify/correct the mistake consistently.

3 With books closed, write the sentences on the board and underline the words in bold in the book. Ss copy them down. Ask questions 1–3 and elicit/check their answers. Elicit/check the form of the underlined verbs: *may/might/will/won't* + infinitive without *to*. Then ask Ss to make the verbs in questions a) and b) negative, e.g. *Food pills* <u>might not</u> *become more popular/In the future we* <u>may not</u> *have …* (NOT *mightn't* or *mayn't*). Ss then underline examples of the verbs in the texts in Ex 2A.

Answers: 1 d) won't (eat)   2 a) might (become) and b) may (have)   3 c) (always) will be

---

⟹ LANGUAGEBANK 6.2 p138–139

Read/check the notes with your Ss. They can refer to them when they do the exercises. *Weaker Ss* should do Ex A and B in class.

Answers:
A 1 e)   2 d)   3 a)   4 f)   5 b)   6 c)
B 1 ~~don't will~~ *won't* know my exam results until August. 2 Will you ~~to~~ go to university next year?   3 Anna is very busy so she may not ~~comes~~ tonight.   4 The traffic is heavy so they may ~~to~~ be late.   5 Edson might~~s~~ be the best player we have ever seen.   6 I might ~~go not~~ *not go* to the exercise class today.   7 We'll ~~to~~ be back at 6p.m.

PRACTICE

4A Check the example and ask *Is it possible/probable/certain?* Ss then work alone and write the most suitable responses. Monitor and provide support.

Suggested answers: 2 You might lose weight. 3 It might be expensive.   4 You'll feel healthier.   5 It might not be open.   6 You might not like it.   7 You'll enjoy it.

B Check/drill the example conversation. Ss then work in pairs. Monitor and encourage them to extend their responses. In feedback, nominate pairs to say a sentence/respond in open pairs across the class. Give feedback as needed.

SPEAKING

5A Check the rubric and statements. Discuss question 1 with the class. Ask *Do you think it will happen? It might./No, I don't think it will.* Give Ss 4–5 mins to decide on their choices and write a response. They must be able to give reasons for their choices. Monitor closely and prompt Ss to self-/peer correct.

B Check the example. Ss work with another pair/pairs and compare answers. While Ss talk, make notes on the use of the language they've studied in this lesson and do remedial work as required in feedback. Invite members of each group to talk about one of their choices and discuss it with the class. Give feedback if necessary.

WRITING   sentence structure

6A Ss read the title and introduction to the article. Check where Sri Lanka is. Show Ss a map if possible and ask *Have you ever eaten food from Sri Lanka? What's it like?* (Curries, rice, fish, vegetables). Ss then read and discuss their answers to the questions.

Answers: 1 Because she runs a restaurant and it is her hobby and passion.   2 She's a restaurant owner/chef.   3 She started by reading cook books, asking friends for help, and did a cooking course.

B Read the two examples with Ss and elicit their answers.

Answers: The first example has three short sentences that don't connect together very well. The second has linked the three short sentences with *when* and *and*. This makes it flow more smoothly and it is easier for the reader to understand.

speakout TIP

Then discuss the speakout tip with Ss. Ss can look at their last piece of writing if they have it with them, or do it later. It might be better to do Ex C first.

C Ss find the sentences and underline *and* and *so*. Elicit the sentences and do another example, e.g. *Last night I met some friends. We went to the cinema. We had dinner together.* Ask Ss to use *and* and *also* to connect them.

Answers: I needed to learn quickly, so I read books *and* asked my friends for help. I *also* went on a cooking course. I learnt to cook traditional Sri Lankan *and* Indian dishes. I *also* cooked English food.

D Brainstorm Ss' responses to the topics, e.g. for cooking, they could say *I love/hate cooking. I can't cook, I'm a very good cook, I'd like to learn how to cook.* Ss then choose a topic and write a paragraph of 50–60 words. They can use the text in Ex 6A as a model. Monitor and support Ss while they write and encourage them to help each other. Ss then show their paragraphs to other Ss, who should find the different sentence lengths. Alternatively, nominate Ss to read out their paragraphs to the class. Ss should also respond to the paragraph and ask questions about it. Give feedback as required.

Homework ideas

- Ex 6C: write a paragraph about a different topic.
- Language bank 6.2 Ex A–B p139
- Workbook Ex 1–6, p35–36

HOW ARE YOU FEELING?

Introduction

Ss learn and practise language for visiting the doctor and talking about illness. They also learn how to predict language used in common everyday situations.

SUPPLEMENTARY MATERIALS

Resource bank p168

Warm up: bilingual dictionaries should be available.

Ex 2A: bring/download pictures of (people with) various illnesses/injuries for revision.

Warm up

Activate language connected to health/sickness. Ask, e.g. *When was the last time you were ill/injured? What was wrong/ What happened? Did you go to the doctor? What medicine/ treatment did you have? Did you take time off work? How long?* Give Ss 4–5 mins to answer the questions in pairs. They can ask you/each other for words they need, or use bilingual dictionaries. They then report back to the class about their partners.

READING

1A Ss cover the text and look at the photo. Give them 2 mins to answer the question. Monitor and provide vocabulary they may need. In feedback, elicit/discuss Ss' answers. They may have different ideas about what the doctors do: write some of their ideas on the board if they contain useful language for the lesson. Then give Ss 2–3 mins to read the text alone, check their predictions and compare answers. In feedback, elicit the answer to the question. Ask Ss *Were your predictions correct?* Finally, teach/check useful new language in the text, e.g. *less likely, solve the problem, wherever.*

Answer: BBC Street Doctors travel to different cities and visit people with health problems wherever they are.

B Check the questions and elicit some initial answers. Ss then talk about the questions for 3 mins and report back to the class. Find out how many Ss think it's a good idea.

VOCABULARY illness

2A Use the photos in the book to revise the words/phrases in bold (supplement these with your own pictures if possible). You can also use mime to check words Ss don't remember (or they can use dictionaries). Ss then match the problems and advice alone and check in pairs. Tell them there might be more than one possible answer. Elicit/discuss Ss' answers in feedback and check the pronunciation of difficult words, e.g. *cough, sore throat.*

Answers: 1 d) 2 c) 3 b) 4 a)

B Check the example and give Ss 2 mins to discuss their answers. In feedback, find out who has the best remedy for these ailments.

FUNCTION seeing the doctor

3 Check the rubric. Ss should take notes and focus on answering the two questions. They should try not to get distracted by unknown language. Ss listen, note down their answers and then compare them. Play the recording again for them to check/add to their notes. In feedback, check Ss' answers (in bold in the audio script) and teach/check new vocabulary, e.g. *painful.* During this stage, elicit more information about the conversations, e.g. ask *Is the woman worried or under pressure? Does she have a healthy diet? How many cups of tea and coffee does she drink?*

Answers:
Conversation 1: 1 The woman feels terrible. She gets headaches and feels sick. She can't sleep at night because her head hurts. 2 The doctor says she should stop drinking so much tea and coffee, only one small cup a day. She gives her some painkillers and says she should take two three times a day.
Conversation 2: 1 The man is worried about his foot. It hurts when he walks. It's very painful. 2 The doctor thinks it's broken and that he should go to the hospital for an X-ray.

Unit 6 Recording 4
Conversation 1
D=Doctor W=Woman

D: Hello. I'm Dr Andrews. Now, <u>what's the matter?</u>

W: Well, doctor, <u>*I feel terrible.*</u> I get these headaches and I feel sick.

D: Oh. <u>How long have you had this problem?</u>

W: A few weeks now. And <u>*I can't sleep*</u> at night because my head hurts.

D: You can't sleep?

W: That's right.

D: And are you very worried or under pressure at the moment?

W: No, I don't think so.

D: Do you have a healthy diet?

W: Hmm. Quite healthy.

D: Do you drink tea or coffee?

W: Yes, I do.

D: How much?

W: Tea? Probably about eight cups, or ten.

D: A day?

W: Yes.

D: I see. And has that changed in the last few weeks?

W: Not really.

D: OK. Well the first thing is **I think you should stop drinking so much tea and coffee.** Try to drink just one small cup a day. <u>**I'll give you some**</u> painkillers for the headaches. Take two of these three times a day. I don't think it's anything to worry about, but if …

Conversation 2
D=Doctor M=Man

D: Good morning. How can I help?

M: Well, <u>*I'm worried about my foot.*</u>

D: Your foot?

M: Yes. <u>*It hurts when I walk.*</u>

D: I see. Did you do anything to it? Did you have an accident?

M: Um. Well, sort of.

D: What happened?

M: I kicked a wall.

D: I see. When did you do that?

M: About a week ago.

D: OK. Did you go to hospital?

M: No.

D: <u>Can I have a look?</u>

M: Yes, of course.

D: <u>Where does it hurt?</u> Here?

M: Argh. Yes, there.

D: Can you move it?

M: Yes, a little, but *it's very painful.*

D: Hmm. I think it might be broken. <u>It's nothing to worry about,</u> but I think you should go to the hospital for an X-ray. I'll write you a note and if …

4A The sentences are extracts from the doctor's part of the recording (the underlined words in the audio script). Ss complete them and compare their answers. Check and practise the pronunciation of the sentences in feedback.

Answers: 2 problem 3 pills 4 look 5 hurt 6 worry

B The sentences are extracts from what the patients say in the recording (the text is underlined and in italics in the audio script). Follow the same procedures as in Ex 4A.

Answers: 1 sick 2 sleep 3 worried 4 hurts 5 painful

C Ss listen and repeat the phrases (from Ex 4A and B above). Play the recording as many times as necessary until Ss are confident with their pronunciation. Drill the phrases both chorally (as a class) and individually. Prompt Ss to correct themselves/each other during the individual repetition stage.

Unit 6 Recording 5

Doctor

1 What's the matter?

2 How long have you had this problem?

3 I'll give you some pills.

4 Can I have a look?

5 Where does it hurt?

6 It's nothing to worry about.

Patient

1 I feel sick.

2 I can't sleep.

3 I'm worried about …

4 It hurts when I walk.

5 It's very painful.

⟹ **LANGUAGEBANK** 6.3 p138–139

Ss should refer to the information in the tables when they do this exercise.

Answers:
A 1 What's the matter/problem 2 I feel terrible 3 How long have you had this problem 4 Can I have a look 5 very painful 6 It hurts 7 I'll give you

5 Elicit the answer to question 1. Ss work alone, compare their answers and report back to the class in feedback. With *stronger classes*, ask *Why are the other two options (pain/sore) not possible?* Because a verb is needed after the subject *My head. Pain* is a noun and *sore* is an adjective. You could ask Ss to write sentences using *pain/sore*, e.g. *I've got a terrible <u>pain</u> in my leg/back. I've got a <u>sore</u> throat.* Elicit/check them in feedback.

Answers: 1 hurts 2 cold 3 sick 4 broken 5 hurt 6 worry 7 give 8 problem

LEARN TO predict information

6A Elicit the first two answers. Read the speakout tip with Ss before they do the exercise. This should motivate Ss and give real purpose to the exercise. Give Ss 3–4 mins to discuss and complete the answers. Monitor while they work to check how well they have remembered and can use the language.

B Ss check their answers in the audio script and compare them. In feedback, you could play the recording again to check their answers. Ss could then practise reading the conversations in pairs. Monitor and help them with the sentence stress and intonation if necessary. *Stronger Ss* could rehearse/memorise and act out extracts to the class. Alternatively, Ss take turns to read out parts of each conversation to the class. Prompt other Ss to suggest pronunciation corrections after each pair has read an extract, if appropriate. This should be done sensitively so as not to undermine Ss' confidence. Finally, relate this exercise back to the speakout tip. Ask Ss to choose 6–8 words/phrases they think are the most useful for a visit to the doctor's. They work in pairs/groups and report back to the class. Find out which words Ss found most useful.

Answers:
Extract 1: 1 what's the matter? 2 I feel terrible 3 headaches 4 sick 5 have you had this problem 6 weeks 7 can't sleep 8 head 9 Do you have a 10 Do you drink
Extract 2: 1 I'm worried about 2 hurts when I 3 Did you do 4 Did you have 5 I have 6 does it hurt 7 very painful 8 it might be 9 to worry 10 to the hospital

speakout TIP

Encourage Ss to use the speakout tip with Ex 6A and in real-life situations.

7 Check the first question. Ss write the sentences alone and compare answers. Elicit/drill them with the class. Ss can then rehearse/memorise the conversation in pairs and act it out in groups.

Answers: 1 What's the matter? 2 I've got a cough. 3 I feel terrible. 4 How long have you had the problem? 5 About a week. 6 Can I have a look? 7 It's very painful. 8 I'll give you some painkillers.

8 Divide the class into Ss A and B. They look at the relevant exercises on p161 or p163 and prepare their roles in A or B pairs. Monitor closely while Ss do this and provide support where necessary. Ss then work in A/B pairs and take turns to be the doctor and patient. Monitor and make notes of problems for feedback. Invite Ss to act out their role-plays to the class and give feedback on their performance as needed. Alternatively, record Ss doing their role-plays. Play the recordings in feedback and invite Ss to suggest corrections for language/pronunciation.

Homework ideas

- Ex 8: write one of the conversations from p161 and 163 between the doctor and patient.
- Language bank 6.3, Ex A, p139
- Workbook Ex 1–4, p37

A GAME OF SQUASH

Introduction

Ss watch an entertaining extract from an episode of the BBC comedy *The Two Ronnies*. They then do a sports survey and write about a sporting memory.

SUPPLEMENTARY MATERIALS

Resource bank p165

Photo bank p157

Ex 1B: bring/download pictures of the sports.

Ex 1C: dictionaries should be available.

Ex 5A: bring pictures of famous sports heroes, including Pelé.

Warm up

Introduce the topic of the lesson and revise sports vocabulary. Ss cover the text and look at the large photo on p64–65. Ask, e.g. *What do you know about this game? What equipment are they using? Where are they playing? What are they wearing?* Elicit Ss' answers: *squash; a racket and a hard ball; on a (squash) court; shorts, sports shirt, socks and trainers.* Teach new words using the photo.

DVD PREVIEW

1A Give Ss 2–3 mins to answer the question. In feedback, find out which sports Ss most enjoy watching/playing.

B Teach/check the sports words using mime or pictures. Ss then make two lists of sports that collocate with *play/go* and compare answers. After checking the answers, elicit/tell Ss that we use *play* with sports played with a ball, and *go* with sports words that are made with verb +-*ing*. Elicit other sports Ss know to add to the *play/go* lists.

Answers:
play: basketball, badminton, rugby, cricket, volleyball, squash, football, tennis
go: surfing, running, horse racing, jogging, cycling, swimming, rollerblading, skiing, windsurfing

C Teach/check new words, e.g. *bat, try*. Alternatively, Ss can use dictionaries.

Answers: 1 a) ball: basketball, rugby, cricket, volleyball, squash, football, tennis b) racket: badminton, squash, tennis c) bat: cricket 2 a) score a try: rugby b) score points: basketball, badminton, volleyball, squash, tennis c) score goals: football 3 a) boots: horse racing, rugby, rollerblading, football, skiing b) trainers: basketball, running, badminton, jogging, volleyball, squash, tennis c) a swimsuit: swimming, (surfing) 4 a) Wimbledon: tennis b) Lords: cricket c) Wembley: football d) Ascot: horse racing

---

PHOTOBANK p157

1A Check the meaning of each sport by asking Ss to mime it. If necessary, Ss could do the exercise at home, using their dictionaries.

Answers: 1B: A 15 B 1 C 5 D 2 E 4 F 16 G 22 H 30 I 27 J 29 K 25 L 17 M 10

2 Ss could do this exercise before Ex 5A or Ex 7.

---

2 Check what Ss know about *The Two Ronnies*. They then read the text to check. Elicit Ss' answers to the question in the rubric. They will find out the correct answer in Ex 3A.

DVD VIEW

3A Ss watch the DVD and circle the answers.

Alternative approach
In Ex 3A, Ss could watch the DVD without sound first. They concentrate on the men's actions and expressions and should be able to speculate about the answers. Play the DVD again with the sound to confirm Ss' answers.

B Check Ss' answers. Ask *What did Ronnie Barker call* cricket *in sentence 3B?* Cracket (a mixture of *cricket/racket*). Elicit other reasons why Ronnie Corbett got angry (or do this after Ex 4).

Answers: 1 a) 2 b) 3 b)

4 Check the sentences and the meaning of *work* (meaning function), *captain* (v), *love* (in tennis). In feedback, play the DVD to check Ss' answers. Pause the DVD after each answer and ask further comprehension questions to highlight the humour of the sketch, e.g. question 1: *What's Corbett's reaction to this sentence?* Question 2: *Why does Barker say* thingies *and* whatevers?

Answers: 2 B 3 C 4 C 5 B 6 C 7 B 8 C

DVD 6 The Two Ronnies

B=Ronnie Barker C=Ronnie Corbett

B: I say, that was, that was really, jolly good that was. I must say I really enjoyed that. Thanks very much.

C: That's fine. Fine.

B: I say, it's a super game, isn't it? I can't understand why I've never tried it before. Absolutely lovely. I loved it. But thanks to you, old boy, of course, from now on, I shall be a dedicated squish player.

C: Squash.

B: Pardon?

C: The game is called *squash*.

B: Oh squash, yes, that's right. I'm sorry. Who actually won? I mean I couldn't quite grasp the scoring-mechanism. I mean, did I, did I win?

C: Yes, you … yes, you won, you won.

B: Oh that's good. How many goals did I get?

C: Goals?!

B: Well, you know, er …, thingies, er …, whatevers, runs …

C: Points!

B: … runs … ah, points!

C: Points!

B: Points, yes.

C: Points!

B: How many points did I get?

C: Well the score was, if you want to know, game-love, game-love, game-love, game-love. You see. You won four games to love.

B: Oh, I see. So, I got four and you got love.

C: Yes.

B: I see. How many is love?

C: Love is nothing.

B: Oh no, no. That's not right I'm sure. Because I'm sure you got a goal earlier on, right at the beginning.

C: A point.

B: A point, I mean.

C: A point, yes, well of course I did. That was when you …

B: Oh, I know, I was holding the thing by the wrong end. I must remember, hold the bat by the thin end.

C: The racket!

B: Racket, I mean.

C: The racket!

B: Yes.

C: This is … this is a ball.

B: Yes.

C: The game is called squash.

B: Yes.

C: Let's start from basic principles.

B: Yes.

C: The whole thing is called squash.

B: Squash..

C: This is a ball.

B: Yes.

C: This is a … racket when you do that. That's what that is, that is a racket.

B: I see. Will it work now you've done that?

C: Ah … I don't much care, to be honest. I mean … I'm not going to be playing squash anymore ever!

B: Oh, I say. That's a pity, because I was hoping we could have another game next week. I mean, I thought, well you know, I thought I might get a bit better.

C: A bit better? A bit better? Look matey, I'm the secretary of this squash club. You know. I mean, I captain the A-team. You know. I'm one of the best players round here, as a matter of fact. You know, I won the area finals last year, and all that sort of thing, you know. You know, I'm good. You know, good. And you come along here, if I may say so, you've never played the game before, you're vastly overweight, if I may say so, you're very slow on the court, you've gone out on that court, and you've thrashed me, you've pounded me into the ground, you pulverised me, in front of my friends, four games to love. Well, how do you do it?

B: Beginner's luck?

C: It's a fluke. That's what it is, a fluke, mate. It won't happen again. I'll tell you what … It won't happen the next time.

B: No, well there won't be a next time, will there? Because you've broken your rocket.

C: My racket! I'll get a new one. I don't care. I'll get a new one. Look mate. I'll get a new one, and tomorrow morning, here, 10 o'clock, things will be different!

B: Oh no, no. Sorry, old boy. No, not tomorrow. No can do.

C: What do you mean, 'No can do'?

B: Well, I've got to go up to a place called Lords tomorrow. I've got to play a game called *cricket* or something.

speakout a sports survey

5A If you have pictures of famous sports heroes, use them as examples here. Ss then listen and order the questions. They compare answers but don't check them until after Ex B.

B Ss read and check the **key phrases**. Play the recording again for Ss to check their answers and tick the **key phrases**. In feedback, play the recording again, pausing at each **key phrase** (in bold in the audio script). Elicit/drill the complete sentences. Ask further comprehension questions, e.g. question 1: *How does sport make him feel?*

Answers:
order of questions: b) 4 c) 3 d) 2
key phrases: ✓ it's difficult to find time to exercise, but …, (I go to the gym once or twice …), I think he is one of the greatest football players ever

Optional extra activity
Stronger Ss read the audio script and write questions to ask other Ss.

Unit 6 Recording 7

A: Does exercise make you feel relaxed?

B: Yes, I think it really does. Sometimes **it's difficult to find time to exercise, but** I play football after work on a Monday, and I play tennis at the weekend, and I feel so much better. If I don't play one week, I feel terrible. So, yes, doing sport makes you feel really good. You feel much better, and more relaxed.

A: How much exercise do you do in a week?

C: In a week, well I probably do about two or three hours of exercise, maybe more. **I go to the gym once or twice**, if I have time, and I sometimes go swimming. Oh, and I ride my bike at the weekend, so actually, probably three or four hours a week. More than I thought. Yeah, four hours, that's OK.

A: Do you have a sporting hero?

D: Oh yes, Pelé. He's a hero, not just for me, but probably for all Brazilians. **I think he is one of the greatest football players ever**. He was such a good athlete, and he had so much talent. He was 'King of Football', and scored more goals for Brazil than anyone else. And he was born very poor. You know he didn't have money for a football so he used to practise kicking a grapefruit, or a sock stuffed with paper.

A: How much do you walk a day?

E: Oh my goodness. Well, I suppose, I don't walk very much actually. I … um … I drive, the car everywhere. That's terrible, isn't it? Um. Yes, I probably only walk about, about maybe five mins every day.

C Ss write their answers and compare them in groups. In feedback, ask *How similar were your answers?*

6A Elicit questions Ss could ask about the ideas on the page. Ss then work in pairs and write their questions. Monitor to ensure the questions are accurate.

B Depending on your teaching situation, Ss can walk around the class asking/answering the questions, or do it in groups.

C Give Ss time to prepare the results of their survey before reporting back to the class. They should use the **key phrases**, e.g. *Most people/Nobody in the class wants to try a new sport.*

writeback a sporting memory

7 Ask *Do you remember the World Cup in 2006?* Ss then read the text and answer the questions. Elicit/check answers and teach *sounding their car horns*.

Answers: 1 No. 2 When Italy won the World Cup. 3 In Florence. She was having a meal with friends when suddenly they heard a lot of noise. They realised that Italy had won the World Cup. There was a huge party in the streets all night.

8 Give Ss 8–10 mins to write their text. Provide support where needed.

Homework ideas
• Ex 6: write the results of your survey.
• Ex 8: write a final draft of your sporting memory.

LOOKBACK

Introduction

Lookback activities are designed to provide revision and communicative practice in a motivating way. This helps the Ss and gives you the opportunity to assess their ability to use the language they've learnt in the unit. It's a good idea to monitor and assess individual Ss while they do the activities, and compare their performance with their results in more formal tests.

HEALTH

1A Elicit a question for question 1, e.g. *Do you get lots of sleep?* Ss then work alone/in pairs to write the other questions. Monitor to assess how well Ss are using question forms and check/drill the questions in feedback as preparation for Ex B.

> **Possible answers:** 1 Do you get lots of sleep? 2 How much exercise do you do in a week?/Do you do much exercise? 3 Do you eat junk food? 4 Do you work with computers? Would you prefer/like not to work with computers? 5 Do you miss breakfast? 6 Do you take vitamins every day? 7 Do you drink caffeine? 8 Do you like oily fish?

B Tell Ss that this is a survey and give clear instructions. Ask a question from Ex 1A and elicit answers from several Ss. Summarise or ask Ss to summarise the answers, e.g. *Three people in my group don't need much sleep. The others sleep for at least eight hours every night.* Ss then work in groups and note down other group members' answers. They then prepare a summary of each answer for Ex C. Monitor and prompt Ss to correct any mistakes in their sentences. Make notes of persistent problems for remedial feedback after Ex C, and/or for assessment.

C Ss from each group take turns to give a summary of each answer to the questions to the class. The other groups should note down how similar/different their own findings are in preparation for feedback. Ss could then prepare a summary of the similarities and differences, in the class e.g. *Most of the Ss in our class need eight hours sleep every night but some of them only sleep for 6–7 hours.*

PRESENT PERFECT + FOR/SINCE

2A Elicit examples for question 1 to show Ss what to do, e.g. *I haven't been to the USA since I was a child.* Give Ss 4–5 mins to write their sentences. Monitor and note down problems they're having in terms of the present perfect and the use of *for/since*. Give feedback on this before Ss do Ex B. Ss can correct their sentences if necessary before they do Ex B.

> **Possible answers:** 1 I haven't been to the zoo since I was a child. 2 I've only had this bike for a few months. 3 I've known my friend Nicola since I was a teenager. 4 I haven't sung in a concert since I left school. 5 I've wanted to learn karate for a long time. 6 I've played rugby for eight years.

B Check/drill the example dialogue and encourage Ss to respond and expand their answers in a similar way when they work in pairs. Monitor and assess how well they do this, and give feedback afterwards.

FOOD

3 Give Ss thirty seconds to find the words. Elicit the words, but don't check meaning/pronunciation until after Ex 4A.

> **Answers:** onion, cream, pineapple, lemon, carrot, wheat, chicken, cake, oats, jelly, cheese, mussels

> **Optional extra activity**
> Ss write another word snake using food and drink words, and give it to a partner/another pair to find the words.

4A Give Ss 3–4 mins to put the words in the correct category. *Weaker Ss* could look at p60 or p156 if necessary. Elicit, check and drill the words in feedback.

> **Answers:** desserts: cake, jelly; **dairy:** cream, cheese; fruit: pineapple, lemon; **vegetables:** onion, carrot; grains: wheat, oats; **meat/seafood:** chicken, mussels

B Ss add words they remember and then check their answers on p60 or p156. Alternatively, make this into a race between pairs/teams. Give Ss 3 mins to add as many words as possible. The pair/team with the most words wins.

MAY, MIGHT, WILL

5A Ss do the exercise alone/in pairs. Elicit and check answers, and do remedial teaching as required.

> **Answers:** 1 f) 2 e) 3 a) 4 c) 5 b) 6 d)

B Check the example and elicit two more responses, e.g. *You'll love it! You may find it boring.* Monitor while Ss do the task and make notes of the appropriacy of their responses. In feedback, check Ss' answers in open pairs across the class. Invite other Ss to make corrections and/or suggest other answers. Write the most relevant problems you noted on the board in feedback. Ss correct them in pairs.

6 Elicit some example answers: encourage Ss to use *may, might, will, won't,* e.g. *I think there will be more jobs for young people in a few years' time.* Give Ss 10 mins to ask/answer the questions. Monitor their use of the modal verbs and do remedial teaching if necessary, after discussing Ss' answers as a class.

SEEING THE DOCTOR

7A Ss complete the questions and compare their answers.

> **Answers:** 1 broken 2 catch 3 have 4 can 5 gave 6 feel

B While Ss ask/answer the questions, monitor and note how well they are using language to talk about health problems. Give feedback and/or use your notes for assessment as required.

> **Homework ideas**
> • Workbook Review and Check 2, p38–39
> • Workbook Test 2, p40

OVERVIEW

STUCK IN A RUT

Introduction

Ss learn/practise *used to* and verbs with prepositions in the context of listening to and talking about life changes.

SUPPLEMENTARY MATERIALS

Resource bank p169 and p170

Warm up: bring/download pictures of famous people as they look now and as they looked in the past.

Warm up

Show Ss recent pictures of two famous people, e.g. J.K. Rowling or David Beckham. Ask *What are they famous for? What are they like? What have they done recently?* Then show pictures of the same people in the past. Ask *What were they like then? What did they do? How have they changed?* Elicit statements, e.g. *J.K. Rowling didn't have any money in 1995. Now she's one of the richest women in the world.* Show/distribute more pictures. Ss work in pairs and describe how the people have changed. Elicit/discuss their answers. N.B. If you haven't got pictures, Ss could talk about their country/town as it was ten years ago and as it is now. Give them prompts, e.g. *entertainment and leisure, transport, housing, health, shopping, education, employment/salaries/cost of living, politics.*

VOCABULARY verbs + prepositions

1A Check the title of the lesson and ask *Are you stuck in a rut? Do you know anyone who is? In what way?* Elicit and discuss Ss' answers. Then give them 3–4 mins to discuss the questions here and report back to the class.

B Give Ss 2–3 mins to read the text and answer the questions. Check the answers and ask *What do people think about doing when they're stuck in a rut?* Elicit answers about the text. Then ask *Have you ever wanted to do or thought about doing any of these things?*

Answers: 1 a) 2 b) 3 a)

2A Check the example. Ss then do the exercise alone and compare answers.

Answers: 2 move to 3 give up, go back 4 look for, dream about 5 wait for 6 travel around

B After checking the first sentence with Ss, they tick sentences they agree with. Give them 3–4 mins to discuss and compare their ideas. Ss report back to the class about themselves and their partner, e.g. *I wouldn't like to move to another country, but Julia dreams about living by the beach in the Caribbean.*

speakout TIP

After checking Ss' answers, read the speakout tip below with Ss. They copy the verb + preposition phrases into their notebooks, preferably with an example sentence. Take this opportunity to check how well Ss are organising new vocabulary. Ideally, they should create a separate section in their notebooks to make it easier to access and review new words/phrases.

Optional extra activity
Check verb + preposition phrases from the text. Read out the text, pausing at each verb. Ss tell you what the correct preposition is, e.g. *it's time to look ____ (for) something new.* Do this activity now or as a warmer/filler in the next lesson.

LISTENING

Culture notes
Lincoln Center for the Performing Arts is a major venue for music, ballet, opera, film, etc. in New York City.

3A Invite Ss to speculate about the two women in the photos. Give them 2–3 mins to discuss, e.g. *their ages, jobs, how they changed their lives, what they did, where they went.* Elicit Ss' predictions and write them in note form on the board.

B Ss listen and discuss the predictions on the board in pairs. In feedback, refer to the board, and ask *Which predictions were/weren't right?*

Answers: Anita gave up her job in advertising to travel around the world for a year. She worked on a farm in Australia for a while. Jasmin was a doctor but she gave it up to become a professional musician.

4A Ss first read the sentences. Check *follow her dream, look after.* Then give Ss 2–3 mins to discuss the statements and correct the false ones if possible.

B Play the recording again. Ss check their answers and compare them. In feedback, nominate Ss to answer and correct the false statements (see answers in bold in the audio script).

Answers: 1 T 2 F: she was nearly 40 years old when she decided to change her life. 3 T 4 T 5 F: she worked on a farm in Australia. 6 T 7 F: she was a doctor working with elderly patients in a hospital. 8 F: she played the piano, but not well. 9 T 10 T

Optional extra activity
Exploit the recording further. Play it again and pause it at suitable points to ask Ss for more specific details, e.g. *When did Jasmin give up her job? What did Anita sell? Did she enjoy her job?*

Unit 7 Recording 1

P=Presenter A=Anita J=Jasmin

P: Have you ever felt stuck in a rut? Well, this morning we talk to two women who have made big life changes and they are here to tell us about it. Jasmin Wells <u>used to work</u> as a doctor in York. In her thirties she gave up her job and became a professional musician. Anita Jacobs <u>used to work</u> in advertising. But she sold her house, gave up her job, and decided to travel around the world. Anita first, what made you decide to change?

A: Well, **I was nearly forty.** I was in a job that I wasn't really interested in. I <u>used to work</u> long hours and I didn't enjoy the job much any more. So I decided to follow an ambition I've had for a long time. **I always wanted to travel, but I never had the chance.**

P: Your ambition was to travel around the world?

A: That's right. The idea was to take a year off. I started work when I was eighteen and I never had a break in all that time. I never had time to travel or see the world. **So I decided to take a year off and go travelling.** The time was right, so I left my job and went.

P: And you earned some money while you were travelling, didn't you?

A: Well, a little. **I worked on a farm for a while in Australia.** They didn't pay me very much, but I stayed on the farm and ate for free, so I was happy.

P: I see. Now, Jasmin, doctor to musician is quite a big change. What happened?

J: Well, it is a big change. And it happened quite suddenly. **I was working in a hospital doing more than a hundred hours a week, looking after elderly patients.** <u>I didn't use to have time</u> for anything else. It was just work, work, work. And one morning when I left the hospital, I saw a piano in the corner of the room. I sat down and started to play. I remembered that I really enjoyed making music.

P: So, <u>did you use to play</u> the piano before, as a child?

J: Yes, <u>I used to play</u>, but I wasn't very good! Luckily, I'm a bit better now. Anyway, I decided I wanted to learn the piano, so I **started piano lessons, and learnt about writing songs.** It became a passion for me, and I realised that it was something I really wanted to do. So, I decided to make more time for it, and eventually I gave up medicine altogether, and **started playing my own music.**

P: Fascinating, now tell me …

5 Elicit initial responses to the questions before Ss discuss them in pairs. Encourage them to use the phrases with prepositions from Ex 1, particularly when they answer question 2. Note how well they do this while you monitor. In feedback, elicit/discuss Ss' answers. Give feedback on language you noted while monitoring.

GRAMMAR *used to*

Watch out!
Ss may confuse the form and pronunciation of *used to*. They sometimes translate from their L1 and say, e.g. *I'm used to go,* or mix past simple forms, e.g. *I used to went … .* Ss may also pronounce *used* with two syllables /juːsɪd/ instead of /juːst/. It's important to check/drill the forms clearly, and correct errors consistently in order to prevent fossilisation (habitual use).

6A Write sentences a)–c) on the board. Underline the complete verb phrase (*used/didn't use/did you use to* + infinitive without *to*) in each sentence. Then ask concept questions 1–5 and elicit/check Ss' answers carefully. Model/drill the sentences: highlight the pronunciation of *used to* /juːstə/ and write on the board.

Answers: 1 Yes, she did. 2 No, she doesn't. 3 No, she didn't. 4 Yes, she does. 5 The past.

B Ss read the rules and discuss their answers in pairs. In feedback, do a personalised substitution drill to check the form and pronunciation of *used to* further. Give Ss prompts, e.g. *watch cartoons when you were a child.* Elicit/drilll *used to/ didn't use to watch cartoons when I was a child.*

Answers: 1 past simple 2 more than once

▶ **LANGUAGEBANK** 7.1 p140–141

Ss can refer to the notes when they do the exercises. *Weaker classes* should do Ex A and B in class. In Ex B, check *leather jacket.*

Answers:
A 1 used to study 2 used to smoke 3 never used to argue 4 used to live 5 didn't use to like
6 Did (you) use to enjoy 7 used to go out 8 used to do
B 1 used to 2 didn't use to 3 used to 4 used to 5 used to 6 didn't use to 7 used to 8 did (not) use to

---

PRACTICE

7A Ss work alone and compare their answers. Monitor and note any problems they have with the target language (the language they've just learnt).

B Play the recording, pausing after each sentence for Ss to make changes to their answers if necessary. Check the answers with the class. Ss listen again and repeat. Highlight and drill the pronunciation of *use(d) to* /juːstə/ and drill the sentences chorally and individually.

Answers: 1 When I was a child I used to cycle to school yesterday. 2 My brother always used *to* listen to heavy metal music. 3 ✓ 4 ✓ 5 We didn't ~~used~~ use to have any pets.
6 We used to go skiing in the holidays ~~last year~~.

C Elicit sentences for question 1 that are true for your Ss. Give them 3–4 mins to do the exercise alone. In feedback, nominate Ss to tell the class about themselves/their partner, e.g. *When I was a child, I used to walk to school, but Marta used to cycle 5 miles every day.*

Unit 7 Recording 2

1 When I was a child I used to cycle to school.
   used to – I used to cycle to school.
2 My brother always used to listen to heavy metal music.
   used to – He used to listen to music.
3 My family used to live in a different city.
   used to – We used to live in a different city.
4 I used to stay up all night dancing. Now I get tired at 10p.m.
   used to – I used to stay up all night dancing.
5 We didn't use to have any pets.
   didn't use to – We didn't use to have any pets.
6 We used to go skiing in the holidays.
   used to – We used to go skiing in the holidays.

SPEAKING

8A Elicit some examples, e.g. *My life's changed completely. I got married eight years ago and now I have five children.* Ss then write three facts that have significantly changed their lives.

B Ss compare sentences and discuss how their lives have changed. Remind them to use *used to* when possible and monitor to see how successfully they do it. Ss should be prepared to tell the class about their partner. In feedback, Ss decide whose life has changed the most in the last ten years. Do remedial work on *used to* if necessary.

WRITING paragraphs

9A Check unfamiliar language in the sentences. Ss then order them and compare answers. They must be able to justify the order they decide on. Check answers in feedback.

Answers:
Paragraph 1: 2 Before that, I was working for a company, but I didn't enjoy my job. 3 I've always thought that being a teacher would be really interesting. 4 So, I went back to college and did a teacher training course.

Paragraph 2: 2 For example, I had to work to earn money, and find time to do coursework. 3 So I used to study in the evenings. 4 Now, I have a teaching qualification, and I'm doing the job I've always wanted to do.

B Check the meaning of *support/conclude* and elicit the answers for paragraph 1. Ss then check paragraph 2 and discuss whether it follows the same pattern.

Answers: In each paragraph: 1 Sentence 1 contains the main idea. 2 Sentences 2 and 3 support the idea.
3 Sentence 4 finishes/concludes the paragraph.

C Ss can use one of their examples from Ex 8, or invent one. With *weaker classes*, elicit an example first, using the framework here. Give Ss 8–10 mins to write their paragraph. Monitor and support them where necessary. Also encourage them to read/comment on each other's work.

Homework ideas
- Ex 9C: write another paragraph about yourself/someone you know.
- Language bank 7.1 Ex A–B, p141
- Workbook Ex 1–8, p41–42

THE GREAT IMPOSTOR

Introduction

Ss revise and practise the use of linking words (*to, because, so*) to talk about purpose, cause and result in the context of a text about a famous impostor.

SUPPLEMENTARY MATERIALS

Resource bank p171

Ex 2B: Ss may need dictionaries to check new words in the text.

Warm up

Revise vocabulary Ss need for the lesson. Dictate sentences 1–7 about Barney, but in the wrong order. Ss write them down and then put them in the correct order. *1 Barney committed a crime in 2005. 2 The police arrested him in 2006. 3 He escaped from the police station the next day. 4 They caught him again in 2007. 5 He went to prison. 6 He spent two years there. 7 They released him from prison in 2009.* Ss check their answers in pairs. In feedback, elicit the answers or ask Ss to write them on the board. Teach/check the verbs in each sentence.

READING

1 Check the rubric and the definition. Elicit/prompt Ss to give some examples. Then give Ss 3–4 mins to discuss the question in pairs, and then as a class.

Possible answers: fiction: Rosalind dresses as a boy to escape the wicked Duke in Shakespeare's *As You Like It*; **real-life:** Victor Lustig 'sold' the Eiffel tower in 1925; in the 1990s, Christopher Rocancourt tricked rich people out of money while pretending to be a French member of the Rockefeller family; **films:** the imposter Frank Abagnale was played by Leonardo DiCaprio in *Catch Me if You Can*; the characters in *Ocean's 11, 12* and *13* use many disguises; Robin Williams dresses as a female housekeeper in order to be near his children in *Mrs Doubtfire*; **fairy stories:** the wolf pretends to be *Little Red Riding Hood's* grandmother.

Culture notes

Tony Curtis (born Bernard Schwartz, 1925) is an American actor. His first film was in 1949 and he appeared in over 100 films altogether, most famously with Marilyn Monroe in *Some Like it Hot* (1959).

A **State Marshal** is usually involved in law enforcement, e.g. assisting with court security/prisoner transport and seeking fugitives.

2A Ss look at the poster. Ask *What's the poster for?* Elicit: for a film called *The Great Impostor*. Also elicit what Ss know about actor Tony Curtis (see **Culture notes**). Then give Ss 1 min to look at the smaller pictures/text in the poster and answer the question in pairs. In feedback, check Ss' answers and teach new words/phrases, e.g. *pull the wool over someone's eyes.*

Answers: He pretended to be a naval officer (sailor), a US Marine (soldier), a State Marshal, a monk, a dentist.

Culture notes

Ferdinand Waldo Demara, Jr. (1921–1982) was said to have a photographic memory and an extremely high IQ. This is how he memorised techniques from a textbook and perform operations. He's reported to have said that the things he did were like childish pranks; he didn't intend to hurt people.

B Read part 1 of the story with Ss to illustrate what they have to do. Check the dates of the Korean War (1950–1953). Ss then guess the answer to the first question and read part 6 to find the answer. Give them 3–4 mins to read the rest of the text. They can use dictionaries to check unknown vocabulary if necessary. In feedback, ask Ss *How many correct guesses did you make?* Check the answers and ask further comprehension questions about each one. For example, for part 6 ask, *When did he pretend to be a doctor? Who did he pretend to be? Why did the soldiers love him?* Also teach new words/phrases, e.g. *bullet, perform an operation.*

Answers: 1 a) 6 c) 3 b) 5 b) 4 c)

3 Check the questions and elicit one or two initial answers. Give Ss 3 mins to discuss them further. In feedback, elicit Ss' answers: use information from the **Culture notes** to enable them to expand on questions 1 and 2.

Optional extra activity

Ss work in pairs/small teams and write 4 comprehension questions (*stronger Ss* could write more) about the text, e.g. *When was Demara born? When did he appear in a film?* Pairs/teams then exchange questions and must answer them without looking at the texts. The pair/team with the most correct answers wins.

VOCABULARY collocations

4A First check vocabulary, e.g. *role, documentary, murder.* Ss find/underline the collocations in the story before feedback with the class.

Answers: 1 f) 2 c) 3 e) 4 a) 5 d) 6 g) 7 b)

B Elicit/help Ss with the first sentence in the story: *During the Korean War, Demara pretended to be a doctor on a ship. The soldiers loved him because he cured their illnesses.* Ss use the underlined expressions in the text to help them tell the story in pairs. While they do this, monitor and provide support where needed. In feedback, Ss take turns to tell one part of the story. Prompt peer/self-correction during this stage.

speakout TIP

Read the speakout tip with Ss. Advise Ss to write whole phrases in their vocabulary notebooks, such as the collocations in Ex 4A, where possible, rather than single verbs. Elicit some examples of words that collocate with *play/make*, e.g. *play football (a game)/the piano (an instrument), make a cake/mistake.*

GRAMMAR purpose, cause and result

Watch out!

Because of L1 interference, Ss frequently make mistakes with the use of *to* to talk about purpose, e.g. *I went to the shop* for *to buy a newspaper*. It's important to make Ss aware of this problem as early as possible. When teaching the form, ask Ss to compare it with their own language and notice the similarity/difference. Prompt them to self-correct and correct each other whenever they make this mistake.

5A Ss complete the sentences and compare answers. Move on to Ex B.

B Ss find and check their answers. In feedback, ask checking questions, e.g. *Why did he appear in a 1960 film?* To make some money. *Why didn't he go to prison?* Because people thought he was a hero. *What did the mother do when she saw the picture?* She told the police.

Answers: 1 to 2 because 3 so

C Give Ss 2–3 mins to find other examples in the story. In feedback, check Ss' answers. Then write these two sentences on the board: 1 *Demara pretended to be Dr Joseph Cyr* <u>to</u> *work on a ship. 2 Demara pretended to be Dr Joseph Cyr* <u>in order to</u> *work on a ship.* Ask *Do the sentences have the same/a different meaning?* The same. Then ask Ss to find the sentence in the text (in part 6). Elicit and write it on the board. *Demara pretended to be Dr Joseph Cyr* <u>so that</u> <u>he could work</u> *on a ship.* Ask *What's different?* Elicit/underline *so that* and subject + *can/could* + verb (he could work). Ss will read about *in order to* and *so that* in the **Language bank**, p140.

Answers:
Part 4: Instead the police released him and gave him extra money to say 'thank you' for his great work!
Part 5: Demara became famous because of his great work as the ship's doctor … .

⟹ LANGUAGEBANK 7.2 p140–141

Read/check the notes with your Ss if necessary. They can refer to them when they do the exercises. *Weaker Ss* should do Ex A and B in class. In Ex A, check *sales reps* and in Ex B check *wallet, attend a conference.*

Answers:
A 1 to 2 because 3 to 4 so 5 so 6 to 7 because 8 so
B I usually get a newspaper *because* I want to know what's on TV, but today I read a strange story. An Englishman was feeling terrible *because* he was under pressure at work, *so* he decided to disappear. He went to a beach *to* go swimming (he said). Then he left his clothes there *so that* someone could find them. He also left his wallet with a photo and ID *so* the police knew who it was. The police went *to* his home to speak to him but he wasn't there. He was in Australia and had a different name! Three years later he was caught when his cousin, who was in Australia *to* attend a conference, recognised him. Where were they? On a beach!

PRACTICE

6A Do the first question as an example. Ss then work alone, underline the correct alternatives and compare them. In feedback, check Ss' answers. With *stronger classes*, you could ask Ss which sentences can be written with *in order to* or *so that*. *In order to* can be used with questions 1, 4, 6, and *so that* with questions 1 and 6, e.g. *I'm doing an English course* <u>in order to</u> *improve my speaking. I'm doing an English course* <u>so that I can</u> *improve my speaking.*

Answers: 1 to 2 because 3 so 4 to 5 because 6 to 7 so 8 because

B Discuss one or two of the sentences with the class. Then give them 3–4 mins to discuss others that are true for them. In feedback, invite Ss to tell the class about their partners.

7 Check the examples and give Ss 2–3 mins to complete the exercise. While they do this, make notes on their use of the target language (the language they've studied in this lesson) and do remedial work as needed in feedback.

Suggested answers: I wanted to help people so I became a nurse. I went to the doctor because I felt sick. I liked travelling so I became a pilot. I went to university to get a Master's degree. I phoned my friend to invite her to a party. I cycled to work because I couldn't drive. I bought an iPod because I love listening to music.

Optional extra activity

Ss work with a different partner. They take it in turns to make sentences with the phrases in list A, but have to provide different answers, e.g. *I went to the cinema … because I wanted to see the new James Bond film.*

SPEAKING

8A Discuss some answers to question 1 with the class. Then give Ss 4–5 mins to think about and discuss their answers in pairs/groups.

B Ss read the situations. Check unfamiliar language, e.g. *CV, references, a designer bag.* Ss then discuss their answers in pairs. Remind them that they need to give reasons for their answers. To extend the practice, Ss could exchange opinions with another pair. Monitor and make notes on the strengths and weaknesses of the language they use. In feedback, invite pairs to discuss each situation with the class. Find out how far they agree. Give feedback as required.

Homework ideas

- Ex 8B: write your response to each situation here, giving reasons.
- Language bank 7.2 Ex A–B, p141
- Workbook Ex 1–5, p43–44

CAN YOU TELL ME … ?

Introduction

Ss learn and practise how to find out and check information about facilities in a language school/university.

SUPPLEMENTARY MATERIALS

Resource bank p172

Ex 3C: make copies of a plan/map of your school for Ss to describe.

Ex 10: record Ss' role-plays if you have audio/video facilities available.

Warm up

Lead in to the topic of the lesson: Ss discuss facilities in their town. Ask *Is your town a good place for tourists and/or students?* Invite some initial responses and, if necessary, provide prompts of things Ss need to consider (places of interest and facilities), e.g. *museums, monuments, churches, parks, walks, hotels, pubs, cafés, library, internet cafes, art galleries, clubs, bookshops, cinema,* etc. Ss discuss the question in pairs/groups. In *multilingual classes*, put Ss from different countries in different ones. In feedback, discuss Ss' conclusions about their town(s).

READING

1 Ss look at the photos. Ask, e.g. *What's this place? What can you see? Who are the two young people?* Ss then discuss the questions, first in pairs and then as a class.

2 Give Ss 2–3 mins to read the text, answer the questions and compare their answers. In feedback, check answers and then ask further comprehension questions, e.g. *What do you think the Chinese saying means? Why is it difficult for foreign students when they arrive? What kind of things do they have to do?* Elicit and discuss Ss' answers.

Answers: 1 Chinese students find studying abroad hard at first, but then it gets easier and they think it's a great experience. 2 There are 66,000 Chinese students at UK universities.

Optional extra activity

Find/underline four collocations in the text, e.g. *read books, walk 1,000 miles, get easier, open a bank account, get a phone contract.*

VOCABULARY facilities

3A Ss do the exercise alone and compare their answers. In feedback, elicit/check the answers and teach new words, e.g. *register, accommodation, welfare, lecture theatre.* Elicit the stressed syllable in each word/phrase and drill the pronunciation. Ss write new words in their notebooks.

Answers: 1 library 2 stationery shop 3 registration desk 4 cafeteria 5 accommodation/welfare office

B Check/drill the example and elicit another one. Ss then take turns to ask/answer questions about the facilities. Check their answers in open pairs across the class: prompt self- and peer correction.

Other answers: study centre: study by yourself/do your homework; **book shop:** buy textbooks; **cafeteria:** have a coffee/eat something; **main reception:** find out where to go; **classroom:** have a lesson; **photocopying room:** make photocopies; **library:** borrow books/do research; **accommodation/welfare office:** discuss problems; **lecture theatre:** listen to a lecture

C Give Ss 3–4 mins to answer the questions in pairs. If possible, provide a map/plan of your language school, or Ss could draw one to facilitate their answers. In feedback, find out which facilities are most widely used.

FUNCTION finding out information

4A Check the example and give Ss 3–4 mins to write the questions. Monitor and support *weaker Ss* if necessary. Check/drill the questions in feedback (the questions are in bold in the audio script). *Stronger classes* could check their answers in Ex B.

Answers: b) Where's the study centre? c) What time is/does the library open? d) Can you help me find my classroom? e) Where can I use the internet? f) Where can I buy a notebook? g) Where can I get a new student card? h) Can you tell me where to go (for information about …)?

B Ss listen, note down their answers and compare them. Play the recording again to check answers, if they still have doubts.

Answers: 2 b) 3 e) 4 c) 5 g) 6 d) 7 f) 8 h)

5 Give Ss time to read and check the statements before listening. Tell them to correct the false statements when they compare answers. Play the recording twice if necessary. In feedback, nominate Ss to answer with the corrected statements (see answers underlined in the audio script).

Answers: 1 T 2 T 3 T 4 F: the library is open from 9–6 every day. 5 T 6 T 7 F: the stationery shop is downstairs. 8 F: the welfare office is next to the book shop.

Unit 7 Recording 3

Conversation 1

A: *Excuse me,* where do I register for my course?
B: Do you know where the main reception is?
A: Sorry?
B: The main reception.
A: Oh, yes.
B: The registration desk is there.
A: Thank you so much.

Conversation 2

A: Excuse me, **where's the study centre?**
C: It's next to the cafeteria.
A: The cafeteria? Where's that?
C: Follow me. I'll take you there.
A: Thank you. *That's very kind.*

Conversation 3

A: Where can I use the internet?
D: You can use the computers in the library or in the study centre.
A: *Do I have to pay?*
D: No.
A: So it's free for students.
D: Yes, that's right.

Conversation 4

A: Excuse me, *what time is the library open?*
E: It's open every day, from 9a.m. until 6p.m.

A: Did you say 'every day'?
E: Yes, that's right. Every day, from nine in the morning until six in the evening.
A: Thank you.

Conversation 5

A: *Could you help me? Where can I get* a new student card? I've lost mine.
F: OK. If you go to the main reception, you can get a new one.
A: Thank you.

Conversation 6

A: Excuse me, **can you help me find my classroom?**
G: Sure. What number is it?
A: 301.
G: OK. You need to go up to the third floor. And it's on the right.

Conversation 7

A: Where can I buy a notebook?
H: There's a stationery shop downstairs.
A: Sorry?
H: There's a stationery shop downstairs.
A: Thank you so much.

Conversation 8

A: Can you help me?
I: Yes, maybe.
A: *I need to find out about* my accommodation. **Can you tell me where to go?**
I: Accommodation? I think you have to go to the welfare office, over there, next to the book shop.
A: Thank you.

6A Point out/check the three headings for the questions/phrases here. Give Ss 3–4 mins to complete gaps 1–7 and compare their answers.

B Ss check their answers in the audio script. *Fast finishers* could find examples of the other phrases in Ex 6A. In feedback, check the answers (in italics in the audio script) and elicit/drill the complete sentences from the recording, e.g. *Where can I get a new student card? I need to find out about my accommodation.*

Answers: 1 Excuse 2 help 3 can 4 time 5 have 6 need 7 kind

⇒ LANGUAGEBANK 7.3 p140–141

Ss should refer to the information in the tables if necessary.

Answers:
A 1 A: Can you tell me where to ~~can~~ find … B: Yes, there's one just behind ~~of~~ you! 2 A: I need to ~~be~~ find out … B: There's an accommodation office ~~on~~ downstairs. 3 A: … from ~~on~~ 7 o'clock. B: Did you ~~to~~ say 7 o'clock? 4 A: Do you ~~is~~ know … B: Yes, I'll show ~~it~~ you. That's *very kind of you.* 5 A: Is it ~~a~~ free to park … B: No, ~~it's~~ you have to pay.

7 Elicit the answer to question 1. Ss then do the exercise alone and compare their answers. In feedback, Ss read out the dialogues in pairs. Prompt them to self-correct if they make mistakes and invite peer correction if necessary.

Answers: 1 A: Excuse ~~to~~ me … B: … around *the* corner. 2 A: What time ~~do~~ does the … B: … it opens ~~on~~ at eight o'clock. 3 A: Can *you* tell me … B: You need ~~going~~ to go to reception. 4 A: Where ~~I can~~ can I get a coffee? B: … next *to* the library.

8 Divide the class into two groups: Ss A and B. They each check the relevant exercises and maps on p165 or p166 and work with another student from the same group (A or B) to prepare the questions they need to ask in Ex 8A. They also need to check the maps/information for Ex B. Monitor closely while Ss do this and provide support and clarification where necessary. When they are ready, put Ss into A/B pairs. They take turns to ask/answer the questions. Monitor and make a note of problem sentences for feedback. Invite Ss to act out their conversations to the class. Give feedback on problems as needed.

Suggested answers: A 1 Excuse me, what time do the shops open? At 10a.m. every day except Sunday. 2 Excuse me, where's the nearest train station? It's over the bridge on the other side of the river. 3 Excuse me, can you help me? I need to change some money. There's a money exchange next to the railway station. B 1 Excuse me, where's the nearest coffee shop? It's next to classrooms 4 and 5, on the right. 2 Excuse me, where can I buy an English dictionary? There's an English bookshop in the reception area. 3 Excuse me, can you tell me what time the school closes? At 10p.m. from Monday to Saturday and at 1p.m. on Sunday.

LEARN TO check information

9A Ss read and listen to the extracts; tell them to pay attention to the pronunciation of the language highlighted in bold on p73.

B Check the meaning of *repetition/rephrasing*. Elicit the first answer as an example before Ss work alone/in pairs. In feedback, elicit and check the answers.

Answers: a) Extracts 2, 5 b) Extracts 1, 4 c) Extract 3

C Ss listen and repeat the words/phrases that come just before the pause in the recording. Use your hands and arms to conduct/highlight the main stress and fall/rise of the intonation in each question.

Answers: The word is repeated as a question so there is a fall/rise intonation after the stressed syllable.

10 Read and check the rubric and situation with the class. Give Ss 5–6 mins to work in pairs and plan/write notes about what they want to say. In *mixed-ability classes*, put stronger/weaker Ss together. They should prepare both A and B roles and rehearse both parts of the conversation. Monitor closely to provide support with accuracy and pronunciation where needed. Prompt Ss to self-correct any errors. Then put Ss into pairs with a different partner. They take turns to be A/B and role-play the situation. They may have to adjust some of the things they'd planned to say, depending on what their partner says. In feedback, invite pairs to perform the role-plays to the class, or in groups. If you have audio/video recording facilities available, record the role-plays. Ss can watch and comment on them in feedback.

Homework ideas
• Ex 10: write a conversation about a different situation, e.g. you lost your iPod or you can't find the library.
• Language bank 7.3 Ex A, p141
• Workbook Ex 1–3, p45

MY FAMILY AND OTHER ANIMALS

Introduction

Ss watch an extract from a BBC film about the famous Durrell family, who moved to Greece in the 1930s. Ss then learn and practise how to talk and write about a new experience.

SUPPLEMENTARY MATERIALS

Warm up: bring/download a map of Greece, showing the island of Corfu off the north east coast.

Culture notes

Corfu is a large, beautiful, Greek island in the Ionian Sea, off the north east coast of Greece. It has a long history of hospitality to foreign visitors and is a popular tourist destination for British people.

Warm up

Introduce the lesson and subject of the DVD. Ss cover the text and look at the large photo of Corfu on p74–75. Ask, e.g. *What's this place like? Where is it?* Elicit and discuss Ss' answers. If possible, show Ss a map of Greece/the island of Corfu. Ask Ss *Would you leave your country and move to a place like this? Why/Why not? Why do you think people might move there?* Ss discuss their answers in groups and then with the class.

▷ DVD PREVIEW

1 Check the rubric and give Ss 2–3 mins to answer the questions in pairs. In feedback, Ss tell the class about their partner's answers. Discuss ways of communicating when you can't speak the language.

Suggested answers: If you can't speak the language, you can use a dictionary/a phrase book, draw a picture of the object you want, mime an action to illustrate it, e.g. brush your teeth to show toothpaste/toothbrush.

Culture notes

The autobiography *My Family And Other Animals* is by famous naturalist and conservationist **Gerald Durrell** (1925–1995), who spent four years on Corfu with his family from 1935–1939. The book is the first of his Corfu trilogy, together with *Birds, Beasts, and Relatives*, and *The Garden of the Gods*. His brother **Lawrence** (1912–1990) is also a famous author, best known for *The Alexandria Quartet*.

2A Check if Ss know the book/film *My Family And Other Animals*. If so, elicit what they know about it. Ss then read the text and answer the questions. In feedback, check Ss' answers and anything else they know about authors Gerald and Lawrence Durrell. Use the **Culture notes** if necessary.

Answers: They move to Corfu because they want to escape the wet, grey English weather.

B Ss read the information again and discuss their answers in pairs. Tell them to use prepositions, and details about the people's clothes, to help them describe who the people are. Nominate Ss to answer in feedback. Check new words and elicit further information about them, e.g. ask *How old is Gerry? Who's the eldest/an intellectual? Who loves animals?* Also lead in to the DVD extract. Ask *What happens to the family in Corfu? Why are they delighted to meet Spiro? Who do you think Spiro is?*

Answers: The man in the blue shirt on the left is Lawrence, the girl with blonde hair in front of him is Margot, the young man at the top of the stairs in the brown shirt is Leslie, the young boy in the front is Gerry, the older woman on the right in the red dress is their mother.

▷ DVD VIEW

3 Check the rubric/sentences about the DVD and preteach *customs officer*. Ss then watch the DVD, number the scenes and compare answers. In feedback, elicit Ss' answers and as much detail about each scene as they can remember, e.g. in scene 1, ask *Why don't they feel well?* Because Gerry, Margot and Leslie have colds, and mother is tired.

Alternative approach

Ss watch the DVD without sound first. They watch the actions/events and should be able to put most scenes in order. Ss compare their answers, and then watch the DVD again with the sound to check.

Answers: 2 e) 3 b) 4 d) 5 c)

4A Check the rubric and quotes with Ss. Teach/check *bed linen*. They then match the people to each quote and compare answers. Ss should try to remember exactly where the people were/what they were doing when they said these things.

B Ss watch the DVD again and check their answers (in bold in the DVD script). Pause after each answer and ask further comprehension questions to exploit the landscape, actions and events in the DVD to the fullest, e.g. for question 1 ask *What did Lawrence's mother reply? Did the others want to pack up and go?*

Answers: 2 Lawrence 3 Mother 4 Mother 5 Mother 6 Leslie 7 Spiro 8 Spiro 9 Gerry

DVD 7   My Family And Other Animals

Lawrence: Why do we put up with this climate? I mean, look at us! Gerry can't speak.
Gerry: Uh?
Lawrence: Leslie can't hear.
Leslie: What?
Lawrence: Margot's got a face like a plate of red porridge.
Margot: Shut up!
Lawrence: And mother is beginning to look like an Irish washer woman.
Mother: I am not.
Lawrence: It's August! We need sunshine.
Mother: Yes, dear.
Lawrence: I've got a friend. Lives in Greece. Corfu. Says it's wonderful. **Why don't we pack up and go?**
Mother: I can't just go like that. We have a house here.
Lawrence: We'll sell up.
Mother: Don't be ridiculous, Lawrence. Gerry needs an education.
Gerry: No, I'll be fine.
Mother: We can't just up and leave. That would be madness.
Lawrence: I'm a writer. That one's very good.

Customs Officer: Good. This, no.

Mother: It's bed linen.

Customs Officer: Merchandise. Tax.

Mother: It's our bed linen. You silly man.

Margot: Come away, mother. Let's put off annoying people as long as possible.

Mother: I'm sorry but you've shown us ten houses, and none of them has a bathroom.

Gerry: Oh, not again.

Estate agent: Bathroom? What for you want a bathroom? You have the sea.

Mother: This is the cradle of civilisation. They must have bathrooms. We'll find a place ourselves. Uh … no, um, er … Taxi?

Leslie: We don't actually speak Greek.

Margot: We do plan to learn.

Mother: Can't you do something, Larry?

Lawrence: What?

Spiro: Oi!!! You need someone who talks your language? Them's been worrying yous?

Mother: Ah … no, no.

Spiro: Hey! … So, taxi? Where you wants to go, eh? You know what? English always wants bathrooms. I got a bathroom in my house. Eight years I was in Chicago, and then I says, Spiro, you's made enough money, so I come back. I bring this car with me. Best car on the island. I tell you no word of a lie.

Mother: Eyes on the road.

Spiro: All the English tourists, they ask for me when they come to the island. Yeah. You know, if I wasn't Greek, yeah, I likes to be English. There. Villa with bathrooms.

Gerry: We'll take it.

5 Check the questions and elicit some initial answers. In *multilingual classes*, put Ss from the same countries in different pairs. Give Ss 4–5 mins to discuss the questions and make a note of their partner's answers for feedback. Find out who the most popular character is and why, and what the most common problems for tourists are.

speakout a new experience

6A Check the rubric. Remind Ss to focus on answering the three questions and not get distracted by unfamiliar language. Ss listen and make notes of their answers, and then compare them. Play the recording again if necessary. Nominate Ss to answer (in italics in the audio script) and elicit extra information if possible.

Answers: 1 Agata moved to the USA, but she didn't speak very good English. 2 She felt nervous when she had to speak to people. 3 She met some American girls and went out with them. Now, her English is better, she feels more confident; she talks to people all the time.

B Ss read and check the **key phrases**. Ss listen and tick the phrases they hear. In feedback, play the recording again, pausing at each **key phrase** (in bold in the audio script). Elicit/drill the complete sentences and ask further comprehension questions, e.g. *Where did Agata learn English? Why was it different in the USA?*

Answers: ✓ The biggest problem was … , I felt very nervous/shy/excited when … , I couldn't … , Luckily, I met/made friends …

Optional extra activity
Ss work in pairs/groups and re-tell Agata's story using the **key phrases**, e.g. *When Agata moved to the USA, her biggest problem was …*

Unit 7 Recording 6

Well, when I first arrived in the USA, it was a very interesting time for me. *The biggest problem was* that I couldn't really speak the language very well. I learnt English at school and at university in Poland, but it's very different when you are living in the country and you need to speak it all the time. *I felt very nervous when* I had to speak to American people, like in the shops or when you meet friends, and *I couldn't* understand what people were saying to me. It was terrible. I used to stay at home, and watch loads of television to try and understand what people were saying. *Luckily, I made friends very quickly with some American girls, so we used to go out together, and that really helped me.* After a few months my *English was much better. I felt more confident. And now I talk to people all the time,* but it was hard at the beginning.

7A Check the rubric/questions and give Ss 3–4 mins to make notes of their answers. Monitor and help them with language they need.

B Ss should make notes of one of their partners' experiences and prepare to report back to the class in feedback. Monitor and note down examples of good language and errors Ss make for feedback.

writeback a blog/diary

Culture notes
Leeds is a large city in Yorkshire in the north of England.

8A Ss read the text and answer the questions. Discuss Ss' answers and highlight the use of *used to* in the blog.

Answers: 1 Yes. 2 She misses her family and friends. When she first arrived, she used to get lost all the time.

B First elicit examples of what Ss could write, using the prompts given, e.g. *One thing that has really changed in my life is learning to drive. I decided to learn to drive so that I could be more independent. Before that I used to take buses everywhere,* etc. Ss can use their notes from Ex 7 to write their blog/diary. Encourage them to read/comment on each other's work, while you provide support where needed. Ss can display their blogs in the classroom or pass them round for other Ss to read. Then discuss which experience Ss thought was the most unusual/interesting and give feedback on their performance.

Homework ideas
• Ex 5 question 2: write your answer to this question.
• Ex 8B: write another blog/diary and put it on your school website/class blog.

LOOKBACK

Introduction

Use the **Lookback** section to monitor and assess Ss' understanding of the language covered in the unit.

SUPPLEMENTARY MATERIALS

Ex 3: Ss may need dictionaries for this exercise.

VERBS + PREPOSITIONS

1A Elicit/check the answer in question 1. Ss then work alone and complete the exercise before comparing their answers. Monitor to assess how well Ss use the prepositions and do remedial work in feedback if necessary.

Answers: 1 about 2 around 3 up 4 to 5 about 6 back

B Elicit and discuss Ss' answers to question 1. Give them time to prepare their answers before they ask/answer the questions in pairs. They should make notes of their partner's answers for feedback.

Optional extra activity

Ss write one sentence containing one of their partner's most interesting answers on a piece of paper but leave their name blank, e.g. _____ would like to travel around Nepal. Collect the pieces of paper and redistribute them. Ss must then find the person their sentence is about by asking the relevant question, e.g. *Would you like to travel to Nepal?* They walk around the class asking their question or read out the question to the class. Monitor and make notes on Ss' strengths and weaknesses for feedback and/or assessment.

USED TO

2A Elicit the answer to question 1 to show Ss what to do and then give them 3–4 mins to write the questions. Check/drill the questions before Ss do Ex B.

Answers: *When you were a child …* 1 did you use to work hard at school? 2 did you use to eat fast food? 3 did you use to spend time with your grandparents? 4 did you use to get ill often? 5 did you use to have a special friend? 6 did you use to play any sport? 7 did you use to travel to school on public transport? 8 did you use to live in a different place?

B Elicit as many related questions as possible for question 1 in Ex A, e.g. *What subjects did you enjoy? What did you use to be good/bad at? Did you use to get good exam results?* Encourage Ss to use both *used to* and the past simple. *Stronger Ss* can work alone, or in pairs with *weaker Ss*, depending on your aim (for revision/practice or for assessment). It's important that Ss' questions are accurate for Ex C, so monitor and support Ss.

Suggested answers: 2 Did your mother use to cook home-made food? What was your favourite dish? Did she teach you to cook? 3 When did you use to visit them? Where did they live? 4 What sort of illnesses did you use to get? Did you take much time off school? 5 What was his/her name? How old were you? What did you use to do together? Are you still friends now? 6 How often/well did you play? Did you use to play in a school team? 7 How far was it? How long did it take? Did you use to cycle to school? 8 Where did you live? How long did you live there? Did your parents use to move around a lot?

C Check/drill the example dialogue, encouraging Ss to sound interested. While they work in pairs, monitor and assess their use of the target language and give feedback afterwards.

COLLOCATIONS

3A Ss work alone/in pairs and can check their answers on p71. In feedback, check Ss' answers. With *stronger classes*, elicit/check how the other verb in each sentence could be used, e.g. *This hero rescued me.* Alternatively, Ss can use their dictionaries to check the verbs/find examples.

Answers: 1 cured 2 saved 3 become 4 spends 5 for 6 spent 7 played 8 make

B Check the example. Give Ss 4–5 mins to write new sentences in pairs/teams. *Stronger Ss* could write more. Monitor but don't help Ss while they work. In feedback, Ss take turns to read out their extra sentences to the class. The other Ss decide if the sentence makes sense and is grammatically correct. Ss get two points for appropriate/correct sentences, and one point for an appropriate one.

PURPOSE, CAUSE AND RESULT

4A Ss read the two parts of the exercise first. Check *put my feet up.* Ss then do the exercise alone and compare their answers. In feedback, elicit/check answers and prompt peer (Ss correct each other) and/or self-correction where appropriate. Then do remedial teaching if necessary.

Answers: 1 f) 2 g) 3 h) 4 a) 5 e) 6 d) 7 b) 8 c)

B Check the example. Do another one if necessary to illustrate the exercise further. Give Ss 1 min to write the questions before they ask/answer them in pairs. Monitor and make notes of problems Ss have with the linking words. Write them on the board in feedback. Ss correct them in pairs.

FINDING OUT INFORMATION

5A Give Ss 3 mins to order the conversations and compare answers. In feedback, model/drill the sentences to remind Ss of the importance of sentence stress and intonation when asking for/checking information. This will prepare them for the practice in Ex B.

Answers:
Conversation 1: 2 i) 3 e) 4 d) 5 f) 6 c) 7 g) 8 b) 9 h)
Conversation 2: 1 i) 2 b) 3 h) 4 g) 5 a) 6 d) 7 c) 8 f) 9 e)

B Ss practise reading the conversations, and take turns to ask for information. Monitor and note Ss' pronunciation, particularly stress and intonation. In feedback, nominate pairs to act out a conversation and invite the other Ss to comment on their stress/intonation. Ask *Did they sound polite?* Do remedial teaching/give further feedback if necessary.

OVERVIEW

MONEY MAKERS

Introduction
Ss learn/practise the use of relative clauses to describe people, places and things. They also learn and practise vocabulary to talk about money.

SUPPLEMENTARY MATERIALS

Resource bank p173 and 174

Photo bank p158: Ss may need dictionaries.

Warm up: photocopy the matching activity for Ss if possible.

Ex 1: dictionaries should be available for the questionnaire.

Ex 3A: download/bring pictures from the film *2001: A Space Odyssey*.

Ex 8B: Ss may need dictionaries.

Warm up
Lead in to the lesson with a light-hearted matching activity about nicknames for British/US money. If possible, photocopy these two columns of nicknames/definitions. Otherwise, write them on the board: *Column A: 1 a nickel 2 a dime 3 a quarter 4 a buck 5 a quid 6 a fiver 7 a tenner 8 a grand, Column B: a) 5 cents b) £5 c) £1000 d) 10 cents e) £10 f) 25 cents g) £1 h) US$1*. Ss match the words in pairs. Check answers, then ask *Do you have nicknames for money in your country?*

Answers: 1) A nickel = 5 cents (US) 2) a dime = 10 cents (US) 3) a quarter = 25 cents (US) 4) a buck = US$1 5) a quid = £1 (Br) 6) a fiver = £5 (Br) 7) a tenner = £10 (Br) 8) a grand = £1000 (Br)

VOCABULARY money

1A Look at the photos and elicit/check words Ss know in the photos. They then read the questionnaire and tick the words in bold that they know. In pairs, Ss discuss the meaning of the words in bold they don't know, and check any they're not sure of in their dictionaries. In feedback, check and drill each word/phrase, and recap the names of things in the photos.

Answers: cash, credit card, notes, coins, tip (n)

B Ss ask/answer the questions and make notes of their partner's answers. In feedback, Ss tell the class about their partner. Discuss questions of particular interest, e.g. 5, 6, 9 and 10. Some Ss might not want to talk about their finances in class.

⟫ PHOTOBANK p158

1 Give Ss 2–3 mins to match the photos/words and compare answers. They can use their dictionaries if necessary. In feedback, elicit/check and drill the words. N.B. *ATM = automated teller machine.*

Answers: 1 F 2 G 3 C 4 E 5 B 6 A 7 H 8 D

2 Ss prepare their definitions using dictionaries if necessary. Do feedback in open pairs across the class.

LISTENING

Culture notes

Sabrina was directed by Billy Wilder and starred Humphrey Bogart, Audrey Hepburn and William Holden.

2001: A Space Odyssey was actually released in 1968 and was a very ambitious, forward-thinking science fiction film directed by Stanley Kubrick. It's now recognised as one of the greatest films ever made.

2A Elicit the names of the objects in the photos and what Ss know about them. Check language in the questions, e.g. *successful, invented*. Ss then discuss the questions in pairs. As question 2 predicts information from the recording in Ex C, elicit Ss' predictions and note them on the board. Don't confirm them until feedback in Ex 3B.

B Ss first read the rubric/sentences. Check unfamiliar vocabulary, e.g. *rubber, sold, concentration*. This is another prediction exercise, so reassure Ss that they are not expected to know the answers; they should deduce/guess them. Give them 3–4 mins to discuss and note down their answers.

C Ss listen and check their answers. Monitor while they compare them and play the recording again if necessary. In feedback, elicit Ss' answers (in bold in the audio script), but don't do any further comprehension until after Ex 3B.

Answers: 1 mobile phone 2 chewing gum 3 iPod
4 Monopoly 5 chewing gum 6 Monopoly 7 iPod 8 mobile phones

3A Ss read the rubric/sentences. Check *reached the public*. Also ask what Ss know about the two films mentioned here (see **Culture notes**) and show them pictures from *2001: A Space Odyssey* if possible. Ss discuss their answers for 2–3 mins. In feedback, elicit/check if Ss agree with each other, but don't confirm their answers yet. Move to Ex B.

B Ss listen again, check their answers and compare them. If Ss don't agree on the answers, play the recording again, but pause at each answer (underlined in the audio script). Elicit the exact words from the recording and any other details Ss can give you about the answer. Ss can also check their predictions on the board from Ex 2A.

Answers: 2 F: no-one knows who first used chewing gum. 3 F: invented in 1908. 4 T 5 T 6 T 7 T 8 F: Charles Darrow did.

Unit 8 Recording 1

Welcome to *Money Matters*, presented by Jimmy Stevens. Today we're going to talk about four of the best money-making ideas in history. What do you think this is? It's a food which you don't eat. **It's a sweet which is made of rubber. It's chewing gum!** Chewing gum was originally made from chicle, a plant from Central and South America, but now many gum companies use rubber. No one knows who first used chewing gum, but it was in 1891 that Wrigley Company started making and selling it. **Many people say it helps them to concentrate, and the US army gives gum to its soldiers for this reason.** Today the industry is worth nearly twenty billion dollars a year. On to our next big money maker. The first telephone that could be carried around was invented in 1908. **In the 1954 film, Sabrina, a character played by actor Humphrey Bogart made a call from the back of his car!** But it was in 1973 that the modern mobile phone was invented by an American, Martin Cooper, and

in the 1980s 'mobiles' started to become popular. Many countries, including the UK, now have more mobile phones than people. Next is the iPod. It's small and light. It plays and stores music. **A company called Apple invented it,** but Vinnie Chieco was the man that gave the iPod its name. He saw the machine and thought of a line from the film *2001: A Space Odyssey*, 'Open the pod bay door, Hal!' The iPod arrived on the market in 2001. In 2007, from January to March, Apple earned 1.8 billion pounds from iPod sales. Our final big money maker is all about making money. In 1934 Charles Darrow showed a game to a company called Parker Brothers. Did they want to invest in it? No, they didn't. So, with a friend who worked in a printing company, Mr Darrow made 500 copies of the game and started selling them under the name 'Monopoly'. The idea of the game is to buy streets where you can build houses and hotels. It soon became popular and Parker Brothers agreed to produce it. Today the owners say they've sold over 200 million **Monopoly sets and 750 million people have played it.** The game is truly international: it's sold in 103 countries and **in thirty-seven languages.**

4 Give Ss 3–4 mins to discuss their answers and compare them with another pair. Monitor and note how well they use language from this section of the lesson. Elicit and discuss Ss' opinions in feedback. Find out which money-making idea the class thought was the best. Give feedback as necessary.

GRAMMAR   relative clauses

Watch out!

Ss tend to confuse the use of *who/which* for people/things, so highlight the difference clearly. Ss may also translate from their L1 and say, e.g. *He's the man that he sold me my car.* This error is connected to the use of defining/non-defining relative clauses, which is a more advanced language point and is not explicitly focused on here. Correct errors like these when they occur, but avoid any further explanation for now.

5 Ss do the exercise alone and compare answers. Meanwhile, write the sentences on the board. In feedback, elicit/underline the relative pronouns *who, which, that, where* and the clause that follows. Elicit Ss' answers and check the rules carefully. Ask *Is* chewing gum *a thing or a place?* A thing. *Do we use* who *or* which? Which. *Is* a friend *a thing or a person?* A person. *Do we use* who *or* which? Who. *Can we use* that *instead of* where? No, instead of *which or who*.

Answers: 2 that 3 who 4 that 5 where

▶ LANGUAGEBANK 8.1 p142–143

Ss can read the tables/notes in class or at home. However, draw their attention to the last point about the use of *the* not *a/an*. In Ex B teach *insurance, honeymoon*.

Answers:

A 2 which/that I sent you last week 3 restaurant where you can watch the chefs make your food 4 is the shop which/that sells cheap iPods and mobiles 5 accountant who/that helped me complete my tax form 6 where I learnt to do business 7 who/that invested the money was a criminal B 2 who/that borrows $1,000,000 to buy a horse. 3 which/that sells insurance. 4 which/that she lends me. 5 who/that was working as a chef? 6 where we went on our honeymoon.

PRACTICE

6A Check the words in the box and the example. Ss then work alone and compare answers. Elicit/check them in feedback.

Answers: 2 credit card 3 inventor

B Ss work alone to write definitions using relative pronouns and the prompts. Remind Ss to think carefully about which relative pronoun to use in each. Ss compare answers and then give feedback.

Suggested answers: 1 It's a place where people look after your money. (bank) 2 It's a thing that/which you use to carry money and credit cards. (wallet) 3 It's a person who/that gives money to a product or business (to make more money). (investor) 4 It's a place where you go to borrow books. (library) 5 It's a thing that/which you use to watch films. (DVD player)

C Divide the class into two groups: A and B. They look at the relevant exercise on p164 or p167. Working in pairs with another student from the same group (A or B), Ss write the definitions of the words in their crossword. Monitor to provide support where necessary. Also prompt Ss to correct their sentences before the next stage. Then put Ss in A/B pairs. They take turns to ask/give the definitions of the words. In feedback, nominate Ss to ask for/give definitions of their words in open pairs. Prompt Ss to self-correct/correct each other as needed.

Answers:
Student A:
Down: 4 pieces of money which/that are made of metal not paper 10 a person who/that owns something (he/she bought it or was given it)
Across: 6 a thing that/which you use to call someone 8 a place where you find cars, houses, shops, etc. 11 money that /which you use to start a business and make more money 12 a person who/that acts in films or theatre
Student B:
Down: 3 material that/which you use to make car tyres and chewing gum 7 a place where you stay when you are travelling 8 a person who/that fights for his country in wars 9 a thing which/that grows in the earth and is usually green
Across: 1 a thing that/which we use to pay for something (not a credit card) 5 a thing which/that you use to download and listen to music

SPEAKING

7 Elicit the names of the items represented in the photos (Levi jeans, iPhone, DVD, Nike trainers/sports clothes, Coca Cola, Porsche car, baseball cap). Give Ss 4–5 mins to discuss their answers. Monitor and make a note of problems, particularly with language from this lesson. In feedback, find out which things Ss think are the most popular, and why. Give feedback as needed.

WRITING adding emphasis

8A Check the rubric and vocabulary in the advertisement, e.g. *in good condition, features, hard drive, screen.* Ss read and answer the questions alone and then compare them. In feedback, check answers and elicit other examples about Ss' clothes, books, stationery, e.g. *This pen is fairly new. I bought it three weeks ago. This jacket is extremely comfortable. I wear it all the time.*

Answers: 1 adjective 2 extremely 3 fairly

B Ss work in pairs and choose the product they want to write about. Give them 6–8 mins to write the advertisement in 50–60 words. Monitor and support Ss with language they need where necessary; they could also use dictionaries. They might also want to draw/download a picture to illustrate it. Display Ss' advertisements around the class. They read them and choose the most convincing one.

Homework ideas
- Ex 4: write your opinion of the best money-making idea.
- Ex 8B: write an advertisement for another product of your choice.
- Language bank 8.1 Ex A–B, p143
- Workbook Ex 1–6, p46–47

PAY ME MORE!

Introduction

Ss learn and practise the use of *too much/many, enough, very* and multi-word verbs. They read and discuss why certain people/professions should earn the most money.

SUPPLEMENTARY MATERIALS

Resource bank p175

Ex 9A: download/bring pictures of other jobs that are not in the photos here, e.g. plumber, cleaner, dentist, traffic warden.

Warm up

Lead in to the topic of the lesson. Write this statement on the board: *Every job is important, so everybody should earn the same salary.* Ss work in pairs/groups. Give them 3–4 mins to agree/disagree with the statement, giving reasons. Elicit/discuss their answers in feedback.

READING

1A Ss look at the cartoon. Elicit details about it and elicit/check and drill *violin, violinist, flute, orchestra.* Ask *Who's playing harder/faster?* Give Ss 2–3 mins to read the text and then answer the question in pairs. In feedback, elicit Ss' answers and discuss their initial reactions to the opinions in the text (funny/justified/silly). Ask *Who do you agree with – the violinists or the director?*

Answers: The violinists say they play more notes than the other musicians and want more money.

B Check the rubric and questions, including *save the company time/space.* Give Ss 4–5 mins to read and answer the questions, and compare their answers. In feedback, check Ss' answers and incidental vocabulary they ask about, e.g. *5 foot 5 inches, whereas,* but don't check the multi-word verbs yet. This is done in Ex 2A.

Answers: 1 A, D 2 B 3 C, E 4 F

C Give Ss 3–4 mins to discuss their answers in pairs, and then with the class.

VOCABULARY multi-word verbs

2A Give Ss 1 min to find/underline the verbs. Then elicit them.

Answers: A give back B take back C give up D took over E give in F take up

B Ss complete the verbs and check them against the texts to confirm they're correct. Ss check their answers in Ex C.

C Ss listen and check their answers from Ex B. In feedback, elicit the answers and ask comprehension questions about the text to check meaning further, e.g. *give up: What do people give up doing at work? Why should they get more money?* Point out that all the verbs except *give in* can be followed by an object. Ss then listen to the verbs again and repeat. Elicit the words that are stressed.

Answers: 2 in 3 back (something) 4 up (something)
5 back (something) 6 over (something)
The preposition is usually stressed.

Unit 8 Recording 2

1 give up
2 give in
3 give back
4 take up
5 take back
6 take over

3A Check the sentences and elicit some examples. Give Ss 2–3 mins to note down their answers. Monitor and provide support where needed.

B Check/drill the example. Highlight the importance of showing interest in what their partners say and extending the conversation. Monitor while Ss exchange information and note Ss' problems with meaning/form with the multi-word verbs. In feedback, nominate Ss to speak/respond in open pairs. Prompt them to correct themselves/each other during this stage and give feedback as necessary.

speakout TIP

Read the speakout tip with Ss and emphasise the importance of recording multi-word verbs in sentences. They should do this now with the verbs they've just learnt. Then elicit other verbs Ss know and write them on the board, e.g. *get up, go out, come back, get back.* Ss work in pairs and think of example sentences.

GRAMMAR *too much/many, enough, very*

Watch out!

It takes time for Ss to acquire confidence with quantifiers as most languages use them in different ways, e.g. they don't distinguish between countable/uncountable nouns, the word order is different. Ss will therefore make mistakes as part of the learning process, e.g. *There are too much cars/too many traffics in the streets. I'm not enough paid.* It's important to present the language clearly and correct errors with quantifiers at every opportunity.

4A Do the first sentence as an example. Ss then work alone and compare their answers. In feedback, elicit Ss' answers and check the words/meanings in bold carefully.

Answers: 1 b) 2 c) 3 d) 4 f) 5 e) 6 a)

B Ss look at the cartoons and describe what's happening there. Ask *Why is it too much work but too many jobs?* Because work is uncountable and jobs are countable. Elicit Ss' answers and check them with the rules on the page. Check further. Give Ss countable/uncountable nouns. They have to make a sentence with *too*, e.g. *books/money: I've got too many books. He's got too much money.*

Answers: 1 too many (jobs) 2 too much (work)

> **LANGUAGEBANK** 8.2 p142–143
>
> Check the table/notes with your Ss, paying special attention to the notes on the different uses of *enough*. Ss can refer to the notes when they do the exercises. *Weaker Ss* should do Ex A and B in class.
>
> **Answers:**
> A 1 The film was great. It was ~~too~~ *very* funny. 2 There aren't *enough* eggs ~~enough~~ to make a cake. 3 That child eats too ~~much~~ *many* sweets. 4 Do you earn *enough* money ~~enough~~ to pay the bills? 5 I spent too ~~many~~ *much* time on the first question. 6 ✓ 7 ✓ 8 There isn't enough ~~of~~ time to do this exercise.
> B 1 too much 2 enough 3 too 4 too many 5 very 6 too 7 too much 8 not enough

PRACTICE

5 Do the first question as an example. Ss work alone and then compare answers. They should refer to the rules and examples in Ex 4 to check. *Weaker Ss* can also refer to the **Language bank** for help. In feedback, check the answers carefully, referring back to the rules and examples in Ex 4.

Answers: 1 enough time 2 too much 3 very 4 too 5 too many 6 enough

6A Elicit examples for question 1. While Ss write their answers, monitor and prompt them to correct their own mistakes if possible. Try to check all Ss' sentences before they do Ex B.

B Ss compare their sentences and find out what they have/don't have in common. They should prepare to report back to the class about themselves/their partner in feedback, e.g. *I worry too much about my health, but Juan doesn't worry about anything!*

SPEAKING

7A Check the rubric and give Ss 1 min to predict the professions on the recording. Elicit their answers and write them on the board. Ss listen and check. Discuss which professions on the board were correct (see answers in bold in the audio script).

Answers: footballers, fire fighters, doctors, teachers

B Ss discuss their answers in pairs. Elicit Ss' answers and write a list of possible answers for each question on the board.

C Ss listen and check the answers on the board against the recording. In feedback, elicit Ss' answers (underlined in the audio script) and any other details they remember about each answer, e.g. *Why do footballers earn too much money? Because they're twenty-years-old and they're already millionaires. It's crazy.*

Answers: 1 footballers 2 footballers 3 fire fighters 4 doctors 5 doctors 6 teachers

Unit 8 Recording 3

A: Personally, I think these **footballers** earn too much money. They're twenty-years-old and they're already millionaires. I think it's crazy.

B: I agree. They earn enough money in one week to buy a house, a car – anything. Now if you look at, say, fire fighters, who risk their lives …

A: **Fire fighters** don't earn enough.

B: They don't earn enough.

A: Or what about **doctors**? Certainly in Britain they work very hard.

B: They work too hard. One of my friends is a doctor and he sometimes does eighteen-hour shifts.

A: That's crazy.

B: Eighteen hours without a break. Again, they're saving people's lives.

A: **Teachers**, too. I think they should get much bigger salaries. They also work really long hours.

B: Yeah, although they do get good holidays.

A: Yeah. That's true.

B: Actually, I think they get too many holidays. There's Christmas and half-term and Easter and the summer. What is it in the summer – about six weeks?

A: Yeah, but I think teachers need it 'cause of all the stress.

8A First elicit the names of the professions shown in the photos and write them on the board if necessary. Then check the example answer. Give Ss time to think about their own opinions before they work in pairs. *Weaker Ss* could work together so that you can provide more help if necessary. Then give Ss 4–5 mins to discuss the questions. Monitor and note mistakes Ss make, especially those related to the target language in this lesson.

Answers: A security guard B teacher C IT consultant D footballer E surgeon F fire fighter

B Ss compare their ideas and find out what they agree/don't agree about. They should summarise the differences and prepare to report back to the class, e.g. *Two of us think that teachers should earn more because they play a very important role in people's lives, but the other two think doctors should earn more.* In feedback, invite Ss from each group to tell the class about their opinions. Find out which profession Ss think should earn the most money and why. Give feedback on language problems Ss had now or in the next lesson.

9A Put Ss into pairs/groups with Ss who have, or will have, different professions, if possible. Alternatively, show Ss pictures of other jobs they could talk about, or tell them to refer to the jobs in the **Photo bank** on p152. Give Ss 4–5 mins to choose a job and make notes of their answers to the question. They could refer to the text in Ex 1 as a model for a more light-hearted response, or to audio script 8.3 for a more serious one. Provide support where needed. Ss who want to talk about the same profession could work in pairs.

B Ss work with another student/pair and exchange ideas. Monitor and note down examples of good language Ss use, and problems they have. In feedback, invite Ss to give their/their partner's opinions to the class. Ss then vote for the profession they most think should earn more money. Give feedback on language problems Ss had, now or in the next lesson.

Homework ideas
- Ex 8 and 9: write your answer to one of the questions in these exercises.
- Language bank 8.2 Ex A–B, p143
- Workbook Ex 1–6, p48–49

I'M JUST LOOKING

Introduction

Ss learn and practise buying and describing things in the context of shopping.

SUPPLEMENTARY MATERIALS

Resource bank p176

Ex 1, 3A and 4B: Ss should have dictionaries available to check new vocabulary.

Ex 6, 7 and 8: use audio/video recording facilities for one or more of these exercises.

Ex 10A: download/bring pictures of unusual types of clothing, food and household appliances/equipment as prompts. Ss may need dictionaries.

Culture notes

People in the UK are changing the way they shop for food, clothes and consumer goods. Online shopping has become very popular because it's become safer to use credit cards online. People also want to avoid queues and save time and money. As far as food is concerned, there's a movement towards growing and eating 'real' food. People are more aware of their health and want fresh, ethically sourced ingredients rather than take-away or ready-prepared meals. More and more people are growing their own vegetables again, as they did 30–40 years ago.

Warm up

Lead in to the lesson via the photos. Elicit the different shopping situation in each photo: *online shopping, shopping in a street market/supermarket* and ask Ss to give more detail, e.g. *What are the people in each photo doing/buying? Are they enjoying it? Why/Why not?* Then ask Ss to think of two reasons why shopping in each of these ways is positive/negative, e.g. *quicker, cheaper*. Give them 3 mins to discuss this in pairs and report back to the class.

VOCABULARY shopping

1 Check the words/phrases in the word webs and elicit one more word for each section (see suggested answers below). Ss work in pairs and think of one or two more, using dictionaries if necessary. In feedback, elicit/check Ss' answers and write new words on the board.

Suggested answers:

shops: grocer's, baker's, chemist's
other places/ways: catalogues, ads in newspapers/shops, yard sale, car boot sale, mall, boutique, shopping channel, market seller, department stores, money exchange
people/services: sales assistant, tailor, personal shopper, exchange desk
product: price tag, wrapping/container, size, colour

2 Elicit one or two answers to each question. Ss discuss the questions for 2–3 mins and compare their answers with another pair. In feedback, check their answers and find out what they have in common.

READING

3A Ss cover the text and read the phrases in the box. Check the meaning of the title and elicit an example of a *do/don't* using phrases from the box, e.g. *DO: shop in markets because the food is fresh.* Give Ss 2–3 mins to make five more predictions about the article and compare them. Elicit their predictions and write them in note form on the board. Give Ss 2 mins to read the text and underline predictions from the board. In feedback, ask *Which predictions were right? Why/Why not?* Then check essential vocabulary Ss need for Ex B, e.g. *taste, eye level, ingredients, taxes, handling charges, waste money.* Alternatively, Ss can check it themselves in their dictionaries.

B Read and check the three parts of the rubric with Ss. They work in pairs and discuss each answer for 2 mins. For the last question, they should think of at least two pieces of advice for shoppers. In feedback, elicit/discuss the advice and ask *Which is the most useful?* Ask for a show of hands to decide this.

Optional extra activity

In pairs, Ss write a short advice list of their own Dos and don'ts for shoppers, or shop assistants.

FUNCTION buying things

4A Check the rubric and unfamiliar words on the list, e.g. *candle, hair product.* Ss listen to the five conversations and circle their answers. Play the recording again if necessary, and check Ss' answers (in bold in the audio script).

Answers: 1 b) 2 c) 3 a) 4 c) 5 c)

B Give Ss time to read the phrases from the recording and ask about unfamiliar words/phrases, e.g. *fitting room, fit, in particular, PIN (Personal Identification Number)*. Alternatively, they could use dictionaries to check new language. They then complete the phrases and compare their answers.

C Ss listen again and check their answers. In feedback, play the recording again, pausing after each answer to elicit/check it (underlined in the audio script).

Answers: 1 me 2 of 3 on 4 for 5 cash 6 here 7 enter

Optional extra activity

Ss listen again and number all the phrases in Ex 4B in the order they hear them. They then check their answers in the audio script on p173.

Unit 8 Recording 4
Conversation 1
W=Woman S=Shop assistant
S: Can I help you?
W: No, thanks. I'm just looking.
S: OK, just let me know if you need anything.
W: Thanks.
Conversation 2
M=Man S=Shop assistant
S: Hi there. <u>Are you looking for anything in particular?</u>
M: Yeah, do you sell those things that soldiers wear? Er … it's like a jacket.
S: Um, a type of jacket?
M: Yeah, a light green jacket with lots of pockets.
S: Ah, you mean **a flak jacket?**
M: Yes.

S: They're just on your left.

M: Ah, yes. Thank you. <u>Can I try this on?</u>

S: Of course.

M: Where's the fitting room?

S: Just over there.

M: Thanks.

Conversation 3

M=Man S=Shop assistant

M: <u>Excuse me. Do you have one of these in a larger size?</u> It doesn't fit.

S: Is that the Large? I'll just go and check for you. I'm sorry. This is all we've got in stock at the moment. There are some **other T-shirts** over there on the other side. There might be some Extra Large sizes there.

Conversation 4

W=Woman S=Shop assistant

W: Hello. I was wondering if you've got any of that stuff you use for cleaning swimming pools.

S: Um … yeah, we usually sell **a liquid cleaner**. You pour it into the pool. There's one here.

W: Can I have a look?

S: Yep.

W: How much is it?

S: This one's twenty-eight pounds ninety-nine for a litre bottle.

Conversation 5

M=Man S=Shop assistant W=Woman

S: Hi. <u>Are you paying by cash or credit card?</u>

M: Credit card.

S: <u>Can you enter your PIN, please?</u> Thanks. Here's your card.

M: Thanks.

S: Thank you. Who's next, please?

W: Do you take Mastercard?

S: Yes, that's fine. <u>Can you just sign here, please?</u>

5   Write the questions from recording 8.5 on the board and then play them twice. Tell Ss to listen for the main stressed words in each question. Elicit and underline them (as in the answer key). Then ask Ss to notice how *Do you* and *Can I* are pronounced. Play the questions again and elicit Ss' answers. Point out that *you* is pronounced /juː/ before a consonant and /jə/ before a vowel. Write the phrases in phonemic script on the board: *Do you* /dəjuː/, /dəjə/ and *Can I* /kənaɪ/. Ss listen again and repeat the questions chorally and individually, paying attention to the sentence stress and intonation of the question. Correct and help Ss to sound natural. Prompt them to self-correct or correct each other, if possible.

Answers: 1 Do you /dəjuː/ sell <u>pens</u>? 2 Do you /dəjə/ <u>have</u> one of these in <u>red</u>? 3 Can I /kənaɪ/ <u>try</u> it <u>on</u>? 4 Can I /kənaɪ/ try <u>these</u> on?

Unit 8 Recording 5

1 Do you sell pens?

2 Do you have one of these in red?

3 Can I try it on?

4 Can I try these on?

6   With *weaker classes*, play recording 8.4 again while Ss read it, if you think it will be helpful. They could underline the main stressed words in the sentences as they listen. Monitor while Ss read the conversations, helping and prompting them to self-correct their pronunciation. *Stronger Ss* could rehearse/ memorise one of the conversations and act it out to the class in feedback. If possible, record Ss reading the conversations and watch/invite comments on the recordings in feedback.

▶ **LANGUAGEBANK** 8.3 p142–143

Weaker Ss can refer to the information in the tables when they do the exercise. *Stronger Ss* should cover them.

Answers: A 1 help 2 on 3 fit 4 size 5 one 6 fitting 7 by 8 enter

7   Give Ss time to prepare both A and B roles they'll say. They then take turns to be Student A and practise the conversation. Monitor and make notes on problems of accuracy and pronunciation for feedback. Alternatively, give Ss time to rehearse and then record them. Play the recordings with the class and give feedback as needed.

8   First divide the class into Ss A and B. Student As read the information on p163, and Student Bs on p166. Put Student As into pairs, and Student Bs into pairs. Give them 3–4 mins to prepare their roles using the prompts. Monitor and provide support where needed. Ss then work in A/B pairs, facing each other. They take turns to start the conversations and act out the role-play. They could stand up, as if in a shop, if preferred. Monitor discreetly, making notes for feedback. In feedback, invite Ss to act out the role-plays to the class, or record them if you haven't done so yet. Give feedback and do remedial work as necessary.

LEARN TO   describe things

9A   Ss read the extracts from recording 8.4 and discuss the answers. Check them in feedback, asking Ss to give reasons.

Answers: *things* is used for countable nouns and *stuff* for uncountable nouns.

B   Ss discuss the answers in pairs. Elicit/drill the sentences in feedback. Point out that the phrases can be used with both countable and uncountable nouns.

Answers: 1: *It's a type of* pen. 2: *It's a kind of* oil that you use for cooking.

SPEAKING

10A   Check the rubric and example and elicit a few examples of less common clothing, food and domestic products/ appliances. Alternatively, use pictures as prompts for this exercise if possible, e.g. *a tie, glove, sandal, cucumber, onion, prawns, avocado, tin-opener, corkscrew*. Ss can work in pairs to choose their items and write a description of them. They can use dictionaries to find the words they need if necessary.

B   Ss work with different partners and take turns to describe/ guess the items. Nominate Ss to describe/guess the items in open pairs across the class in feedback.

Homework ideas

• Ex 7 or 8: write a conversation in a shop based on one of these exercises.

• Language bank 8.3 Ex A, p143

• Workbook Ex 1–5, p50

GOOGLE

Introduction

Ss watch an extract from the BBC *The Money Programme* about Google and its founders, Larry Page and Sergey Brin. The programme was broadcast in 2006. Ss then learn and practise how to talk about a money-making idea and write an entry for a competition.

SUPPLEMENTARY MATERIALS

Ex 5: if Ss are unlikely to know much about well-known internet companies, download/bring information about them.

Culture notes

Sergey Brin was born in Moscow in 1973 and moved to the USA with his parents when he was six. He met **Larry Page**, also born in 1973, at Stanford University in San Francisco, where they were both doing a PhD in computer science. They founded the **Google** company in 1998, and it went public in 2004, with a value of $23 billion. Three of the company's main concerns are the world's energy and climate problems, philanthropy and positive employee relations: Google has been voted Best Place to Work several times. The company headquarters is the Googleplex (Google complex) in Mountain View, south of **San Francisco**, in what is known as Silicon Valley, a world famous centre for high-tech computer companies. The name Google originated from a mis-spelling of the word googol, the large number represented by a 1 followed by one hundred zeros. The verb *to google* has now been entered into dictionaries.

Warm up

Lead in and create interest in the lesson via the photos of the San Francisco bridge/Larry Page and Sergey Brin and the Google logo. Ask *Where's this bridge? Who are these two men? What's the connection between the three?* Elicit Ss' answers. Use the **Culture notes** to support what Ss know about Larry and Sergey's biographical details, and the importance of Stanford University/San Francisco/Silicon Valley to Google and the computer industry. However, don't discuss information about Google in too much detail yet as Ss will focus on it in Ex 2 and on the DVD.

▷ DVD PREVIEW

1 Check the rubric and elicit some initial answers. Ss then discuss the questions in pairs. In feedback, find out what the most popular websites in the class are.

Culture notes

The title of this BBC programme is 'inspired' by the title of John Irving's book *The World According to Garp* (1978), a bestseller for several years.

2A Check the rubric and give Ss 2–3 mins to read the information and answer the question. In feedback, elicit brief answers as Ss will check new vocabulary in the text in Ex B.

Answer: It's changed the way people use the internet/ the life of millions of people, it was used by more than 400 million people a month in 2009, it's made its founders very rich.

B Ss read the definitions and match them to the words. Elicit/ check the meaning and pronunciation in feedback. Elicit the main stress in each word and drill it. Ss write the words in their notebooks, underlining the stress. Discuss what Ss think the title of the programme means, e.g. *this is how Google defines the world*.

Answers: 1 software 2 extraordinary 3 search engine 4 founder(s) 5 multibillionaires 6 revolutionised

Culture notes

Stonehenge is one of the most famous World Heritage Sites in the world: a prehistoric monument of standing stones located in the south west of England near Salisbury, and built over 4000 years ago.

▷ DVD VIEW

3 Ss read the sentences and work out what type of word is needed for each gap, e.g. noun/adjective. They can also use any previous knowledge of Google and its founders to guess the words and complete the sentences. Give Ss 1–2 mins to discuss their answers in pairs. Elicit answers and write them on the board. Ss then watch the DVD and check their answers. In feedback, check answers (in bold in the DVD script). Play the relevant sections of the DVD again if Ss have problems.

Answers: 1 students 2 university 3 tour guide 4 software 5 profitable

4 Ss read the statements and then watch the DVD. They compare answers and correct the false ones. Play the DVD again, pausing to check each answer (underlined in the DVD script). Ask more detailed comprehension questions, e.g. *Why do they have lava lamps and bouncy balls in their office? Why do they play hockey at lunchtime? What was the key word they chose as an example?* Also teach/check useful phrases in the script, e.g. *playground, childlike, hit the jackpot*.

Answers: 1 F: they always believed their software/system was a winner. 2 F: the office was a playground of lava lamps and bouncy balls. Lunchtime hockey in the car park was all part of how Google was going to be different. 3 T 4 T

Optional extra activity

Play the DVD again for Ss to watch/enjoy. Invite comments and questions from them as they watch, or afterwards. Discuss how they think Google has changed people's and the founders' lives.

DVD 8   The Money Programme: The World According To Google

P=Presenter SB=Sergey Brin

P: It's the fastest growing company in history, used by 400 million people a month. The internet search engine Google has turned its founders from students, to multibillionaires.
Tonight, *The Money Programme* does its own research on this extraordinary money-making machine and finds out how it's changed the lives of countless millions of people, who now inhabit the 'World According to Google'.
And these are the guys who made it all possible. Google's founders, Larry Page and Sergey Brin, still in their early thirties, and each worth an estimated 6 billion pounds. Theirs is a dramatic tale which began 10 years ago when Larry and Sergey were both **brilliant computer science students. The two met on a day out from Sergey's university. Sergey was acting as tour guide** for some prospective students, and Larry was in the group.

Larry and Sergey developed a piece of software which they believed could revolutionise searching the internet. <u>Larry and Sergey always believed their system was a winner.</u> <u>Lunchtime hockey in the car park was all part of how Google was going to be different.</u>

SB: It's a revolution, and you know, like the Industrial Revolution.

P: <u>Inside, the office was a playground of lava lamps and bouncy balls.</u> Sergey himself created the Google logo, with its childlike colours, to remind users that Google wanted to be a force for good.

In 2000, Larry and Sergey hit the jackpot. <u>And turned the corner from successful search engine, to successful business.</u> <u>Their secret? A special system of advertising.</u>

So how does it work? <u>Well, if you're trying to find out about, say, Stonehenge, here's what you get. These are ordinary search results and over here is a list of ads. They're from companies who have picked</u> *Stonehenge* <u>as a key word which triggers their ad to appear.</u> They are businesses who all think someone searching for Stonehenge might also be interested in them.

And that was how **a humble student project became the fastest growing and one of the most profitable companies ever.**

5 Elicit an initial answer to the questions. Elicit names of well-known internet companies, and provide information about them if possible. Ss discuss the questions in pairs/groups and report back to the class.

speakout a money-making idea

6A Ss read the summary and then listen and underline the answers. Play the recording again if they still have doubts. Elicit/check answers in feedback.

> **Answers:** 1 Cake 2 children 3 markets 4 doesn't need
> 5 website.

B Ss copy the **key phrases** into their notebooks and add sentences 1–5 where they think they should go. They then listen again to check. Ss correct any wrong answers and check them in pairs. In feedback, play the recording again. Pause at each key phrase (in bold in the audio script) to elicit/drill the complete sentences. Ask further comprehension questions, e.g. *What sort of shapes will the cakes be? What else will they put on the cakes? Where will they sell the cakes? How much money do they need? Where will they advertise?*

> **Answers:** 1 We plan to … 2 Our idea is to …
> 3 Our business is called … 4 To be successful, we need
> to … 5 We hope to make money by …

Unit 8 Recording 6

Our business is called The Very Special Cake Company. **Our idea is to** make delicious birthday cakes for children. We want to make interesting cakes shaped like animals or trains or faces. In fact, you can choose any shape you want and we'll make it for you. We'll also make the cake personal, by writing your name or a special message on it. **We hope to make money by** selling the cakes at local markets, in shops and on the internet. We don't need very much to start our business, because we can make the cakes at home. **To be successful, we need to** advertise in schools and have a beautiful website with lots of colourful photos. And **we plan to** go to markets and give people a free taste of the cakes, so they can try them, and then they'll definitely want to buy them!

7A Read/check the rubric and questions. Ss discuss hobbies/interests they have for 2–3 mins. Elicit/discuss some ideas for making money briefly and decide which are workable. Ss then work in groups and make notes of their ideas in more detail, using the checklist of questions. Provide help where needed.

B Remind them to use the **key phrases** as well as their notes from Ex 7A. While they prepare the presentation, monitor and prompt Ss to correct their notes if necessary. They should decide which part of the presentation each of them will present to the class, and rehearse what they'll say.

C While Ss present their ideas, the rest of the class listen and note down interesting/useful ideas. Monitor discreetly and make your own notes with examples of good language and problems. In feedback, Ss discuss the presentations and vote for the best idea. Give feedback as needed.

writeback a website entry

8A Ss read the advertisement for the competition. Check *entrepreneur* and ask *How much will the winner receive? What's the money for?* Ss then reread the entry and answer the question. In feedback, check the answer and the meaning of *a fair price.* Ask *Why is this different, do you think?*

> **Answers:** They will pay a fair price to the people making the clothes in their own country.

B Ss work alone/in pairs with partners they worked with for Ex 7. They write a draft of their entry, using the model in Ex 6 and their ideas from Ex 7.

Teaching tip

Encourage Ss to show their drafts to each other and ask for/give opinions and advice. Ss write a final draft of the entry when they're ready. They can email it to you or other Ss to be 'judged'. Alternatively, display Ss' entries around the classroom. Divide the class into different groups of 'judges'. They read the entries and decide which one most deserves to win the competition.

Homework ideas

• Ex 8B: write a final draft of the competition entry or write an entry for a different idea.

LOOKBACK

Introduction

Lookback exercises are designed to provide you and your Ss with an informal assessment of the language and skills covered in the unit. However, you might want sometimes to make them into a more formal test. In this case, set aside a lesson for Ss to do all the exercises with no help from you or their books. Monitor the speaking activities and make notes of Ss' performance (Ex 1B, 2C, 4, 5B). At the end of the lesson, check answers formally, awarding marks where relevant (Ex 1A, 2A, 3, 5A). Assess Ss' speaking skills from your notes and give them marks out of 20 (five marks each for fluency, accuracy, pronunciation, interaction).

MONEY

1A Read the first two lines of the poem with Ss. Ask *What is the poem about?* Elicit Ss' answers/predictions. Then elicit the two rhyming words at the end of each line *thin/win*. Tell Ss that rhyming words like these will help them complete the poem. Give them 1–2 mins to do this.

B Elicit/check Ss' answers after they've compared them. Then ask *What happened to Brenda Bones?* Elicit answers for the whole story, e.g. *First, she paid her bills. Then she … . After that she … .* Check/teach new language during this stage, e.g. *super-size hot air balloon, crash.* (Cameroon is in central/west Africa.) Read the poem aloud with Ss to give them confidence. Do this twice or more if necessary. They then practise reading it in pairs, saying alternate lines. Monitor and prompt them to correct mistakes with their pronunciation. In feedback, invite Ss to read the poem to the class. Ask Ss *What did Brenda learn? Do you agree?*

Answers: 1 bills 2 invest 3 lent 4 cash 5 borrowed
6 coins 7 tips 8 earn

RELATIVE CLAUSES

2A Check the example and ask *What other word can you use here? Why?* Answer: *which* for things. Tell Ss that they can sometimes use *who/that* in the exercise. Give Ss 3–4 mins to write the complete sentences and compare them. Monitor and note down problems with relative clauses for feedback. Check Ss' answers. Ask *Where could you also use* which? In question 2 (and also in question 4 and 6 + *in*).

Answers: 2 Pasta is the type of food *that* I eat most often. 3 My mother is the person *who/that* has helped me the most. 4 The town *where* I grew up is really beautiful.
5 My brother and sister are the only people *who/that* understand me. 6 The restaurant *where* I usually have lunch is expensive.

B Elicit one or two examples, e.g. *Saturday is the day I like best, Monday is the day I hate most.* Then give Ss 3–4 mins to rewrite the sentences. Monitor to provide support and encourage Ss to self-correct any errors they make.

C Check the example. Ss then work in pairs and compare and respond to each other's statements in the same way. Monitor and make notes for feedback or assessment. In feedback, nominate Ss to say their sentences/respond in open pairs. Give feedback as needed.

MULTI-WORD VERBS

3 Check the example. Ss then do the exercise in pairs, taking it in turns to ask the questions. Elicit/check Ss' answers in feedback.

Answers: 2 gave up 3 gave (it) back 4 took up 5 took (it) back 6 took over

TOO MUCH/MANY, ENOUGH, VERY

4 Look at picture A and elicit sentences about the problem, e.g. *There are too many people. There isn't enough space in the lift. The lift is very/too crowded.* Ss work alone/in pairs. Give them 4 mins to write as many sentences as possible about the other 3 pictures. Elicit/check the answers in feedback. Ss with the most correct sentences win.

Suggested answers:
A There are too many people. There isn't enough space in the lift. The lift is too/very crowded. B It's too/very cold. The woman isn't wearing enough clothes. There's too much snow. It isn't warm enough. C There's too much water in the bath. The bath is too/very full. D The plant doesn't have enough water. The earth is too/very dry.

BUYING THINGS

5A Do an example. Give Ss 5 mins to write out the conversations, and then compare answers. In feedback, check Ss' answers. To prepare them for Ex B, elicit the main stress in each sentence. Also remind Ss of the pronunciation of the weak forms and word linking in *Do you … ?* and *Can I … ?* Drill selected sentences to illustrate this.

Answers:
1 A: Can I help you? B: I'm just looking.
2 A: Can I help? B: Do you sell gardening tools? A: I'll just check.
3 A: Are you looking for anything in particular? B: Do you have one of these in red?
4 A: How is it? B: It doesn't fit. Do you have one of these in a bigger size? A: I'll have a look. Here you are. B: Thanks. It fits OK.
5 A: Who's next? Are you paying by cash (credit card) or credit card (cash)? B: Credit card, please. A: Can you just sign here, please?
6 A: Excuse me. Can I try this on? B: Yes, certainly sir. A: Where's the fitting room? B: It's on the left.

B Monitor while Ss practise the conversations to assess/help them with their pronunciation. Invite pairs to read them to the class. Do remedial pronunciation work with sentence stress, weak forms and linking if necessary.

OVERVIEW

WONDERFUL WORLD

Introduction

Ss revise and practise the comparative/superlative forms and vocabulary to describe nature in the context of talking about the environment.

SUPPLEMENTARY MATERIALS

Resource bank p178

Photo bank p158: download/bring maps of Ss' country/countries.

Warm up: photocopy the list of activities.

Ex 1B/3A: use a map of the world for Ss to name/find deserts, rainforests, etc.

Ex 7A: download/copy information about how to be 'greener' for the survey.

Warm up

Prepare Ss for the lesson. Write the list of activities below on the board (or photocopy them for Ss): *have a picnic in the park, take a boat trip on the river, walk in the mountains, go horse riding in the countryside, swim in a lake, watch the sunset on a beach, go surfing in the ocean, drive a 4x4 in the desert.* Ask Ss *Which of these activities would you most like to do this weekend? Why?* Elicit one or two answers. Then give Ss 1–2 mins to put the activities in order of importance for them. Ss then compare their lists in pairs and give reasons for their choices.

VOCABULARY nature

1A Use the photos to check the vocabulary in the questions. Then elicit a sample dialogue, e.g. A: *Have you ever swum in an ocean?* B: *Yes, I've swum in the Atlantic and Pacific Oceans.* A: *Really? Where exactly?* B: *I've swum on both sides of the Atlantic ... .* Ss ask/answer the questions in pairs and report back to the class.

B Read the word box and check *mountain range* in the example. Show Ss a map of the world if possible, and elicit examples of the things in the box. Give Ss 2–3 mins to think of or find more examples. In feedback, invite Ss to answer, and show the places on the map if available.

Suggested answers:
oceans: Pacific, Arctic, Indian, Antarctic
lakes: Michigan (USA), Toba (Indonesia), Baikal (Russia)
deserts: Sahara, Kalahari (Africa), Gobi (China/Mongolia)
rivers: Nile (Egypt), Amazon (Brazil, Peru, Bolivia, Colombia, Ecuador, Venezuela, Guyana), Yangtze (China), Mississippi (USA)
falls: Angel (Venezuela), Niagara (USA), Victoria (Zambia/Zimbabwe)
mountain ranges: Alps, Andes, Himalayas, Blue Mountains (Australia)
rain forests: Amazon, The Congo Basin Forest of Central Africa

▐▶ **PHOTOBANK** p158

1 Check *glacier, coastline.* Give Ss 4–5 mins to discuss their answers in pairs/groups. In *multilingual classes*, provide maps of Ss' countries if possible.

LISTENING

2A Check the rubric and example. Ss then discuss other problems related to the places in the photos here and on p158. Elicit Ss' ideas and write them on the board for Ss to copy.

Suggested answers: climate change/global warming means there's less water/food in hot countries, melting icecaps/glaciers so sea levels are rising, people throw rubbish/plastic bags in the oceans which causes water pollution, we cut down trees and don't plant more, we throw away too much food, there is too much packaging on food/products, we don't recycle enough, the population of the world is getting bigger, cars/traffic produce too much air pollution

B Ss listen to the programme and tick their ideas from Ex 2A if/when they hear them. They compare answers and report back to the class. Elicit any other details Ss remember about the problems mentioned on the programme.

Answers: The problems:
Big population: a big population causes big problems.
Water: many people have difficulty getting clean water. The deserts are getting bigger.
Animals: for the animals, there is less space than before. People are destroying the rain forests, so many species will become extinct.
Weather: the world is getting warmer. The ice is melting. Sea levels are rising,

3A Ss read the factfile, but don't check the words in bold until Ex B. If you have a map of the world, show the places mentioned in the factfile. Play the recording again. Ss underline the five mistakes and compare their answers. In feedback, play the recording again, pausing at each mistake to elicit the correct answer (in bold in the audio script). Check the meaning of *less/more*. Ask comprehension questions to check the answers further, e.g. *What's the largest desert in the world? What's happening to it?*

Answers: 1 there might be more than *nine* billion 2 But in the US, it's *600* litres. 3 And the deserts are getting *bigger*. 4 People destroy the rain forest to make more space for *houses*, roads and farms. 5 on Mount Everest there is *less* snow every year

Unit 9 Recording 1

Welcome to *Save the Planet* where we talk about the world's environmental problems. Now, did you know there are more than six billion people on the planet, and by 2050 **there might be more than nine billion?** People are living longer and healthier lives than ever before, but a big population means big problems for the planet. Let's look at three of the most important problems. The first problem is water. Many people in the world can't get enough water. But in some countries we use too much. A person in Gambia, Africa, for example, uses much less water than someone in the United States. In Gambia, one person uses four and a half litres of water a day. **But in the US it's 600 litres.** And to make the problem worse, the deserts are getting bigger. The Sahara desert is one of the hottest places in the world, and is already the largest desert. But each year it gets bigger than before, so it gets more difficult to find clean water. Our second problem is the animals. There are more people on the earth than ever before. This means we use more space. And for the animals this means that there is less space than before. One example is the Amazon rain forest. It has the highest number of plant and animal species in the world, but it's getting smaller every year. **People are destroying the rain**

forest to make more space for houses, roads and farms. In the last ten years we have destroyed more than 150,000 square kilometres of forest – that's an area larger than Greece! So in the future, many plants and animal species will become extinct. And the last problem on our list, but not the least important, is the weather. The world is getting warmer. The ice in Greenland is melting faster than ever before and on Mount Everest there is less snow every year. Also sea levels are rising. This means that soon some of the world's most important cities, like New York, London, Bangkok, Sydney and Rio de Janeiro might all be under water.

B Ss look at the words in bold and try to work out the meaning from context. In feedback, elicit/check and drill the words. Also check *species, go up, damage, exist, heat*.

Answers: 1 extinct 2 sea levels 3 population 4 destroy 5 melting

GRAMMAR comparatives/superlatives

Watch out!

The short/long comparative and superlative forms in English often cause problems for Ss as their L1 probably won't make this distinction. Ss tend to mix up the forms, e.g. *The most bigger problems are because of climate change.* It's therefore very important to highlight form clearly and give Ss adequate spoken and written practice in *full sentences*. Monitor and correct errors consistently to prevent fossilisation, i.e. to prevent mistakes from becoming acquired/habitual.

4A Ss should be familiar with the basic comparative/superlative forms so give them 1–2 mins to complete the rules and compare their answers. Then elicit/check them, referring to sentences 1–4. With *weaker classes*, read the sentences and rules with Ss and elicit other examples, e.g. *shorter, bigger, friendlier, more important, more/less time.*

Answers: With short adjectives, add + -er or + -ier to the end of the adjective (+ *than*); With longer adjectives use *more* + adjective. We also use *more/less* + noun to compare things.

B Follow the same procedures as in Ex 4A for the superlative form.

Answers: With short adjectives: use *the* and add -est to the end of the adjective. With longer adjectives use *the* + *most/least* + adjective.

C Give Ss 3–4 mins to do the exercise and compare answers. Play recording 9.1 again. Tell Ss to say *Stop!* at each answer (underlined in the audio script).

Answers: longer and healthier, the most important, less water than, worse, the hottest, the largest, bigger than, more difficult, more people, more space, less space than, the highest, smaller, larger than, the least, warmer, faster than, less snow, the world's most important

⯈ **LANGUAGE**BANK 9.1 p144–145

Read/check the tables and notes with Ss, especially the irregular forms and use of *as … as* (Ss are not expected to use *as … as*). Ss can refer to the tables when they do Ex A/B. N.B. *CVC* = consonant-vowel-consonant. In Ex B, Ss can use both the present/past tense of the verb *be* when possible.

> **Answers:**
> A 2 longer, than 3 noisier 4 more interesting than
> 5 more expensive than 6 more dangerous than 7 hotter
> than 8 more exciting than 9 less cold
> B 2 You're the best friend I've ever had. 3 That was/is
> the most boring film I've ever seen. 4 This is the shortest
> day of the year. 5 That was/is the longest run I've ever
> done. 6 This is the oldest building I've ever seen. 7 That
> was/is the hardest job I've ever done.

PRACTICE

5A Check the rules for the examples in the table. Ss then complete it and compare answers.

B Ss listen, check and compare their answers. Check the form/spelling of the answers, using the rules in Ex 4.

> **Answers:** higher, the highest; healthier, the healthiest; more difficult, the most difficult

Unit 9 Recording 2

1 long, longer, the longest
2 high, higher, the highest
3 healthy, healthier, the healthiest
4 difficult, more difficult, the most difficult

C Play the recording twice. Ss listen and underline the main stress. Check answers and highlight the unstressed *than* in sentences 2–4. Ss listen again and repeat chorally/individually. Prompt self- or peer correction of pronunciation mistakes.

> **Answers:** 1 It's the most <u>beau</u>tiful place I've <u>ever</u> been to.
> 2 It's <u>hotter</u> than I ex<u>pected</u>. 3 The food is <u>cheaper</u> than at
> <u>home</u>. 4 It's more <u>dangerous</u> than I <u>thought</u>.

Unit 9 Recording 3

1 It's the most beautiful place I've ever been to.
2 It's hotter than I expected.
3 The food is cheaper than at home.
4 It's more dangerous than I thought.

6A Do an example. Ss complete the exercise alone and compare answers. N.B. Tell them that more than one answer is possible in two sentences.

> **Answers:** 1 the most beautiful 2 warmer than
> 3 the nicest 4 healthier than 5 the furthest 6 bigger than
> 7 less friendly/friendlier than 8 the most/least polluted

B Ss prepare their answers before they work in pairs. Monitor and note how well they use comparative/superlative forms. Discuss Ss' answers and give feedback on persistent mistakes.

SPEAKING

7A Read/check the survey with Ss and elicit one or two answers to the questions. While they work, monitor and check the accuracy of Ss' questions before Ex B.

> **Suggested answers:** Do you … plant trees/turn off lights and electrical appliances/take showers not baths/ reuse plastic bags?

B First Ss should make a note of their own answers to the questions, giving reasons. Monitor and support Ss with language they need during this stage. They then take turns to answer/discuss each question, and make a note of the *yes/no* answers. Make notes of good use of comparatives/ superlatives and mistakes. Each group reports the results of their survey back to the class. Find out who is the 'greenest' group/person and why. Give feedback on Ss' performance as needed.

WRITING similar sounding words

8A Do question 1 as an example and ask *Why do people often spell these words wrongly?* Because they sound the same. Then elicit the difference in meaning between *you are* and *your*. Ss then do the exercise and compare answers. In feedback, check answers and elicit other words Ss know that have the same sound but a different meaning (homophones).

> **Answers:** 1 your 2 wear 3 two 4 write 5 see 6 their

B Ask *What does the writer do to protect the environment?* Ss read the comment and discuss the answers in pairs. They then underline the six mistakes and correct them. After checking Ss' answers, tell Ss to check their written work for mistakes before they give it to you.

> **Answers:** I think everyone should recycle. I've done this since I was a child and it's not difficult. Children need to be educated about the ~~write~~ right way to look after the world we live in. I use a bicycle to get to work every day, and I get very angry when I ~~sea~~ see people use a car to drive around the corner to the shops. ~~Their~~ There are lots of small things we can do to help the environment like turning off the television when ~~your~~ you're not watching it, using plastic bags for ~~you're~~ your rubbish, and recycling, ~~two~~ too.

C Ss work alone/in pairs to choose the topic they want to write about. Give them 10 mins to write it, using 70–100 words. Monitor and support them with language where necessary. In feedback, Ss can work in groups and read out their comments, or read them to the class. Alternatively, they can put them on the class blog for other Ss to respond to.

> **Homework ideas**
> • Ex 8C: write a comment about a different topic from Ex 7A.
> • Language bank 9.1 Ex A–B, p145
> • Workbook Ex 1–8, p51–52

INTO THE WILD

Introduction

Ss revise and practise the use of articles in the context of reading and talking about nature and the outdoors.

SUPPLEMENTARY MATERIALS

Resource bank p179

Ex 2A, 4 and 5A: Ss need dictionaries to check new words.

Warm up

Lead in to the topic of the outdoors. Ask Ss *Which would you choose for a two-week holiday: a walking/camping holiday around the countryside or beach holiday in a hotel? Why?* Ss discuss their answers in pairs/groups and report back to the class. Find out which kind of holiday is most popular with your Ss.

VOCABULARY the outdoors

1 Check the rubric/questions and elicit examples of *wild places*. Give Ss 3–4 mins to discuss the questions in groups and prepare to report back to the class, e.g. *Two of us like wild places, but three of us don't.* They should also give reasons for their answers.

2A Elicit a definition of *rural area* in question 1. Tell Ss to try to work out the meaning of *rural* from the context if they don't know the word. If they can't, they should check the meaning/pronunciation in their dictionaries. Don't ask for examples of the words here as Ss will talk about this in Ex B. Give Ss 3–4 mins to discuss/find out about the words and check their answers in feedback.

Suggested answers: 1 a place in the countryside 2 a place in the countryside which is very pretty 3 natural features that you can see that are very pretty 4 land which is protected by the government because it is very pretty and people can visit it 5 a building/place used for the study and protection of animals and plants that people can visit 6 a hot, wet area of very tall trees 7 natural parts of the land such as mountains or lakes 8 clean air found in areas which are not polluted

B Find out if question 1 is true for your Ss. If so, elicit/discuss their reasons for this. Ss then work alone and decide which sentences are true for them, making notes of the details, e.g. *The north of my country has an area of natural beauty called the Lake District. It's very popular with tourists.* Ss then work in pairs/groups and take turns to give their answers. In *multilingual classes*, put Ss from the same countries/areas of the world in different groups. Invite Ss to tell the class about sentences that are true for them. Give feedback on errors with the new vocabulary.

C Ss write the words in bold in their notebooks. Play the sentences several times: Ss listen and underline the main stress in each word. In feedback, elicit the pronunciation and stressed syllables in the collocations.

Teaching tip

Use finger highlighting to help Ss. Say the words naturally first, e.g. *natural beauty*. Then hold up the fingers of one hand and ask *How many syllables in 'natural beauty'?* Elicit/say *Five.* /ˈnætʃərəl ˈbjuːtɪ/. Ask *Where's the stress?* Elicit/say *On the first and fourth syllables.* At the same time, point to the thumb and fourth finger. Say the words again naturally, beating the stress, and drill them chorally and individually.

Answers: 1 <u>ru</u>ral <u>a</u>rea 2 <u>na</u>tural <u>beau</u>ty 3 <u>beau</u>tiful <u>sce</u>nery 4 <u>na</u>tional <u>park</u> 5 <u>wild</u>life <u>cen</u>tre 6 <u>tro</u>pical <u>rain</u> forest 7 geo<u>gra</u>phical <u>fea</u>tures 8 <u>fresh</u> <u>air</u>

D Ss listen and repeat the sentences chorally and individually. Prompt Ss to self-correct or correct each other where necessary.

Unit 9 Recording 4

1 I'd like to live in a rural area when I'm older.

2 The north of my country is an area of natural beauty.

3 Where I live there is a lot of beautiful scenery.

4 I went camping in a national park.

5 We visited the wildlife centre.

6 I'd like to visit a tropical rain forest.

7 My country has interesting geographical features.

8 I like being out in the fresh air.

READING

Culture notes

Tarzan was a fictional jungle hero character created by the writer Edgar Rice Burroughs in 1914, and popularised in cartoons and *Tarzan* films starring actor Johnny Weissmuller.

3A Elicit details of the pictures and teach *bees, nest, insect* and *jaguar*. Give Ss 2 mins to discuss the titles and predict what happened in each story. Elicit their ideas and note them on the board if necessary.

B Give Ss 2–3 mins to read the stories and check their predictions from Ex 3A in pairs. Ask *What was the same/ different in the stories?* In feedback, discuss which predictions were correct/incorrect. Ss will deal with unknown vocabulary in the next two exercises. Elicit what Ss know about Tarzan films.

4 Ss read the questions. Check *screaming, disappointed* and *frightened*. Give Ss 4–5 mins to write their answers and check them in pairs. Ss can check new words in their dictionaries, but only essential words they need for their answers, e.g. *mammal.* Elicit Ss' answers and check new words, e.g. *shy, disappear.*

Answers: 1 A bees' nest. 2 Because the bees were all over her. 3 She didn't see any interesting animals, only insects. 4 Tropical birds and mammals are very shy. 5 He saw a jaguar/A jaguar appeared in front of him. 6 The jaguar disappeared/ran off into the rain forest.

5A Ss find/underline the words in the stories. Do question 1 together. Ask *What do you think* disturb *means from the context?* Elicit answers, then tell Ss to check the word in their dictionaries.

Teaching tip

It would be good to focus on the usefulness of dictionaries at this point. Ask *What other information can you find out about the word* disturb *in your dictionary?* Elicit part of speech (verb), pronunciation, example sentence. Encourage Ss to become more autonomous and use their dictionaries more often. Give Ss 4–5 mins to complete the exercise with their dictionaries. In feedback, elicit/check the pronunciation, part of speech and an example sentence from the dictionary.

Suggested answers: 1 upset s.o. or sth by interrupting them 2 touch s.o or sth quickly and hard with your hand, a stick, etc. 3 take off clothing 4 move suddenly from side to side or up and down, usually with a lot of force 5 deliberately use violence to hurt a person or damage a place 6 become impossible to see any longer

B Ss cover the text and look at the pictures/words. Elicit ideas about how to start the stories, e.g. *Frances was on a jungle trip in Bolivia and there was a bees' nest in a tree … .* Ss then practise telling the stories in pairs. In feedback, nominate Ss to take turns telling different parts of the stories (in chronological order). The rest of the class listen and add/correct details where appropriate.

GRAMMAR articles

Watch out!

Articles cause confusion for learners because either they're used in a different way in their L1, or they're not used at all. However, there are patterns in the use of articles which help, e.g. *no article before plural nouns.* Patterns like these are revised in this lesson. It's particularly important that Ss learn, keep a record of and practise phrases with articles as fixed/semi-fixed phrases.

6 Ss read the rules/examples. Check the answer to question 1 as an example. Ss then work alone and compare their answers. In feedback, elicit Ss' answers and check each rule carefully. Elicit more example sentences for each rule, or read further examples in the notes in the **Language bank** on p144.

Answers: a) 1 b) 5 c) 4 d) 2 e) 3

⮕ LANGUAGEBANK 9.2 p144–145

Ask Ss to read the notes and tick ones that are the same as in Ex 6 on p91. Then check the other notes/examples. Ss can refer to the notes when they do the exercises. *Weaker Ss* should do Ex A and B in class. In Ex A, check *whale, bat, blood, squirrel, eagle.* In Ex B, check *zoo.*

Answers:
A 1 – 2 the 3 – 4 the 5 a 6 – 7 an 8 the 9 an 10 the
B I was feeling bored so I went for *a* walk. The trees were green and *the* sky was blue. It was *a* beautiful day. Suddenly I heard a strange noise, like *an* animal. But I knew it wasn't *a* cat because cats don't sound like that. *The* sound continued for a minute or more. I went home and switched on *the* TV to watch the local news. The newsreader said, 'Some animals have escaped from *the* city zoo.'

PRACTICE

7 Check the example. Ss then work alone and compare their answers. They can refer to the rules and examples in Ex 6 to check. In feedback, check the answers carefully, referring back to the rules and examples in Ex 6/the **Language bank**.

Answers: 2 I was one of many tourists in ~~the~~ South America. 3 A guide met us at the airport. The next day, *the* same guide took us hunting. 4 On *the* second day, the guide took us to a river. 5 I sometimes make ~~a~~ programmes in Britain. 6 In my job, I can explain *the* natural world to millions of people. 7 Generally I hate ~~the~~ insects, but especially bees. 8 I carried *a* rucksack for many years.

8 First elicit details about the picture and teach *bow, arrow.* Ask *Why are the boys running away?* Elicit some ideas. Give Ss 1–2 mins to read the text and check their ideas. Discuss the answer in feedback and check new words, e.g. *hunting, jumped up, missed, fortunately, gravity.* Then elicit the answer for gap 1 and ask *What's the rule?* No article with the names of states. Ss complete the text alone and compare answers. They must identify the correct rule. Monitor and prompt them to correct their own mistakes if possible. Check answers in feedback, eliciting the rule for each answer.

Answers: 1 – 2 – 3 – 4 a 5 the 6 the 7 – 8 a

SPEAKING

9A Give Ss 1–2 mins to read the comments. Check comprehension: ask *What's wrong/good about country life?* Ss then discuss the question in pairs. In feedback, elicit answers briefly as they will expand on their answers in Ex B.

B Elicit an example of one good/bad thing about living in the country/city and write them in four lists on the board. Ss copy and add other points to the lists working alone. *Weaker Ss* could work in pairs. Monitor and provide language Ss need if necessary.

C Ss take turns to talk about their preferences. Monitor and note down examples of good language/problems they have. In feedback, invite Ss to tell the class about their partner. Find out how many people prefer country/city life. Give feedback on language problems Ss had, now or in the next lesson.

Homework ideas
• Ex 9C: write two paragraphs explaining why you are a city/country person.
• Language bank 9.2 Ex A–B, p145
• Workbook Ex 1–4, p53–54

IT COULD BE A ...

Introduction

Ss learn/practise making guesses and giving themselves time to think in the context of talking about animals.

SUPPLEMENTARY MATERIALS

Resource bank p177 and p180

Photo bank p159: Ss may need dictionaries.

Warm up: make copies of the fable for the activity.

Ex 3A: download/bring a picture of a Monarch butterfly.

Ex 7B: download/bring pictures of a swift and a python.

Ex 10B: download/bring a picture of a chameleon.

Warm up

Lead in to the topic of the lesson. Use the fable below for a running dictation (or dictate it yourself). Place copies on the walls around the room. Ss work in A/B pairs. Student A runs to read the first sentence of the story, runs back and dictates it to Student B. When they have finished dictating the story, check it with the class, or give Ss a copy to check themselves. Then ask *Do you know this story/fable? What's the message?* Don't believe everything people tell you! (Don't trust people who flatter you!)

The Fox and the Crow

One day, a fox saw a crow in a tree. It was holding a big piece of cheese in its mouth. 'I must have that cheese,' thought the fox. So he said, 'Good morning, Miss Crow. You're looking very well this morning. I'm sure your voice is more beautiful than any other bird. Please sing for me.' The crow was very proud so she opened her beak to sing. Of course, the cheese fell out and the fox ate it!

VOCABULARY animals

1A First elicit/check the names of animals in the photos. Then teach language in the word webs, e.g. *wild, jaguar, insect, bee.* Ss copy the word webs into their notebooks and complete them with words they know. In feedback, draw the word webs on the board and invite Ss to complete them.

Alternative approach

Do the exercises in the **Photo bank** with Ss (see below) before they do Ex 1. Ss can then add the words they learn to the word webs.

Suggested answers: wild: monkey, lion, cheetah domestic/farm: cat, guinea pig, hamster, cow, pig, sheep, chicken insect: mosquito, fly, butterfly reptile: crocodile, lizard, alligator

B Elicit one or two examples and give Ss 2–3 mins to do the exercise. In feedback, go through the alphabet eliciting the names of animals for each letter.

⮕ PHOTOBANK p159

1 Check the headings. Ss can use dictionaries, if necessary. Check answers.

Answers: B dolphin C whale E lion F tiger G leopard I elephant J cow L spider M fly N butterfly O camel P bear Q eagle R ostrich S pigeon T penguin U tortoise V crocodile W snake X chimpanzee Y monkey Z gorilla

2 Ss discuss the questions in pairs/groups and report back to the class.

speakout TIP

Read the speakout tip and ask Ss if they already have a *study buddy* or regularly practise their English with other learners. If not, discuss why it's a good idea and discuss other ways of practising their English together.

LISTENING

2 Give Ss 2–3 mins to discuss and note down their answers to the questions using verbs, e.g. *talk, cook, run.* Discuss Ss' ideas in feedback.

Culture notes

A **triathlete** takes part in a triathlon which is made up of a swim, a cycle ride and then a run.

3A Ss look at the photos and read the introduction. Ask *Why did we invent the plane/boat/car? What's the quiz about?* Elicit Ss' answers. Using the photos, check *sea turtle, triathlete, black bear.* If possible, use your own picture to check *monarch butterfly* (orange with black edging round their wings). Then give Ss 3–4 mins to do the quiz. They should discuss/guess which might be the best answer to each question.

B Ss compare/discuss reasons for their answers and may modify them if they wish. Ss will check the answers in Ex 4.

4 Ss listen and tick the answers they got right, and correct the wrong ones. Check the answers to the quiz in feedback (underlined in the audio script) and find out which ones Ss got correct. Further comprehension will be done in Ex 5A.

Answers: 1 a) a monarch butterfly 2 b) a rat 3 b) a sloth 4 c) a university professor

5A Check language in the sentences first, e.g. *lay eggs, wires, survive, hide.* Ss then write their answers alone/in pairs.

B Ss listen and check their answers, and compare them. Play the recording again, or relevant parts of it, if Ss still have doubts. Nominate Ss to answer (see bold in the audio script). Discuss answers/information that most surprised Ss.

Answers: 2 monarch butterflies 3 rats 4 rats 5 human babies 6 sloths 7 (female) elephants 8 jays

Optional extra activity

Ss work alone/in pairs. They read the audio script and write 4–6 questions to ask other Ss, e.g. *How far do sea turtles travel a year? What do New York taxi drivers know?* Ss ask/answer their questions in groups (as a team game) or across the class.

Unit 9 Recording 5

Question 1

A: The best sense of direction? *Perhaps* it's the butterfly.

B: Er, I'm not sure.

A: It's hard to say. Well, *it could be* sea turtles.

B: *Maybe.*

A: They swim everywhere, don't they?

B: Um, *it might be*, but I think it's the butterfly. *It can't be* the taxi driver, can it?

A: *It's definitely not* the taxi driver.

C: OK, here are the answers. Sea turtles travel 3,000 miles a year. **And when they lay eggs, they go back to the place where they were born.** So they have a great sense of direction. New York taxi drivers drive 37,500 miles a year. They know the fastest way to any address in New York. But sea turtles and taxi drivers do not have the best sense of direction!

B: So *it must be* the butterfly.

C: <u>The winner is the monarch butterfly.</u> **At the end of every summer, they fly from Canada to Mexico.** And no one knows how they do it.

Question 2

A: Er, so who's the best athlete? That's a good question.

B: I'm not sure.

A: It could be triathletes.

B: Or rats.

C: <u>Rats are the winners.</u> A rat is the superman of animals. Rats can kill animals that are much bigger than they are, and **they can eat electric wires.** They can swim a mile and **survive in water for three days.** They can also jump three feet and fall forty-five feet and survive.

A: That's amazing.

Question 3

B: Who sleeps the most? Let me think. Erm, it can't be the human baby, can it? And it's not the black bear.

A: It must be the sloth. They spend most of their lives asleep.

B: So what's the answer?

C: Well, the black bear sleeps for about seven months a year. The females are even half-asleep when they have their babies.

B: Wow.

C: Human babies usually **sleep about eighteen hours a day, but only in their first few months.** <u>So sloths are the winner.</u> They sleep fifteen to eighteen hours a day for their whole life.

Question 4

A: Who has the best memory? That's a good question. It's hard to say.

B: It must be humans. We remember things for years.

A: Or elephants?

C: Here's the answer: **female elephants remember friendly elephant faces** and this helps protect the group. **Jays store their food in secret places and always remember where they put it.** <u>But humans are the winners.</u> We have the best memory because we are able to organise time. We have concepts like 'yesterday', 'last week', and 'tomorrow' and these help us to remember things better. We also have ways to record information like writing and photos.

B: I thought so.

FUNCTION making guesses

6A Ss listen to question 1 in recording 9.5 again and number the phrases in order. Play it again if necessary, and check Ss' answers (in italics in the audio script).

Answers: a) 2 b) 4 c) 3 d) 5 e) 1 f) 6 g) 7

B Elicit the answer to the first question as an example. Ss then complete the table and compare answers. In feedback, play the recording again and elicit/drill the answers in sentences, e.g. *Perhaps it's the butterfly. It could be sea turtles.*

Answers:
It's possible: It could be, It might be, Maybe, Perhaps
It's not possible: It can't be, It's definitely not
It's certain: It must be

C Read the questions with Ss and elicit their answers. Play the recording again if necessary for Ss to notice the silent letters.

Answers: 1 *Could* has a silent *l*. *Might* has a silent *g*. 2 *Must* has a silent *t*.

D Ss listen and repeat the sentences at least twice. Highlight the linking and silent *t* in *must be* /mʌsbiː/ and drill the phrase in isolation. Then drill the sentences chorally and individually, prompting Ss to correct themselves/each other.

Unit 9 Recording 7

1 It could be triathletes.

2 It might be.

3 It must be humans.

➡ **LANGUAGEBANK** 9.3 p144–145

Ss refer to the information in the tables when they do the exercise. Check *smell*.

Answers: A 1 e) 2 g) 3 h) 4 a) 5 b) 6 f) 7 c) 8 d)

7A Ss should do the exercise alone as the answer to the question and the language are sometimes closely related.

B Ss compare answers, and then check them on p164. In feedback, check the language questions in Ex 7A and the answers from p164. Find out how many questions Ss answered correctly. Show Ss pictures of a *swift* and a *python* (or draw them on the board).

Answers: 1 can't be (whale shark) 2 is definitely not (spine-tailed swift) 3 must be (ostrich) 4 It can't be (python) (snake) 5 Maybe it's (cheetah) 6 It's definitely not (mosquito) 7 must be (whale) 8 might be (tortoise)

LEARN TO give yourself time to think

8 Ss read the extracts from recording 9.5 and discuss the answers. Check them in feedback, asking Ss to give reasons.

Answers: B: Er, I'm not sure. A: It's hard to say. B: Um, it might be, B: Let me think. A: That's a good question.

9A Do an example. Ss then correct the other sentences and compare answers. Elicit/check and drill the sentences in feedback to prepare Ss for Ex B.

Answers: 1 A: Er, let me ~~to~~ think. B: Well, I'm not ~~much~~ sure, but I think … 2 A: Um, that's *a* good question. B: It's hard *to* say, but …

B Remind Ss about the pronunciation points in Ex 6C. Monitor while they practise, and help with pronunciation where needed. *Strong Ss* could memorise the conversations and act them out to the class in feedback.

SPEAKING

10A Check the rubric and extend part B's example. Elicit, e.g. *It could/might be a dog./Yes, maybe it's a dog./No, it can't be because … ,* etc. Give Ss 3–4 mins to speculate and discuss why the parts are special. Monitor and make notes on language problems for feedback later.

B Ss work with another pair and compare their answers before checking them on p164. Check how many answers Ss guessed correctly. Also ask what they learnt.

Homework ideas
• Language bank 9.3 Ex A, p145
• Workbook Ex 1–4, p55

THE NORTHERN LIGHTS

Introduction

Ss watch an extract from the BBC documentary *Joanna Lumley In The Land Of The Northern Lights* (2008). They then learn/ practise how to talk about an amazing place and write a travel blog.

SUPPLEMENTARY MATERIALS

Warm up: download/bring pictures of actress Joanna Lumley, e.g. in the TV series *Absolutely Fabulous* or *The Avengers*. Also, bring more pictures of the Northern Lights if possible.

Ex 1: download/bring a map showing Norway and the Svalbard archipelago.

Ex 5: download/bring pictures and a map of Fish River Canyon and Namibia.

Culture notes

The Northern Lights, or *aurora borealis*, most often occur from September to October and from March to April. This natural phenomenon is the result of an interaction between the Earth's magnetic field and solar wind. The Lights are most visible close to the North Pole because of the long periods of darkness and magnetic field.

Joanna Lumley (b. 1946) is an English actress, best known for her role as Patsy in the BBC TV comedy series *Absolutely Fabulous* (*Ab Fab*). She's also famous as a human rights and animal welfare activist. She was born in India and her family moved to Malaysia when she was two. In the programme, she travels up through Norway to Tromso, and then to Svalbard, an archipelago in the Arctic Ocean. It's the most northerly permanently inhabited place on Earth with temperatures of minus 30°C.

Warm up

Lead in and create interest in the lesson. Ss look at the photos in the book and cover the text. Ask *What does the photo show? What are the green lights?* Elicit/discuss Ss' answers, using the **Culture notes** if necessary. Then look at the photo of Joanna Lumley and show more pictures of her if possible. Ask *What do you know about her? Where's she from? What's she famous for?* Elicit/discuss what Ss know using the **Culture notes**.

DVD PREVIEW

1A Ss discuss the questions in pairs for 2–3 mins. In feedback, elicit Ss' answers. Show the map of Norway with Tromso, Svalbard, etc. For question 2, ask *Would you like to go to this place? Why/Why not?*

B Give Ss 2 mins to read and answer the questions in pairs. In feedback, discuss Ss' answers. Ask, e.g. *Why did she dream of being somewhere cold?* Also check/teach *get the chance to, sled.* Ss can discuss/predict the answer to the question at the end of the text.

Answer: She is an actress. She goes to the far north to make her dream of seeing the Northern Lights come true.

DVD VIEW

2A Ss read the information and complete the sentences in pairs. They should use what they know about Joanna Lumley and her journey from Ex 1B.

B Ss watch the DVD and check their answers. In feedback, check them (in bold in the DVD script) and elicit other information they can remember about each answer. Play the relevant sections of the DVD again if Ss aren't sure.

Answers: 1 snow 2 people 3 books 4 dogs 5 lights

3A Ss read the sentences and match the words in bold to the definitions. Do the first one as an example. Encourage Ss to look for clues in the context which will help them decide on the correct definition. Ss finish the exercise alone and compare answers. Check these in feedback.

Answers: a) hot and wet climate b) not definitely good or bad c) difficult to find d) amazing e) necessary f) happy to wait (maybe for a long time)

B Ss listen and order the sentences. After they've compared answers, play the DVD again, or the relevant parts of it, if necessary. In feedback, check Ss' answers (underlined in the DVD script). With *stronger classes*, you could ask more detailed comprehension questions related to each answer, e.g. *What did she look like when she was a child? What sort of books did she read? What were they about?*

Answers: 1 a) 2 c) 3 e) 4 b) 5 f) 6 d)

Optional extra activity

Play the programme again for Ss to watch/enjoy. Invite comments and questions from them as they watch, or at the end. Elicit what the Northern Lights look like and how they would feel if they saw them.

DVD 9 Joanna Lumley In The Land Of The Northern Lights

JL= Joanna Lumley T=Tura KS=Kjetil Skøglie

JL: The far north. Fairytale mountains. It's just fabulously beautiful. The land of the magical Northern Lights is somewhere I've longed for all my life. As a little girl I lived in the steamy heat of tropical Malaysia. I used to yearn to be cold. I'd never even seen snow. But my storybooks were full of snow queens, and now I'm entering that world. This is the journey I've always dreamt of making. I feel I've come into another world now: No people except you and us. And if we're very lucky we might see the elusive Northern Lights. I pack up things that are going to be essential on every trip. So in here I've got, for instance, oil-based pastels; and I've got a lovely little drawing book, but I've got coloured pages so that you can draw in different colours; a lovely old guidebook – it's called *The Land of the Vikings*. It's got beautiful old maps. Look at that. But if it wasn't for one item in my case, I wouldn't be on this journey at all. This is the book: *Ponny the Penguin*. This is when I first heard of the Northern Lights. And there was this picture which haunted me of a sort of rippling curtain and a little tiny penguin. This is not your average taxi rank at the station. I'm in the hands of Tura Christiansen and his team of eleven sled dogs.

Good morning. I'm Joanna.

T: Tura.

JL: Tura. How nice to see you, Tura.

T: Yes

JL: These are wonderful dogs.

T: They like to … to, er …

JL: They like to run?

T: Yes.

JL: The weather near Tromsø is uncertain. But local guide Kjetil Skøglie promises me we'll track down the lights even if it takes till morning. I can't see anything, Kjetil.

KS: No it's … it's nothing yet. You just have to be patient.

JL: OK, so I just wait here.

KS: Yeah, you just wait here.

JL: Yeah.

KS: Good luck.

JL: Thanks, Kjetil.
I stand in the pitch black by the side of the fjord, and wait. Look – much brighter there. Oh, something's happening there. Oh … Look up here! Look what's happening here!
Look at that! Oh … Oh! Look at this! And it just keeps changing and changing.
I can't believe I'm seeing this. It's fantastic and it's coming back again. I have been waiting all my life to see the Northern Lights. I'm as happy as can be. This is the most astonishing thing I have ever, ever seen.

4 Elicit some initial answers to the questions. Ss then discuss them in pairs/groups and report back to the class about their partner(s).

speakout an amazing place

> **Culture notes**
> Fish River Canyon in Namibia, Africa, is a gigantic ravine about 160 km long, up to 27 km wide and almost 550 m deep in places.
> The Grand Canyon in Arizona, USA, is 446 km long, from 6.4 to 29 km wide and 1.83 km deep in places.

5A Check the rubric and questions before Ss listen. They compare answers and listen again if they haven't understood and still have doubts. Elicit/answers in feedback. Show Ss a map and pictures of Namibia and Fish River Canyon if you have them, and discuss details from the **Culture notes**.

> **Suggested answers:** 1 Fish River Canyon is in Namibia, Africa. 2 It is the second biggest canyon in the world. It is silent.

B Ss read the **key phrases** and listen/check them. In feedback, play the recording again. Pause at each **key phrase** (in bold in the audio script) and elicit/drill the complete sentence.

> **Answers:** ✓ What did you think of it? It was amazing/ frightening/wonderful!, The first thing you notice is (how big it is). The best thing about it was (the silence), Would you like to go back?

Unit 9 Recording 8

A: OK, the most beautiful place I've been to. Well, a few years ago I went to Fish River Canyon.

B: Where?

A: Fish River Canyon. It's the second biggest canyon in the world.

B: After the Grand Canyon?

A: After the Grand Canyon.

B: Where is it?

A: It's in Namibia, in Africa.

B: Wow. And **what did you think of it?**

A: **It was amazing. The first thing you notice is** how big it is, of course.

B: Of course.

A: It just goes on and on as far as your eye can see. But **the best thing about it was** the silence.

B: Right.

A: It was so amazingly quiet. We went there in August and there weren't many tourists and it was just so quiet.

B: **Would you like to go back?**

A: I would love to go back. One day!

B: One day.

6 Give Ss 2–3 mins to make notes of their answers to the questions. Monitor and prompt Ss to correct their notes, if necessary. Provide help where needed.

7A First demonstrate the activity. Elicit example sentences using the **key phrases**, e.g. *The highest place I've ever been to is Mont Blanc in Switzerland. It was amazing! The best thing about it was the light.* Give Ss 3–4 mins to prepare what they'll say using the **key phrases**. Monitor and help with language where necessary. Ss then take turns to talk about their experiences in pairs.

B Ss work with another pair/group. First they take turns to talk about their experiences. Then they discuss which were the most interesting/exciting/dangerous. Monitor discreetly and note examples of good language and problems.

C Ss talk about their experiences while the rest of the class note down the most interesting/exciting/relaxing places. The class then decides which place was the most interesting/ exciting/relaxing of all. Give feedback as needed.

writeback a travel blog

8A Check the rubric and give Ss 1 min to answer the question. After eliciting their answers, check/teach *hire, less-than-perfect, chasing, leaves.*

> **Answers:** Namibia, because the Etosha National Park and the wildlife is incredible.

B Check the rubric and questions. Ss choose a place they talked about in Ex 6 (or another place of their choice) and decide if they want to work alone/with a partner from Ex 7. They write a draft of their travel blog, using the model in Ex 8A and the **key phrases**. Encourage Ss to show their drafts to each other and ask for/give opinions and advice. Monitor while they do this, providing support as needed. Ss can put the final draft of their travel blog on the class blog. Alternatively, display Ss' entries around the classroom for the class to read/ discuss.

> **Homework ideas**
> • Ex 8B: write a final draft of your travel blog, adding pictures if possible.

LOOKBACK

Introduction

Lookback activities are designed to provide revision and communicative practice in a motivating way. This helps the Ss and gives you the opportunity to assess their ability to use the language they've learnt in the unit. It's a good idea to monitor and assess individual Ss while they do the activities, and compare their performance with their results in more formal tests.

NATURE

1A Give Ss 2 mins to answer the questions alone with no help.

B Give Ss 2 mins to compare their answers and check them in the key. In feedback, check which pair had the most correct answers. Also ask *Which was the easiest/most difficult question?*

Alternative approach
Give Ss 3–4 mins to work in pairs/teams and discuss the questions together. Check each team's answers and give a point for each correct one. The team(s) with the most correct answers win(s).

Answers: 1 The Andes are higher than the Rockies. 2 Canada has a longer coastline (151,485 miles) than Russia (23,396 miles). 3 Lake Michigan (USA) is bigger than Lake Toba (Sumatra). 4 The Amazon is shorter, but wider than the Nile. 5 The Pacific is the deepest ocean. 6 Angel Falls, Venezuela, is the highest waterfall.

COMPARATIVES AND SUPERLATIVES

2A Do an example with *hot* and write the two forms on the board. Ss then write the correct forms for the other adjectives. Monitor and note down persistent errors Ss make and focus on them in feedback. Elicit/check Ss' answers, including the spelling, and do remedial work if necessary.

Answers: hotter, the hottest; better, the best; more lovely, the most lovely; cheaper, the cheapest; higher, the highest; more boring, the most boring; more healthy, the most healthy; longer, the longest; more exciting, the most exciting; faster, the fastest; older, the oldest; colder, the coldest

B Check the examples. Ss then take it in turns to test each other in pairs. In feedback, nominate Ss to ask/answer in open pairs across the class and prompt other Ss to correct if necessary.

3A Do question 1 with Ss as an example. Ss then complete the answers alone and compare them. Nominate Ss to answer, giving reasons for their choice of form, e.g *hard* is a one-syllable adjective so it ends with *-est*.

Answers: 1 the most organised 2 the hardest
3 the longest 4 the youngest 5 the tallest 6 the most
7 the fastest 8 the furthest/farthest

B Elicit the answer to question 1 as an example. Ss then do the exercise in groups, taking it in turns to ask the questions. Elicit/check Ss' answers in feedback. Find out if the groups have the same names in their answers to each question. Ensure that sensitive Ss don't feel uncomfortable during this exercise.

Optional extra activity
Use the **Photo bank** on p159 for this exercise. Put Ss into pairs/teams and number them 1, 2, 3, etc. Select the names of two/three animals from the pictures and say their names. Team 1 must make a comparative sentence (if you give them two words), or a superlative sentence (if you give them three), e.g. *shark, dolphin, whale. A shark is the most dangerous animal. A whale is the biggest/heaviest.* Ss get two points if they give a correct meaningful sentence, and one point if only the comparative/superlative forms are correct.

ARTICLES

4 Elicit the answer to question 1 as an example. Ask *Why is it the?* Because there's only one: *the nearest*. Ss can check in the **Language bank** on p144 if they know the correct answer but can't say exactly why. They then work in pairs and use the **Language bank** for each question if necessary. In feedback, elicit/check Ss' answers together with the correct rule.

Answers: 1 Excuse me, where's *the* nearest bank? 2 This city is big, but it doesn't have *an* airport. 3 ✓ 4 Hi. Would you like *a* drink? 5 Where's *the* money I lent you? 6 ✓ 7 She goes to *a* small school in the centre of London. 8 We missed the bus and waited an hour for *the* next one. 9 My sister is working in *the* United States at the moment. 10 Is there *an* internet café near here?

5 Again, check the rule. Ss check their answers in the **Language bank** if necessary. Elicit, check and correct Ss' answers in feedback.

Answers: 1 animals 2 the sky 3 a journalist 4 the lion
5 Argentina 6 the first day

ANIMALS

6A Give Ss 2 mins to find the nine words. Stop the activity after 2 mins. Invite Ss to write the answers on the board. The student with the most correctly-spelt words wins.

Answers: Across: crocodile, pig, snake, eagle
Down: chimpanzee, cow, whale, dolphin, turtle

MAKING GUESSES

7A Do picture A as an example. Encourage Ss to make as many sentences as possible with *must/might/can't be*. While they guess the others in pairs, monitor to check how well they are using the target language and give feedback after Ex B.

B Ss check their answers on p165. Give feedback as needed.

Answers: A Chile B France C Japan D Australia

Homework ideas
• Workbook Review and Check 3, p56–57
• Workbook Test 3, p58

OVERVIEW

10.1 TOP TEN CITIES

GRAMMAR | uses of *like*

VOCABULARY | describing a city

HOW TO | talk about where you live

COMMON EUROPEAN FRAMEWORK

Ss can describe their living conditions; can write short simple notes and messages relating to matters of everyday life.

10.2 CRIME AND PUNISHMENT

GRAMMAR | present/past passive

VOCABULARY | crime and punishment

HOW TO | talk about crime

COMMON EUROPEAN FRAMEWORK

Ss can read very straightforward factual texts on subjects related to their field of interest with a satisfactory level of comprehension; can participate in short conversations in routine contexts on topics of interest, e.g. crime.

10.3 THERE'S A PROBLEM

FUNCTION | complaining

VOCABULARY | problems

LEARN TO | sound firm but polite

COMMON EUROPEAN FRAMEWORK

Ss can make a simple complaint; can write personal letters describing experiences, feelings and events in some detail.

10.4 THE ZIMMERS ⦿ BBC DVD

speakout | an issue

writeback | a web comment

COMMON EUROPEAN FRAMEWORK

Ss can briefly explain why something is a problem, discuss what to do next, compare and contrast alternatives; can briefly describe past activities and personal experiences.

10.5 LOOKBACK

Communicative revision activities

BBC VIDEO PODCAST
How do you feel about city life?

This video podcast extends and consolidates Ss' vocabulary of describing a city and extends discussion on the advantages and disadvantages of city life. This video podcast would work well at the end of lesson 10.1, or at the start or end of unit 10.

TOP TEN CITIES

Introduction

Ss revise/practise different uses of *like* as a verb/preposition. They learn vocabulary to describe a city and practise writing a formal letter.

SUPPLEMENTARY MATERIALS

Resource bank p182

Ex 1: download/bring a world map and pictures of well-known cities not on the list on p165, e.g. Madrid, Vancouver, Berlin, Cape Town, Buenos Aires, São Paulo, Moscow, Bangkok.

Ex 3: use a world map here.

Warm up

Lead in to the topic of the lesson. Ask *What do you like about your town/city? Is it a nice place to live in? Why/Why not?* If necessary, write prompts for Ss on the board, e.g. *friendly, safe, clean, attractive, good facilities/nightlife/places to eat and shop, transport, interesting events.* Elicit some examples, then give Ss 4–5 mins to discuss the questions in pairs/groups. In *multilingual classes*, put Ss from different countries in different pairs/groups. In feedback, discuss Ss' answers and find out what Ss like/don't like about their town/city.

SPEAKING

Culture notes

Copenhagen is the capital of Denmark.

Dubai is one of the seven United Arab Emirates and the most populated/expensive.

Munich is the third largest city in Germany.

Sydney is the largest city in Australia, but Canberra is the capital.

Tokyo was named the world's most expensive city for expatriates in 2009.

1A If you've brought pictures of well-known cities, use them as prompts for the discussion. If not, elicit some examples of the best cities to live in. Give Ss 3–4 mins to discuss their choices in pairs, using the prompts from the warm up. In feedback, discuss Ss' answers and write their top ten favourites on the board.

B Ss read the text and then check the list of cities on the board against the list on p165. In feedback, ask *How many are the same/different? Do you agree with those on the list?* Elicit/discuss Ss' answers.

VOCABULARY describing a city

2A Give Ss 2–3 mins to answer the question alone or in pairs. Elicit and discuss reasons for their answers.

Answers: 1 + 2 − 3 − 4 + 5 + 6 − 7 − 8 + 9 + 10 + 11 − 12 −

B There are six positive sentences. Give Ss 3–4 mins to decide on the three most important ones, giving reasons for their choices.

C Ss compare their ideas with another pair and should try to come to an agreement on the three most important things for a city. In feedback, discuss Ss' answers. They should agree on/vote for the top three points.

LISTENING

3A First elicit what Ss know about the cities in the photos. If possible, elicit their locations on a world map. Check the rubric and play the recording. Ss should make notes of the positive/negative things mentioned, and compare their answers. In feedback, elicit as much detail as possible about the three cities.

Answers:
Speaker 1: Dubai. Good things: great shopping and nightlife, not much crime/the streets are safe, cheap taxis; problems: crowded, the traffic is terrible
Speaker 2: Tokyo. Good things: cheap Japanese food in supermarkets/restaurants, good public transport system, the metro is fast and cheap, lots of parks/green spaces; problems: metro gets very crowded
Speaker 3: Sydney. Good things: friendly young people, good atmosphere, streets are clean and safe, lots of things to see and do, beautiful buildings, one of the most beautiful coastlines in the world, perfect weather, great café culture; problems: too much traffic/terrible public transport system

B Ss read the questions first. *Stronger Ss* might be able to write some of the answers before they listen. Play the recording again. Ss write their answers and compare them. In feedback, play the recording. Tell Ss to say *Stop!* at each answer (in bold in the audio script).

Answers: 2 Tokyo 3 Sydney 4 Dubai 5 Tokyo 6 Dubai 7 Sydney

4 Give Ss 3–4 mins to read and underline the phrases. Tell them the words are not always exactly the same. Elicit/check the phrases in feedback (underlined in audio script 10.1) Then ask *Which of the three cities would you like to live in?* Ss answer the question in pairs/as a class.

Suggested answers: it's very crowded (question 12), It's a great city for shopping (question 9), it has really good nightlife (question 9), There are lots of parks and green spaces (question 8), There are lots of young, friendly people (question 5), The streets are clean and safe (question 1), There are beautiful buildings (question 4), Too much traffic and a terrible public transport system (questions 2 and 3)

Unit 10 Recording 1

Conversation 1
I=Interviewer R=Rick
I: Rick, you've lived in Dubai for … what, four years, right?
R: Yeah, four years.
I: So what's it like, living in Dubai?
R: Well, I read that Dubai is one of the world's fastest growing cities, so there are a lot of people, and it's very crowded. It's a great city for shopping, and going out. And it has really good nightlife, with lots of bars and clubs.
I: Is it a safe city?
R: Yes, there isn't a lot of crime. The streets are very safe. But one of the biggest problems is the traffic. Everyone drives a car here – petrol is still cheap, so the traffic's terrible. One good thing is the taxis though. There are lots of them, and they're cheap, so you don't have to drive.
Conversation 2
I=Interviewer S=Sasha
I: Sasha, you live in Tokyo, don't you?

S: That's right.
I: And, do you … do you like it? Do you like living in Tokyo?
S: Yes, Tokyo is a great city to live in. People think it's very expensive, but actually you can buy Japanese food in the supermarkets quite cheaply, and eating out in Japanese restaurants isn't expensive either.
I: How about getting around? What's the public transport like?
S: There's a really good public transport system here. The metro system is fantastic. It's very fast, and it's cheap, so lots of people use it. That's the only problem. It gets very crowded.
I: And what do you like best about living in Tokyo?
S: The food, definitely. I love Japanese food! And the green spaces. There are lots of parks and green spaces, so it's less polluted than you think.
Conversation 3
I=Interviewer C=Charlie
I: What about Sydney? What's Sydney like, Charlie?
C: Sydney is one of the best cities in the world. There are lots of young, friendly people living here, so there's a really good atmosphere. The streets are clean and safe and there are lots of things to see and do. There are beautiful buildings, like the Opera House. You can sit and watch the boats on the harbour. And it has one of the most beautiful coastlines in the world.
I: What's the weather like? Is it really hot?
C: The weather is perfect. It's never too hot and never too cold. You can eat outside all year round, so there's a great café culture with lots of places on the streets selling really good coffee.
I: So, are there any problems?
C: Problems? Not really. Traffic, I suppose. Too much traffic and a terrible public transport system.

GRAMMAR uses of *like*

Watch out!
Ss often translate from their L1 and say, e.g. *How is your city?* or confuse the forms in English, e.g. *How is it like your city?* Highlight/check the two forms clearly and correct errors at all stages of the lesson.

5A Ss match the sentences and compare answers before feedback.

Answers: 1 b) 2 c) 3 a) 4 e) 5 d)

B Write questions 1 and 3 on the board. Elicit Ss' answers and underline *be like* and *do you like* in the sentences. Ask *Which questions ask for a description/an opinion?* Questions 1, 2 and 4.

Answers:
rule 1: 3, 5
rule 2: 1, 2, 4

⟫ LANGUAGEBANK 10.1 p146–147
Ss can refer to the tables/notes when they do the exercises. In Ex B, check *peaceful*.

Answers:
A 1 What's your new job like? 2 Do you like my new dress? 3 What is tapas like? 4 What's the weather like there? 5 Do you like living in the country?
B 1 d) 2 b) 3 c) 4 e) 5 a)
C 1 I like ~~listen~~ listening to music. 2 ~~How~~ What is the flat like? 3 Did you like it? 4 What's he like ~~he~~? 5 What's ~~like~~ the weather *like*? 6 ~~Are~~ Do you like speaking English?

PRACTICE

6A Do an example and check the rule. Ss then do the exercise alone and compare answers.

B Ss listen and check their answers. Recheck the rules in feedback. Play the recording again for Ss to listen and repeat the questions.

> **Answers:** 1 it like 2 you like 3 What's (your new flat) like 4 do you like

C Elicit example questions for question 1. Ss then write their own. Monitor and help with with accuracy, prompting them to self-correct.

D Elicit example questions/answers for question 1. Monitor while Ss take turns to ask/answer their questions. Again, prompt Ss to correct their mistakes. In feedback, nominate Ss to ask/answer their questions in open pairs across the class. Encourage Ss to correct each other's errors and do remedial work if necessary.

> **Suggested answers:**
>
> 1 A: I've never been to Stockholm? What's it like?
> B: It's great. It's a big city, with lots of good shopping, and good nightlife.
> 2 A: Do you like living in Paris?
> B: Yes. I love it! It's one of the most beautiful cities in the world.
> 3 A: What's your flat like?
> B: It's lovely. It's big and modern, but it's a long way from the city centre.
> 4 A: What do you like best about living in Barcelona?
> B: The nightlife. There are lots of clubs and bars, with lots of young, friendly people.

Unit 10 Recording 2

Conversation 1

A: I've never been to Madrid. What's it like?
B: It's a lovely city. There's a great atmosphere and the people are really friendly.
A: What's it like?

Conversation 2

A: Do you like living in Moscow?
B: I love it! It's one of the best cities in the world.
A: Do you like living in Moscow?

Conversation 3

A: What's your new flat like?
B: It's very small, but it's near the city centre.
A: What's your new flat like?

Conversation 4

A: What do you like best about living in Rome?
B: The food. I love Italian food!
A: What do you like best about living in Rome?

SPEAKING

7A Elicit/discuss some cities Ss know well, including those Ss talked about in the warm up. Give Ss 4–5 mins to write their notes. Help Ss with language if they need it.

B In *multilingual classes*, put Ss from the same country in the same groups. Monitor discreetly while Ss describe their chosen cities, making notes of examples of good language and problems. They should discuss/agree on one city which should be in the top ten places to live in the world. In feedback, nominate Ss from each group to tell the class about the city they've chosen to be in the top ten, giving reasons. The class then vote for one of them. Write examples of Ss' errors and good language on the board. Ss discuss and correct the errors in pairs.

WRITING using formal expressions

8A Give Ss 2 mins to answer the question. Discuss their answers and write useful new vocabulary on the board.

B Give Ss 1 min to read the letters quickly and answer the question. Check the answers. Ask *Where do they intend to build the new car park?* Check *stadium*. Ss can then read the letters again and underline the reasons given to support the writers' opinions. In feedback, elicit/check them and ask Ss who they agree with most.

> **Answer:** Greg

C Check the rubric/example. Ss underline the informal expressions in the second letter. In feedback, discuss which style they should use to write to the city/town council.

> **Answers:** informal: Just a quick note, Also, Speak to you soon, Best wishes

D Check the meaning of *mayor* and *issue* in the rubric. Then give Ss 3–4 mins to discuss issues in their town/city and decide on the most important. In *multilingual classes*, put Ss of the same nationality together. Elicit/discuss the issues and write useful language on the board. Ss then write their letter alone. While Ss write the first draft, monitor and provide support. Also encourage them to show their work to a partner before they write a final draft. If you have a class blog, Ss could post their letter on it, or send it to you.

> **Homework ideas**
> - Ex 8D: write a final draft of the letter, or another one about a different problem in your town.
> - Language bank 10.1 Ex A–C, p147
> - Workbook Ex 1–9, p59–60

CRIME AND PUNISHMENT

Introduction

Ss learn/practise the use of the present/past passive forms in the context of reading and talking about crime and punishment.

SUPPLEMENTARY MATERIALS

Resource bank p181 and p183

Photo bank p159: Ss may need dictionaries.

Ex 2C: dictionaries should be available for Ss to check words they need.

Warm up

Lead in to the topic and language of the lesson. Write examples of 'modern' crimes on the board, e.g. illegal downloading of music/films/books, etc. from the internet, DVD piracy. Ask *What do you think of this crime? Is it serious? Do you think material on the internet should be free for everybody? Should people who commit this crime be punished? How? Should they go to prison or get a fine?* Give Ss 3–4 mins to discuss the questions in pairs/groups, and then as a class.

SPEAKING

1A Ss read the words in the box, but don't check them until they've tried to match them to the photos. In feedback, elicit/teach the words Ss know/don't know and drill the pronunciation. Ss copy the words and underline the main stress.

Answers: A speeding B drink driving C graffiti D murder E credit card fraud

B Check the rubric with Ss.

Teaching tip

Do this exercise as a ranking activity. Ss first decide on the order alone, making notes of their reasons. They compare their answers in pairs, and must persuade each other to agree on the same order. They then work with another pair, and do the same thing. Monitor and help Ss with language they need. In feedback, elicit each group's order and write it on the board. Ss should then discuss/come to an agreement on the same order as a class.

C Elicit some examples briefly. Ss discuss the question for 3–4 mins and report back to the class. In *multilingual classes*, put Ss of different nationalities in the same pairs/groups.

READING

2A Check the rubric and the title of the text. Give Ss 3–4 mins to answer the questions and compare answers. In feedback, nominate Ss to answer. Check *fine/prison sentence*.

Answers: 1 He stole books from a bookshop. 2 He was sent to read books to hospital patients. 3 Giving punishments that fit the crime, e.g. not prison sentences.

B Check the example and elicit other alternative sentences for this crime. Ss then discuss the other crimes for 4–5 mins and note down their ideas. Elicit/check all answers in feedback. Ss should make notes and vote for the best alternative sentences for each crime.

C Give Ss 4–5 mins to read and check the ideas mentioned there. They should use dictionaries to check essential vocabulary. In feedback, nominate Ss to talk about the ideas from Ex B that were mentioned. Check new words if necessary.

D Check the rubric and elicit an example for each opinion e.g. *I think it's a great idea because it helps criminals to learn from their crimes/helps other people.* Divide the class into As/Bs. Student As work in pairs and think about the advantages; Student Bs work in pairs and think about the disadvantages. Give them 3–4 mins to discuss/make notes of their ideas. Monitor and support Ss with language they need if necessary. Ss then work in A/B pairs and exchange opinions. Monitor and make notes on good language/errors Ss make for feedback. In feedback, nominate Ss from each pair to take turns to tell the class about an advantage/disadvantage. The class then discuss/vote on whether alternative sentencing is a good idea or not. Give feedback as required.

Optional extra activity

In groups, Ss discuss alternative sentencing for more serious crimes, e.g. murder, bank robbery, kidnapping. They should refer to the questions in paragraph 3 of the article in Ex C, to help them, e.g. *Is it possible? What does it depend on?*

VOCABULARY crime and punishment

3A Check the example. Give Ss 2 mins to write and compare their answers. In feedback, check/drill the words.

Answers: 2 prison sentence 3 graffiti 4 community service 5 theft 6 shoplifter 7 fraud 8 shoplifting 9 fine

B Give Ss 2 mins to complete the tables, and check their answers.

Answers: criminal: thief, shoplifter; crime: theft, fraud, shoplifting; punishment: prison sentence, community service, fine

speakout TIP

Read/check the speakout tip with Ss. Elicit other examples from the lesson so far, e.g. *punish/punishment, crime/criminal.*

▶ PHOTOBANK p159

1 Ss can use their dictionaries if they have difficulty matching the words. In feedback, elicit/check and drill the answers.

Answers:
People: 1 B, D, E, F, G 2 A, E, (C) 3 B 4 A
Verbs: 5 D 6 F 7 G 8 E 9 C

2 Give Ss 3–4 mins to write sentences. Check them in feedback.

Suggested answers: Police officers arrest criminals, help victims and investigate crimes. Judges give prison sentences/fines to criminals.

GRAMMAR present/past passive

Watch out!

Ss usually find the passive form easy to understand but may make mistakes with the form/past participle, e.g. *He didn't was arrested. The thief was never catched.* They may also use the passive when the active would be more appropriate, e.g. *I'm sorry. The money was stolen by me.* vs *I'm sorry. I stole the money.* It's important to check the form/use of the passive carefully and provide appropriate practice in natural contexts.

4A Ss complete the tables alone and compare answers. In feedback, elicit and write the passive sentences on the board. Underline the form: *be + past participle.* Refer Ss to the irregular verb tables on p127 and remind them to review the past participle forms as often as possible.

Answers:
present passive: A man *is caught* stealing books from a bookshop.
past passive: The man *was sent* to read stories.

B Check the rubric with Ss and read the sentences in Ex 4A again. Elicit their answer to the question and complete the rule.

Answers: The *active* sentences say *who* does the actions.
Rule: Form the passive with: subject + verb *to be* + past participle.

C Give Ss 3–4 mins to find/underline other examples of the passive in the article and compare answers. In feedback, elicit the examples and check form/meaning. Ask, e.g. *Are they in the present or past passive? Do we know who caught the man/ boys/shoplifter? No. Is it important? No.* Then ask *What do we say if we want to say who did the action?* Elicit/teach and write on the board *The shoplifter was caught by the manager/police. She was sent by the judge to speak to shop owners.*

Answers: A man is caught … , The man is sent to read stories … , Two boys were caught writing graffiti … , the boys were told to do community service, A shoplifter was caught shoplifting … , She was sent to speak to shop owners, … he was told to keep all the equipment …

⇒ LANGUAGEBANK 10.2 p146–147

Ss can refer to the tables/notes when they do the exercises. *Weaker Ss* should do Ex A and B in class. In Ex B, check *snails*.

Answers:
A 1 is served 2 was given 3 aren't caught 4 was written 5 are shown 6 are arrested 7 wasn't told 8 were sent
B 1 Snails are eaten by the French 2 *Crime and Punishment* was written by Dostoyevsky 3 I was asked some questions by a journalist 4 All of our programmes are produced by Alejandro Ledesma 5 Most of the roles in that film were played by Alec Guinness 6 The best chocolate is made by Swiss companies

PRACTICE

5A Check the example. Ss then write the sentences alone and check in pairs. In feedback, nominate Ss to write the answers on the board, using contracted verb forms.

Answers: 2 I'm called Jim by my friends. 3 I'm told that I am like my father. 4 When I was younger, I was helped by many teachers. 5 On my last birthday, I was taken to Disneyland. 6 Last Christmas I was given an iPod. 7 I'm paid every month by my company. 8 I was chosen as captain of my football team when I was at school.

B Check the example and elicit similar examples which are true for your Ss, e.g. *When I was a child, I was taught to be polite.* Give Ss 4–5 mins to write personalised sentences and compare them. Monitor and help Ss with language they need, and prompt them to correct their own mistakes. Ss then compare their sentences with a different partner(s) and find out what they have in common. In feedback, they should tell the class about their similarities/differences, e.g. *I'm told I'm like my mother, but Hiroshi is told he's like his uncle.*

SPEAKING

6A First ask *What crime did the people in each story commit?* Give Ss 3–4 mins to read and answer the question. Check their answers (stealing sweets, internet fraud, art theft). Check vocabulary if necessary, e.g. *gun, water pistol.* Ss then complete the stories with the correct verb forms.

Answers: 1 were arrested 2 started 3 were stopped 4 was sent 5 asked 6 bought 7 stole 8 was taken 9 were caught

B Check the rubric and refer Ss back to the alternative sentencing in the article in Ex 2A. Elicit how the sentencing in the cases there fitted the crimes. Give Ss 5–6 mins to discuss alternative punishments like the ones above. Monitor closely to provide help with ideas and vocabulary where needed. Ss should then prepare their presentation to the class, decide who is going to talk about which story, etc. While Ss present their ideas, the class should make notes of the ideas they liked. At the same time, make notes on Ss' use of the language they've studied in this lesson for feedback/remedial work later. When Ss have finished their presentations, the class discusses/votes for the best idea for each crime.

Optional extra activity

Ss role-play the 'trial' for one of the crimes in groups. Each student chooses his/her role: the judge, the lawyers for the prosecution/defence, and the criminal(s); there could also be witnesses for the prosecution/defence. Ss choose the crime they want to role-play and then prepare/rehearse their roles. Provide support where needed. Ss then act out their role-plays to the class.

Homework ideas

• Ex 6: write an article about the arrest and sentencing of the criminals in one of the stories.
  Language bank 10.2 Ex A–B, p147
• Workbook Ex 1–7, p61–62

THERE'S A PROBLEM

Introduction

Ss learn/practise ways of complaining about problems and how to sound firm but polite. They also practise how to complain politely in an email.

SUPPLEMENTARY MATERIALS

Resource bank p180

Warm up: photocopy the sentence stems for Ss.

Ex 1A: Ss may need to use dictionaries here.

Ex 7 and 8: use audio/video recording facilities for the role-plays if available.

Warm up

Lead in and prepare Ss for the lesson. Write/dictate these questions: *When did you last make a complaint about something? What was the problem? Who did you complain to? What did you say? How did the other person respond? Were you happy with the result of the complaint? Why/Why not?* Elicit answers to the first two questions, e.g. *Two months ago. My neighbours were having very noisy parties every weekend.* Ss work in pairs/groups. They take turns to ask/answer the questions and make notes of their partners' answers. In feedback, Ss report back to the class. *Do you complain if something is not as it should be? Usually, sometimes, rarely, never. When was the last time you complained?*

VOCABULARY problems

1A Ss first look at the photos. Elicit a description of each one, e.g. *traffic jams.* Ss then read the phrases and check the words in bold. They could use dictionaries to check unfamiliar words. In feedback, check answers and the meaning of the words in bold.

Answers: A 7 a traffic jam B 2 litter C 4 faulty equipment D 1 delays E 5 someone speaking loudly on a mobile phone

B Check the rubric and example. Ss then work in pairs and choose three things from Ex A that most annoy them. Check answers in feedback and find out which single thing most annoys the class.

FUNCTION complaining

2A Check the rubric. Tell Ss to focus only on the two questions, and not get distracted by the other information. They listen, note down their answers and then compare them. In feedback, check answers (in bold in the audio script) and play the relevant part of the recording again if Ss have problems.

Answers:
1 Conversation 1: in a hotel Conversation 2: in a restaurant Conversation 3: at a train station
2 Conversation 1: the air conditioning doesn't work Conversation 2: slow service and an extra charge on the bill Conversation 3: train delays

B Ss read the questions first. They then listen, make notes of their answers and compare them. Monitor to check if they need to listen again to add more details to their notes. In feedback, elicit/check Ss' answers (underlined in the audio script). Ask *Why is the problem of the snow so surprising?* Teach *kidding* (a colloquial word for *joking*).

Answers: 1 to look into it right away and send someone up 2 polite 3 twenty minutes 4 he waited another hour 5 he said it's a very busy time of year 6 for over an hour 7 because the cause of the delay is the wrong type of snow

3A Check the example and the meaning of *look into it.* Ss do the exercise and compare answers.

B Give Ss 2–3 mins to check their answers in the audio script. In feedback, elicit/check answers.

Answers: 2 R 3 R 4 C 5 R 6 C

Unit 10 Recording 3

Conversation 1

G=Guest R=Receptionist

G: Oh hello. Could you help me? **There's a problem with the air conditioning.**

R: Oh yes?

G: I've just tried to switch it on, but it doesn't work.

R: Is it completely dead?

G: Completely. Absolutely nothing.

R: OK, we'll look into it right away. I'll send someone up. It'll be about five minutes, OK?

G: Thanks.

R: You're welcome. And sorry about that.

Conversation 2

W=Waitress D=Diner M=Manager

D: I'm afraid I have a complaint. Could I speak to the manager, please?

W: Yes, of course.

M: Good evening, sir. I understand there's a problem.

D: Yes. I'm afraid I have a complaint.

M: Oh?

D: Well, we got here at eight. And then **we waited about twenty minutes for a table.**

M: Right.

D: This is for a table we'd booked for eight, OK? Then **we waited another hour for our meal.**

M: Right.

D: One hour. Then when the bill arrived they put this **extra charge** on it.

M: An extra charge? That's probably the service charge.

D: Well, could you check this for me, please?

M: Yes, that's service.

D: Well, to be honest, I don't want to pay this.

M: Of course not. Well, sir, I am really sorry about that. It's a very busy time of year.

Conversation 3

W=Woman M=Man

W: Excuse me. Do you work here?

M: Yes.

W: Do you know when the next train will be arriving? I mean, I've been here for over an hour.

M: I'm sorry but there's nothing we can do at the moment. **Everything is delayed.**

W: And you don't know when the next train is coming?

M: No.

W: Or why there's a delay?

M: Snow.

W: What?

M: Snow on the track. It was the wrong type of snow.

W: What do you mean 'the wrong type of snow'? You're kidding, right?

▶ LANGUAGEBANK 10.3 p146–147

Ss can refer to the information in the tables to help them with this exercise.

Answers:
A 1 A: Excuse me. I'm afraid I have a complaint. B: What's the problem? A: The shower doesn't work. B: We'll look into it right away.
2 A: Excuse me. Could you help me? B: Yes. A: There's a problem with the internet connection. B: I'm sorry but there's nothing we can do at the moment.
3 A: Excuse me. Could I speak to the manager? B: Yes. A: I've been here for over an hour. B: I'm really sorry about that.

4 Ss read the sentences first. Check *appointment, flight delay, faulty engine, right away*. In feedback, elicit and drill the complaints/responses.

Answers: 1 d) 2 a) 3 b) 4 c)

LEARN TO sound firm but polite

5A Give Ss 1 min to discuss their answers. In feedback, check Ss' answers. Refer to the speakout tip, if necessary.

Answer: We use the phrases before making a complaint.

B Ss listen to the sentences, underline the stressed syllables and compare their answers. Play the recording as many times as necessary for Ss to be sure. For feedback, write the sentences on the board and elicit/underline the stressed words (see answer key). When Ss listen again, show Ss how the voice rises on the stressed words in polite intonation by using your hands/arms, as if you were conducting an orchestra. They then listen again and repeat. Again, play the recording several times until Ss are confident. Then do individual repetition and correction as needed.

Answers: 1 <u>Could</u> you <u>help</u> me? 2 I'm <u>afraid</u> I have a <u>complaint.</u> 3 Ex<u>cuse</u> me, <u>could</u> I speak to the <u>manager?</u>

speakout TIP

Read the speakout tip with Ss and discuss their answers.

6 Check the word box and do an example. Ss work alone and check their answers in pairs. In feedback, elicit/drill the answers. Ss can then practise reading the conversations in pairs to help prepare them for Ex 7. Monitor and help Ss with their pronunciation while they practise.

Answers: 1 A: Excuse me. Could I *speak* to the manager? A: There's a *problem* with the TV in my room. It *doesn't* work. 2 A: Excuse me. I ordered room service over an hour *ago*. Can you look *into* it, please? 3 A: *Could* you help me? I'm *afraid* I have a complaint.

7 Set up the role-play carefully. First divide the class into As and Bs. Student As look at p165 and Student Bs at p166. They check the instructions and ask for clarification if necessary. They then work in pairs to prepare for the role-play. Monitor closely and support Ss where needed. Then put Ss into A/B pairs for the role-play. Monitor and make notes of how well they use the target language for feedback later. Invite pairs to act out their role-plays to the class. Ss must listen and decide which pair was the most firm, but polite. If possible, record Ss' role-plays.

SPEAKING

8A Check the rubric/sentences with Ss. Then give them 2 mins to work alone and decide which they find most annoying.

B Prepare Ss for this role-play in the same way as in Ex 7 above. They should refer to the language in the previous exercises for help. Provide support while they do this, especially with polite intonation. During the activity, monitor discreetly, making notes of both good language and errors for feedback.

WRITING

9A Check the rubric carefully and elicit an example before Ss do the exercise. In feedback, check Ss' answers and move to Ex B where they will find specific examples.

Answer: Parts of the email are too direct/rude.

B Give Ss 2 mins to underline the words/phrases and compare answers. In feedback, elicit suggestions for making the words/phrases more polite.

Answers: 1 … very mad about 2 (the equipment was) rubbish 3 Give me (a refund) 4 Write back to me now. 5 Goodbye!

C Ss rewrite the letter using the words/phrases in the box. In feedback, nominate Ss to take turns to read out each sentence. Prompt Ss to correct themselves/each other.

Answers:
Dear Mr Ripoff,
I *would like* to complain about my course at the Noparlo School of English. Firstly, I was very *disappointed with* the classes. The teacher was always late. Secondly, your advertisement said there was a Self Access Centre with modern equipment, but a lot of the equipment was *faulty*. Finally, the classrooms were dirty and full of litter. *I would like to receive* a refund for the last two weeks of my course. *I look forward to hearing from you soon.*
Yours sincerely,
Katya Szabo

D Ss write the letter alone, though *weaker Ss* might like to work together. Give them 6–7 mins to draft and write the letter, using their answer from Ex C as a model. Monitor and prompt Ss to self-correct where possible. Ss then compare their letters and make changes to it for the final draft if necessary.

Homework ideas
- Ex 9D: write an email from the person in conversation 2 or 3 in Ex 2 complaining about what happened in the restaurant/at the train station. Alternatively, write a complaint about something that happened to you.
- Language bank 10.3 Ex A, p147
- Workbook Ex 1–4, p63

THE ZIMMERS

Introduction
Ss watch an extract from the BBC documentary *The Zimmers Go To Hollywood* (broadcast in 2007) about a group of elderly people who form a rock band. They then learn/practise how to talk about an issue they feel strongly about and write a web comment about it.

SUPPLEMENTARY MATERIALS
Warm up: download/bring a recording of the song *My Generation* and copy the lyrics of the song. Also bring pictures of The Who.

Ex 3A: download/bring a picture of the album cover of the Beatles *Abbey Road*.

Culture notes
The Who (1964) is an English rock band formed by guitarist Pete Townshend, singer Roger Daltry, bass player John Entwistle and drummer Keith Moon (Moon and Entwistle died in 1978/2002). They were famous for smashing their instruments at live performances. Among their albums are *My Generation, Quadrophenia* and the rock opera *Tommy* which was made into a film. *My Generation* (1965) became one of The Who's most recognisable songs and is considered one of the 100 best rock songs of all time. It was written by group member Pete Townshend for rebellious British youths in the 1960s and expressed their feeling that older people didn't understand the younger generation.

Warm up
Show Ss pictures of The Who and elicit what Ss know about them (see **Culture notes**). If you don't have a recording of the song, play a few seconds of the first scene of the DVD, showing the old people singing and smashing things (as The Who did). If you have them, give each student (or pair) a copy of the song lyrics. Play the song while Ss read the lyrics. Ask *What's the message of the song? Do young people still think about older people in the same way?* Elicit and discuss Ss' answers and check vocabulary in feedback.

DVD PREVIEW
1 Give Ss 3–4 mins to discuss the questions. In feedback, elicit/discuss their answers and list problems they mention on the board. They can refer back to them in Ex 3.

Culture notes
The cover of the Beatles' album, *Abbey Road* (1969), has become one of the most imitated in recording history.

2 Check the title of the text and read the glossary for a *zimmer frame* at the bottom. Ss then read and answer the questions. In feedback, check answers and show them a picture of the *Abbey Road* album if possible. (They will see the Zimmers crossing Abbey Road in the same way as on the album cover in the DVD.)

Answers: 1 The Zimmers are a group of old people who formed a band. 2 They're the world's oldest rock band. 3 They had a successful song on YouTube. Tim Samuels made a film about them. 4 They are going to be interviewed on a chat show.

Culture notes
Richard and Judy and Graham Norton are well-known British TV presenters, while Jay Leno has a famous TV chat show in the USA.

George Clooney, the American actor, became famous on the TV series *ER* and in the *Ocean's 11/12/13* films. He now acts and directs films.

A care home is a residential home for elderly people. It has qualified staff and nurses who provide personal care to residents if necessary, e.g. help with washing, dressing, eating, medication, etc. There are both public and private care homes in Britain.

▷ DVD VIEW
3 Ss should read the descriptions before they watch the DVD. Check *injured, care homes, bingo club.* Ss watch the DVD and then compare their answers. In feedback, elicit answers (in bold in the DVD script). Also refer back to the list of problems on the board from Ex 1. Ask *Were any of these problems shown on the DVD?* Elicit and discuss Ss' answers.

Answers: 1 Joan 2 Winnie 3 Alf

4 Ss read the facts. Check the meaning of *combined age* before they watch the DVD again. After they've compared answers, play the DVD again, or the relevant parts of it, if Ss haven't been able to answer all the questions. Alternatively, play the DVD again in feedback, pausing at each answer for Ss to check (underlined in the DVD script).

Answers: 2) 3,000 3) 82 4) 16 5) 90 6) 2 million

Optional extra activity
Play the DVD again, pausing at suitable points. Ask questions/elicit descriptions of the contrasts they see: the old people's lives at home, the glamour of Hollywood and the fun they had making the record/video.

DVD 10 Power To The People: The Zimmers Go To Hollywood

R&J=Richard and Judy JL=Jay Leno GN=Graham Norton TS= Tim Samuels G=George Clooney J=Joan W=Winnie A=Alf

R&J: The Zimmers. Hurray.

JL: The Zimmers.

GN: The Zimmers!

TS: Who'd have thought it would come to this? <u>When forty isolated old people formed a rock band.</u> This is the story of how <u>The Zimmers, with a combined age of nearly 3,000,</u> took the rock world by storm. And even took their message all the way to Hollywood.

G: Congratulations, you guys. Hello. Hi, I'm George. How are you? I hear you're all over the chart.

TS: Four months ago, we set about making a film about what it's like being old in Britain today. We found many who were lonely and forgotten, cast aside by society.

J: Hello.

TS: Hello, Joan. I'm Tim.

<u>82-year-old Joan</u> had been stuck indoors since a bad fall three years ago.

J: When I have left the flat, it's only ever for something like that, the doctor's, the dentist ... you know, not ... I haven't been for pleasure.

TS: 99-year-old Winnie was a serial care-home mover. She just couldn't find one that felt right. Over the last decade, <u>she'd moved care homes 16 times.</u> Boredom drove Winnie from her last home. How do you feel about leaving this place?

W: Nothing but joy.

TS: And 90-year-old Alf was facing the closure of his local bingo club, which meant there would be nowhere to meet his friends.

A: I'm gonna lose these people, when that closes, because I've gotta find new friends. And at our ages, it's so difficult.

TS: So, we thought we would try and get these cast-aside old people heard again. And what better way than record a charity single, and try and storm the charts.
All we had to do was convince them we were serious. Eventually, forty pensioners took a leap of faith and came together at the world famous Abbey Road Studios, to record a cover version of The Who's *My Generation*. The name of their band, The Zimmers. It was a day when people made friends, and came alive again.

W: I've never kissed a hundred-and-one-year-old yet.

TS: What's more, it looked like we might even have a decent single on our hands. And when we made the video available online, it proved a sensation. Two million people watched it in the first few days.

5 In *multilingual classes*, put Ss from different countries together. Ss discuss the questions and make notes about question 3: problems for old people in their countries. In feedback, discuss their answers as a class. Discuss the question briefly with Ss. Then give them 2–3 mins to talk about other ideas and report back to the class.

> **Suggested answers:** 1 Their lives probably changed when they became famous because they got more money. They travelled the world and made new friends. They did interviews and had their photographs taken. They were probably able to have better lives after being famous. 2 and 3 Ss' own answers

speakout an issue

6A Ss read the word box. Check the meaning/pronunciation of *issue* and any other words they have doubts about. Ss then listen to the recording and tick their answers. Check them in feedback.

> **Answers:** food, public transport

B Ss read the summaries, then listen and complete them. Give them 1 min to check their answers in pairs. Play the recording again if Ss don't agree on the answers, or they haven't completed all the gaps. Ss will check their answers in Ex C.

> **Answers:** 1 food 2 abroad/other countries (New Zealand, South Africa)/the other side of the world 3 delayed/cancelled 4 better

C Ss read the **key phrases** first. Check *get fed up with*. Then give them 3–4 mins to read audio script 10.5 and do the exercise. In feedback, check answers to Ex B (in italics in the audio script). Then check the **key phrases** (underlined in the audio script) and ask more detailed comprehension questions. e.g. *Where do the apples in supermarkets come from? What does the government say about using cars?*

> **Answers:** One thing that really annoys me, I don't understand why, I get fed up with, I think … should

Unit 10 Recording 5

A: One of the things that really annoys me is *when I buy food in the supermarket*, and I see that, for example, I buy apples, yeah, and here in the UK we grow a lot of apples. And I go to the supermarket to buy some apples, and *they come from New Zealand, or South Africa, or something*. And, I just think it's crazy. I mean, I don't understand why we pay for apples *to come millions of kilometres, from the other side of the world, when we grow them right here in this country*. It really makes me angry.

B: I get very fed up with public transport, you know, buses and trains, and that kind of thing. I mean the government says that we shouldn't use our cars, and we should travel by public transport. But it's horrible. It's crowded and *there are delays*. I use the train to get to work, and so many *times I arrive late because the train gets cancelled, or delayed*, and you know I'm paying a lot of money for my ticket, *so I just think it should be better*. I think the service should be better.

D Ss discuss their chosen issues and make notes of their answers to the questions. Monitor and provide support or language Ss need if necessary.

E While Ss work in groups, monitor and note down examples of **key phrases** Ss use well or not. In feedback, first find out about the issues Ss talked about, and then if they agreed with other people's ideas or not. Give feedback on Ss' use of **key phrases**.

writeback a web comment

7A Give Ss 2–3 mins to answer the questions. Then elicit the answers and teach/check, e.g. *clear it away, collect/drop litter, dirty/dirtier.*

> **Answers:** 1 Rubbish/litter left on the streets and beaches. 2 The writer feels angry. 3 Ss' own answers

B With *weaker classes*, first elicit answers for the prompts. Ss can use an issue from Ex D or E. Provide support where needed.

> **Homework ideas**
> * Ex 5: write your answer to question 2.
> * Ex 7B: write about another issue you feel strongly about using the prompts.

LOOKBACK

Introduction

If you have a *stronger class*, it's a good idea to ask Ss to write their own versions of some of the discrete-item test types, e.g. *gap fills for vocabulary/grammar, jumbled words for vocabulary, word ordering in sentences, questions/answers to match, sentences with a mistake to correct.* See the optional extra activity after Ex 2B as an example of what Ss can do. Use Ex A/B test types in the **Lookback** sections for more ideas. Ss can write one or two short tests in pairs/groups and then give them to another pair/group to answer. Ss usually find this kind of activity quite rewarding as it is not only competitive but shows them how much language they know.

SUPPLEMENTARY MATERIALS

Ex 1: bring pictures of famous cities/buildings in your Ss' country or other countries as prompts.

Ex 5B and 6: use audio/video recording facilities if they are available

DESCRIBING A CITY

1A Ss can do this exercise as a race between pairs/teams. The first to finish with all the correct answers wins.

Answers: 1 traffic 2 buildings 3 polite 4 transport 5 crime 6 streets 7 nightlife 8 expensive

B In *monolingual classes*, Ss could describe the place but not mention its name. The other person must guess where it is. Alternatively, display pictures of famous cities/buildings as prompts. Ss take turns to describe a place and their partner has to guess which it is.

Possible answers: 1 There's a lot of traffic in the city centre, and on the road around the city. 2 There are a lot of beautiful buildings in the city, but I never have time to see them! 3 Many people in the city are not friendly and polite. They are too busy. 4 There is a good public transport system here. The metro is fast and cheap. 5 There isn't a lot of crime here. 6 There streets are not very clean, and at night they are not very safe. 7 There isn't good nightlife here. You have to go to a bigger city for that. 8 It's expensive to live here now. Going out is very expensive.

Optional extra activity
Ss work in pairs and write 4–5 more sentences with an extra word, using the different forms/uses of *like*. They exchange sentences with another pair and correct the sentences.

USES OF *LIKE*

2A Give Ss 2–3 mins to rewrite the sentences and compare answers.

Answers: 2 What food do you ~~to~~ like most? 3 What's your capital city ~~it~~ like? 4 What do you like about where ~~do~~ you live? 5 What's ~~about~~ the food in your country like? 6 What ~~like~~ are the people like where you live?

B In *multilingual classes*, put Ss of different nationalities together. While Ss ask/answer the questions, monitor and note down problems they have with the use of *like*. Give feedback/do remedial work on this, or use the information for assessment.

Suggested answers: 1 Today, it's hot and sunny. 2 I like Italian food, like pasta and pizza. 3 Warsaw? It's a big city, and very busy. It has good shopping and nightlife, but there's a lot of traffic. 4 Where I live is a very small town, so there aren't a lot of things to see and do, but it's very friendly. 5 The food in my country is very good. We eat a lot of meat and fresh vegetables. 6 Where I live there are a lot of old people. And many of them are not very friendly!

Optional extra activity
Ss write two or three more sentences each with *like* as a verb/preposition and ask and answer them in groups. They can choose any topic they like.

CRIME AND PUNISHMENT

3 Give Ss 3–4 mins for the exercise and to compare answers. As a follow-up, Ss write new sentences with the words, e.g. *She was given a 5-year prison sentence for theft.* Alternatively, Ss write the sentences but leave a gap for the word. They give their sentences to another student/pair to complete.

Answers: 1 prison sentence 2 community service 3 shoplifter 4 theft 5 fraud 6 fine 7 thief 8 writing graffiti

PRESENT/PAST PASSIVE

4A Ss do the exercise without any help. In feedback, check the answers but don't discuss them further until after Ex B. Check answers after the next exercise.

Answers: 1 b) 2 d) 3 f) 4 e) 5 c) 6 a)

B Ss discuss their answers and decide if they are true/false. In feedback, check answers and elicit what Ss know about *penicillin* and the other names/places in the exercise.

Answers: All are true except 3 (the answer is Alexander Fleming – Ian Fleming wrote the James Bond books) and 5 (Hawaiian).

COMPLAINING

5A Do an example first. Ss then do the exercise alone and compare answers before feedback. Monitor and assess how well Ss can use the language. Do remedial work in feedback if necessary.

Answers: 1 afraid 2 into 3 have 4 doesn't

B Monitor and assess Ss' pronunciation while they practise. Encourage them to memorise the dialogue and rehearse it. Help them with their pronunciation. Invite pairs to act out the conversations to the class. If you have recording facilities available, record Ss and use the recordings for feedback or assessment.

6 Check the situations carefully. With *weaker classes*, put Ss into pairs first (As or Bs together) to prepare their roles. Monitor closely and prompt/help them if necessary (depending on your aim: fluency practice or assessment). While Ss do the role-plays, record them if possible for feedback or assessment. Otherwise, invite pairs to act out one of the role-plays to the class. Give feedback as required.

OVERVIEW

This video podcast extends discussion on technology and consolidates Ss' vocabulary of communication and the key phrases from lesson 11.4. This video podcast would work well at the end of lesson 11.4, or at the start or end of unit 11.

KEEPING IN TOUCH

Introduction

Ss revise/practise the present perfect with the adverbs *just/already/yet* in the context of talking about types of communication. They also learn how to use pronouns for back-referencing to avoid repetition in their writing.

SUPPLEMENTARY MATERIALS

Resource bank p186

Ex 8C: bring/download simple texts containing a variety of pronouns for the optional extra activity.

Warm up

Lead in to the topic with a game of Chinese whispers. Organise Ss into large groups of at least 8 people: they need to be able to whisper to each other without being overheard. Then check the lesson heading *Keeping in touch*. Give one student in each group a sentence on a piece of paper, e.g. *The large black dog bought a new mobile phone.* The student whispers the message to the person on his/her right, who then whispers it to the next person, and so on. They mustn't say the message more than once. The last person in the group writes the message they heard on the board. It will probably not be exactly the same as people often don't catch the exact words they hear, which can be very amusing. Discuss this in feedback.

VOCABULARY   communication

1A Give Ss 2 mins to look at the photos and discuss the different types of communication. In feedback, check answers and teach/drill new vocabulary, e.g. *social networking site*. If necessary, check the meaning of the abbreviation *SMS = Short Message Service*

Answers: A postcard B internet phone/webcam
C SMS (text message) D mobile phone E fax F social networking site

B Check the rubric and language in the table. Do an example to check instructions. Ss then take turns to ask/answer the question and complete the table. They then work with another pair to compare answers and exchange information. Ss should find out how often they use the different ways of communicating. In feedback, elicit answers from each group and find out which of the activities the class does most/least often.

LISTENING

2A Elicit some positive/negative points about *social networking sites*. Give Ss 4–5 mins to discuss the other three things in the word box, and note down one positive and one negative point for each one. In feedback, elicit/write their ideas on the board. (Ss will be able to use them after Ex 3B.)

Suggested answers:
social networking sites: (+) you can keep in touch with friends you don't see very often, (–) sometimes the site is very slow/you can waste a lot of time.
blogs: (+) you can publish your ideas to the world, (–) anybody can read your blog so it's not very private/personal.
text messages: (+) it's quick and cheap, (–) sometimes it's better to talk face to face
internet phones (e.g., skype): (+) you can see the person with a webcam, it's very cheap, (–) the computer crashes

B Check the rubric. Ss then listen to the recording, write their answers and then compare them. Elicit/check them in feedback.

Answers: Speaker 1: text messages; **Speaker 2:** internet phones; **Speaker 3:** blog; **Speaker 4:** social networking sites

3A Check the example and new language in the sentences, e.g. *keep (looking), crash, post (photos)*. Ss then do the exercise and compare answers before they listen and check. In feedback, nominate Ss to answer (see answers in bold in the audio script). With *stronger classes*, ask further comprehension questions, e.g. *Why is a blog better than writing postcards? Who reads the blog?*

Answers: 2) Speaker 1 3) Speaker 4 4) Speaker 2
5) Speaker 4 6) Speaker 1 7) Speaker 3 8) Speaker 2

B Elicit/discuss Ss' answers to question 1. Encourage them to relate the sentence to their own lives, e.g. *I wrote a blog when I was on holiday in Turkey last year. I think I'll use a blog on my next holiday.* Give Ss 3–4 mins to talk about the other sentences in pairs. In feedback, discuss Ss' answers. To follow-up from Ex 2A, refer students to their ideas on the board and discuss which ones were not mentioned in the listening.

Answers: positive: 1, 5, 6, 8; negative: 2, 3, 4, 7

Unit II Recording I

1 I use my phone for everything. **I text most of the time because it's quick and cheap,** so I text my friends and my boyfriend. We send each other texts during the day. It's a nice way to keep in touch. I like texts because they are quiet – nobody knows what you are saying. My mum used to call me all the time to check that I'm OK, but now she can text me, which is much better. **I get really annoyed when you're talking to someone though, and they are texting someone else.** I think that's really rude.

2 I use the internet a lot now. I use it for phone calls – you know – what's it called … Skype. **I use Skype to keep in touch with my family** because my daughter lives in France, you see, so I don't see her very often and the phone is expensive. With the internet I can see my grandchildren – it's wonderful. My son sets up the computer for me. I haven't learnt how to do that yet. **And sometimes it crashes during the phone call,** which is annoying, or I can't see the picture properly. But usually it's fine. Generally, I think the technology is wonderful. When I was younger, we only dreamed of having video phone calls, but now it's possible and it's free.

3 We use a blog. We've never done it before, but **it's a great way to tell people about your travel experiences.** We've been to so many places already and it's nice to be able to tell people about them. And you can put photos there of the people you meet and the places you visit. It's better than writing postcards because you don't have to wait for them to arrive. As soon as you write the blog, people all over the world can read it. And you only have to write it once! **The only problem we have is when we can't find an internet café.**

4 I've just started to use networking sites, like Facebook and MySpace. They're a great way to keep in touch with people you don't see very often. **You can post photos or send jokes and funny videos.** I found some friends I haven't seen for years and it was great to see their pages. **The only problem is that I keep looking at the website when I should be working.**

GRAMMAR present perfect

Watch out!
Ss are familiar with the present perfect but may have problems with the meaning of the adverbs *just, yet* and *already* and their position in a sentence, e.g. *I've just done it three days ago. Has he yet come?* Check the meaning carefully and monitor/correct word order consistently.

4A Ss can do the exercise alone and check in pairs. In feedback, elicit the answers but move on to Ex B to check the meaning of the words in bold.

Answers: 1 c) 2 a) 3 b)

B Ss complete the rules alone and compare their answers. With *weaker Ss*, read and elicit the answers as a class. In feedback, check the meaning of each adverb using the sentences in Ex 4A, e.g. for sentence 1 ask: *Can you do it yourself?* No. *Did you expect to learn it before now?* Yes. *Is the sentence positive or negative?* Negative. Then elicit/check the position of each adverb in the sentences (see **Language bank** II.I on p148). If possible, elicit personalised examples for each adverb, e.g. *We haven't had lunch yet. I've already got 500 friends on Facebook.*

Answers: 1 yet 2 just 3 already

⟶ **LANGUAGE BANK** II.I p148–149

Stronger classes can study the tables and notes at home when they do the exercises. Otherwise, read/check the notes with Ss. *Weaker Ss* should do Exs A and B in class. In Ex A, check *lift, confirmation*.

Answers:
A 1 already 2 yet 3 just 4 already 5 yet 6 already 7 just
8 already/(just)
B 1 B: Yes, I've *just* finished it ~~just~~. 2 B: Imelda hasn't called ~~yet~~ us yet. 3 B: We've (*already*) been ~~already~~ there (*already*). 4 B: Well, ~~just~~ she's *just* run five miles.
5 B: I'd love to come out, but I haven't finished ~~yet~~ my work yet. 6 B: Yes, but ~~already~~ I've (*already*) seen it three times (*already*)!

PRACTICE

5A Check the example. Ss then do the exercise alone and compare answers. Monitor and prompt them to self-correct. Recheck the meaning of the adverbs and their position in the sentences in feedback.

Answers: 2 I haven't done any sport yet this week. 3 My best friend has just had a baby. 4 I've *already* had a holiday this year *(already)*. 5 I haven't finished my studies yet. 6 I've *already* seen the new James Bond film *(already)*. 7 I've just moved house. 8 I've *already* paid for my next English course *(already)*.

B Check the example and elicit Ss' answers for question 2 in Ex 5A. Monitor and support them while they write. Encourage Ss to read/check each other's sentences for accuracy as it's important for them to use correct sentences in the next exercise.

C Ss work with another partner to compare their answers. In feedback, nominate Ss to tell the class one thing about their partners, e.g. *Maria's already been to the gym three times this week.*

6 First elicit information about the cartoon, e.g. *There are some clean shirts and an iron on the ironing board. The man's carrying a bag of shopping.* Ss then write six sentences alone/in pairs. Elicit/check their answers in feedback.

Answers: 1 He's already been to the supermarket. 2 He hasn't cleaned the floor yet. 3 He has already done the washing. 4 He's just ironed his shirts. 5 He hasn't cooked dinner yet. 6 He hasn't watered the plants yet.

SPEAKING

7A First check the phrases in the box and elicit Ss' answers to question 1, e.g. *I have already created my own webpage.* Give Ss 4–5 mins to take turns answering the questions. Encourage them to show interest in their partner's answers and extend the conversation. Monitor closely and note how well they use the adverbs. In feedback, elicit Ss' answers and prompt them to self-correct.

B Elicit examples of things Ss need/want to do this week. Then give them 2–3 mins to write their lists.

C Check the example. Monitor discreetly while Ss work in pairs, making notes of examples of good language and problems. In feedback, write examples of Ss' errors and good language on the board. Ss discuss and correct the errors in pairs.

speakout TIP

Read the speakout tip with Ss and elicit other things they could do to improve their English. They then write five things they want to do in their notebooks. Tell them you will check how many things they've done in a month's time. Make a note of this in your diary!

WRITING pronouns

8A Elicit an example answer. Ss then work alone and compare answers before feedback.

Answers: them – my new friends, they – my new friends, Our – my new friends' and my, it – the course, her – Laura, she – Laura, there – the city centre

B Elicit the answer and emphasise how important the use of pronouns in writing is.

Answer: to avoid repetition of words

C Ss read the travel blog first. Elicit/check that Bucharest is the capital of Romania, which borders on Hungary in Central Europe. Then give them 3 mins to rewrite the blog and compare answers before feedback.

Answers: we, it, our, there, He, them, here, it, us

Optional extra activity

Ss work alone. Give them a simple text from a newspaper/magazine, or tell them to look at a text they've seen before in a previous unit/the **Communication bank**, e.g. on p100, p160–163. Give them 3–4 mins to find/underline the pronouns and draw a line to the word/s they refer to. Ss then compare answers. Tell Ss to practise noticing the use of pronouns in all the texts they read.

Homework ideas

- Write a travel blog about a place you visited recently. Underline all pronouns in the text which avoid repetition.
- **Language bank** 11.1 Ex A–B, p149
- **Workbook** Ex 1–8, p64

IT'S JUST A GAME

Introduction

Ss revise and practise the first conditional + *if/when* in the context of a text about the computer game *The Sims*.

SUPPLEMENTARY MATERIALS

Resource bank p185 and p187

Warm up: bring examples/download pictures and information about current computer games which are popular at the moment. See the **Culture notes** below for types/names of games.

Culture notes

There are many different types of computer games but the basic ones are: action adventure, e.g. *Grand Theft Auto*; fighting, e.g. *Street Fighter II*; first-person shooter (FPS) (where the player shoots a weapon), e.g. *Call of Duty 4*; puzzle, e.g. *Sudoku*; role-playing games (RPG), e.g. *Diablo 3*; simulation, e.g. *The Sims* series; sports, e.g. *World Cup football*; car racing, e.g. *Burnout Paradise*; strategy, e.g. *Warhammer 40,000*.

Warm up

Introduce the topic of the lesson. If you've brought pictures/examples of computer games, use them as prompts here. If not, write the names of different types of games on the board (see **Culture notes** above). Ask *What do you know about these games? What type of games are they? Have you played any of them?* N.B. The aim is for Ss to describe, not evaluate, the games as they do this in Ex 1 below. Avoid asking, e.g. *What do you think of these games?* Ss discuss the question in pair/groups. If possible, put Ss who know/play the games together with those who don't. In feedback, elicit/check Ss' answers and find out which games are well-known/the most popular.

SPEAKING

1A Give Ss 2–3 mins to answer the questions in pairs. Discuss their answers in feedback. Teach/provide adjectives/phrases to describe their opinions of computer games, e.g. *a waste of time, very entertaining, relaxing*.

B Ss read and check the opinions. Teach/check *aliens, shoot, virtual worlds*. Elicit Ss' answers to the first opinion. Tell them to consider the people's ages in their answers. Give Ss 2 mins to think about their responses to the other opinions, and then compare/discuss their answers. In feedback, elicit Ss' reasons for their answers, and find out which opinion is the closest to their own.

C Give Ss 2 mins to complete their sentence. They can compare them in pairs/groups. In feedback, nominate Ss to read out their sentences and invite other Ss to agree/disagree.

Suggested answer: I think computer games are really interesting because you can play with people from all over the world who have the same game/you can compare scores.

Culture notes

The Sims is an American strategic life-simulation game for computers. It was first released in 2000, after *Sim City*. In 2002, it became the top-selling PC game in history, with sales of 6.3 million. Since then, *The Sims 2* and *3* have been released. By March 2009, the games had sold more than 100 million copies. *The Sims* was created by game designer Will Wright. It's a simulation of the daily activities of one or more virtual people (Sims) in a suburb near Sim City. The player controls their virtual 'world'. He creates their homes, and supervises their daily activities and needs, such as sleeping, eating and bathing.

READING

2A First look at the photos. Ask *What can you seen in the photos? Who are these people? What's this place?* Elicit some answers to find out which students are familiar with *The Sims*. Then put students who know *The Sims* in pairs/groups with those who don't. Check the rubric and questions, and give Ss 3–4 mins to read the introduction to the article and discuss their answers. They should cover the rest of the text while they do this. In feedback, elicit Ss' answers and write their predictions for question 2 on the board. Don't confirm them yet. Ss will check them in Ex B.

B Give Ss 3–4 mins to read the article alone and check their answers. They then compare answers and check them with their predictions on the board. In feedback, refer to the predictions on the board and elicit/discuss which of them were correct.

Answers: 1 The Sims are computer-simulated people (people in a computer game). 2 The journalist chooses her characters, builds a house, meets other Sims, makes new friends, etc.

C Check the questions. Give Ss 4–5 mins to underline their answers for questions 1 and 2 in the text, and discuss their ideas for question 3. In feedback, elicit and discuss Ss' answers, but don't check the words in bold yet as these will be checked in Ex 3A. However, teach/check other new words, e.g. *brochure, straight onto, achievement, bubble, type*. N.B. Further comprehension is suggested in the Optional extra activity after Ex 3B.

Answers: 1 She enjoys building a house on the beach, and dancing. 2 She finds it difficult to make friends when she first starts to play.

VOCABULARY feelings

3A Check the rubric and the example. Tell Ss to find the word *bored* in the article and look at the sentences before and after it. This will illustrate how the context helps them to work out the meaning of the word *bored*. Then give Ss 3–4 mins to match the definitions to the other words. In feedback, check Ss' answers and drill the pronunciation of each word. Elicit the stress in each word, e.g. *uncomfortable*.

Answers: 2 confused 3 lonely 4 excited 5 uncomfortable 6 amazed 7 worried 8 nervous

B Check the rubric and examples. Give students time to think about their answers before they work in pairs. Monitor while they work to check how well they are using the vocabulary. In feedback, asks Ss to tell the class about their partner's answers, e.g. *The last time Paula was worried was before her maths test!*

Optional extra activity
Ss work in pairs and write four questions about the article in Ex 2 to ask another pair. Monitor while they do this and check their questions for accuracy.

GRAMMAR first conditional + when

Watch out!
Unlike many other languages, English doesn't use subjunctive forms in conditional sentences. In first conditional sentences referring to the future, Ss often make the mistake of using *will* in the *if/when* clause, e.g. *If/When I will see you, I'll tell you.* It's therefore important to highlight the use of a present tense in *if/when* clauses, and provide sufficient practice and feedback.

4 Ss should first read the sentences (from the article in Ex 2) and rules. While they circle their answers and compare them, write sentences a)–d) on the board. Refer to these in feedback: elicit Ss' answers and underline the verb forms in the sentences. Check the concept of *if/when* sentences. Point to sentence a). Ask *Will I go there?* Maybe. *Will I meet new people?* Yes, you will – if you go there. Then point to sentence c). Ask *Will he walk in?* Yes. *Will people start talking to him?* Yes. If appropriate, ask Ss how they would say these sentences in their own language(s) and elicit any similarities/differences.

Answers: 1 future 2 the present tense 3 a future form

⟶ LANGUAGEBANK 11.2 p148–149

Read/check the notes with your Ss if necessary. Highlight the use of modal verbs in main clauses. *Weaker Ss* should do Ex A and B in class. In Ex A, check *pay rise, get time off work.* In Ex B, check *behaves badly.*

Answers:
A 1 'll leave, finish 2 miss, 'll take 3 see, 'll ask 4 won't have, leaves 5 ask, won't give 6 'll cook, do 7 is, 'll go 8 'll go, gets
B 1 If you ~~will be~~ 're in the office tomorrow, we'll talk about it then. 2 ✓ 3 ✓ 4 We'll ask the doctor when we ~~will~~ get to the hospital. 5 If Theo behaves badly in class, the teacher *will* speak to his parents. 6 They'll move into the house as soon as Mark ~~will finish~~ finishes building it.

PRACTICE

5A First give students 1–2 mins to read the text quickly. Check *disease, depressed.* Discuss what the text is about and ask *Did any of the information surprise you?* Ss then complete the text and compare their answers. In feedback, nominate Ss to answer and say what kind of clause the verb is part of: an *if/when* clause or a main clause.

Answers: 1 don't have 2 will die 3 is 4 won't have 5 doesn't make 6 will get 7 won't listen 8 will fall 9 doesn't sleep 10 sits 11 will be

B Do an example and give Ss 3–4 mins to write their sentences. Monitor and prompt Ss to make any necessary corrections. Answers are checked in Ex C.

C Ss listen and check their answers, making corrections if necessary. In feedback, check answers and then focus on the pronunciation of *will.* Play the first two sentences again and elicit/drill the pronunciation of the contracted form *he'll.*

Suggested answers: 1 If Troy gets a job as a policeman, he'll earn lots of money. 2 If he earns lots of money, he'll buy nice things for the house. 3 If he buys nice things for the house, they'll have a lot of fun. 4 If they have a lot of fun, they'll make new friends. 5 If they make new friends, maybe Troy will find a new girlfriend. 6 If Troy finds a new girlfriend, Sadie won't be happy. 7 If Sadie isn't happy, they'll fight. 8 If they fight, maybe Troy will have to move house.

D Ss listen and repeat the sentences chorally, and then individually. Prompt students to correct their pronunciation. To follow-up, Ss could take turns to say one sentence each around the class.

Optional extra activity
Do a chain drill around the class. Start off with, e.g. *If I win the lottery, I'll take a trip around the world.* Choose a student to continue with *If I take a trip around the world, I'll … .* Continue the activity until Ss can't think of any more sentences.

Unit 11 Recording 2
1 If Troy gets a job as a policeman, he'll earn lots of money.
2 If he earns lots money, he'll buy nice things for the house.
3 If he buys nice things for the house, they'll have a lot of fun.
4 If they have a lot of fun, they'll make new friends.
5 If they make new friends, maybe Troy will find a new girlfriend.
6 If Troy finds a new girlfriend, Sadie won't be happy.
7 If Sadie isn't happy, they'll fight.
8 If they fight, maybe Troy will have to move house.

6A Check the rubric and elicit more examples of situations, e.g. *get a job, get married, have a baby.* Give Ss 4–5 mins to write four sentences. *Stronger Ss* could write more. Monitor and provide support if needed.

B While Ss compare their ideas, monitor and make notes of problems with the target language. In feedback, nominate Ss to read out the most interesting sentences and choose the best one. Prompt them to correct language/pronunciation errors during this stage.

SPEAKING

7A Check the rubric/questions and elicit sample answers for question 1. While Ss complete their sentences, provide help to those who need it. *Weaker students* could work together.

B While Ss compare answers, make notes on the use of language they've studied in this lesson and do any remedial work needed afterwards. In feedback, invite each pair to tell the class about themselves, e.g. *When I next go on holiday, I'll go with a friend, but Sam will go with his family.*

Homework ideas
- Ex 7: write 80–100 words about things you/your friends and family will/won't do next year if they have enough money/time.
- Language bank 11.2 Ex A–B, p149
- Workbook Ex 1–8, p66–67

I TOTALLY DISAGREE

Introduction

Ss learn and practise ways of giving opinions, and disagreeing politely, in the context of talking about using the internet.

SUPPLEMENTARY MATERIALS

Resource bank p188

Warm up: prepare a class survey as described below.

Ex 1: Ss could use bilingual dictionaries.

Ex 8C: use recording facilities here if available.

Warm up

Lead in to the lesson with a *find someone who ...* activity asking what Ss use their computers for. Prepare a survey sheet using 8–10 items from this list: *chat with friends, buy things, play games, surf the internet, read/write emails, listen to the radio, watch films/TV, check spelling, write documents, check information in a dictionary/encyclopaedia, do research for work/studies, write programs, organise your finances, find entertainment, earn money.* Use this sample for your survey sheet:

Activity	Name	How often?
watch films/TV	Maria	rarely
check spelling	Frank	sometimes

Make a copy for each student in your class. In class, hand them out and ask, e.g. *Do you use the computer to watch TV?* If the answer is *Yes,* ask *How often do you do it?* Elicit, e.g. *sometimes/always/not very often,* etc. Ss then walk round the class (or work in groups) and ask/answer the questions. In larger classes, they should try not to write information about the same person more than twice. In feedback, elicit information about each activity, e.g. *Maria rarely uses the computer to watch TV.* N.B. If you don't have a survey prepared, Ss can work in groups and find out the five most common things their partners use the computer for.

VOCABULARY   internet terms

1 Check the words in the box, or Ss could check words they're not sure of in bilingual dictionaries. Give them 3–4 mins to ask/answer the questions in pairs/groups. Discuss their answers in feedback and find out which things Ss use most/least.

READING

2A Look at the cartoon with Ss. Ask *What's the man thinking? Why?* Elicit answers and encourage them to speculate. Then elicit what Ss think *wilfing* is. Give them 2 mins to read the article to find out. Discuss their answers in feedback and teach/check *distracted, get off the computer, get on with your life.*

Answer: *Wilf* means *What was I looking for?* and refers to the habit of wasting time while you are supposed to be working/studying on the computer.

B Check the questions. Give Ss 3–4 mins to read the text again and underline/note down their answers before comparing them. Nominate Ss to answer, quoting the relevant information from the text.

Answers: 1 up to two days per month 2 work/study 3 People argue when one partner spends too much time in front of their computer.

3 Prepare the role-play/debate carefully. First check the rubric and elicit reasons for each opinion, e.g. *people don't talk to their partners, it's very useful for finding out information.* With *weaker classes,* divide the class into As and Bs. Put Student As and Student Bs in separate pairs to prepare their roles first. Monitor and help Ss with this. Then put Ss into A/B pairs for the role-play. Monitor discreetly and notice how well Ss use the language of giving opinions, agreeing and disagreeing. They will learn/practise this in Ex 4–8 so it would be a good idea for them to repeat this role-play after Ex 8C. They should be able to use a wider range of more appropriate language by then. In feedback, invite pairs to act out their role-plays to the class. Discuss the points Ss made in their role-plays and find out which opinion Ss hold most strongly.

FUNCTION   giving opinions

4 Check the rubric and statements. Ss then listen and compare their answers. Play the recording again if there is strong disagreement. Otherwise, elicit/check answers.

Answers: 1 T 2 T 3 F

5A Ss read the statements. Check the meaning and pronunciation of *an addict, to be addicted to, addictive.* Ss tick their answers and compare them.

B Play the recording again. Tell Ss to say *Stop!* at each answer they ticked (underlined in audio script 11.3). Ask further comprehension questions about each ticked answer.

Answers: ✓ 1, 4, 5, 6

Unit 11 Recording 3

A=Man 1 B=Man 2 C=Woman

A: I use the internet all day at work. I 'wilf' and I get my work done.

B: Yeah, me too.

A: I'm sorry, but I really don't see what the problem is.

C: I think the problem is that lots of workers spend all day on the internet instead of doing their work.

A: Hmm.

C: And students at university are failing their degrees because they spend all their time checking Facebook and watching the videos that friends send them.

B: Yes, that's true, but ... um ... I don't think, you know, I don't think that the problem is the internet. You know, I think the problem is with the websites like Facebook.

A: Yeah, MySpace ...

B: Some companies stop you from using certain websites. And I think that's OK.

C: But it's such a waste of time. I don't think people should use the internet at work, unless you need it for your work.

A: I'm not sure about that. Using the internet helps to give you a break. It's like having a cup of coffee or talking to someone in the office. People should use the internet as much as they like.

B: Yes, that's right. I think it's good to use the internet. I run a small business and all my staff use the internet as much as they want to. I don't check what they are doing. They do all their work and they are happy. I don't think it's a waste of time at all. It's the same as going to a bookshop ...

C: No, but …

B: … or looking through a pile of magazines.

C: I'm afraid I **totally disagree**. <u>The problem is that people are addicts. People aren't addicted to reading books, but the internet is different.</u> <u>People spend too much time in front of the computer.</u> They choose the internet over sports and going out. They forget how to live in the real world, and 'wilfing' is a part of that.

6A Check the headings and elicit possible answers. Check the meaning of *totally*. Ss then listen to phrases from audio script 11.3 (in bold in the audio script) and compare answers. Write the headings on the board and elicit/write Ss' answers in the correct column. They then listen and repeat the phrases, and copy the table into their notebooks.

> **Answers:** agreeing: That's *right*, *That's* true, disagreeing: I totally *disagree*, I'm not *sure* about that giving an opinion: I *think*, I *don't* think

B Check the phrases in the box. Ss then add them to the correct column.

> **Answers:** agreeing: definitely; disagreeing: I don't think so; giving an opinion: in my opinion

Unit 11 Recording 4

Yes, that's right. I think it's good.

Yes, that's true.

I'm afraid I totally disagree.

I'm not sure about that.

I think it's good to use the internet.

I don't think it's a waste of time at all.

⟶ LANGUAGEBANK 11.3 p148–149

Ss can refer to the tables/notes to help them with this exercise. In Ex B, check *hunt animals*.

> **Answers:**
> A 1 I'm *sorry*, but I don't think … 2 I don't *think* we should spend … 3 I have to say I think *that's/you're* right. 4 I'm afraid I totally disagree. 5 Make them pay fines? I'm not sure *about* that. 6 In *my* opinion, we should start …
> B 1 I think 2 not sure about 3 I'm afraid 4 totally disagree 5 my opinion 6 Definitely

7A Ss read the conversations first. Check unfamiliar language and the example. Give Ss 2–3 mins to correct and compare their answers before you check them.

> **Answers:** 2 That's ~~not~~ true. 3 I'm *not* sure about that. 4 Definitely ~~not~~. 5 I ~~am~~ totally disagree. 6 I don't think *so*.

B Elicit/discuss Ss' opinions of the first statement. Prompt them to use phrases they learnt in Ex 6, e.g. *In my opinion, everybody should learn at least two other languages. Yes, I totally agree./No, I don't think so.* Before they work in pairs, give Ss time to make notes of their own opinions, and reasons for them.

LEARN TO disagree politely

8A Do question 1 as an example. You may wish to read the speakout tip with Ss now. Then elicit the introductory phrase used in question 1A *I'm sorry, but …* Ss then finish the exercise alone and compare answers. They'll check them in Ex B.

B Play question 1A/B as examples. Ask *Which sounds more polite? Why?* Elicit answer A. First of all, because the speaker uses a softening introductory phrase. More importantly, her voice is softer/gentler and the pitch of her voice on the stressed syllables is lower. The person in B speaks more loudly/aggressively and her voice on the stressed syllables is higher/louder. Play the rest of the recording. Ss listen, note down their answers and compare them. Play the recording again. Stop after each pair of sentences and elicit/check answers.

> **Answers:** 1 A 2 B 3 A 4 A 5 B

C Ss then listen again and repeat both polite/impolite sentences. Encourage them to copy the intonation and extend/soften their voice range accordingly (see the stressed words in the audio script). Play the recording as many times as necessary until Ss are confident. Ss then practise in pairs. Monitor and help Ss with their pronunciation.

> **Teaching tip**
> If you have recording facilities, Ss can record the phrases and compare their pronunciation with the recording. This will help Ss' to become more aware of their pronunciation.

> **Optional extra activity**
> Ss read audio script 11.3 and find/underline examples of phrases from Ex 6 and 8A (in bold in the audio script).

Unit 11 Recording 5

1 A: I'm <u>sorry</u>, but I <u>really</u> don't see what the <u>problem</u> is.

  B: I <u>really</u> don't <u>see</u> what the <u>problem</u> is.

2 A: I <u>disagree</u>.

  B: <u>I'm</u> not <u>sure</u> about <u>that</u>.

3 A: <u>I</u> don't think it's a <u>waste</u> of time at <u>all</u>.

  B: It's <u>not</u> a <u>waste</u> of <u>time</u>.

4 A: That's <u>true</u>, but I <u>don't</u> think the <u>problem</u> is the <u>internet</u>.

  B: The <u>problem</u> is not using the <u>internet</u>.

5 A: I <u>totally</u> <u>disagree</u>.

  B: I'm <u>afraid</u> I <u>totally</u> disagree.

speak out TIP

Read the speakout tip with Ss before Ex 8B or at the end of Ex 8.

SPEAKING

9A Check the rubric and statements with Ss. Elicit sample answers to the first one. Then give Ss 4–5 mins to work alone and make notes of their opinions. They should include examples of language for giving opinions from Ex 6. Monitor and support *weaker Ss*.

B Demonstrate what Ss have to do. Elicit an opinion and prompt other Ss to agree/disagree using phrases from Ex 6 and 8. Ss then work in groups and compare their ideas in the same way. Monitor discreetly, making notes of how well Ss use the language they've practised in the lesson. Note down examples for feedback. In feedback, elicit opposing opinions for each statement. Give feedback as needed.

> **Homework ideas**
> • Ex 9: write your opinion for each statement.
> • Language bank 11.3 Ex A–B, p149
> • Workbook Ex 1–4, p68

IS TV BAD FOR MY KIDS?

Introduction

Ss watch an extract from the BBC documentary series *Panorama* which explores the effect TV has on families and children. Ss then learn and practise how to talk about technology, and write a comment about it on a website.

Warm up

Lead in to the lesson. Read the title of the lesson and write two prompts on the board: *TV is good for kids because …/ TV is bad for kids because …* . Elicit a sample answer for each one, e.g. *TV is good for kids because there are lots of educational programmes and documentaries.* Ss then work in pairs and complete each sentence with at least three reasons. In feedback, elicit/discuss their answers. Then ask Ss *Do you think TV is bad for kids? Yes or no?* Ss vote for their answer with a show of hands.

DVD PREVIEW

1 Check the rubric/word box. Give Ss 2–3 mins to discuss the questions. In feedback, invite them to tell the class about their partner. Find out which things Ss think save or waste time.

2A Ss read the text. Check *concentrating, meaningful conversations.* They then discuss their answers in pairs and decide what they'll write. Elicit some answers for each gap. Ss then check them on p166. In feedback, ask *Which answers surprised you? Why?*

> **Answers:** 2) 60 percent 3) 3.5 years eating, 12 years watching TV 4) 1 5) 3.5 mins, 1,600 mins a week

B Check the rubric and elicit some answers before Ss discuss the questions in pairs/groups. They should make a note of what they have/don't have in common and report back to the class in feedback.

3 Give Ss 1 min to read the programme information and answer the questions. In feedback, elicit Ss' predictions and note them on the board. Ss will check them in Ex 4. Also teach new vocabulary, e.g. *do an experiment, survive.*

> **Possible answers:** 1 The children will get bored/angry, they will think it's fun/interesting. 2 The parents will feel stressed, find it difficult, enjoy spending more time with their kids

DVD VIEW

4 Ss watch the DVD and focus on checking their predictions on the board with how the children/parents reacted to the experiment. After watching, give them 1 min to compare answers. Then elicit/discuss how the children and parents reacted to the experiment, and compare this with Ss' predictions. Which were correct/incorrect?

> **Alternative approach**
> Ss could watch the DVD without the sound first. Tell them to pay careful attention to the faces/expressions of the parents and children, the activities they do, etc. This should give them information about their answers from Ex 3. Elicit/check their answers as above and play the DVD again with sound.

> **Answers:** 1 The children watched less TV but seemed to enjoy playing games and spending more time with their parents. 2 The parents found the experiment very positive. There was a lot more laughter in the house. They laughed a lot and were more of a family.

5 Ss read the sentences. Check *microwaves.* They watch the DVD again, write their answers and then compare them. *Stronger classes* could write their answers before they watch the DVD. In feedback, play the DVD and tell Ss to say *Stop!* when they hear/see the answers (underlined in the DVD script). Ask further comprehension questions and check/teach useful words/phrases.

> **Answers:** 1 T 2 F: they went to a primary school in Manchester. 3 F: they took the TVs, computers and computer games. 4 T 5 T 6 F: they watched less TV.

DVD 11 Panorama: Is TV Bad For My Kids?

JV=Jeremy Vine

JV: Hello, I'm Jeremy Vine, and this is *Panorama.* Is it time to admit that TV is damaging our children? Doing the job we should be doing ourselves …

Dad 1: Are you going to miss TV?

JV: … and making family life without TV seem like just too much hard work. <u>It makes our kids fat</u>, teaches them to be violent, and rots their brains. If, as some argue, TV, computer games are guilty of all that, then surely they should be banned, or at least severely rationed. But hang on, if the kids were unglued from the screen, could we, the parents, cope? Many of us depend on the TV far more than we'd ever admit. Eighty-four percent of children over five have a telly in their bedroom. In the year before he turns nine, the average child will watch thirty-two whole days of television. <u>This is Park Road Primary School, on the outskirts of Manchester.</u> A very friendly place, as we are about to see. This is Year 3 in here. Hi there!

Kids: Hello.

JV: Seven and eight years old. James, what are you studying?

James: Numeracy.

JV: Numeracy. Well, they have agreed to take part in our experiment to see what happens when <u>televisions and computers are removed from their lives</u>. And just over here on the wall, we've got cameras to record the impact of what goes on. Stand by for the short, sharp shock.

Man: You can't have that. I'll have to take that with me. Thank you. Say goodbye.

JV: We'll be going to their homes and <u>removing the screens, the telly, the PC, the games, everything but the microwave.</u> In exchange, they <u>get one new piece of electrical equipment, a camera,</u> to film what happens.

Dad 2: Station number one is warm up.

JV: <u>Without the TV, it's clear the parents will have to work a lot harder.</u>

Boy 1: Go.

Dad 2: A burger? Hotdog? Sandwich?

Boy 1: Yeah.

Dad 2: So one, two, three. Arms straight out. One, two …

Boy 2: I wonder what to do.

Mum 1: Just look at all those games.

Boy 2: Buckaroo!!

Mum 1: It's only been four hours, and I think I will crack very soon without my TV.

Boy 1: I win.

Mum 2: Yay finally, he wins.

JV: Come in. Come in.

Ten weeks on, I met some of the parents to see if they are making any long term changes at home.

You've come back to a different kind of viewing, have you?

Woman 1: <u>Yes, we've changed it so that they can only watch telly, once they've done homework.</u> And they can only watch the telly up until Bernie comes home from, from work.

JV: Has anyone else got, got rules here, as a result of this? The Ropers, you got any rules now?

Woman 2: What's our rule?

Child: Umm … there's not really any TV in the morning, apart from the news.

Woman 2: Yeah.

Boy 3: On a school day.

JV: OK.

Woman 2: Yes, on the school days. Yes.

Man 2: I think most people have done that, haven't we? We definitely don't have any TV …

Woman 2: We started that beforehand.

JV: You know, we were looking for results in the classroom, and we found them in the home, and that was the big thing for us. Does that … ? Mr Breen … Is your … ?

Man 2: Um … I think we definitely found it very positive.

Woman 1: Well it was … it's just there was a lot more laughter in the house. We were having a good laugh, um … and we kind of, you know, we were more of a family.

6 Give Ss 3–4 mins to answer the questions. In feedback, elicit/discuss Ss' answers. Find out how many Ss think the experiment was a good idea, and why/why not.

> **Answers:** 1 Most parents decided to stop the children watching TV in the mornings on a school day, or to make sure that the children do their homework before watching TV. They said it was hard work, but they noticed positive effects on the children. They laughed and were more of a family.

speakout technology

7A Check the rubric and teach *gadget*. Ss listen and write their answers, and compare them. Play the recording again if Ss don't agree/have all the answers. Nominate Ss to answer.

> **Answers:**
> **speaker 1:** essential: laptop not essential: TV, digital camera
> **speaker 2:** essential: mobile phone, TV, DVD player, laptop not essential: digital camera, MP3 player

B First read and check the **key phrases** with Ss. They then listen, tick the answers and then compare them. In feedback, play the recording again, pausing at each **key phrase** (in bold in the audio script). Elicit/drill the complete sentences and ask, e.g. *Why is his mobile phone essential? Why isn't a TV/digital camera essential? Why does she need her mobile phone?*

> **Answers:** ✓ That's essential. I love it. I use it all the time. I couldn't live without … , I don't go anywhere without … , I need it in case … , I suppose I don't need … , I can live without …

Unit 11 Recording 6

1 OK – mobile phone? **That's essential. I love it. I use it all the time.** I love talking to people, and texting. **I couldn't live without** my mobile. MP3 player? **I suppose** it's not essential, although I do like listening to music. Television? Not essential. I don't watch much television. Digital camera? Not essential. I'm terrible at taking photos anyway. So, what's left? Er … laptop? **That's essential** really. I use my laptop for work, so yes, I need that.

2 Which are essential? All of them! Goodness. Right. Mobile phone? Essential. **I don't go anywhere without** my phone. **I need it in case** there's an emergency and I have to call someone. Or if there's a problem with one of the children. Yes, I definitely need my phone. TV? **That's essential** really. **I couldn't live without** my television and DVD player. Umm. Laptop? Well, I need a computer to go on the internet and keep in touch with people. So, **that's essential.** Digital camera? **I suppose I don't need that.** Someone else can take the photos! What else? MP3 player. No. **I can live without that.**

C Elicit some examples using the **key phrases**. Then give Ss 4–5 mins to make notes. Monitor and provide support with language where needed.

D While Ss compare answers in groups, monitor and make notes of language problems, especially with the **key phrases**. In feedback, find out which gadgets are the most popular. Then do a correction slot: write problem sentences on the board. Ss correct them in pairs.

writeback a web comment

8A Check the questions. Give Ss 3 mins to answer them and compare their answers in pairs/groups. In feedback, elicit Ss' answers and teach/check new words in the text, e.g. *interact, humans.*

> **Answers:** Shantanu thinks technology is bad. Jake thinks technology is good.

B Elicit sample answers using the framework provided. Give Ss 3–4 mins to write their own comment and read it to other Ss. Ss discuss the similarities/differences in their opinions.

> **Homework ideas**
> - Ex 8B: write a different comment for the website/your class blog responding to the statement *TV is very bad for children/people.*

LOOKBACK

Introduction

The main aim of the **Lookback** exercises is to give Ss fluency practice of the language they've learnt in the lesson. Fluency practice is usually provided in Ex B of each section, and provides the opportunity for you to assess your Ss' speaking skills. When doing this, you need to consider four things: accuracy of grammar, range of vocabulary used, fluency and pronunciation. For a balanced assessment, give Ss marks out of five for each area, making a total of 20 marks.

COMMUNICATION

1 Ss complete the words alone and check their answers in pairs. In feedback, elicit the words and check the meaning/pronunciation.

> **Answers:** 1 mobile phone 2 web page 3 postcards, blog 4 fax 5 SMS (text message) 6 chat

B Elicit Ss' answers to question 1. Give them 2–3 mins to ask/answer the other questions in pairs, and make notes. In feedback, nominate Ss to tell the class about their partner.

PRESENT PERFECT

2A Ss first read sentences 1–6. Draw a circle on the board and do an example. Elicit short one-word answers to question 1 and write them randomly in the circle. Ss then draw a circle in their notebooks and write their answers to the questions in it: remind them to write them randomly, not in order.

B First check the example conversation, and drill it if necessary. Tell Ss they should use the present perfect in their first question, and then ask further questions to show interest and extend the conversation. While Ss work, monitor to check they are doing the exercise correctly. Take notes on their performance for remedial work if required. Invite/nominate pairs to act out their conversations in feedback and prompt self-/peer correction.

FEELINGS

3A Check the example and the words in the box if necessary. *Weaker Ss* could check them in Ex 3, p111. Give Ss 3–4 mins to do the exercise. Monitor and prompt Ss to correct errors they make.

B Check the rubric and elicit sample answers, e.g. *I feel nervous when I have to do an exam so I study hard to give me confidence/go to bed early the night before/breathe deeply before the exam starts/take my lucky charm with me.* Give Ss time to prepare their answers, and provide help with language if needed. Ss then work in pairs and take turns to tell exchange details of what they do in each situation. Monitor and make notes of their performance for feedback, and/or assessment. Elicit some examples in feedback and find out who has the best ideas/advice.

FIRST CONDITIONAL

4A Do an example and check vocabulary in the sentences, e.g. *ladder*. Give Ss 2–3 mins to do the exercise and compare answers. Elicit Ss' answers and check the form/use of the first conditional in the sentences.

> **Answers:** 1 e) 2 c) 3 f) 4 a) 5 d) 6 b)

B Read the rubric and check the meaning of *superstitions*. Give Ss 5 mins to answer the questions in pairs. In *multilingual classes*, pair Ss from different countries. They should note down examples of superstitions in their partner's countries. In feedback, nominate Ss to tell the class about their partner's answers. Find out which superstitions are universal/unique.

5A Check the example and elicit another one to demonstrate the activity clearly. Give Ss 1–2 mins to write their sentences. Monitor to ensure they are accurate.

B Check/drill the example. Ss then take turns to read out their sentences and extend the conversation. In feedback, nominate Ss to act out their conversations to the class. Give feedback on their use of the first conditional as needed.

> **Optional extra activity**
> Play the consequences game in groups of ten. Write on the board *If you go on holiday next year, where will you go?* Elicit Ss' answers. Then give Ss one sheet of A4 paper each. They all write their answer to the question at the top of their paper. They then fold the paper over the answer, and pass it to the student on their right. Then ask *Who will you go with?* Ss write their answer, fold the paper over it again and pass it on. Follow the same procedures with the following questions *Where will you go if you have lots of money? When will you go? How long will you stay? Where will you stay? What will you take with you? What will you do there? What will you bring back? How will you feel when you get home?* Finally, collect the folded papers up and redistribute them to different Ss. In their groups, they unfold the papers and read out the series of answers. These are usually very amusing.

GIVING OPINIONS

6A Do conversation 1 as an example. Ss then write the sentences in order and check their answers in pairs. In feedback, nominate Ss to read parts A/B in open pairs across the class. Prompt Ss to correct themselves/each other when necessary.

> **Answers:** 1 B: I'm afraid I totally disagree. 2 B: I'm not sure about that. 3 A: In my opinion, all drugs should be legal. 4 B: That's right. I think so, too. 5 A: Do you really think the next government will be better? 6 I don't think so. 7 That's true. I agree. 8 I totally disagree.

B Check/drill the example and remind Ss how to use polite intonation. Give them time to prepare their responses to each opinion. They should also rehearse the polite intonation in each conversation. Monitor and help Ss with their pronunciation where needed. Then in pairs, they take it in turns to give/respond to each opinion. Monitor discreetly, making notes of Ss' performance, especially their pronunciation/intonation. In feedback, elicit/discuss Ss' opinions and do remedial work as required.

OVERVIEW

12.1 CAUGHT ON FILM
GRAMMAR | reported speech
VOCABULARY | film
HOW TO | report other people's words

COMMON EUROPEAN FRAMEWORK
Ss can ask and answer questions and exchange ideas and information on familiar topics in predictable everyday situations; can express some thoughts on more abstract cultural topics such as books, music, films, etc.

12.2 WEB CELEBS
GRAMMAR | second conditional
VOCABULARY | suffixes
HOW TO | talk about hypothetical situations

COMMON EUROPEAN FRAMEWORK
Ss can generally understand clear, standard speech on familiar matters; can describe events, real or imagined in simple terms.

12.3 WHAT CAN I DO FOR YOU?
FUNCTION | requests and offers
VOCABULARY | collocations
LEARN TO | ask for more time

COMMON EUROPEAN FRAMEWORK
Ss can communicate in simple and routine tasks using simple phrases to ask for and provide things, to get simple information and to discuss what to do next.

12.4 BILLION DOLLAR MAN
 **BBC** DVD
speakout | dreams and ambitions
writeback | a web comment

COMMON EUROPEAN FRAMEWORK
Ss can briefly describe dreams, hopes and ambitions.

12.5 LOOKBACK
Communicative revision activities

BBC VIDEO PODCAST
Would you like to be famous?

This video podcast extends discussion on the advantages and disadvantages of being famous. People also describe which famous people they'd like to meet. It would work well at the end of lesson 12.2, or at the start or end of unit 12.

CAUGHT ON FILM

Introduction
Ss learn/practise reported speech and film vocabulary in the context of reading and talking about film extras and film quotes.

SUPPLEMENTARY MATERIALS
Resource bank p189 and p190

Warm up: download/bring cinema listings of films being shown this week.

Ex 4 optional extra activity: Ss can do research using computer facilities if available.

Warm up
Lead in to the topic of the lesson. Dictate/write these questions on the board *What's on at the cinema this week? Which one(s) would you like to see? When? Where? Why?* Put Ss in pairs/groups and give each one a copy of the film listings for this week. Ss ask/answer the questions, using the listings. They should then try to decide on a film they could all go to and make arrangements for a day/time/place. In feedback, elicit/discuss Ss' answers/arrangements. N.B. If you haven't got any listings, elicit what Ss know about current films in their area using the questions above.

Culture notes
The Dark Knight (2008) is a superhero crime thriller in the *Batman* series. It stars Christian Bale as Batman and the late Heath Ledger as the 'Joker'.

Atonement (2007) is a drama based on the novel by Ian McEwan. Set in the 1930s/40s, it stars Keira Knightley and James McEvoy.

An Inconvenient Truth (2006) is a documentary film directed by Davis Guggenheim. It's about former USA Vice President Al Gore's campaign to teach people about global warming.

Seraphim Falls (2007) is an American western set after the end of the Civil War. It stars Pierce Brosnan and Liam Neeson in a story of revenge for a wrong committed against Neeson's character.

The *Scream* series of satirical horror films are directed by Wes Craven. *Scream 1* came out in 1996, *Scream 2* in 1997, *Scream 3* in 2000 and *Scream 4* in 2010. The plot involves a serial killer in a Halloween costume trying to kill one of the main characters in the films. The films star Neve Campbell, Courtney Cox Arquette and David Arquette.

High School Musical 3: Senior Year (2008) is a teen musical film directed by Kenny Ortega. It stars Zac Efron and Vanessa Hudgens. It is the third film in Disney's *High School Musical* film franchise.

VOCABULARY film

1 Look at the film posters with Ss and elicit what they know about each film (see **Culture notes** above). Elicit what type of films they are if possible. Give Ss 2 mins to match the films to the film types and compare their answers. In feedback, check the meaning/pronunciation of each type. Then elicit examples of a science fiction film/historical drama.

Suggested answers: *Atonement*: drama; *An Inconvenient Truth*: documentary; *Seraphim Falls*: western; *The Dark Knight*: action film/fantasy/thriller; *Scream 3*: horror; *High School Musical 3*: musical

2 Check the questions. Ss then ask/answer them in pairs and compare their answers with another pair. In feedback, elicit Ss' opinions of the films on the page and find out what the most popular type of film is in your class.

READING

3A Ss cover the text but read the title. Check the meaning of *fascinating* and *film extra*. Then read/check new words in the statements, e.g. *film studio, speaking/non-speaking role*. Give Ss 2 mins to discuss which statements are true/false. In feedback, elicit and write their answers on the board.

B Give Ss 2–3 mins to read the text quickly and check their answers. Tell them not to worry about unfamiliar words at this stage. In feedback, refer to the answers on the board and check which Ss guessed correctly. You may need to check words in the text which are relevant to the answers, e.g. *Native American, sign language, volunteers*.

Answers: 1 T 2 F 3 F 4 T

4 Ss read the definitions first and ask for clarification of unfamiliar words if necessary. Invite other Ss to explain these words if possible. Give Ss 2–3 mins to match the words in bold and definitions, and compare answers. In feedback, check answers and elicit the pronunciation/main stress in longer words.

Answers: 1 scene 2 director 3 producer 4 actors 5 extras 6 studio 7 roles 8 stars

Optional extra activity
Do further comprehension of the text in Ex 3. Alternatively, Ss work in pairs and write 4–6 comprehension questions to ask another pair.

5A Brainstorm examples of films Ss love/hate and write some of them on the board. Then use phrases 1–6 to elicit information about one of the films as an example. Give Ss 3–4 mins to compete their own phrases. Monitor and support them if needed. Also check the accuracy of their sentences.

B Ss take turns to describe their films in pairs/groups. In feedback, nominate Ss to tell the class about a film they liked/didn't like, and why. Find out how popular each film is with the class.

GRAMMAR reported speech

Watch out!
The rules of form in reported speech are quite complex so it's important not to expose Ss to too much information at first. In this lesson, Ss learn only four tense changes, present/past simple, present/past continuous, *will/would, can/could,* and two reporting verbs, *say/tell*.

To help Ss acquire the rules of form, give them extensive controlled practice and feedback.

6 Check the rubric and questions. Also check *union* and *badly treated* in the text box if you haven't done so already. Ss then answer the questions alone and compare answers. Meanwhile, write the first and third example of direct/reported speech on the board. In feedback, refer to these sentences as you elicit/check Ss' answers. Underline the verb forms e.g. *They don't have speaking roles. The studio said they didn't have speaking roles.* Then check the reporting verbs. Ask *Which verb has an object:* said or told? Elicit *told* (everyone/the union) and elicit other examples, e.g. *me, you, him/her, it, us, them,* [name], etc. Finally, teach Ss that habits in the present simple don't change in reported speech. Elicit an example of a habit, e.g. *I have cereal for breakfast everyday* and ask Ss to change it to reported speech, e.g. *Olga said she has cereal for breakfast everyday.*

Answers: 1 The verb tenses change from the present to the past in reported speech. 2 say, tell

⟹ LANGUAGEBANK 12.1 p150–1

Stronger classes can study the tables notes at home and refer to them when they do the exercises. Otherwise, check the tables and notes with Ss, especially the use of *say/tell*. *Weaker Ss* should do Ex A and B in class. In Ex A, check *invisible, reminds (me)*. In Ex B, check *lecture*.

Answers:
A 1 She told me her favourite film was about an invisible man. 2 He said he didn't like westerns. 3 She told us they could act. 4 He said the film wasn't really about fashion.
5 He told me he was working for a film studio. 6 We told her that director would become famous. 7 She said she was writing a thriller. 8 He said the scene reminded him of another film.
B 2 I will (I'll) be at home by six. 3 I don't want to do my homework. 4 We are busy. 5 I can't understand the lecture. 6 I don't like flying. 7 I am going back to China.

PRACTICE

7 Check the example. Ss then rewrite the paragraph alone and compare answers. Monitor and prompt them to self-correct. Recheck the tense changes and use of reporting verbs in feedback.

Answers: He *told me/said* he could play any role, but he didn't like playing criminals. He *told me/said* he was moving to Hollywood and he was going to be a big star. He *told me/said* he would stay in touch.

Culture notes

Quote 1: Marlon Brando played Don Vito Corleone, the head of a Mafia family, in *The Godfather Part 1* (1972), the first of a trilogy. The quote refers to how he will bribe the producer of a movie to give a part in it to his actor godson. It was voted the second most memorable line in cinema history.

Quote 2 is the last line of the World War II romantic drama *Casablanca* (1942). Police officer Captain Louis Renault and night club owner Rick Blaine (Humphrey Bogart) have just helped Isla Lund (Ingrid Bergman) and her husband escape to Paris and Rick has killed a German officer. Renault suggests they go to join the Free French fighters. Rick replies with this line.

Quote 3: Terminator Arnold Schwarzenegger (*Terminator*, 1984) says this line when the security guard at the hospital where Sarah Connor is a prisoner ignores his questions. He comes crashing back into the building in a car.

Quote 4: Dorothy Gale is a young Kansas girl who falls asleep and finds herself in a fantasy world in the musical *The Wizard of Oz* (1939). She says this line when she 'wakes up' in Oz with Toto, her dog. She adds 'We must be over the rainbow.'

Quote 5: Jack Dawson, played by Leonardo DiCaprio in *Titanic* (1997), says this at the beginning of the film when he and a friend are at the front of the ship watching the dolphins swimming ahead of them. He will later stand in the same place with Rose (Kate Winslet).

Quote 6: This is the last thing Hannibal Lector says on the phone to Clarice in crime thriller *The Silence of the Lambs* (1991). The implication is that cannibal Lector will literally 'have' an old friend for dinner, as we see him watching two men get off a plane.

8A This exercise checks the use of *said/told* and is also a light-hearted quiz about well-known films, many of which Ss will be familiar with. It would, however, be a good idea to reassure Ss that they are not expected to know all the films, or the answers. Check the meaning of *film quotes* in the title of the quiz and do the first question with Ss as an example. If Ss don't know who said the quote, tell them they'll find out later. Give them 2–3 mins to complete the gaps and choose their answers. They can then compare and discuss answers in pairs/groups.

Answers: 1 said 2 told 3 said 4 told 5 said 6 said

B After Ss have checked their answers on p166, elicit more information about the quotes, using the **Culture notes** if necessary. Ask e.g. *What do you know about this film? Who was in it? When/where did this quote come in the film?* Also discuss the other films if Ss know/want to talk about them.

Answers: 1 a) 2 b) 3 c) 4 c) 5 c) 6 a)

C Check the example. Give Ss 3 mins to write their answers and compare them. In feedback, elicit the answers and check the verb changes made.

Answers: 2 He said he thought this was the beginning of a beautiful friendship. 3 He said he'd be back. 4 She said she had a feeling they weren't in Kansas any more. 5 He said he was the king of the world. 6 He said he was having an old friend for dinner.

SPEAKING

9A First read/check the questions with Ss. Elicit ideas for other questions Ss could add. Give Ss 3–4 mins to think about and note down their answers before they do Ex B. If they find it difficult to think of a film, they can use one from Ex 8. *Weaker Ss* could work together. Monitor and provide support where needed.

B Ss take turns to ask/answer the questions. Remind them to take notes for Ex C. Monitor discreetly while Ss work in groups, and make notes of examples of good language and problems.

C Give Ss 2–3 mins to rewrite their notes and put them in reported speech. They then take turns to talk about their partner's answers in groups. Monitor and make notes on problems Ss have with reported speech. Nominate Ss to tell the class about their partners in feedback. Find out if any particular film was chosen more than once. Write examples of Ss' errors and good language on the board. Ss discuss and correct them in pairs.

Homework ideas

- Ex 5: write your description of a film you know well.
- Ex 9B or C: write what your partner said about his/her favourite film.
- Language bank 12.1 Ex A–B, p151
- Workbook Ex 1–5, p69–70

WEB CELEBS

Introduction

Ss learn and practise the second conditional in the context of talking about hypothetical situations. They also study word patterns with suffixes.

SUPPLEMENTARY MATERIALS

Resource bank p191

Ex 3A and 9: dictionaries should be available for Ss.

Ex 9C: Ss can use internet facilities for research if available.

Warm up

Lead in to the topic of the lesson. Ask *Have you ever been in the local or national newspaper, or on TV? Why? When? How did you feel? Did you like it?* Give Ss 3–4 mins to discuss the questions in pairs/groups. If they haven't been in the newspapers/on TV themselves, they could talk about someone they know who has. In feedback, discuss Ss' answers.

VOCABULARY suffixes

1 Check the rubric and question and elicit Ss' answers related to the first photo. Teach *paparazzi*. Give Ss 3–4 mins to talk about the other photos. Elicit/discuss Ss' answers and find out what Ss think are the top three positive/negative things about being famous. N.B. The woman in the photo with the designer handbag is American actress Uma Thurman.

Suggested answers: positive: you're always in newspapers/magazines, companies want you to advertise their products, you have famous friends/(a) lovely home(s), you can buy expensive things, e.g. cars, jewellery, etc., you can talk to politicians to try and change the world **negative:** photographers/the paparazzi follow you and take your photograph wherever you go, you and your family have no privacy

2A Ask the question in the rubric and elicit Ss' answers. Then give them 2 mins to read the article and check. In feedback, check the answer and teach *embarrassing*.

Answer: An ordinary person who becomes famous because of the internet.

B Check the questions. Give Ss 4–5 mins to do the exercise and then compare answers. In feedback, check Ss' answers and discuss other web celebrities they've heard of. Also ask if they agree with Andy Warhol's quote.

Answers: 1 In the past, you had to be good at something to be famous (an actor, musician, sportsperson, etc.). Now, ordinary people can become famous on the internet on YouTube/for their weblog, etc. 2 Both Ghyslain Raza and Gary Brolsma had very popular/successful videos on YouTube. 3 Ss' own answers

3A Check the example with the suffix *-ful*. Ss then copy the table into their notebooks and find the other words in the text. In feedback, elicit the words and the pronunciation.

Answers: *-ous* (adj) famous; *-ion* (noun) invention; *-ity* (noun) celebrity; *-er/-or/-ian* (jobs) actor, musician

B Ss work alone/in pairs to do the exercise, using dictionaries if available. They will check their answers in Ex C.

C Ss listen and check that their answers are in the correct suffix columns. They listen again to underline the main stress. In feedback, play the recording again, pausing after each word for Ss to repeat. Drill each word chorally and individually if necessary.

Answers: *-ful* su<u>cc</u>essful, <u>help</u>ful, <u>won</u>derful; *-ous* <u>fa</u>mous, ad<u>ven</u>turous, <u>dan</u>gerous; *-ion* in<u>ven</u>tion, cele<u>bra</u>tion; *-ity* ce<u>leb</u>rity, popu<u>lar</u>ity; *-er/-or/-ian* pho<u>tog</u>rapher, <u>ac</u>tor, mu<u>si</u>cian, poli<u>ti</u>cian

D Give Ss 2–3 mins to think of other words. Elicit/add them to the correct column on the board.

Suggested answers: *-ity:* familiarity; *-ful:* painful; *-ous:* ridiculous; *-ion:* education; *-er:* teacher; *-or:* instructor; *-ian:* electrician

LISTENING

4A Check the rubric and give Ss 3–4 mins to answer the questions. In feedback, find out what Ss have in common, or not.

B Check the words in the box. Ss listen and write the answers, then check them in pairs. Play the recording again if students don't agree. Elicit Ss' answers in feedback (in bold in the audio script).

Answers: Speaker 2: a politician; Speaker 3: a footballer; Speaker 4: a singer/dancer; Speaker 5: a writer; Speaker 6: a (beautiful) actress; Speaker 7: a scientist/inventor; Speaker 8: –

5A Ss first read the sentences, and then listen and complete them. While they check their answers in pairs, monitor to see if they have the correct answers. If not, play the recording again, and then check answers with the class (underlined in the audio script). N.B. Don't focus on the second conditional yet.

Answers: 1 time 2 museum 3 change 4 World 5 sing 6 writer 7 rich 8 lives 9 happy

B Check the example and elicit Ss' opinions. Give them 3–4 mins to decide which speakers they agree with. Elicit and discuss their answers in feedback.

Unit 12 Recording 2

1 If I could be famous for anything, it would be art. I love painting and <u>if I had more time, I would love to **paint** seriously. If I could have a painting in a museum, I'd be really happy.</u>

2 I'd be a famous **politician**. <u>If I was a politician, I would try to change the world.</u> To stop all these wars and do something to help poor countries. You know, I think it's terrible how most politicians don't seem to worry about things like that.

3 If I could do anything, um … I think I'd be a famous **footballer** or something like that. <u>Imagine if you scored a goal for your country in the World Cup, that would be such a good feeling.</u> You would remember something like that forever.

4 <u>I'd love to sing. If I could be famous for anything, I think I'd be a singer.</u> Or a dancer. I'd love to be a famous dancer. I'm terrible at both of those things – I can't sing or dance! I guess that's why we have dreams, isn't it?

5 I would love to be a famous **writer, or poet,** like Shakespeare. I think it's a wonderful thing to be able to write a book that people all around the world want to read. To be able to speak to people in that way. Yes, <u>I'd like to be remembered as a great writer.</u> But I don't think that'll happen.

6 If I could be famous for anything, well, let me see … for being beautiful! That would be good. **One of those beautiful actresses** who wins at the Oscars. If I was famous, I would be rich, live in a big house, and have all those clothes. Oh yes, that would be nice.

7 If I could be famous for anything, it would be for **inventing something, like a medicine or a cure for cancer.** Not for being an actor, or a musician. If I invented something that made people's lives better, that would be good.

8 What would I want to be famous for? Hmm. I wouldn't like to be famous. If I was famous, I wouldn't be happy. No, I prefer just being me, thank you.

GRAMMAR second conditional

Watch out!

Conditional forms in English are relatively easy compared to many other languages as they don't use the subjunctive. It might be useful to point this out to Ss. However, they often confuse the second conditional forms in the main clause/*if* clause, and say, e.g. *If I would have more time, I would learn other languages.* (N.B. This is common usage in US English.) To help Ss with this problem, provide sufficient practice and feedback.

6A Ss refer to Ex 5A to complete the table, then compare their answers. In feedback, write the table on the board and elicit Ss' answers. They then copy the table into their notebooks.

Answers: 1 past 2 would/wouldn't 3 had 4 wouldn't 5 was

B Read the rules with Ss and elicit/check their answers. Also point out that the order of the *If*/main clause can change. Write an example on the board and show the position of the comma when the *if* clause is used first.

Answers: 1 imaginary 2 unlikely (impossible)

➡ LANGUAGEBANK 12.2 p150–151

Read/check the notes with your Ss, especially the use of *were* for giving advice. In Ex A, check *trains were running*. In Ex B, check *mess*.

Answers:
A 1 c) 2 f) 3 a) 4 d) 5 b) 6 e)
B 1 would go, were 2 sold, would (you) buy 3 would help, could 4 had, would call 5 had, would ask 6 lived, would see 7 Would (your brother) be, didn't work 8 didn't (always) make, would be

PRACTICE

7 Do an example. Ss then underline the correct answer and check in pairs. In feedback, check the form and rules of the second conditional again.

Answers: 1 would feel 2 had 3 didn't 4 didn't have 5 would use

8A Check the example. Give Ss 2–3 mins to write the questions and compare them. Check/drill the questions in feedback.

Answers: 2 If you could have dinner with any two living people, who would you choose? 3 If you had no money, what would you do? 4 If you had more time, what would you do? 5 If you could change one thing about yourself, what would you change?

B Elicit Ss' answers to the first question. While they work in pairs, make notes of problems they have with the second conditional. In feedback, nominate Ss to tell the class about their partners. Do remedial work on the second conditional if necessary.

WRITING paragraphs

9A Check the rubric and elicit briefly what Ss know about Albert Schweitzer. Give them 3–4 mins to do the exercise and compare answers. In feedback, check answers and ask Ss what they learnt about Schweitzer.

Answers: 1 c) 2 a) 3 d) 4 b)

B Check the meaning of *achievements, rise to fame*. Elicit the correct heading to each paragraph.

Answers: 1 Introduction 2 Childhood/education 3 Rise to fame 4 Achievements and later life

C If internet facilities are available in your school, Ss could do research for their profile. Otherwise, use the profile of Nelson Mandela on p167. Ss should use the model in Ex 9A and the speakout tip to help them. Monitor to support Ss and prompt them to correct their writing. Ss can display their final drafts around the classroom or put them on the class blog.

speakout TIP

Read and discuss the speakout tip with Ss before doing Ex 9C. Remind students to always write a plan before they write.

Model answer:

Nelson Rolihlahla Mandela was born in a village near Umtata in the Transkei, South Africa, on 18 July 1918. He went to a mission school where the teacher gave him his English name 'Nelson'. He later studied law at Fort Hare University and the University of Witwatersrand and qualified in 1942.

As a young man, Nelson moved to Johannesburg, where he started a law firm to help fight for the political rights of young black people. He was also an active member of the ANC (African National Congress) party.

In 1962, he was arrested for political activities. He spent nearly 27 years in prison and was released on 27 February 1990. He became head of the ANC, and was the first black man to be elected President of South Africa in 1994.

In 1993, he won the Nobel Peace Prize and was a world famous statesman. He retired from public life in 1999.

Homework ideas

- Ex 9C: write a final draft of your profile of a famous person, or write another profile.
- Language bank 12.2 Ex A–B, p151
- Workbook Ex 1–9, p71–72

WHAT CAN I DO FOR YOU?

Introduction

Ss learn/practise requests and offers in the context of dealing with a personal concierge. They also learn collocations related to the topic and how to ask for more time.

SUPPLEMENTARY MATERIALS

Resource bank p192

Ex 2B: download/bring pictures of *The Lion King* musical, the red carpet at the Oscars ceremony, the Rolling Stones, Madonna, Jennifer Lopez, Bill Clinton.

Ex 9B: use recording facilities if available.

Warm up

Lead in to the topic of the lesson. Ask/write these questions on the board: *If you could be a millionaire for one day … where would you go? What would you do? Would you invite other people? Who?* Elicit some initial answers and tell Ss to write down 4–6 things they would do. Encourage them to be imaginative. Ss then work in pairs/groups and take turns to exchange information. In feedback, discuss Ss' answers and find out who had the most original ideas.

VOCABULARY collocations

1A Check the words in the box and the example. Ss work alone and then compare answers. In feedback, check Ss' answers and elicit other examples that collocate with the verbs, e.g. *recommend a good film/book.*

Answers: 2 rent 3 book 4 invite 5 recommend 6 organise

B Ask *What can you see in each photo?* Elicit details and teach/check useful vocabulary, e.g. *it's a table for two in a restaurant; a chauffeur's opening the door of a car; a singer's performing at a concert, she's on the stage.* Then elicit collocations from Ex 1A to match each photo.

Answers: A book a table for two B organise a private tour/(rent a car) C get tickets for a concert

C Model/drill the question *How often do you get tickets for a concert?* Do a substitution drill using the collocations from Ex 1A: *How often do you rent a car/book a table/invite someone to dinner?*, etc. Ss then ask/answer the questions in pairs and report back to the class about their partner.

READING

2A Read/check the rubric and definition. Elicit one or two things Ss think a personal concierge can do. Then give them 2–3 mins to discuss and write a list of others. In feedback, elicit Ss' ideas and write them on the board.

B Give Ss 3 mins to read the text and underline what a personal concierge does. Ss discuss and compare them to their ideas on the board. In feedback, use pictures of the people/places mentioned as prompts, if possible. Elicit the things Ss have underlined and check them with their ideas on the board. Discuss their reactions to the 'amazing' things a personal concierge does. Also check *red carpet at the Oscars, former, client.*

Answers: book a table at the world's top restaurants, get the best seats for a popular musical, find you a private plane, organise a red carpet at the Oscars, get twenty tickets for a Rolling Stones concert, fly your favourite tea from one country to another, find rare birds, organise dinner with an ex-US President

FUNCTION requests and offers

3A Check the rubric. Ss listen, note down their answers and compare them. In feedback, check answers (in bold in the audio script). Also check *The White House, space flight, the Eiffel Tower.*

Answers: Client 1: wants to go on a private tour of the White House. Client 2: wants a ticket for a space flight. Client 3: wants to rent a boat (for 80 people) and take it down the River Thames for about three or four days. Client 4: wants to go for lunch in Paris.

B Ss read the sentences first, then listen again and complete them. Check/drill the answers in feedback (see underlined phrases in the audio script).

Answers: 1 like 2 possible 3 Would 4 able 5 want 6 Could 7 Shall

C Read/check the rubric and questions with Ss and elicit an example of a request/offer. Give them 3 mins to answer the questions before they compare answers. In feedback, elicit and check Ss' answers.

Answers: a) 1, 2, 4, 6 are requests. 3, 5 and 7 are offers. b) 1 c) 2 and 4 d) 6

Optional extra activity

Stronger classes could read the audio script and underline more examples of requests/offers.

Unit 12 Recording 3

Conversation 1

A: Hello Mr Pietersen. What can I do for you?
B: Hello, Tom. Um, I'd like to go on a private tour of the White House.
A: The White House? In Washington?
B: Yes.
A: OK.
B: And I'd like to go maybe tomorrow afternoon.
A: Tomorrow afternoon in the White House. OK.
B: Yes. If it's OK with the President.
A: Right, let me see if I have a number … hang on … ah, here it is. OK, I'll call the President's office and I'll get back to you later.
B: OK.

Conversation 2

A: Hello, Clara. What can I do for you today?
C: Hello, Tom. Would it be possible to book a ticket for that space flight?
A: What space flight is that?
C: I just saw it on TV. They're sending a flight into space next week and I would really like to go.
A: OK. I know the one you're talking about. Would you like me to get a ticket for your husband too?
C: Yes, please.
A: OK. Just a moment. I'll call Mr Branson.

Conversation 3

A: Hi there, David.

D: Hi, Tom. We'd like to **rent a boat** and take it down the River Thames for about three or four days. And it needs to be a big boat for about eighty people.

A: Eighty?

D: Yes, we're inviting a few friends along.

A: And when would you like it?

D: We told our friends this weekend. <u>Would you be able to organise it</u> for us?

A: Yes, of course. Can you give me a moment? I'll make a few calls. <u>Do you want me to get a</u> boat with a cook and restaurant service?

D: That would be wonderful.

Conversation 4

A: Hi, Maggie. How can I help?

E: Hi, Tom. We're in London and **we're going out for lunch** and we were wondering … well, <u>could you recommend somewhere</u> in **Paris**?

A: In Paris?

E: Yes, we're going to take the helicopter.

A: What type of food?

E: Any type really. Well, French.

A: French. OK. Um, there's a very good restaurant near the Eiffel Tower.

E: Oh good. That's perfect.

A: <u>Shall I book it?</u>

E: Yes, please. And can you give us directions?

A: Have you got your laptop with you?

E: Yes.

A: Hold on. I'll email you a map.

⟱ **LANGUAGE BANK** 12.3 p150–151

Ss can refer to the tables for help with this exercise. Check *plumber*.

Answers:
A Conversation 1: A: *Could* you recommend … ?
B: Would you like *me* to show you … ?
Conversation 2: A: I'd like *to* eat out tonight. B: OK. Do you *want* me to choose? B: OK. And *shall* I book … ?
Conversation 3: A: Would you be *able* to get me … ?
B: *No* problem. A: Would *it* be possible … ? B: Yes, *of* course.

4A Do an example with Ss. Monitor while they write the sentences to check how well they have understood the target language. In feedback, check Ss' answers.

Answers: 1 I'd like to try some local food. 2 Could you recommend a good nightclub? 3 Would you be able to book three tickets? 4 Would it be possible to rent a car? 5 Shall I buy your ticket? 6 Do you want me to book a table? 7 Would you like me to call the manager?

B First check *print out, daily rates, box office* with **weaker classes**. Otherwise do it in feedback. Give Ss 2 mins to match the responses and check in pairs. Elicit/ask Ss to justify their answers by giving you key words, e.g. in answer 1b), *local food, restaurants*.

Answers: 1 b) 2 c) 3 d) 4 a) 5 g) 6 e) 7 f)

5A Elicit details of places/activities in the picture, e.g. *zoo/ museum/gym, go dancing/skiing, go to Disneyland, see a film, eat fish and chips.* Then elicit example answers for question 1, e.g. *Could you recommend a good gym/a film/a place where we can dance?* Ss then write their own requests. Monitor and help them with accuracy in preparation for Ex B.

B Check the example and elicit the offer of help in B's response. Tell Ss to make similar offers in their responses. Monitor while Ss work and make notes of good use of the target language, and problems. In feedback, invite pairs to act out their conversations to the class. Do a correction slot using your notes.

LEARN TO ask for more time

6A Do the example. Then give Ss 2 mins to underline three more phrases and compare answers. Elicit/check them in feedback.

Answers: Just a moment. Can you give me a moment? Hold on.

B Read the rubric and elicit/check Ss' answers.

Answers: The phrases are informal. *Can you give me a moment?* is the most formal.

7A Do an example for conversation 1, using language from Ex 6. Ss then work alone. Tell them to ignore the underlined words for now. After Ss have compared their answers, elicit/ check them.

Answers: 1 Hang *on.* 2 Can you give *me* a moment? 3 *Just* a moment. 4 Hold *on.*

B Ss first listen to the stress and intonation of the answers from Ex 7A. Play the recording again for them to listen and repeat. Beat the stress/intonation while Ss repeat if necessary (see underlined stressed words/syllables in the answer key below). Drill the sentences both chorally and individually, prompting Ss to correct themselves/each other.

Answers: 1 <u>Hang</u> <u>on.</u> <u>I'll</u> <u>call</u> him on his <u>mobile.</u> 2 Can you <u>give</u> me a <u>moment?</u> I <u>need</u> to make a <u>call.</u> 3 Just a <u>moment.</u> I'll <u>speak</u> to him. 4 Hold <u>on.</u> I'll <u>call</u> the <u>airline.</u>

C Check the underlined words and elicit what Ss know about the famous names/places. Then check the example. Give Ss 2–3 mins to plan and rehearse what they are going to say. Provide support if necessary. Monitor while Ss read the conversations. In feedback, invite pairs to read them to the class.

SPEAKING

8 Divide the class into As and Bs. They read their roles on p165 and p167. Ss first prepare their roles in pairs while you monitor and provide support. Then Ss work in A/B pairs and do the role-plays. Make notes of their performance for feedback.

9A Ss write one of their conversations in pairs using the information provided in the rubric. Monitor to check they do this and prompt them if necessary. Also support them while they rehearse their conversations for Ex B.

B If you have recording facilities, use them here to record Ss' role-plays for feedback.

Homework ideas
- Ex 9: write another conversation from p165–167.
- Language bank 12.3 Ex A, p151
- Workbook Ex 1–5, p73

BILLION DOLLAR MAN

Introduction

Ss watch an extract from the BBC documentary about Formula 1 driver Lewis Hamilton. They then learn and practise how to talk/write about their dreams and ambitions.

SUPPLEMENTARY MATERIALS

Warm up: download/bring pictures of people doing extreme sports, e.g. rock climbing, surfing, skydiving, snowboarding, scuba diving, skiing, F1 racing.

Ex 1: bring/download pictures of famous contemporary Formula 1 drivers.

Warm up

Lead in and create interest in the lesson. Elicit the names of 6–8 extreme sports, as listed in the supplementary materials box above, and write them on the board. If you have pictures of these sports, use them as prompts. Ask *Which are the most dangerous/exciting sports? Which have you done? Which would you like to try?* Give Ss 3–4 min to discuss their answers in pairs/groups. Ss could put the sports in order of most dangerous/exciting. Elicit/discuss Ss' answers in feedback and find out which sports Ss would most/least like to try.

DVD PREVIEW

1 Give Ss 3–4 mins to discuss the questions. If possible, use pictures of famous F1 drivers from their countries/worldwide as prompts for question 1. In feedback, elicit what Ss know about F1 drivers and check/teach language to describe what type of people they are, e.g. *ambitious, brave/courageous, talented, excellent driving skills, very fit, able to concentrate.* Elicit/drill the pronunciation of the longer words and write them on the board.

Culture notes

British F1 champion **Lewis Hamilton** was born in 1985. He began driving remote-controlled cars in 1990. His father bought him a go-kart in 1993 and worked very hard to support his son's racing career. In 1998, Lewis joined McLaren's young driver programme. He first drove in Formula 1 in 2007 and won the F1 World Championship in 2008, the youngest British F1 champion ever. The BBC documentary *Lewis Hamilton: Billion Dollar Man* was first broadcast in November 2008.

2A First look at the photos of Lewis Hamilton. Ask *What do you know about him?* Elicit Ss' answers. They then read the text to check their ideas, and answer the questions in the rubric. In feedback, check Ss' answers to the questions and find out if any of their ideas were in the text. They will find out more about Hamilton in the DVD.

Answers: 1 He was in his early twenties (21–24). 2 Yes. He came from a normal family and says his life is now like a dream which has come true.

B Do the first one as an example. Ss then do the exercise alone and compare their answers. In feedback, elicit/check Ss' answers. While doing this, teach *glory, though, attitude, sponsors.*

Answers: 1 ordinary 2 sponsors 3 ambitious 4 progression 5 attitude 6 celebrity 7 impact

DVD VIEW

Culture notes

British athlete **Denise Lewis** is an Olympic gold medal winner in the heptathlon.

Blue Peter is a long-running BBC TV programme for children.

John Leslie was a *Blue Peter* presenter in the 1980s.

3 Check the questions and play the DVD. Ss note down their answers and then compare them. Play the relevant sections of the DVD again if necessary. In feedback, nominate Ss to give the answers (in bold in the DVD script). Elicit/discuss Ss' initial impressions of the DVD.

Answers: 1 'Millionaires and heroes' 2 He was racing electric cars. He was seven. 3 He wanted to be a Formula 1 champion before he was twenty. He likes the speed, to be with all the important 'big' guys, and making lots of money.

4 Ss read the sentences first. Check *loads, passionate, absolutely, unreal* either here or in feedback, if you have a **stronger class.** Ss watch the DVD and number the answers. Monitor while Ss compare them to check if they need to watch the DVD again. In feedback, check Ss' answers (underlined in the DVD script).

Answers: 1 f) 2 b) 3 c) 4 a) 5 e) 6 d)

Optional extra activity

Exploit the context and language of the DVD further. Play it again, pausing at suitable points. Ask questions about what Ss can see/hear, e.g. *What's Lewis doing? Where is he? How long is the Formula 1 season? Where does it take place? What was he like when he was seven/a teenager?*

DVD 12 Lewis Hamilton: Billion Dollar Man

VO=Voiceover W1=Woman 1 W2= Woman 2 DL=Denise Lewis JL=John Leslie LH=Lewis Hamilton NR= Newsreader

VO: This is Lewis Hamilton, Formula 1 driver, model, celebrity, winner.

MAN: He has a face, an attitude, a style and a talent that the sponsors love.

W1: Everybody's talking about Lewis Hamilton. Everyone wants to talk to me about Lewis Hamilton. I want to talk to them about Lewis Hamilton.

W2: He's my new hero. He really is. He's a hero for loads of people.

DL: I feel so passionate about his story, his progression and the impact he's made on Formula 1.

VO: This is the story of how Lewis Hamilton went from this – to this.

Formula 1 is all about speed. In this world, only the fastest survive. The season lasts from March to October, and it takes place in some of the world's richest locations. **It's the sport of millionaires – and heroes.** Speed on the track, money in the bank, fame and glory. And nobody does it better than Lewis Hamilton, the billion dollar man. A hero today. But where did it all start?

JL: Cars like these are getting ready to compete in the World Championships. Someone who's preparing for those very same championships is Lewis Hamilton, who is only seven years old. So how long have you been racing cars for already, Lewis?

LH: About a year.

JL: So you must be pretty good at it. Is it easy to do?

LH: No.

JL: What do you have to do then?

LH: This is the brake.

JL: That's the brake. Oh, you need the brake.

LH: And these are the turns for steering.

JL: That's your steering wheel, right and left. OK, now, do you think I'd be able to have a go?

LH: Yes.

JL: You sure? Well, they're under starter's orders for the *Blue Peter* mini-Grand Prix. Three, two, one. Go! And I'm last already. I hope you're allowed to do that. Put it back on the track. I'm going to be lapped. It's been brought back on. And cars are over me all the time. And we have a winner. Who won the race?

LH: Me!

JL: Lewis! Well done! Congratulations!

LH: The reason I want to be a Formula 1 driver is because it's got a lot of speed in it. When I saw the actual speed that they were doing, it was amazing because you don't actually think about it when you're watching on TV. And my kart feels really powerful when I'm in it but imagine being in a Formula 1 car. It must be very powerful.

NR: Lewis Hamilton has won four British go-karting championships. Now he says he wants to be World Formula 1 champion by the time he's twenty.

LH: My ambition is to get to Formula 1. Definitely. I enjoy the speed. I like to be with all the … the big guys, and I like to be making lots of money.

VO: After go-karting, Lewis moved on to Formula 3, which is two levels below Formula 1. Formula 3 is fast, dangerous, and full of young, ambitious drivers. The best of the drivers are seen by Formula 1 managers. And Lewis, of course, was the best. After two years of winning everything, he moved up to the next level, and then to Formula 1.

LH: It's so different to what I'm used to. Before, I was just a driver, but now it seems to change absolutely everything, and it's just an unreal feeling. It's my dream come true basically.

5 Elicit Ss' definition of a *hero*. They then give their opinions in pairs/groups. In feedback, elicit/discuss them.

speakout dreams and ambitions

> **Culture notes**
> Jimi Hendrix (1942–1970) was an American guitarist, singer and songwriter.
>
> Keith Moon (1946–1978) was the drummer of the rock group The Who.
>
> Jim Morrison (1943 –1971) was an American singer, songwriter, poet, writer and filmmaker. He was the lead singer and lyricist of the band The Doors.
>
> Nick Drake (1948–1974) was a singer/songwriter whose album *Pink Moon* became famous in the 1990s.

6A Check the rubric/questions and the words *inspire, special skill, achieve a dream*. Ss then listen and tick the answers, and then compare them. Elicit/check them in feedback. Find out what Ss know about Jimi Hendrix, Keith Moon (The Who), Jim Morrison (The Doors), Nick Drake (see **Culture notes**).

> **Answers:** ✓ 1, 2, 3, 5

B Ss discuss what Rhodri said in more detail. Play the recording again if Ss need more information. In feedback, elicit answers and Ss' reasons for them (see bold in the audio script).

> **Answers:** 1 He grew up in South Wales. 2 He wanted to be a rock star. 3 He was inspired by listening to his father's records on a Sunday afternoon. 4 No, he didn't. 5 He never became a famous rock star, but he was a musician and had songs on the radio.

Unit 12 Recording 5

I'm 28 and I live in South Wales. I've grown up here. My dream began from an early age. As a child, I always used to listen to my Dad's records on a Sunday afternoon. And the music really excited me. I knew I wanted to be a rock star. As a teenager, I had music idols: Jimi Hendrix, Keith Moon, Jim Morrison, Nick Drake. Many of them died before they were 27. It made me think that I had to do something about my dream, before it was too late. When I was 15 I bought myself a second-hand drum kit. I joined bands, and we played concerts. And then I started to write songs. I played all the time. I played for pleasure, I played for money, I played when I was angry. It was like everything I ever wanted. But although we had songs on the radio, we never got famous. I don't know when my dream started to change. But at 28 it was like I woke up and I realised there was something else. I was watching my son grow up, to have his own dreams and ambitions. I woke up to my family, and my friends. I still play, but it's just for fun because I'm 28 now and it's time to live.

C First check the rubric and **key phrases**. Elicit sample answers to the questions in Ex 6A. Give Ss 4–5 mins to write their notes. Monitor closely to provide support where needed.

D Ss work in pairs and take turns to talk about their dreams and ambitions. They should make notes of similarities in their answers. Monitor and make notes on Ss' performance for feedback later. In feedback, Ss report back to the class about their group. Find out which ambitions the class shares now.

writeback a web comment

7 Give Ss 2–3 mins to read the text and answer the questions. Check Ss' answers and check *Sociology, law/lawyer*.

> **Answers:** 1 a teacher 2 He wants to go back to college, study to become a lawyer and work in international law.

8 Ss write a web comment in answer to the three questions, using their notes from Ex 6. Provide support if needed.

> **Homework ideas**
> • Ex 6D: write about a partner's dreams and ambitions for a website or your class blog.

LOOKBACK

Introduction

With *stronger classes*, you could exploit the last **Lookback** section in a slightly different way. Put Ss in pairs/groups and ask *Which areas of the language here do you feel most/least confident about? Which would you like to do first?* Give Ss 15–20 mins to do the sections they choose. Monitor and provide support as needed, while you also assess Ss' performance. In feedback, check Ss' answers as far as possible, or give them a copy of the answer key for them to check their own work. Ask, e.g. *Why did you choose these sections? How well did you do them? What did you learn?* Discuss Ss' answers.

FILM

1A Check the words in the box (unless you want this exercise to be a test). Ss then complete the text alone and check their answers in pairs. In feedback, elicit/check Ss' answers.

Answers: 1 thriller 2 director 3 actors 4 star 5 role 6 scene 7 extras

B Give Ss 3–4 mins to prepare and make notes. *Weaker Ss* could refer to SB p118–119 for help. While Ss describe their favourite film, monitor and take notes for feedback and/or assessment. In feedback, find out how many Ss chose the same film.

REPORTED SPEECH

2A Do an example and find out what Ss know about the *Lethal Weapon* films. Give them 4–5 mins to write their sentences and compare answers. Monitor and note down problems they have with reported speech. Nominate Ss to answer and give feedback/do remedial work as needed. Elicit what Ss know about the films mentioned, and what they know about the context of the quotes.

Answers: 1 He said he was too old for this. 2 He said it was a strange world. 3 He said where they were going, they didn't need roads. 4 He said he could see now. 5 He said it was too bad she wouldn't live, but then again who did.

B Ss discuss the question and compare answers with another pair. In feedback, discuss Ss answers and reasons for their choices.

SUFFIXES

3A Give Ss 3–4 mins to do the exercise and then compare answers. In feedback, check the meaning/pronunciation of each word. Drill the questions if necessary.

Answers: 1 dangerous 2 wonderful 3 celebration 4 famous 5 politician, musician 6 successful

B Give Ss time to prepare their answers. They then take turns to ask/answer the questions. They should note down their partner's answers and report back to the class in feedback. Monitor discreetly, making notes of Ss' errors. In feedback, Ss tell the class/group about their partner. Do remedial work as required.

SECOND CONDITIONAL

4 Ss read the sentences first. If necessary, check *upset, scarf, desert island, ideal partners*. Give Ss 4–5 mins to complete the sentences and compare answers. Check Ss' answers and do remedial work on the second conditional if needed.

Answers: 1 didn't have to, would take 2 would be, lost 3 were able to, would (you) choose 4 lived, would be 5 wouldn't say, knew 6 would be, didn't argue

5 Do the example with Ss around the class, each one adding a new 'consequence' for as long as possible. They then do the exercise in pairs/groups. Monitor and make notes of Ss' problems for feedback. In feedback, invite pairs/groups to act out their longest exchange to the class. Find out who has the longest.

Optional extra activity

Ss work in pairs/groups. Ask *If you had a time machine, which year would you go to? Where would you go? Why? What would you do? Who would you meet?* Elicit sample answers, e.g. *If I had a time machine, I'd go to the year 1500. I'd go to Florence and meet Leonardo da Vinci. I'd ask him lots of questions and take his photo on my mobile.* Ss ask/answer the questions and report back to the class.

REQUESTS AND OFFERS

6A Ss underline the correct alternative and compare answers. In feedback, elicit/drill the answers and ask *Which is a request/offer?*

Answers: 1 to see 2 me to buy 3 able to 4 recommend 5 I call you 6 me to get 7 like to visit

B Check the rubric and *wildest dreams*. Give Ss time to choose their three things from the box, or use their own ideas. Encourage them to be imaginative.

C Check the example and the meaning of *whereabouts*. Give Ss time to prepare how they want to make their requests and provide support if necessary. Ss should take turns to be the concierge. Monitor and make notes of their performance for feedback and/or assessment. In feedback, invite pairs to act out their conversations to the class. Do remedial work as needed.

Homework ideas
- **Workbook** Review and Check 4, p74–75
- **Workbook** Test 4, p76

PAGE	UNIT	PHOTOCOPIABLE	LANGUAGE POINT	TIME
145	1	Love story	**Vocabulary: relationships** • recycle vocabulary of relationships • practise structured story telling using the past simple	30–35
146	1	Heads and tails	**Grammar: question forms** • practise forming questions • practise speaking skills by talking about free time activities using the present simple and the past simple	25–30
147	1	Talk about it!	**Grammar: past simple** • practise speaking skills using the past simple	30–35
148	1	Party time!	**Functional language: making conversation** • practise functional language for making polite conversation	30–35
149	2	What do I do?	**Vocabulary: jobs** • review vocabulary of professions, work and the workplace • practise speaking skills in the context of a guessing game	20–30
150	2	Grammar maze	**Grammar: present simple and continuous** • practise the present simple and present continuous • practise speaking skills by asking and answering questions	30–40
151	2	How often do you … ?	**Grammar: adverbs of frequency** • use adverbs of frequency to talk about habits and free time activities • practise speaking skills in the context of a game	20–30
152	2	I can't stand cheese!	**Functional language: expressing likes/dislikes** • practise functional phrases for expressing likes and dislikes	20–30
153	3	You've hit my composer!	**Vocabulary: the arts** • review vocabulary of culture and the arts • review letters and spelling	20–30
154	3	Bank Holiday weekend	**Grammar: present continuous/*be going to* for future** • use the present continuous and *be going to* to make future arrangements • practise speaking skills by accepting and refusing invitations	30–40
155	3	Is it art?	**Grammar: questions without auxiliaries** • use questions without auxiliaries to complete a text about Banksy • practise speaking skills by asking and answering questions	20–30
156	3	Who's calling?	**Functional language: making a phone call** • practise functional language for making and receiving phone calls	25–35
157	4	Collocation football	**Vocabulary: *make* and *do*; education** • review collocations with *make, do, give, play, study, tell* and *wear* • practise speaking skills by talking about education and school	15–25
158	4	Have you ever … ?	**Grammar: present perfect + *ever/never*** • use the present perfect and past simple to talk about life experiences • review the past participles of irregular verbs	25–35
159	4	Class rules	**Grammar: *can, have to, must*** • use *can, have to* and *must* to write rules for the class • practise speaking skills by discussing rules and obligations	25–35
160	4	Save our school!	**Functional language: giving advice** • practise functional language of giving advice and responding to advice for schools	30–40
161	5	Getting around	**Vocabulary: transport** • review of vocabulary of types of transport • practise speaking skills by describing types of transport	20–25
162	5	Missing money	**Grammar: past simple and past continuous** • use the past simple and past continuous to talk about a crime	20–30
163	5	20 things about you	**Grammar: verb patterns** • use verb patterns to talk about yourself	20–30
164	5	Tipton tour	**Functional language: asking for/giving directions** • practise functional language for giving and following directions around a town	25–30
165	6	A healthy city	**Vocabulary: sports** • review vocabulary of sports • practise speaking skills – agreeing and disagreeing	20–30
166	6	How long … ?	**Grammar: present perfect + *for/since*** • use the present perfect + *for/since* to talk about sports stars • review some sports vocabulary	25–30
167	6	Predictions	**Grammar: *may, might, will*** • use *may, may not, might, might not* and *will/won't* to talk about future predictions	25–30
168	6	Where does it hurt?	**Functional language: seeing the doctor** • practise functional language for visiting the doctor	20–30

RESOURCE BANK

Index of photocopiables

PAGE	UNIT	PHOTOCOPIABLE	LANGUAGE POINT	
169	7	Another life	**Vocabulary: verbs + prepositions** • use verbs with prepositions to talk about life changes • practise speaking skills – sharing personal information	2
170	7	Did you know … ?	**Grammar: *used to*** • use *used to* to describe past states and habits of famous people and things • practise speaking skills in the context of a quiz	2
171	7	I went home to …	**Grammar: purpose, cause and result** • use *to, because* and *so* to express purpose, cause and result in the context of a game	2
172	7	Career change	**Functional language: finding out information** • practise functional language for finding out information in the context of changing careers	2
173	8	Amazing money	**Vocabulary: money** • review vocabulary for money • practise speaking skills by doing a quiz	2
174	8	Four guesses	**Grammar: relative clauses** • use relative clauses to describe familiar and successful things and places for a guessing game	3
175	8	Let's celebrate!	**Grammar: *too much/many, enough, very*** • use *too much/too many, enough/not enough* and *very* in the context of planning a party	3
176	8	Can I help you?	**Functional language: buying things** • practise functional language for shopping and buying things	2
177	9	It's a cheetah!	**Vocabulary: animals** • review the names of animals in the context of a game	2
178	9	Compare it!	**Grammar: comparatives/superlatives** • use comparatives and superlatives to make comparisons in a board game	2
179	9	Race to the South Pole	**Grammar: articles** • practise recognising incorrect article use in a text about an explorer	2
180	9	It might be …	**Functional language: making guesses** • practise functional language for making guesses and speculating about objects	2
181	10	Crime crossword	**Vocabulary: crime and punishment** • review vocabulary of crime and punishment	2
182	10	What's it like?	**Grammar: uses of *like*** • use *like* for descriptions, opinions and positive and negative attributes in a snakes and ladders game	3
183	10	I don't believe it!	**Grammar: present/past passive** • use the passive in the context of discussing surprising facts • revise irregular verb forms	3
184	10	Excuse me …	**Functional language: complaining** • practise functional language for making and dealing with complaints in a variety of situations	3
185	11	Dominoes	**Vocabulary: feelings** • practise recognising adjectives to describe feelings	2
186	11	Who am I?	**Grammar: present perfect (+ *just, yet, already*)** • use the present perfect and *just, already* and *yet* in a guessing game	2
187	11	Conditional wheels	**Grammar: first conditional** • use the first conditional to make sentence chains	3
188	11	Gadgets	**Functional language: giving opinions** • practise functional language for giving opinions and disagreeing politely about new ideas	3
189	12	Noughts and crosses	**Vocabulary: film** • review vocabulary of films in the context of a game	1
190	12	Star interview	**Grammar: reported speech** • practise speaking skills in the context of an interview • use reported speech to repeat information from an interview	3
191	12	Three in a row	**Grammar: second conditional** • use the second conditional to describe imaginary situations in a game	3
192	12	All in a day's work	**Functional language: requests and offers** • practise functional language for making requests and offers	3

1 Match pictures A–H with the words and phrases in the box below.

didn't have a girlfriend **A**	fell in love	met	argued	got married	accepted
got back together again	got divorced	asked her to marry him	got on well	

2 Put the pictures in order to make a story.

When did you last	buy something expensive?
When did you last	go on holiday or have time off?
What is	your favourite book?
What is	your favourite sport?
Were you	feeling happy yesterday?
Were you	at home last night?
Do you have	a best friend?
Do you spend	a lot of money?
How often do you play	or watch sport?
How often do you cook	for other people?
Where do you go	out with friends?
Where do your	family live?

Talk about a journey you took.

1

Talk about your best holiday.

5

Talk about the last time you met your friends.

1

Talk about an easy subject at school.

4

Talk about your first English lesson.

2

Talk about what you last saw at the cinema.

4

Talk about your first bike or car.

4

Talk about the last time you cried or laughed a lot.

2

Talk about your favourite toy when you were a child.

5

Talk about the last time you worked or studied hard.

3

Talk about your first day at school.

3

Talk about how you met your best friend.

6

Talk about what you cooked/ate yesterday.

1

Talk about a difficult subject at school.

3

Talk about the last present you bought.

2

Talk about the last party you went to.

5

PARTY TIME!

Functional language: making conversation

Role card 1

Tom from Scotland

Family	wife: Elizabeth
Occupation	actor
Recreation	going shopping and cooking
Education	parents – at home
Task	Find out who is an architect.

Role card 2

Sarah from Australia

Family	boyfriend: Brad
Occupation	dancer
Recreation	driving fast cars and riding horses
Education	went to a school for actors and dancers
Task	Find out who went to school in Japan.

Role card 3

Joe from Wales

Family	wife: Maria, five children and ten pets
Occupation	doctor
Recreation	gardening and having barbecues
Education	went to school in Canada
Task	Find out who is a lawyer.

Role card 4

Annie from Ireland

Family	husband: James
Occupation	TV Presenter
Recreation	playing football and learning languages
Education	Bath University
Task	Find out who likes fishing.

Role card 5

David from England

Family	married twice, three children
Occupation	fire fighter
Recreation	karate and painting
Education	didn't go to school very much
Task	Find out who is a dancer.

Role card 6

Jenny from New Zealand

Family	no husband, one child
Occupation	chef
Recreation	playing golf and travelling
Education	went to school in Japan
Task	Find out who comes from Scotland.

Role card 7

Andrew from Northern Ireland

Family	wife: Angela and a pet crocodile
Occupation	singer
Recreation	running and making cakes
Education	went to an expensive private school
Task	Find out who has ten pets.

Role card 8

Laura from the United States of America

Family	husband: John
Occupation	architect
Recreation	reading and playing the guitar
Education	Harvard University
Task	Find out who went to Bath University.

Role card 9

Ewan from England

Family	wife: Kate
Occupation	businessman
Recreation	boxing and fishing
Education	went to eleven different schools
Task	Find out who likes making cakes.

Role card 10

Rachel from South Africa

Family	three sisters
Occupation	lawyer
Recreation	swimming and having barbecues
Education	went to school in Cape Town
Task	Find out who has three children.

START

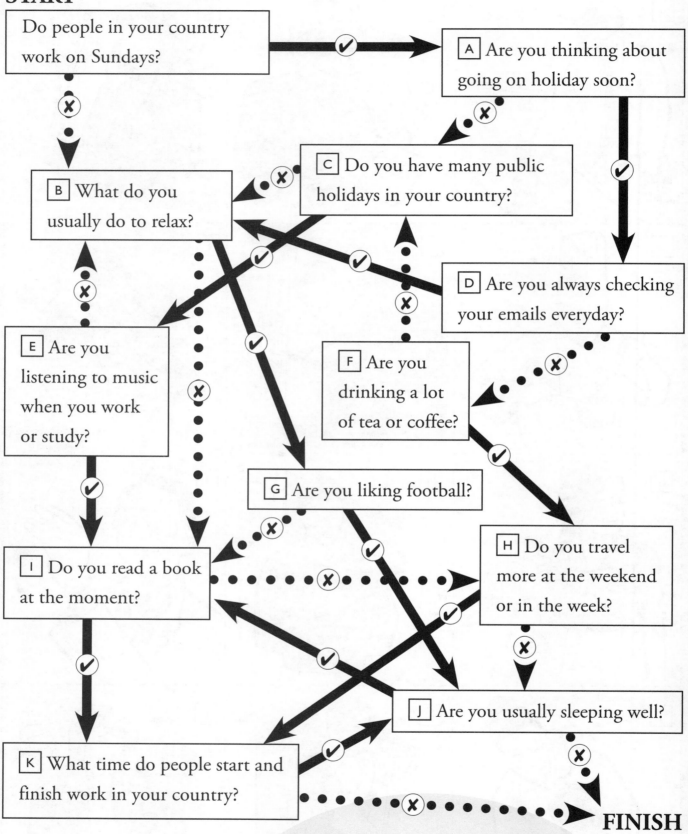

Do people in your country work on Sundays?

A Are you thinking about going on holiday soon?

B What do you usually do to relax?

C Do you have many public holidays in your country?

D Are you always checking your emails everyday?

E Are you listening to music when you work or study?

F Are you drinking a lot of tea or coffee?

G Are you liking football?

H Do you travel more at the weekend or in the week?

I Do you read a book at the moment?

J Are you usually sleeping well?

K What time do people start and finish work in your country?

FINISH

Read the questions. If the grammar is correct follow the black arrow. If the grammar is incorrect follow the dotted arrow to the next box.

Write the order here: Start __ __ __ __ __ __ __ __ __ __ Finish

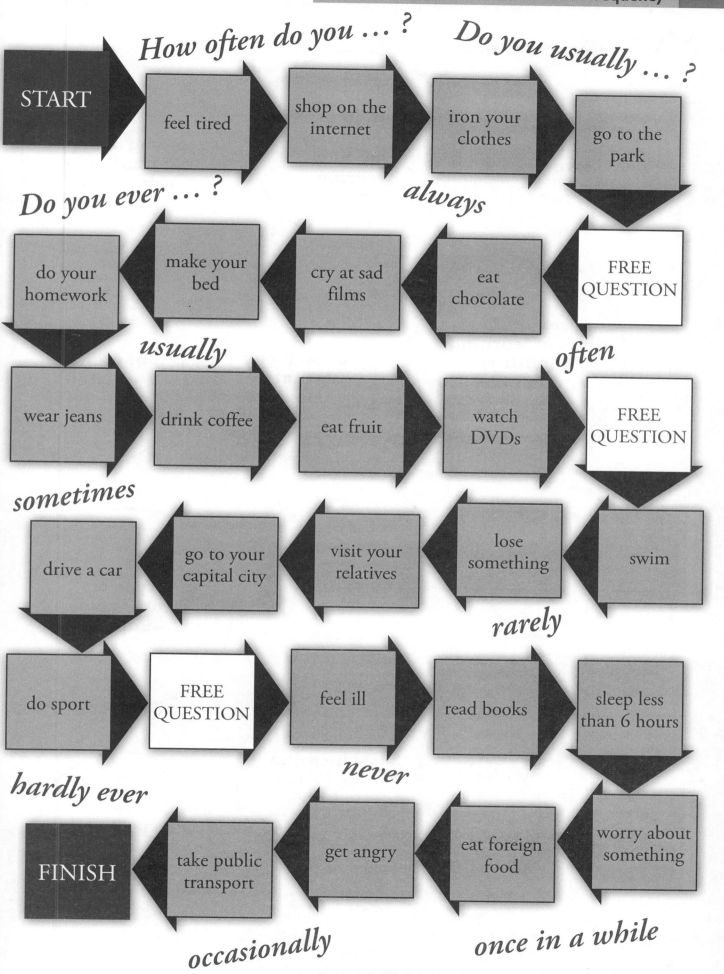

I CAN'T STAND CHEESE!

Functional language: expressing likes/dislikes

Write the name of …

1
a food you absolutely love

_____

2
an item of clothing you like wearing

_____

3
a song or type of music you can't stand

_____

4
something about learning English you don't like

_____

5
a smell you absolutely love

_____

6
housework you don't mind doing

_____

7
a food you can't stand

_____

8
a building you don't like in your hometown

_____

9
a type of weather you hate

_____

10
a colour you like

_____

11
something on TV you hate

_____

12
a sport you are keen on

_____

Student A

Put these words somewhere in the grid:

| audience | actor | concert | exhibition | singer | jazz | painter | band |

	1	2	3	4	5	6	7	8	9	10
A										
B										
C										
D										
E										
F										
G										
H										
I										
J										

Miss!

Hit 'a'!

You've hit my (play)!

Student B

Put these words somewhere in the grid:

| composer | rock | classical | painting (n) | pop | sculpture | play (n) | artist |

	1	2	3	4	5	6	7	8	9	10
A										
B										
C										
D										
E										
F										
G										
H										
I										
J										

Miss!

Hit 'a'!

You've hit my (composer)!

The *London* Guide:

The best of what's on in London this Bank Holiday

Art/Dance/Culture	Cinema/Theatre	Special Events	Sport
Art Exhibition See the work of the great artist Salvador Dali at The National Gallery. All weekend from 10a.m. until 5p.m. £15	**Shakespeare at Night** See *Romeo and Juliet* outside at Regent's Park Theatre. Saturday, 7p.m. until 11p.m. £30	**International Food Fair** Taste food from all over the world and meet famous chefs in Brick Lane. All weekend from 10a.m. until 5p.m. £15	**Brazil v Argentina** Two great football teams and both here in London! It will be a great match at Wembley Stadium. Saturday, 3p.m. £30
Russian Ballet See the world's best ballet dancers in Covent Garden. Saturday/Sunday, 7.30p.m. until 10p.m. £30	**Horror Film Day** See lots of famous horror films and meet actors, directors and monsters in Covent Garden. Saturday, 1p.m. until 11p.m. £15	**Rock Concert** See the best London and international rock bands in Hyde Park. Saturday, 1p.m. until late Free	**Extreme Sports Fair** Watch and try extreme sports at the ExCeL Exhibition Centre. All weekend from 11a.m. until 5p.m. £25
French Circus See the world's best circus in Camden Town. Everyday from 7p.m. until 10p.m. £25	**Star Wars Film Fair** Meet some of the actors, thousands of fans and watch the films in Leicester Square. Sunday, 11a.m. until 5p.m. £15	**Street Carnival** A celebration of London's different cultures: music, food, dancing and lots more in Notting Hill. Sunday, 12p.m. until late Free	**Fun Run** Run 5km from Buckingham Palace to the Tower of London with thousands of people or just watch! Sunday, 10a.m. until 4p.m. Free

Saturday 27

morning	9a.m. breakfast with Sarah at The Corner Café
afternoon	
evening	

Sunday 28

morning	
afternoon	
evening	

Monday 29 BANK HOLIDAY

morning	
afternoon	
evening	

Worksheet A

Ask your partner questions to find the missing information in your text. Use the words in brackets.

Banksy is a ¹_____ (who). He is probably the most famous one in the world. He became famous in the early 2000s, but we know very little about him. We know he was born in 1974, in Bristol, UK and lives and works in Shoreditch, London. Perhaps his real name is ²_____ or _____ (what). There are no photos of Banksy because he doesn't want people to know who he is.

Banksy makes 'street art' and it is in many countries including ³_____ , _____ , and _____ (where). His art is successful because it's powerful, it's simple and often funny. Animals such as ⁴_____ and _____ (which) are often in his pictures as well as people like police officers, soldiers and children. However, a London council painted over one of Banksy's famous paintings in 2009 because they thought it looked like graffiti.

Banksy's art now sells for hundreds of thousands of dollars and he sells art to many famous people. In 2007 ⁵_____ and _____ (who) spent $2 million on his work. His most successful exhibition was in Bristol in 2009. There were over 8,500 visitors every day. However, his parents don't even know what he does. They think his job is painting houses!

Worksheet B

Ask your partner questions to find the missing information in your text. Use the words in brackets.

Banksy is a famous graffiti artist. He is probably the most famous one in the world. He became famous in the early 2000s, but we know very little about him. We know he was born in ¹_____ (when), in Bristol, UK and lives and works in Shoreditch, London. Perhaps his real name is Robert or Robin Banks. There are no photos of Banksy because ²_____ (why).

Banksy makes 'street art' and it is in many countries including USA, Australia, and Israel. His art is successful because it's ³_____ , it's _____ and often _____ (why). Animals such as rats and monkeys are often in his pictures as well as people like police officers, soldiers and children. However, ⁴_____ (who) painted over one of Banksy's famous paintings in 2009 because they thought it looked like graffiti.

Banksy's art now sells for hundreds of thousands of dollars and he sells art to many famous people. In 2007 Brad Pitt and Angelina Jolie spent $2 million on his work. His most successful exhibition was in ⁵_____ (where) in 2009. There were over 8,500 visitors every day. However, his parents don't even know what he does. They think his job is painting houses!

Role card 1A

You booked a General English course for two weeks at The English School.

The course starts next Monday, but you want to change it to a course one month later.

Phone the school.

Role card 1B

You are a receptionist at The English School.

There are courses available next month.

Students who change courses must pay an extra £50.

Role card 2A

You work for HBS and you are Mrs Forster's secretary.

Mrs Forster is busy – she is in a meeting.

Ask if you can take a message.

Role card 2B

You need to phone a company called HBS for your job.

You want to speak to Mrs Forster.

If you can't speak to her, you would like her to call you back.

Phone the company.

Role card 3A

You are at home and you are bored. You want to do something with your friend.

You would like to go to the cinema or see a play.

Ask your friend for ideas.

Phone your friend.

Role card 3B

You are at home and you are bored. You want to meet a friend.

The weather is nice and so you would like to do something outside.

Role card 4A

Your uncle owns a restaurant called The Borough Lounge (spell this to your friend).

The phone number is 020 87973 2047.

It is best to phone in the afternoon when the restaurant is not busy.

Role card 4B

You are looking for a job in a restaurant as a waiter/waitress.

Your friend's uncle owns a restaurant, but you can't remember the name of the restaurant.

You need the restaurant's telephone number.

Phone your friend.

		START		
GOAL				GOAL
A				**B**

Worksheet A

1 I am really healthy, I <u>make</u> a lot of sport. ✗ (play/do)

2 I studied English online, but it was quite boring. ✓

3 I need to <u>do</u> a very important decision. ✗ (make)

4 At my school, I studied French and Spanish. ✓

5 When I arrived at this school, I did a test. ✓

6 I can play a musical instrument. ✓

7 At school I <u>made</u> a project on Roman history. ✗ (did)

8 I once <u>did</u> a meal for six friends. ✗ (made)

9 We didn't wear a uniform at school. ✓

10 My company <u>makes</u> business with many foreign customers. ✗ (does)

Worksheet B

1 I am so nervous when I <u>do</u> speeches. ✗ (give)

2 I am studying a lot because I am <u>making</u> an exam soon. ✗ (doing/taking)

3 When I was a child, I played card games with my grandparents. ✓

4 I <u>do</u> a lot of mistakes when I write in English. ✗ (makes)

5 My father did really badly at school. ✓

6 After the lesson, I need to <u>do</u> a phone call. ✗ (make)

7 I was in a play at school and gave an amazing performance. ✓

8 It was hard for me to make friends at school. ✓

9 I am not doing anything this weekend. ✓

10 I'm a really bad student, I never <u>make</u> my homework. ✗ (do)

4 HAVE YOU EVER ... ?

Grammar: present perfect + *ever/never*

Find someone who ...	Name
1 has _____ (swim) with dolphins.	
2 has _____ (keep) a pair of shoes for more than ten years.	
3 has _____ (do) a test online.	
4 has _____ (drive) a lorry.	
5 has _____ (win) some money.	
6 has _____ (grow) vegetables.	
7 has _____ (fly) in a helicopter.	
8 has _____ (make) a birthday cake for someone.	
9 has _____ (buy) an animal.	
10 has _____ (lose) their passport on holiday.	
11 has _____ (give) a present to a teacher.	
12 has _____ (not pay) a bill.	
13 has _____ (sleep) outside, but not in a tent.	
14 has _____ (catch) a train from one country to another.	
15 has _____ (write) a letter to a newspaper.	
16 has _____ (meet) someone famous.	

The class contract

The students

- The students don't have to switch their mobiles off in class.

- The students must arrive ten minutes before lessons start.

- The students mustn't sit in the same place everyday.

- The students can talk when the teacher is talking.

- The students can't sit next to who they want.

- The students can eat and drink during the lesson.

- The students must stand up when the teacher enters the class.

- The students have to bring the teacher a cake on Fridays.

The teacher

- The teacher doesn't have to mark the students' homework.

-

-

-

-

-

-

Signed _____ and _____ (students)

Signed _____ (teacher)

St William's Grammar School

Many students arrive late for school and they are tired in lessons.

New Wood Senior School

The students steal books from the library and vandalise computers during lunchtimes.

Oxbridge Comprehensive

The students don't eat the school lunches and say they are hungry in the afternoon.

East Village College

You want students to start wearing a uniform. You want something smart, but also comfortable.

Forest Green School

The school sports teams always lose and a lot of students don't want to do sport.

The Edward Long School

The school's exam results are bad. Many students leave school with few qualifications.

Foxbury School

The school needs money for a new computer lab. You asked the government, but they didn't help.

Manchester High School

The students often text their friends in class and don't listen to the teacher.

Crossword A

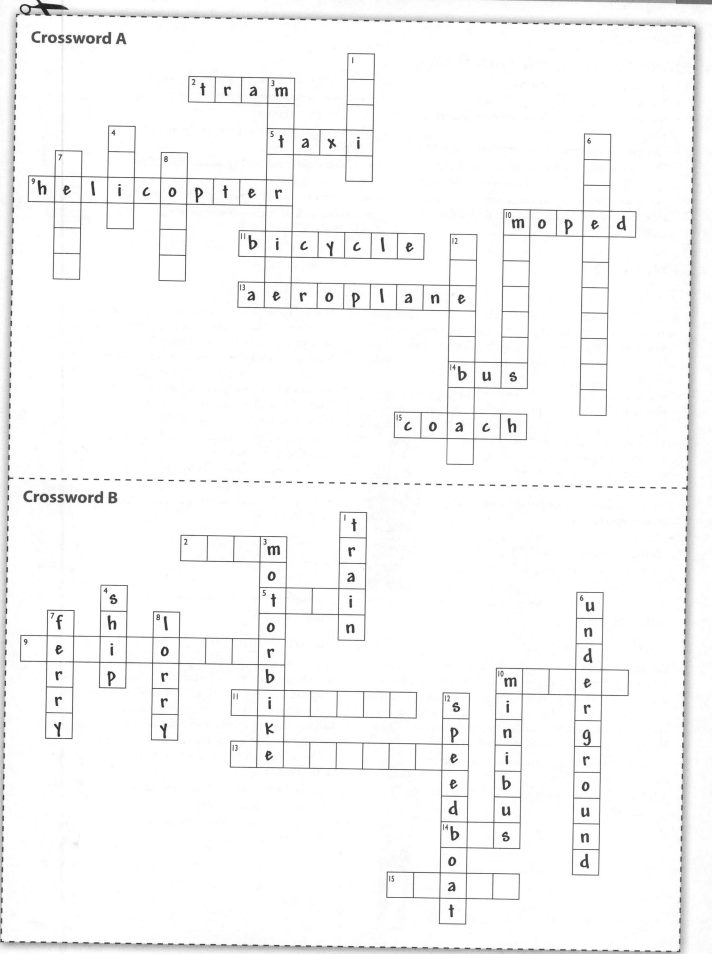

Crossword B

5 MISSING MONEY

Grammar: past simple and past continuous

Role card 1

Detective Inspector Dick Brown

You know the following information:

- The train was travelling from London to Manchester. It left London at 6p.m. and arrived in Manchester at 8.15p.m.
- The money was stolen between 7p.m. and 7.30p.m.
- There were only five passengers on the train.
- At 7.30p.m., when Chris Hinds realised his money was missing, he stood up and shouted; 'Somebody stole my money!' That's when the train driver called you.

Interview the other passengers and find out:

- what time the other passengers got on the train
- where they were going
- what everyone was doing between 7p.m. and 7.30p.m.
- what everyone did after they heard Chris Hinds say his money was missing
- any other questions you need to ask.

After you've spoken to the other passengers, decide who you think did it.

Role card 2

Richard Cagney, 36

You are Shirley Cagney's husband. You both got on the train at 6p.m. and were travelling to Manchester to visit your wife's mother. You stole the money, because you were having problems with your business, and you didn't want your wife to know.

Between 7p.m. and 7.30p.m., you were sitting with your wife and reading the newspaper. At 7.15p.m. you told your wife you were going to the toilet, but on the way you stopped because you saw Chris Hinds with his bag open and his wallet inside. You asked him where the toilet was, but then fell over and took the wallet.

Prepare the following information before the detective speaks to you:

- What will you tell the detective you were doing between 7p.m. and 7.30p.m.?
- What did you do when you heard Chris Hinds shout?

Role card 4

Jack Brown, 25

You got on the train in London at 6p.m., and were travelling to Manchester to play in a football match. You were sitting in the same carriage as Chris Hinds, you were looking at him because you thought you knew him – he looks like someone you went to school with. At 7.15p.m. you saw a man in a suit come into the carriage and talk to Chris Hinds. You didn't hear what they said, but you saw the man in a suit fall onto the chair.

Prepare the following information before the detective speaks to you:

- What were you doing before you heard Chris Hinds shout?
- What did you do when you heard Chris Hinds shout?

Role card 3

Shirley Cagney, 29

You are Richard Cagney's wife. You both got on the train at 6p.m. and were travelling to Manchester to visit your mother. Between 7p.m. and 7.30p.m. you were sitting with your husband and reading a book. Around 7.15p.m., you saw Susan Wright come running out of the carriage Chris Hinds was in. She was looking nervous.

Prepare the following information before the detective speaks to you:

- What did you do when you heard Chris Hinds shout?

Role card 5

Susan Wight, 31

You got on the train at 6.45p.m., and were travelling to Manchester to visit your friends. You were sitting in the same carriage as Chris Hinds and another young man who was wearing a sports tracksuit. The man in the tracksuit was looking at Chris Hinds before the money was taken. That evening you had a stomach-ache, and at about 7.15p.m. you felt sick and ran to the toilet in the next carriage.

Prepare the following information before the detective speaks to you:

- What did you do when you heard Chris Hinds shout?

162 PHOTOCOPIABLE © Pearson Education Limited 2011

1 Underline the correct alternative.

1 a place you wouldn't **choose** *to go/going* on holiday _____

2 something you **enjoyed** *to do/doing* as a child _____

3 a job you **hope** *to do/doing* in the future _____

4 something you **needed** *to do/doing* last week _____

5 housework you **hate** *to do/doing* _____

6 something you can't **imagine** *to wear/wearing* _____

7 what you **expect** *to do/doing* next summer _____

8 a place you **avoid** *to go/going* to in your town/city _____

9 a book you **didn't finish** *to read/reading* _____

10 someone you **need** *to email/emailing* soon _____

11 another language you **want** *to learn/learning* _____

12 a song you **love** *to listen/listening* to _____

13 some food you **would like** *to eat/eating* tonight _____

14 someone famous you **would like** *to meet/meeting* _____

15 a present you **chose** *to buy/buying* recently _____

16 where you **imagine** *to live/living* in ten years' time _____

17 the next expensive thing you **expect** *to buy/buying* _____

18 a person you **want** *to talk/talking* to after the lesson _____

19 some advice you **decided not** *to listen/listening* to _____

20 a place you **hope** *to visit/visiting* in the future _____

2 Think of an example for 1–20.

Map A

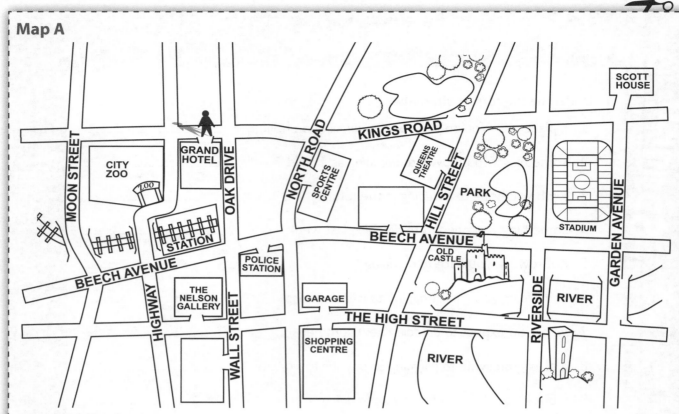

Ask how to get from:

1 The Grand Hotel to The National Museum

2 The National Museum to The Old Tower

3 The Old Tower to The Summer Palace

4 The Summer Palace to King's Park

Map B

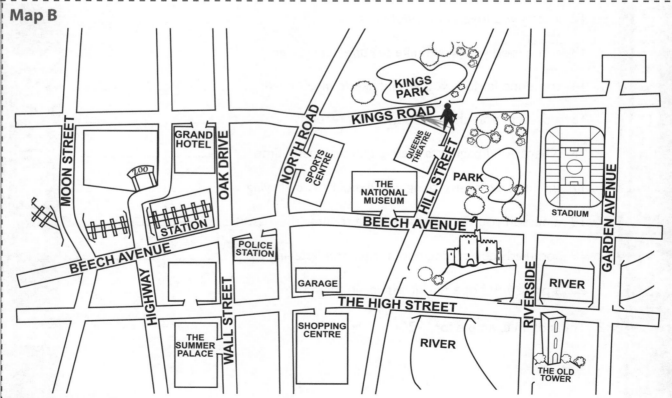

Ask how to get from:

1 The Queen's Theatre to The Old Castle

2 The Old Castle to City Zoo

3 City Zoo to Scott House

4 Scott House to The Nelson Gallery

Worksheet A

1 You are a town councillor, and your job is to develop sports in your area which will be good for the following categories. Choose three sports for each category.

Good for older people:

1 _____

2 _____

3 _____

Urban sports:

1 _____

2 _____

3 _____

Expensive sports:

1 _____

2 _____

3 _____

Dangerous sports:

1 _____

2 _____

3 _____

Sports that are easy to learn:

1 _____

2 _____

3 _____

2 Work in pairs and discuss your ideas. Decide on the best sport for each category.

3 Present your ideas to the class.

Worksheet B

1 You are a town councillor, and your job is to develop sports in your area which will be good for the following categories. Choose three sports for each category.

Good for younger people:

1 _____

2 _____

3 _____

Rural sports:

1 _____

2 _____

3 _____

Cheap sports:

1 _____

2 _____

3 _____

Safe sports:

1 _____

2 _____

3 _____

Sports that are difficult to learn:

1 _____

2 _____

3 _____

2 Work in pairs and discuss your ideas. Decide on the best sport for each category.

3 Present your ideas to the class.

Felipe Massa
Formula 1

First played
this sport: *he was 8 years old*

Became
professional: *1998*
For: _____

Became
famous: *2003*
For: _____

Number of
competitions won: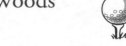

Lionel Messi
Football

First played
this sport: *he was 5 years old*

Became
professional: *1995*
For: _____

Became
famous: *2005*
For: _____

Number of
competitions won:

Tom Brady
American football

First played
this sport: *he was 3 years old*

Became
professional: *2000*
For: _____

Became
famous: *2001*
For: _____

Number of
competitions won: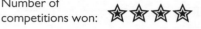

Tiger Woods
Golf

First played
this sport: *he was 2 years old*

Became
professional: *1996*
For: _____

Became
famous: *1999*
For: _____

Number of
competitions won:

Maria Sharapova
Tennis

First played
this sport: *she was 4 years old*

Became
professional: *2001*
For: _____

Became
famous: *2003*
For: _____

Number of
competitions won:

Usain Bolt
Running

First played
this sport: *he was 12 years old*

Became
professional: *2003*
For: _____

Became
famous: *2008*
For: _____

Number of
competitions won: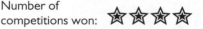

Lebron James
Basketball

First played
this sport: *he was 2 years old*

Became
professional: *2003*
For: _____

Became
famous: *2004*
For: _____

Number of
competitions won: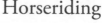

Jonny Wilkinson
Rugby

First played
this sport: *he was 4 years old*

Became
professional: *1998*
For: _____

Became
famous: *2007*
For: _____

Number of
competitions won:

Michael Phelps
Swimming

First played
this sport: *he was 7 years old*

Became
professional: *2000*
For: _____

Became
famous: *2004*
For: _____

Number of
competitions won:

Misty May-Treanor
Beach volleyball

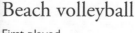

First played
this sport: *she was 8 years old*

Became
professional: *1999*
For: _____

Became
famous: *2004*
For: _____

Number of
competitions won:

Beezie Madden
Horseriding

First played
this sport: *she was 3 years old*

Became
professional: *1985*
For: _____

Became
famous: *2004*
For: _____

Number of
competitions won:

Stephanie Gilmore
Surfing

First played
this sport: *she was 10 years old*

Became
professional: *2005*
For: _____

Became
famous: *2007*
For: _____

Number of
competitions won: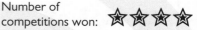

Student A

In the next twenty-four hours, do you think you will:	will	may/might	may/might not	won't
eat some junk food?				
walk in a park?				
tell someone you love them?				
use a computer?				
drink more than three cups of coffee?				

Student B

In the next seven days, do you think you will:	will	may/might	may/might not	won't
cry?				
buy something new to wear?				
sleep less than five hours one night?				
forget to do something important?				
tell a lie?				

Student C

In the next twelve months, do you think you will:	will	may/might	may/might not	won't
buy a car?				
lose weight or gain weight?				
visit another country?				
move house?				
start a new hobby?				

Student D

In the next twelve years, do you think you will:	will	may/might	may/might not	won't
start or end a relationship?				
have (more) children?				
live in another country?				
be happier than now?				
learn a foreign language?				

Patient	Doctor
	Ask the patient: • what the problem is • how long he/she has had it • where it hurts Tell him/her what he/she should do and not to worry!

Patient	Doctor
	Ask the patient: • what the problem is • how long he/she has had it • where it hurts Tell him/her what he/she should do and not to worry!

Patient	Doctor
	Ask the patient: • what the problem is • how long he/she has had it • where it hurts Tell him/her what he/she should do and not to worry!

Patient	Doctor
	Ask the patient: • what the problem is • how long he/she has had it • where it hurts Tell him/her what he/she should do and not to worry!

Patient	Doctor
	Ask the patient: • what the problem is • how long he/she has had it • where it hurts Tell him/her what he/she should do and not to worry!

Patient	Doctor
	Ask the patient: • what the problem is • how long he/she has had it • where it hurts Tell him/her what he/she should do and not to worry!

Patient	Doctor
	Ask the patient: • what the problem is • how long he/she has had it • where it hurts Tell him/her what he/she should do and not to worry!

Patient	Doctor
	Ask the patient: • what the problem is • how long he/she has had it • where it hurts Tell him/her what he/she should do and not to worry!

Who ...	Name	Extra information
1 ... dreams _____ working in another country?		
2 ... is looking _____ a new job?		
3 ... has given _____ something difficult?		
4 ... has travelled _____ their country?		
5 ... is waiting _____ someone to call them?		
6 ... is thinking _____ starting a new hobby?		
7 ... would like to go _____ to school or university?		
8 ... has moved _____ another city?		
9 ... is thinking _____ buying a new car?		
10 ... is looking _____ a new house/flat?		

7 DID YOU KNOW ... ?

Grammar: *used to*

Team A

1 Which company used to be called Blue Ribbon Sports?
   a) Nike
   b) Adidas
   c) Puma

2 What did sports car company Lamborghini use to make?
   a) fridges
   b) lorries
   c) tractors

3 Which actor used to be a security guard?
   a) Sylvester Stallone
   b) Bruce Willis
   c) Arnold Schwarzenegger

4 Which American city didn't use to be in Mexico?
   a) Los Angeles
   b) San Francisco
   c) Chicago

Team B

5 Which politician didn't use to be a lawyer?
   a) Tony Blair
   b) George W. Bush
   c) Bill Clinton

6 Which country used to be called New Holland?
   a) Australia
   b) New Zealand
   c) The USA

7 Which English word used to mean *teacher*?
   a) architect
   b) doctor
   c) lawyer

8 Which famous product used to be called *Yum Yum*?
   a) Coco-Cola
   b) Kit Kat
   c) Kellogg's Cornflakes

Team C

9 Which political leader used to be a spy?
   a) Nelson Mandela
   b) Margaret Thatcher
   c) Vladimir Putin

10 Which football team used to be called Newton Heath?
   a) Chelsea
   b) Liverpool
   c) Manchester United

11 Who used to work in the fast food restaurant Dunkin Donuts?
   a) Madonna
   b) Mariah Carey
   c) Shakira

12 In which country did people use to drive on the left?
   a) Australia
   b) The USA
   c) Brazil

Team D

13 Which job did J. K. Rowling (author of Harry Potter) use to do?
   a) an English teacher
   b) a hairdresser
   c) a worker in McDonald's

14 Which footballer used to be so poor that he played with a grapefruit not a ball?
   a) Maradona
   b) Pelé
   c) David Beckham

15 Which city used to be the capital city of Australia?
   a) Sydney
   b) Melbourne
   c) Adelaide

16 Which country's flag used to have three lions on it?
   a) England
   b) South Africa
   c) Russia

Grammar: purpose, cause, result

Purpose – I went to university **to** study Economics.

Cause – I moved to Australia **because** I wanted a better life.

Result – I left my job **so** I had very little money.

Role card 1

Web Design Course at Eastbury Technical College

The college	• large modern college with 12,000 students • near Eastbury train station
Course information	• courses from September to May or March to November • 6.30p.m. to 9.30p.m., three evenings a week • maximum thirty-five students
Price	• $1,500
Materials	• about five books • a personal computer to do homework
Extra information	• computer rooms are open until 11p.m. Monday to Saturday • library is open until 8p.m. Monday to Saturday • need to be a creative person

Role card 2

Massage Course at Longton Adult Education Centre

The college	• small college in old house in beautiful gardens, outside the city centre
Course information	• two months long, starting every month • 6p.m. to 8.30p.m. two evenings a week • maximum twelve students
Price	• $1,500
Materials	• one book ($45) • massage oils (quite expensive)
Extra information	• practise massage on friends and family for homework • need strong hands • library is closed after 5p.m.

Role card 3

Teaching Course at Oxford International College

The college	• busy international college with 1,500 students in the city centre
Course information	• one year full time • 9a.m. to 6p.m. • maximum fifteen students
Price	• $1,200
Materials	• two books • lots of paper, pens and your own computer
Extra information	• courses are very stressful • library is open from 8a.m. to 8p.m.

Role card 4

You need to find out information about:

• the college
• the course
• times and dates
• materials you need
• when the library and facilities are open
• price

Role card 5

You need to find out information about:

• the college
• the course
• times and dates
• materials you need
• when the library and facilities are open
• price

Role card 6

You need to find out information about:

• the college
• the course
• times and dates
• materials you need
• when the library and facilities are open
• price

Team name: _____

1 How big were the largest notes ever made?

a) about the size of printer paper

b) about the size of a door

c) about the size of a football pitch

2 Who were the first cheques used by?

a) the ancient Greeks

b) the Chinese

c) the ancient Romans

3 How much should you leave as a tip in a US restaurant?

a) about 50%

b) about 5%

c) about 15%

4 How much is the world's most expensive mobile phone worth?

a) $500,000

b) $1,300,000

c) $10,000,000

5 What was unusual about some coins issued in Somalia in 2004?

a) They were made of plastic.

b) They were square.

c) They were shaped liked guitars.

6 Where was the note with the biggest number made?

a) Zimbabwe

b) Russia

c) Peru

7 How small was the smallest ever note?

a) 11 mm x 19 mm

b) 69 mm x 135 mm

c) 32 mm x 41 mm

8 Which company invented the first credit cards?

a) Visa

b) Diner's Club

c) Mastercard

9 When was the first electronic ATM used?

a) 1939

b) 1952

c) 1967

10 How much did Will Smith earn for his first movie, in 1992?

a) $50,000

b) $500,000

c) $5,000,000

11 Where was the first bank note used?

a) The USA

b) Rome

c) China

12 Where does the US dollar sign '$' come from?

a) a **U** over an **S**, representing the United States of America

b) The Spanish Peso

c) Russia

Team A

The internet	Chocolate	
It's something which North American universities used first. (4 points)	It's something which Central Americans first made 3,000 years ago. (4 points)	_____ (4 points)
It's something which over half a billion people use. (3 points)	It's something which you can eat or drink. (3 points)	_____ (3 points)
It's something which you need a computer to use. (2 points)	It's something which can be brown or white. (2 points)	_____ (2 points)
It's something which you can surf. (1 point)	Nestle, Mars and Lindt are companies which make it. (1 point)	_____ (1 point)

Team B

Computer	Sandwich	
It's something which Charles Babbage invented in the 1820s. (4 points)	It's something which an English man invented in 1770. (4 points)	_____ (4 points)
It is something which is getting smaller and smaller. (3 points)	It's something which you eat. (3 points)	_____ (3 points)
It is something which is electronic. (2 points)	It's something which you eat when you want a snack. (2 points)	_____ (2 points)
Apple is one of the companies that makes it. (1 point)	It's something which you make with two slices of bread. (1 point)	_____ (1 point)

Team C

Microwave oven	Monaco	
It's something which Percy Spencer invented in 1945. (4 points)	It's a place which is on the Mediterranean coast. (4 points)	_____ (4 points)
It's something which some people think is dangerous. (3 points)	It's a place where you can find lots of casinos. (3 points)	_____ (3 points)
It's something that you can find in a kitchen. (2 points)	It's the place where lots of millionaires live. (2 points)	_____ (2 points)
It's something which you use to cook food quickly. (1 point)	It's the place where there is a famous Grand Prix. (1 point)	_____ (1 point)

Team D

CD	McDonald's	
It's something that Philips first sold in 1980. (4 points)	It's a company which started in California in 1948. (4 points)	_____ (4 points)
It's something which contains information. (3 points)	It's a company which has a Scottish name. (3 points)	_____ (3 points)
It's something which is round and silver. (2 points)	It's a company which sells food to 58 million people a day. (2 points)	_____ (2 points)
It's something which you play to listen to music. (1 point)	It's a company which sells fast food. (1 point)	_____ (1 point)

Team E

Bicycle	Jeans	
It's something which John Starley invented in 1885. (4 points)	They're something that sailors and miners first wore. (4 points)	_____ (4 points)
It's something which people use for transport and sport. (3 points)	They're something which young people often wear. (3 points)	_____ (3 points)
It's something which is very common in Holland and China. (2 points)	They're something which is usually blue. (2 points)	_____ (2 points)
It's something which you ride. (1 point)	They're something which Levi Strauss & Co. make. (1 point)	_____ (1 point)

Party Planner Card

Reason: Why are you having a party?	birthday ☐ engagement ☐ wedding ☐ anniversary ☐ graduation ☐ festival ☐ other ☐
Requirements: What do you need for the party?	food ☐ drinks ☐ food and drinks ☐ dancing ☐ DJ ☐ other ☐
Budget: How much do you want to spend?	Under $1000 ☐ $1000–1500 ☐ $1500–3000 ☐ $3000+ ☐ other ☐
Numbers: How many guests?	under 50 ☐ 50–100 ☐ 100+ ☐
Car parking: How many guests are coming by car?	none ☐ some ☐ all ☐
Accommodation: How many guests need to stay the night?	none ☐ some ☐ all ☐
Hours: What time does the party start and finish?	from: 6p.m. ☐ 7p.m. ☐ 8p.m. ☐ 9p.m. ☐ 10p.m. ☐ to: 11p.m. ☐ 12a.m. ☐ 1a.m. ☐ 2a.m. ☐ 3a.m. ☐

The Plaza Hotel

Costs	• $1000–2000 • free drinks, food $20 per person
Numbers	• up to 50 guests (Regency Room) • 50–150 guests (The Ball Room)
Extra information	• 4 bars, 3 restaurants, swimming pool • 500 parking spaces • rooms for 500 guests ($150 a night) • parties from 8p.m.–2a.m.

The Country House Hotel

Costs	• $800 • drinks not included, food $20 per person
Numbers	• 100 guests maximum
Extra information	• DJ not included • free parking • rooms for 50 guests • big old house in beautiful gardens • parties from 8p.m.–3a.m.

THE MOON RIVER BOAT

COSTS	• $100 an hour or $600 all night • free drinks, food $10 per person
NUMBERS	• 70 guests maximum
EXTRA INFORMATION	• 2 bars, 2 DJs • 10 parking spaces • no accommodation for guests on the boat but 25% discount at 3 star hotel which is very near • parties from 6p.m.–1a.m.

The Diamond Nightclub

Costs	• $325 • drinks not included, food $15 per person
Numbers	• 45 guests maximum
Extra information	• 1 bar, free DJ • 15 parking spaces, no accommodation • nightclub in centre of the city • parties from 7p.m.–3a.m.

Role card 1

Bob's Boutique

Tick (✓) when you sell	Price
shirt (large, white)	$40
shoes (size 40)	$50
jeans (size 28)	$35
coat (long, green)	$95
hat (grey)	$40

Role card 3

Claire's Clothes

Tick (✓) when you sell	Price
shirt (medium, white)	$20
shoes (size 38)	$50
jeans (size 30)	$65
coat (short, black)	$85
hat (yellow)	$10

Role card 2

Fran's Fashions

Tick (✓) when you sell	Price
shirt (large, blue)	$45
shoes (size 44)	$30
jeans (size 32)	$90
coat (short, black)	$100
hat (green)	$25

Role card 4

Gary's Gear

Tick (✓) when you sell	Price
shirt (medium, blue)	$25
shoes (size 40)	$30
jeans (size 32)	$70
coat (long, green)	$120
hat (grey)	$15

Role card 5

Shopping list A

Tick (✓) when you buy	Budget
shoes (size 40)	$30
jeans (size 32)	$90
shirt (large, white)	$50

Role card 7

Shopping list C

Tick (✓) when you buy	Budget
coat (short, black)	$100
hat (grey)	$20
shoes (size 40)	$60

Role card 6

Shopping list B

Tick (✓) when you buy	Budget
shirt (medium, white)	$20
coat (long, green)	$100
hat (yellow)	$20

Role card 8

Shopping list D

Tick (✓) when you buy	Budget
hat (green)	$35
shoes (size 38)	$60
jeans (size 32)	$80

Worksheet A

1 It lives in the sea.

2 This animal can fly but it's not a bird.

3 It's a very big fish.

4 It's a big dangerous mammal.

5 It can run as fast as a horse.

6 This animal is the biggest in the world.

7 This animal is quite dangerous.

8 This animal eats lots of fish.

9 This wild animal lives in Africa.

10 It's a very small insect.

11 This animal is very slow.

12 This animal is very good at climbing trees.

13 It's the biggest animal on land.

14 This animal begins with **e**.

15 People use this animal to carry things.

16 This animal lives in all cities.

Worksheet B

1 It's an intelligent and friendly mammal.

2 It's an insect.

3 It has lots of teeth.

4 This wild animal lives in the forest or mountains.

5 It's the biggest bird.

6 It lives in the sea.

7 This reptile lives in rivers.

8 It's a bird but can't fly.

9 It has spots.

10 This animal can bite you.

11 This reptile carries its 'home' on its back.

12 It is a very intelligent wild animal.

13 It has a very good memory.

14 This animal is the symbol of some countries.

15 This animal lives in the desert.

16 Most people don't like this bird.

Worksheet C

1 It begins with **d**.

2 It has beautiful coloured wings.

3 This animal can be very dangerous.

4 It likes honey.

5 It can't fly.

6 It is not a fish.

7 It has a long body and lots of teeth.

8 It lives in Antarctica.

9 It's the fastest animal on land.

10 This animal can give you malaria.

11 It can live for a very long time.

12 This mammal is very similar to humans.

13 It has a trunk and very big ears.

14 It's the king of the birds.

15 It can live without eating or drinking for two weeks.

16 It begins with **p**.

Answer sheet

Team name:

1 □□□□□□□
2 □□□□□□□□□
3 □□□□□
4 □□□□
5 □□□□□□□
6 □□□□□
7 □□□□□□□□
8 □□□□□□□

9 □□□□□□
10 □□□□□□□□
11 □□□□□□□□
12 □□□□□□□□□
13 □□□□□□□□
14 □□□□□
15 □□□□□
16 □□□□□□

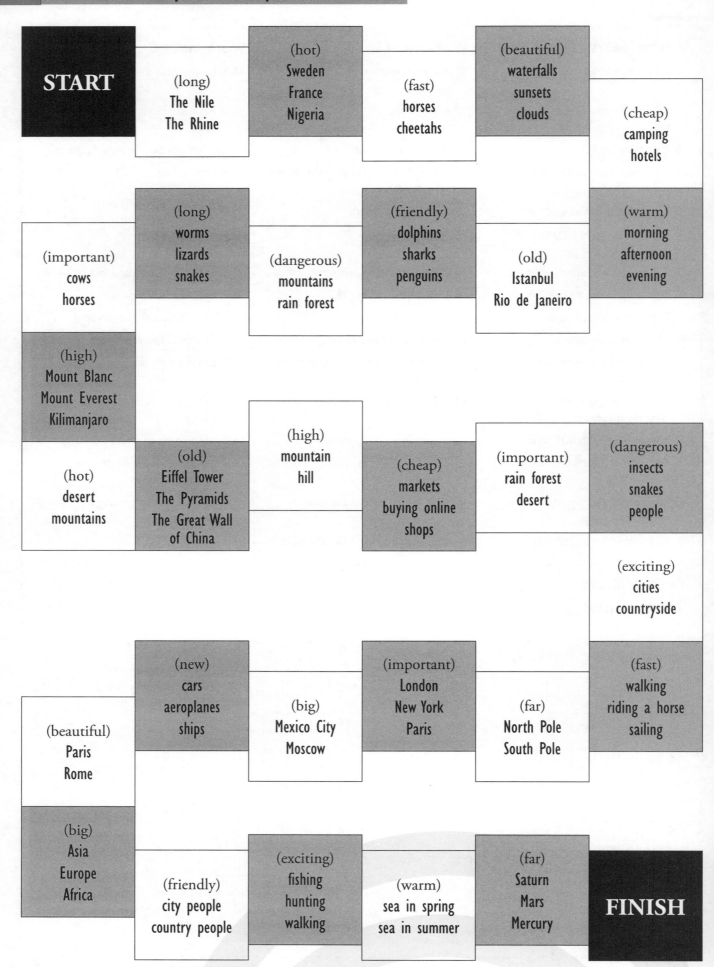

START

(long)
The Nile
The Rhine

(hot)
Sweden
France
Nigeria

(fast)
horses
cheetahs

(beautiful)
waterfalls
sunsets
clouds

(cheap)
camping
hotels

(important)
cows
horses

(long)
worms
lizards
snakes

(dangerous)
mountains
rain forest

(friendly)
dolphins
sharks
penguins

(old)
Istanbul
Rio de Janeiro

(warm)
morning
afternoon
evening

(high)
Mount Blanc
Mount Everest
Kilimanjaro

(hot)
desert
mountains

(old)
Eiffel Tower
The Pyramids
The Great Wall
of China

(high)
mountain
hill

(cheap)
markets
buying online
shops

(important)
rain forest
desert

(dangerous)
insects
snakes
people

(exciting)
cities
countryside

(beautiful)
Paris
Rome

(new)
cars
aeroplanes
ships

(big)
Mexico City
Moscow

(important)
London
New York
Paris

(far)
North Pole
South Pole

(fast)
walking
riding a horse
sailing

(big)
Asia
Europe
Africa

(friendly)
city people
country people

(exciting)
fishing
hunting
walking

(warm)
sea in spring
sea in summer

(far)
Saturn
Mars
Mercury

FINISH

The frozen continent

1	In the winter of 1911, there was the race to be the first country to reach	
2	the South Pole. Captain Scott, a famous explorer from the Great Britain,	
3	led the British team and Roald Amundsen led a Norwegian one.	
4	Scott's team took the horses, motor vehicles and a few dogs, but	
5	Amundsen was clever and took only the dogs. In November 1911,	
6	Scott's group started journey, but there were many problems;	
7	the horses died and the motor vehicles stopped working. In an end,	
8	Scott and a four men (Wilson, Bowers, Evans and Oates) continued on	
9	foot. They reached South Pole in January 1912, but they had a	
10	terrible shock when they arrived. Amundsen had arrived the five weeks	
11	earlier and they had lost a race. Scott's men were extremely tired	
12	and disappointed but they still needed to walk back 800 miles to coast.	
13	Weather got worse and worse and all the men became ill. First Evans	
14	died at the night and soon after so did Oates. The other three died in	
15	their tent only 11 miles (18 km) from their base. They were found an eight	
16	months later. Scott's diary tells a story of their final terrible days.	

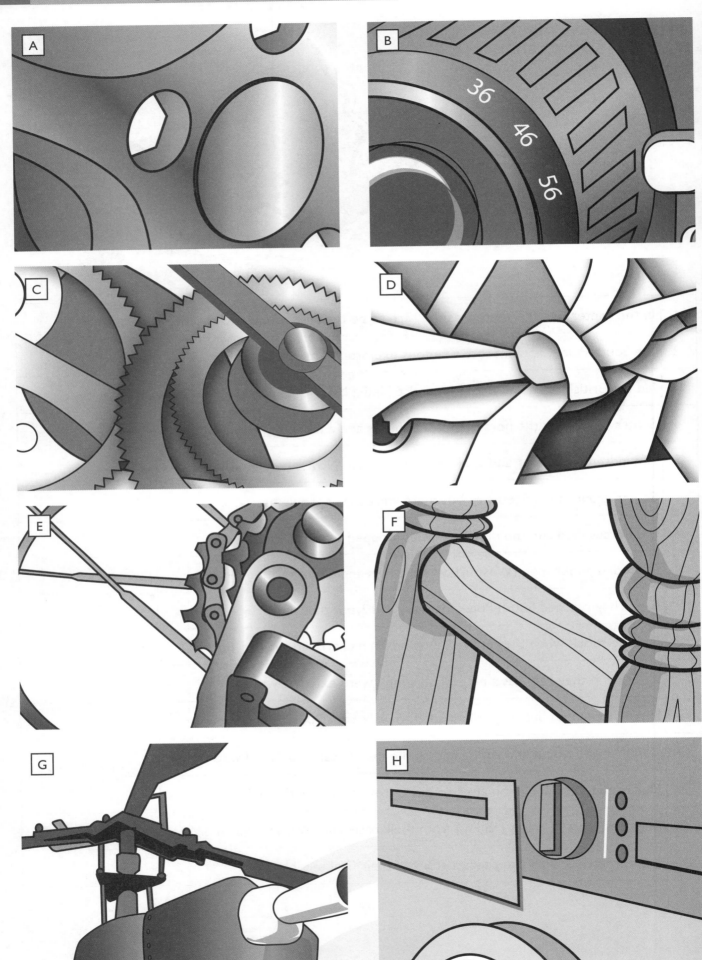

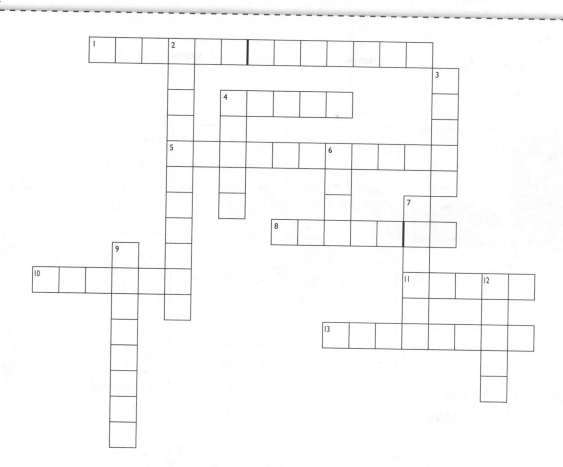

Student A

Across

1 A person who catches criminals (6, 7)
   (police officer)

4 To take things which are not yours (5)
   (steal)

5 The crime of stealing things from shops (11)
   (shoplifting)

8 To go into a building illegally (5, 2)
   (break in)

10 When the police catch criminals (6)
   (arrest)

11 The crime of stealing things (5)
   (theft)

13 A person who breaks the law (8)
   (criminal)

Student B

Down

2 When the police look for a criminal (11)
   (investigate)

3 The person who decides a punishment (5)
   (judge)

4 What you do with a gun (5)
   (shoot)

6 An amount of money you have to pay as a
   punishment (4)
   (fine)

7 The person who the criminal affects/hurts (6)
   (victim)

9 Another word for punishment (8)
   (sentence)

12 The crime of cheating people to make
   money from them (5)
   (fraud)

Tell your group ...

... what these things are like.

... what you like or dislike about them.

FINISH	③④ your mobile phone	③③	③② your car or a car you would like	③① a typical food from your country	③⓪
② your country's flag	②⑤ people from your country	②⑥	②⑦ your capital city	②⑧ your bedroom	②⑨ your best friend
②③ your workplace or your ideal work place	②② your favourite building	②① your neighbour	②⓪ someone in your family	⑲ an animal or pet	⑱ your garden or balcony
⑫ your favourite clothes	⑬ your sitting room	⑭ your favourite teacher	⑮ your favourite park	⑯ your best holiday	⑰ your boss or an ideal boss
⑪ your computer/a computer	⑩ a traditional game or sport	⑨	⑧ your school or university	⑦	⑥ your bike or motorcycle/ a bike or motorcycle
START	① a famous person	② an important possession	③ your kitchen	④ the weather today	⑤ a traditional festival

Student A

1 Coca-Cola _____ (make) with colouring so it's not green. (true)

2 Alaska _____ (buy) from Russia for $7 million in 1867. (true)

3 The Statue of Liberty _____ (give) to the United States by Great Britain in 1886. (false)

4 In 2006, a whale _____ (see) swimming up the River Thames in London. (true)

5 The first underground system in the world _____ (build) in London in the 1860s. (true)

6 Potatoes _____ (not grow) in Europe until 1536. (true)

7 **Necessary** _____ (spell) incorrectly more than any other word in English. (false)

8 **The Da Vinci Code** _____ (write) by Dan Brown in just three weeks. (false)

Student B

1 The giant panda _____ (find) only in two countries – China and Burma. (false)

2 The British prime minister _____ (choose) by the queen or king. (false)

3 The first photo _____ (take) by the Chinese in the early 1700s. (false)

4 In Sweden, coffee _____ (drink) by children on their birthday. (false)

5 **The Mona Lisa** _____ (steal) in 1911 and lost for two years. (true)

6 **Happy Birthday** _____ (sing) more than any other English song. (true)

7 Macadamia nuts _____ (not sell) in their shells because people can't break them. (true)

8 In some parts of Wales, sheep _____ (ride) by local farmers for transport. (false)

Student C

1 **The Simpsons** cartoon _____ (show) for the first time in 1989. (true)

2 Cars _____ (drive) on the left in Sweden until 1967. (true)

3 Originally, Mickey Mouse _____ (know) as Mortimer Mouse. (true)

4 More chocolate _____ (eat) by Italians than any other nationality. (false – Swiss)

5 Traditionally, skirts _____ (wear) by men in Ireland. (false)

6 Queen Elizabeth II went to hospital in 1991 after she _____ (bite) by one of her dogs. (true)

7 English school children _____ (not teach) foreign languages at school. (false)

8 The Pyramids in Egypt _____ (hide) under sand for 2,000 years. (false)

A

B

C

D

E

F

Your teacher is explaining some grammar badly.	**worried**	Your classmate is talking about a big *chicken* in her house. (She means *kitchen*!)	**worried**
It's 11.30p.m. and your 14-year-old child is late home.	**nervous**	Your friend has just called you and told you he's in hospital.	**nervous**
You're going to take your driving test this afternoon.	**excited**	You're going to have an important job interview today.	**excited**
You have two tickets to see your favourite pop singer.	**amazed**	Your best friend is coming home after two years away.	**amazed**
You see a boy fall from an upstairs window and then get up and walk.	**lonely**	Your friend has just won $10 million on the lottery.	**lonely**
All your friends are on holiday and you have no-one to go out with.	**bored**	You're in a new country and don't know anyone.	**bored**
The teacher is talking a lot and it's not interesting.	**uncomfortable**	You're at home. It's raining and there is nothing to do.	**uncomfortable**
You're staying in a hotel. It's too hot and the bed is very hard. You can't sleep.	**confused**	You're wearing some new jeans, but they are too small.	**confused**

Worksheet A

Adam
1 not / finish / school / yet
2 already / learn / a foreign language
3 just / ride / bike / for the first time

Sam
1 just / climb / Mount Everest
2 already / climb / it / six times
3 not / be / Africa / yet

Hugh
1 already / travel / around the world
2 just / buy / a sports car
3 not / pass / driving test / yet

Johnny
1 not / find / girlfriend / yet
2 already / make / lots of money
3 just / start / playing the guitar

Colin
1 already / retire
2 just / become a grandparent
3 not / see / grandchild / yet

_____ _____ _____ _____ _____

Worksheet B

Debbie
1 just / move / house
2 not / meet / neighbours / yet
3 already / live / ten different homes

Marcia
1 already / become / grandparent
2 just / win / lottery
3 not / fly / in aeroplane / yet

Emma
1 just / visit / hairdresser's
2 already / divorce / first husband
3 not / finish / university / yet

Angelina
1 already / make / $1million
2 just / sell / hotel
3 not / leave / home / yet

Jessica
1 already / read / lots of books
2 just / eat / ice cream
3 not / learn / swim / yet

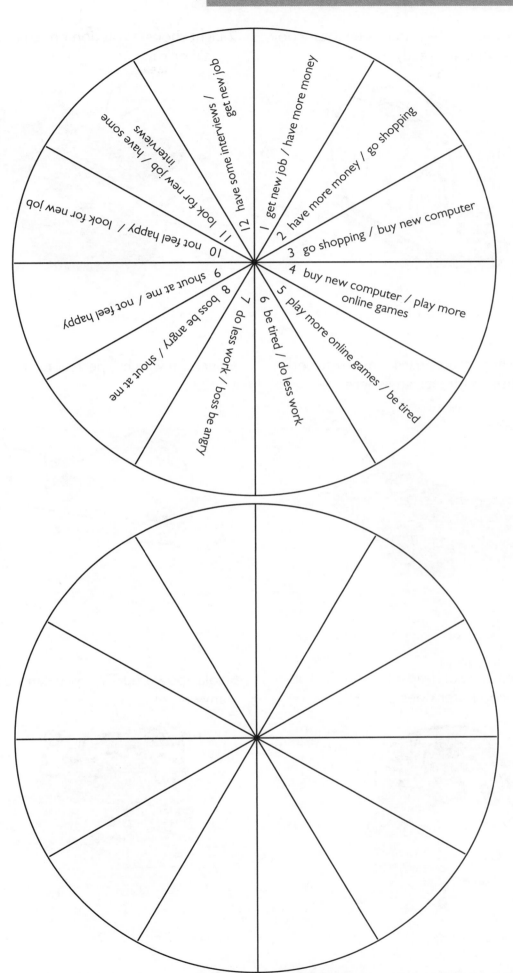

1 get new job / have more money
2 have more money / go shopping
3 go shopping / buy new computer
4 buy new computer / play more online games
5 play more online games / be tired
6 be tired / do less work
7 do less work / boss be angry
8 boss be angry / shout at me
9 shout at me / not feel happy
10 not feel happy / look for new job
11 look for new job / have some interviews
12 have some interviews / get new job

1 Transparent toaster – watch your toast cook and decide when it's ready

2 Light shoes – you don't need batteries, just walk or run

3 Go-anywhere skateboard – use in streets, on beaches, in forests, anywhere

4 Stick-on watch – perfect for travelling light

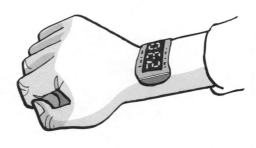

5 Computer control headset – you think it and your computer does it

6 Solar-powered TV – you can watch TV anywhere!

a person who performs in a film or play	the company that makes films	a short part of a film	the part a person has in a film or play
a film which makes you very scared	people in films who don't have important parts	a film which is not like real-life	a film which is about the past
the person who tells the actors what to do	a film which is about the future	a film or play that makes you laugh	a film which is about real life
a film with lots of singing and dancing in it and uses songs to tell the story	the most important actor in the film	the person who organises the whole film	a very exciting film about murder or crime

Referee's answers

an actor	a studio	a scene	a role
a horror film	extras	a fantasy film	a historical drama
a director	a science fiction film	a comedy	a documentary
a musical	a star	a producer	a thriller

STAR INTERVIEW

Grammar: reported speech

1 Imagine you are a film star and complete the following information.

STAR CARD

Personal information

Name	
Age and birthday	
Marital status	
Home(s) and car(s)	
Three things you love	
Three things you hate	
Talents	

Career information

Best career moment	
Worst career moment	
Present film: • type • role • actors	

2 Now interview your film star partner and make notes.

INTERVIEW CARD

Personal information

What's your name?	
How old are you? When is your birthday?	
Are you married?	
Tell me about your home(s) and car(s).	
What three things do you love?	
What three things do you hate?	
What are your talents?	

Career information

What was the best moment in your career?	
What was the worst moment in your career?	
Tell me about what you are filming at the moment. • type • role • actors	

Example: If I saw a spider, I would scream

Hot lava

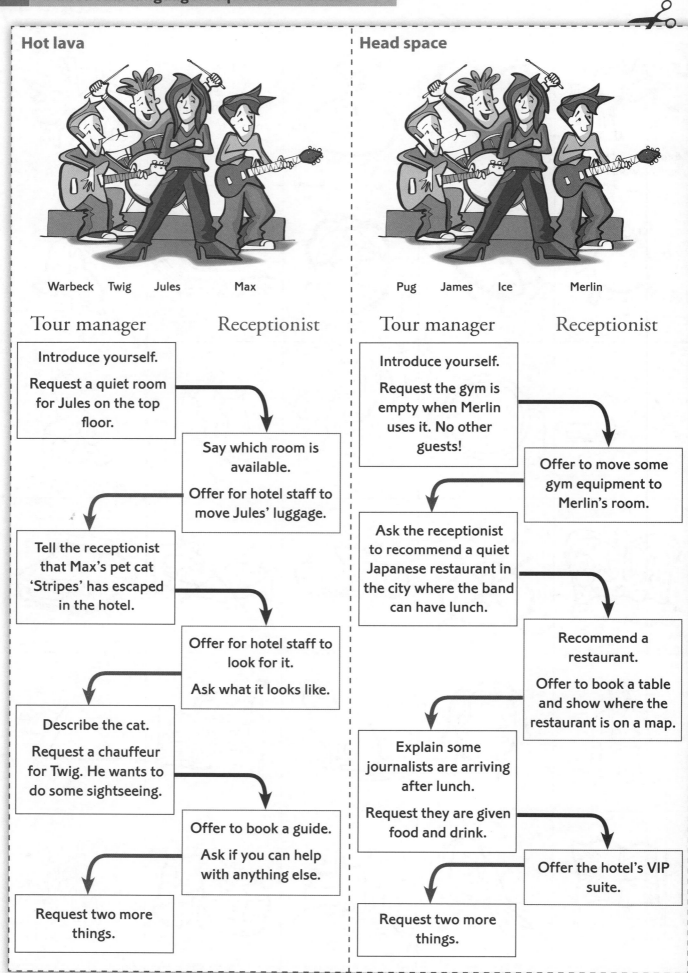

Warbeck Twig Jules Max

Tour manager   **Receptionist**

Introduce yourself.

Request a quiet room for Jules on the top floor.

Say which room is available.

Offer for hotel staff to move Jules' luggage.

Tell the receptionist that Max's pet cat 'Stripes' has escaped in the hotel.

Offer for hotel staff to look for it.

Ask what it looks like.

Describe the cat.

Request a chauffeur for Twig. He wants to do some sightseeing.

Offer to book a guide.

Ask if you can help with anything else.

Request two more things.

Head space

Pug James Ice Merlin

Tour manager   **Receptionist**

Introduce yourself.

Request the gym is empty when Merlin uses it. No other guests!

Offer to move some gym equipment to Merlin's room.

Ask the receptionist to recommend a quiet Japanese restaurant in the city where the band can have lunch.

Recommend a restaurant.

Offer to book a table and show where the restaurant is on a map.

Explain some journalists are arriving after lunch.

Request they are given food and drink.

Offer the hotel's VIP suite.

Request two more things.

Unit 1

LOVE STORY

Materials: One copy of the worksheet per pair of students

Preteach *lifeguard* and elicit the job's good and bad points. Tell Ss they are going to tell a story about a lifeguard. Arrange Ss into pairs and distribute one worksheet per pair. They match the pictures with the words and phrases.

Answers: A didn't have a girlfriend B got divorced C fell in love D met/got on well E argued F got married G got back together again H asked her to marry him/accepted

Then tell Ss to work together to put the pictures into the right order by thinking about the logical order of events in the story. You can check the correct order with the whole class.

Answers: A, D, C, H, F, E, B, G

Ss then practise telling the story together by taking it in turns to describe pictures. Remind Ss to use the past simple. At the end, you can ask the class questions about the characters, e.g. *Why do you think they got divorced?*

HEADS AND TAILS

Materials: One copy of the worksheet per group

Arrange Ss into groups of four and distribute one set of cut up cards per group. One student deals the cards and each player places their cards face up in front of them. Explain the rules. The first student puts down a card. If the second player has the other half, they place it next to the first card. If the group agree that the two cards make a question, the second player can take the cards and put them to one side. The same student then puts down a new card. If the next student can't put down the other half of the question they miss a turn. Ss take it in turns completing and winning questions until all the questions have been formed. The winner is the student with the most questions. Monitor to ensure that Ss form correct (and plausible) questions.

Then tell Ss to ask each other their questions. Encourage Ss to ask for extra information, especially if the questions are closed questions.

Answers: (as on the worksheet)

When did you last buy something expensive?

When did you last go on holiday or have time off?

What is your favourite book?

What is your favourite sport?

Were you feeling happy yesterday?

Were you at home last night?

Do you have a best friend?

Do you spend a lot of money?

How often do you play or watch sport?

How often do you cook for other people?

Where do you go out with friends?

Where do your family live?

TALK ABOUT IT!

Materials: One copy of the worksheet and a dice per pair of students

Put the Ss into pairs. Give one worksheet to each pair. Explain the rules. Student A starts and rolls the dice. The number on the dice corresponds to the numbers in the boxes. If the dice lands on number two he/she chooses any topic numbered two and then talks about it for thirty seconds using the past simple. If Student B is satisfied, the topic is crossed out and Student A wins the box. Student A can write his/her initials in the box. It is then Student B's turn. If a student rolls the dice and there are no more topics left with that number, they lose a turn. This continues until all the topics have been crossed out. The student who wins the most boxes is the winner.

PARTY TIME!

Materials: One role card per student

Tell Ss that they are going to a party where they are going to meet lots of other interesting people.

Review how to ask about someone's occupation and the kind of questions you need to ask about people's families, hobbies, etc. Demonstrate the language from unit 1.3 used to make conversation and sound natural when you meet and say goodbye to people in social situations.

Distribute a role card to each student. Give Ss a few minutes to read it and check they understand all the information on the card. Help with vocabulary if necessary. It does not matter if two Ss have the same role card, they will have a lot in common when they meet!

Tell Ss that they are at the party and to circulate to meet the other guests. The object of the activity is for the Ss to make natural conversation based on the topics listed and also to do the task at the bottom of the cards. Encourage the students to elaborate on the information on the cards so they appear as interesting as possible to the people they meet.

At the end of the activity, ask the class who they met and who was the most interesting person.

Unit 2

WHAT DO I DO?

Materials: One set of cards per group

Review useful vocabulary from the unit related to describing jobs and write it on the board, e.g. *I work in an office/in a company/outside/in a team/with animals/with my hands. I work under pressure, the salary is high/low. My job is boring/dangerous/exciting/creative. I wear a uniform/smart clothes/casual clothes/special clothes.*

Arrange Ss into groups of four and distribute one set of cut up cards per group. These are placed face down in the middle of the group.

Tell the first student to pick up a card and describe the job to the group, pretending that it is their job. They can describe various aspects of it, e.g. workplace, customers/colleagues, pay, etc. Invite the other Ss to guess what the job is and the student who guesses it correctly first wins that card. It is then the next student's turn. Ss must not show their cards to the others while they are describing them. This continues until all the jobs have been guessed. The winner is the student with the most cards.

It is also possible to do the activity without cutting it up. Ss choose a job but don't say or show which one it is. The procedure is the same and the first student to guess it correctly wins that job. The student writes their initials on the job card. The student who has won the most jobs at the end of the activity is the winner.

As follow up, invite Ss to decide the best three and worst three jobs in groups and then to compare with the other groups. Encourage them to reach some kind of class consensus.

GRAMMAR MAZE

Materials: One worksheet per pair of students

Arrange Ss into pairs and distribute one worksheet per pair. Elicit the difference between present continuous (used for temporary things happening now or around now) and present simple (used for more permanent situations).

Explain the game and demonstrate. Tell Ss to begin at the start box and to decide whether the question is in the correct tense form. If they think the question is correct, tell them to follow the solid black arrow to the next box. If they think it is incorrect, tell them to follow the dotted arrow. Ss record the order of the boxes they visit by writing the letters at the bottom of the worksheet. This continues until Ss arrive at the finish.

If Ss arrive at the finish before visiting every box or if they revisit a box then they have made a mistake and need to go back and consider carefully where they went wrong. Ss also need to make written corrections to the incorrect questions. Help Ss if they cannot see where they have gone wrong.

As follow up, arrange Ss into larger groups to ask and answer the questions.

> **Answers:** Start ✓, A ✓, D ✗ (*Do you always check … ?*), F ✗ (*Do you drink … ?*), C ✓, E ✗ (*Do you listen … ?*), B ✓, G ✗ (*Do you like … ?*), I ✗ (*Are you reading … ?*), H ✓, K ✓, J ✗ (*Do you usually sleep … ?*), Finish

HOW OFTEN DO YOU … ?

Materials: One copy of the board and a dice per group and a counter per student

Arrange Ss into groups of three or four and distribute a dice and a board (enlarged to A3 size if possible) to each group. If you don't have a dice, Ss can use a coin and move one space for heads and two spaces for tails. Ss also need a small object like a counter or coin to move around the board. Ss place these at the start.

Explain the rules. The first student rolls the dice, moves the number of places shown and makes a question from the words in the box and appropriate question phrase from those listed on the board, e.g. *go to the park* becomes *How often do you go to the park?* The student asking the question can ask whoever they want and the student answering can respond using any of the adverbs of frequency listed on the board. Encourage the group to ask additional questions to find out more information, e.g. *Do you usually go alone?* Tell Ss to make their own questions if they land on a free question box. While you are monitoring, pay attention to the appropriateness and accuracy of the questions as well as more general language problems. The winner is the first student to reach the finish.

I CAN'T STAND CHEESE!

Materials: One worksheet per student

Distribute the worksheets. Ask Ss to write in the circle the name of something they like/dislike, etc. Monitor and help Ss with any vocabulary needed.

After all the worksheets have been filled in, Tell Ss to mingle with the objective of finding people with the same answers and noting their names. Ss should also find out some additional information, e.g. *What food do you absolutely love? I absolutely love pizza. What about you? Me too! How often do you eat it?*

At the end, ask whether anybody had similar likes and dislikes and also what was the most interesting, amusing or unusual thing anybody heard.

Unit 3

YOU'VE HIT MY COMPOSER!

Materials: One copy of worksheet A and worksheet B per pair of students

Arrange Ss into A and B pairs. Distribute the worksheets and tell Ss to work alone and write the eight words from the box into their grids. The words can be written horizontally, vertically or diagonally and can also cross each other.

When Ss have finished, explain the activity and demonstrate. Tell Ss that they have to find their partner's eight words. To do this, Ss give grid references to each other, e.g. Student A starts and asks for 1A. If there is nothing written in Student B's grid, they say *Miss!* and Student A should record the miss as an X in their grid. Student B then gives a reference, 3C, and if there is a letter written in Student A's grid, they say *Hit!* as well as the letter Student B has hit. Student B writes the letter in the correct place. This continues until one student has found all eight words.

Once Ss start 'hitting' words, the process becomes much easier and a student can guess the word from the letters if they think they know it. If they are correct, the other student replies, *Yes, you've hit my (composer).*

It is imperative to remind Ss that they must not show their worksheet to each other or look at each other's worksheet.

BANK HOLIDAY WEEKEND

Materials: One worksheet per student

Start by asking Ss if they have many public holidays in their country, when they are and what they celebrate. Also ask Ss whether the day of the holiday is changed so people can have a long weekend.

Preteach *extreme sports*, *circus*, *fair* and any other words you think Ss might not know. Give The London Guide listings and a diary page to each student.

Tell Ss to work on their own and to choose four activities they would like to do and to write them in their diaries in the correct place. Remind Ss that don't have to go for the whole event unless it is a performance or a football match: they can just go for a few hours. Tell Ss to leave the other slots free. Give Ss a few minutes to fill in their activities. Monitor and help with vocabulary if necessary.

When they have finished, tell Ss to mingle and to discuss their plans and to make further arrangements for the bank holiday weekend. Tell Ss to try to fill the blank slots in their diary and to find people to do their four activities with, e.g.

A: *What are you doing on Saturday afternoon?*
B: *Nothing, I'm free.*
A: *I'm going to the Extreme Sports Fair. Do you want to come?*

Students should write down the new arrangements they make and the names of the students who are coming with them for their four activities. Ss continue to mingle until they have a full diary but they should only make one arrangement per person and don't have to make arrangements with everyone they meet, especially if they don't like what they are doing!

When they have finished, ask students what they have planned to do at certain times.

IS IT ART?

Materials: One copy of worksheet A and worksheet B per pair of students

Try to get some images of Banksy's work and ask students if they are familiar with it or if they have heard of him.

Arrange Ss in A and B pairs and distribute the worksheets. Give Ss a few minutes to read the text before they start the activity. Both Ss have the same text but different information is missing from each one.

Tell Ss to ask their partner questions in order to fill in the gaps in their text using the question word in brackets to help them. Monitor the activity paying attention to the question forms and correcting any errors.

When they have finished, check answers with the class.

Answers:

Student A's questions: 1 Who is Banksy? 2 What (perhaps) is Banksy's real name? 3 Where is his art? 4 Which animals are often in his pictures? 5 Who spent $2 million on his art in 2007?

Student B's questions: 1 When was he born? 2 Why are there no photos of Banksy? 3 Why is his art successful? 4 Who painted over one of Banksy's famous paintings? 5 Where was his most successful exhibition?

WHO'S CALLING?

Materials: One set of role cards per pair of students

Arrange Ss in A and B pairs and distribute the A and B role cards. Give Ss a few minutes to read through the information, check what they need to do and to think about the functional language they need.

Get Ss to sit back-to-back to make it a little more like a telephone conversation. Tell Ss that there are two role-plays where they make the phone call and two in which they answer phone calls. Encourage Ss to add their own ideas where appropriate during the role-plays.

During the activity, monitor and listen for correct use of the functional language.

You may wish to change Ss' partners so they have a new partner for every role-play. One way to do this is to have an inner circle of Student As and an outer circle of Student Bs. For every new role-play the outer circle rotates so every student gets a new partner.

Unit 4

COLLOCATION FOOTBALL

Materials: One copy of worksheet A and worksheet B, one coin and one goal per pair of students

Write an incorrect sentence from the activity on the board and ask Ss to correct it. Tell Ss they are going to try to identify whether other collocations are correct or incorrect.

Arrange Ss into A and B pairs and distribute the A and B worksheets and goal. Tell Ss not to look at their partner's worksheet.

Explain the rules and demonstrate. Student A places a coin on start. Student B reads the first sentence to Student A who decides if it is correct or incorrect. If it is an incorrect sentence, Student A should try to correct the sentence. If Student A is successful, they move the coin one space towards their goal. It's in then Student B's turn.

If Student B is successful, he/she moves the coin back towards their goal. Ss continue to take it in turns. If a student makes a mistake, the coin doesn't move. The object is to reach the goal squares and 'score a goal'. When a goal is scored Ss return the coin to the start.

Remind Ss to read slowly and clearly to each other and that it is only collocations that they are correcting and not grammatical mistakes.

When Ss have finished the game, they can look at each other's worksheet and discuss which statements are true for them. If the statements are not true, they can make the sentences true for them and tell their partner about the real situation. Encourage Ss to ask additional questions.

HAVE YOU EVER … ?

Materials: One worksheet per student

Arrange Ss into pairs and distribute the worksheets. Tell Ss to work together to complete the sentences with the past participle of the verbs, which are given in brackets. Check the answers and pronunciation.

Answers: 1 swum 2 kept 3 done 4 driven 5 won 6 grown 7 flown 8 made 9 bought 10 lost 11 given 12 not paid 13 slept 14 caught 15 written 16 met

Then tell Ss to mingle and ask each other *Have you ever … ?* questions using the prompts on their worksheets. They can choose any questions and in any order. Encourage Ss to ask further questions if they get a positive answer and record the name of the person they spoke to. Remind them to use the past simple for any further questions and answers, e.g. *Have you ever swum with dolphins? Yes, I have. Where did you swim with them? In Florida, two years ago. I was on holiday. It was in a big swimming pool …*

For negative answers, remind Ss they can use *never*, e.g. *Have you ever swum with dolphins? No, I have never swum with dolphins* or *No, I haven't/No, never.*

Tell Ss to find new partners after they have both asked and answered a question. Encourage Ss to speak to as many different partners as possible and not spend too much time with one person or just copy each other's answers.

CLASS RULES

Materials: One worksheet per pair of students

Elicit or preteach the noun *contract* and clarify the idea that it is a legal document that is signed and has to be respected. Arrange Ss into pairs and distribute one contract per pair of students. Ask them to look at the list of rules and decide if they are true for your class. If the rule is not true, Ss change it.

> **Suggested answers:** 1 … must/have to switch their mobiles off … 2 … don't have to arrive ten minutes before lessons start. 3 … don't have to/can sit in the same place … 4 … mustn't/can't talk when the teacher is … 5 … can sit next to who they want. 6 … mustn't eat and drink (except water) during the lesson. 7 … don't have to stand up when the teacher … (this depends) 8 … don't have to/can bring the teacher a cake … 9 … has to/must mark the students' …

After Ss have discussed and agreed the alterations, in pairs, they add their own ideas to complete the contract using the modals. When the contracts are complete, pin them to the walls and Ss can move around the class reading them to decide which one is the best. There could be a vote to decide this and the winning contract becomes the contract for the whole class. While Ss are reading, note any problems with the modals and deal with them at the end of the activity.

SAVE OUR SCHOOL!

Materials: One role card per Head Teacher

Lead into the topic by asking students about the quality of schools in their country and elicit some common problems and possible solutions.

Preteach or check *vandalise* and *uniform*. Divide the class into half. One half is Head Teachers and the other half is Educational Advisors. Sit each group in a row facing each other – one line is the Head Teachers and the other is the Educational Advisors. Give a card to each Head Teacher.

Tell the Head Teachers to explain their problem to the advisor opposite who responds by giving advice. After a few minutes tell the Head Teachers to move along one space so they can speak to a new advisor. The Head Teacher at the end of the row moves to the start of the row. Head Teacher's should speak to all the advisors. Monitor and ensure that Ss are using the functional language.

When they have finished, ask the Head Teachers to describe the best advice they were given.

Unit 5

GETTING AROUND

Materials: One copy of crossword A and crossword B per pair of students

Arrange Ss into A and B pairs and distribute worksheets A and B. Make sure they are sitting face-to-face so they can't see each other's answers. Tell Ss the object of the activity is to fill in the missing words in their crossword by asking their partner to describe them, e.g. Student A asks Student B for 1 down. Student B says *It carries lots of people. You can see them in the city, but also if you go to another city you can take one.* Student A guesses *train* and then it is Student B's turn. This continues until both Ss have completed their grids.

You may wish to preteach the following useful phrases:

What's 1 down?

It's something you ride/drive/fly/catch/sail.

You can see them in the city/in the sky/on the water.

It carries one person/four people/lots of people.

It's slow/fast/expensive/cheap/quiet/dangerous.

Tell Ss not to look at each other's crossword, show their crossword to each other or use the word they are describing.

When they have finished, they can check their answers by looking at each other's worksheets.

MISSING MONEY

Materials: One set of role cards per group

Arrange the students into groups of up to five Ss. If you have less than five Ss in a group, make sure at least the following roles are included: Dick Brown, Richard Cagney, Shirley Cagney. Preteach *wallet, steal, to be missing*.

Explain the situation, to set the scene. The Manchester Express was travelling from London to Manchester one evening, when one of the passengers realised his money was missing. Distribute the role cards to individuals within each group, ask them to read the information and prepare what they are going to say, on their own. Go round and help out with vocabulary and ideas. Give the Dick Brown role card to a stronger student, as this role involves thinking on their feet, as they ask further questions.

When they are ready, instruct Ss to carry out the role-plays. The detective asks each student questions in turn. Encourage them to ask as many questions as possible, in order to find out as much information as they can. Monitor carefully, prompting Ss where necessary, and taking notes on their use of language for later feedback/correction.

When they have finished, ask the 'detective(s)' who they think stole Chris Hinds' money. Give Ss feedback on their use of language, paying particular attention to the past simple and past continuous.

> **Answer:** Richard Cagney stole Chris Hinds' wallet. He was having problems with his business, but couldn't tell his wife. At 7.15p.m., he was reading the newspaper when he got up and told his wife he was going to the toilet. On the way he saw Chris Hinds sitting with an open bag, with the wallet showing. The train stopped and Richard Cagney pretended to 'fall' onto Chris' bag, and stole his money. He then returned and sat with his wife, but looked nervous.

20 THINGS ABOUT YOU

Materials: One worksheet per student

Arrange Ss in pairs and distribute the worksheets. Tell Ss to decide which verb form is correct in each prompt. Give Ss a few minutes and then check the answers.

> **Answers:** 1 choose to go 2 enjoyed doing 3 hope to do 4 needed to do 5 hate doing 6 can't imagine wearing 7 expect to do 8 avoid going 9 didn't finish reading 10 need to email 11 want to learn 12 love to listen/listening 13 would like to eat 14 would like to meet 15 chose to buy 16 imagine living 17 expect to buy 18 want to talk 19 decided not to listen 20 hope to visit

Ss spend five minutes writing an idea for each prompt in the gap. Monitor and provide vocabulary for Ss if they need it.

Arrange Ss into groups of four and tell Ss to tell each other their ideas and ask each other additional questions.

TIPTON TOUR

Materials: One copy of map A and map B per pair of students

Arrange Ss into pairs and distribute map A and B. Sit Ss face-to-face so they can't see each other's maps. Tell Ss they are going to visit the famous, historical town of Tipton. (It's not a real place.) Tell Ss to take turns to guide each other around the city and to label the boxes/places with the correct place name of the four destinations on their itinerary, e.g. Student A starts as a tourist and Student B (the tour guide) directs them from The Grand Hotel to The National Museum, by looking at their map. You should remind Ss not to look at each other's worksheet or show their worksheet to their partner. When Student A arrives, he/she labels the correct box. Then it is Student B's turn.

Tell Ss to take it in turns until they have visited all the places on their list and correctly labelled the places. When they have finished, they can check their answers by comparing maps.

Unit 6

A HEALTHY CITY

Materials: One copy of worksheet A and worksheet B per pair of students

Divide the class into half and explain the situation. The students are town councillors/planners, and as part of their job they are going to decide which sports (and facilities) should be developed for different categories in their area. Preteach *urban* and *rural*. Distribute worksheet A to one half of the class and worksheet B to the other half. Give Ss time to complete their questions. Refer them to the **Photo bank** on SB p157 to help with the names of sports.

Put Ss into A/B pairs and explain the activity. Each student shares his/her list with the other student, and elicits ideas from their partner, and vice-versa. They then need to agree on one sport which best fits each category.

When they have finished, Ss present their ideas to the class.

HOW LONG … ?

Materials: One set of cards per pair of students

Arrange Ss into pairs and distribute the cards. Ask Ss to work together to complete the *For: _____* gaps on each card, using the information given, e.g. Became professional: 1998 For: *13 years* (assuming now is 2011).

When they have finished, tell Ss to put the cards back in a pile face down, then divide them up between them. They must not show their cards to their partner.

Elicit the questions they will need for the activity, and drill them round the class:

How long has he/she played this sport?

How long has he/she been professional?

How long has he/she been famous?

How many competitions has he/she won?

N.B. The first question/answer may sound more natural if the present perfect continuous is used (*How long has he/she been playing this sport? She has been playing tennis since she was four years old*). If Ss use this form when doing the activity, allow it, but avoid lengthy explanations as to why at this point.

Demonstrate the activity with a stronger student. Each turn, a student picks a category on their topmost card to compare. The other student then responds using *for* or *since* and their answer. Whoever's answer is the longest/biggest, wins their partner's card. If the numbers are the same, then both Ss keep their cards. The winner is the student who gets all of the cards.

PREDICTIONS

Materials: One set of cards per group

Revise the differences between *might/may* and *might not/may not* and the fact that the latter sounds less of a possibility.

Arrange Ss into groups of four and distribute one card to each student. Tell Ss to ask each other questions using the prompts on the card and to write names of the people they interview in the appropriate column. Encourage the Ss to ask supplementary questions and note the answers, e.g. *In the next seven days, do you think you'll sleep less than five hours? Yes, I will. Why? Because I have to work.*

When Ss have finished, depending on the number of students, you can group the Ss with the same card together and they can compare their information.

You can then ask the different groups more general questions, e.g. *Do many people think they will use a computer in the next twenty-four hours?*

WHERE DOES IT HURT?

Materials: One role card per student

Preteach *rash* and *stomach ache*.

Distribute the cards. Fold the cards so there is a patient and a doctor side. On the patient side there is a medical problem and on the doctor side there are prompts for the doctor to ask the patient.

Tell Ss to mingle and show the doctor side of their card to other student. The other student takes the role of doctor and asks for information about the patient's condition before telling the patient what they should do. If there is an odd number of students, there can be three-way conversations.

After Ss have spoken to a few doctors, they can change cards with each other so they have a new problem to ask advice for. Try to do this a few times during the mingle.

When Ss have finished, ask them to describe which illnesses they had, what advice they were given by the different doctors and who gave the best advice.

Unit 7

ANOTHER LIFE

Materials: One worksheet per student

Distribute the worksheets and check Ss understand the sentences.

Arrange Ss in pairs and tell them to complete the questions with the correct preposition. Give Ss five minutes before checking answers.

Answers: 1 about 2 for 3 up 4 around 5 for 6 about 7 back 8 to 9 about 10 for

Demonstrate the activity by using the first question and going round the class asking: *Do you dream about working in another country?* Continue asking the question until someone answers *Yes!* Write their name in the correct column. Ask follow up questions (e.g. *Why? Where?*) and write notes in the Extra information column. Model the other question forms with the class.

Instruct Ss to mingle and find people who can answer *yes* to the questions, and write their names in the correct column. Encourage them to ask follow-up questions, and monitor their language, taking notes for later feedback/correction.

When they have finished, ask Ss to tell the class what they found out.

DID YOU KNOW … ?

Materials: One card per group

Arrange Ss into four teams of between two to four people and give each team the appropriate worksheet.

Tell the first team to read out one of their questions and the three possible answers to the other three teams. The other teams listen and then discuss what they think the correct answer is and write it down. When all three teams have decided and are ready to listen, you can ask the first team to tell the others the correct answer. This is indicated in bold. Ss should not shout out their answers.

You can keep score on the board, awarding ten points for each correct guess. The winners are the team with the highest score.

I WENT HOME TO …

Materials: One copy of the board per group and one counter per student

Arrange Ss into groups of four and give each group a board, enlarged to A3 if possible. Assign each student with a letter from A to D. Each student needs a small object, like a coin or a counter, which they can move around the board. These are placed on their letter.

Explain the rules and demonstrate. The object is for Ss to cross the board and reach the opposite corner by making sentences using infinitives of purpose, *because* or *so*. Ss make sentences using a verb (in a light grey circle) and *so*, *to* or *because* in an adjacent black circle, e.g. Student A starts and says *I bought a sandwich because I was hungry*, Student D might say, *I needed help so I phoned my brother*. Ss can use the verbs before or after *so*, *to*, or *because*. Therefore, the verbs and *so*, *to*, or *because* can be in the same clause or different clauses. However, the sentence must contain the two words and clearly express purpose, cause or result.

If the other Ss agree that the sentence is correct, the student moves their counter to the either of the two circles which is nearest their destination. Ss may move horizontally and vertically but not diagonally.

Tell Ss not to use the circle they are on again for their next turn but to use one which is either horizontally or vertically adjacent.

Throughout the activity, monitor closely to check Ss are using the three forms correctly.

CAREER CHANGE

Materials: One role card per student

Start by explaining the situation. Tell Ss that they are bored with their jobs and want to change their lives completely. Tell Ss they are going to a careers fair to find out about new careers and training courses.

Arrange Ss into groups of six. There are three Ss who work as representatives for colleges (Role cards 1, 2 and 3) and three Ss who need information (Role cards 4, 5, and 6). If there is an odd number of Ss, then there can be two career changers or reps together.

Preteach *massage* and *stressful*. Distribute the role cards. Give Ss five minutes to read the role cards and prepare their questions/information. Then sit reps and career changers face-to-face.

The object is for career changers to visit each college rep and ask for information. The reps should try to convince the career changers to book a course with them. College reps have to be persuasive, but truthful and career changers should ask additional questions. Every eight minutes or so, tell the career changers to move to the next rep.

When Ss have finished, ask the career changers to tell the class which new course they thought was the best for them and also who the best college rep was.

Unit 8

AMAZING MONEY

Materials: One copy of the worksheet per group

Arrange the class into groups of three. Give each group a copy of the quiz and ask them to think of a name for their group and write it at the top of the worksheet. Tell them to discuss the questions and circle the correct answers.

When they've finished, collect in their worksheets and give each one to a different group. Go through the answers, and tell them to award one point for each correct answer. The group with the most points wins.

Answers: 1 a) These were issued in The Phillipines and worth 100,000 pisos. 2 c) They were called *praescriptiones* and used in the first century BC. 3 c) However, this can vary, depending on how happy you are with the service. 4 b) The Goldfish 'Le Million' phone, certified by the Guiness Book of Records on January 29th 2008, was made of white gold and covered in diamonds. 5 c) They were issued in 2004 to commemorate '50 years of Rock 'n' Roll'. 6 a) They were issued in 2009 and worth 100 trillion Zimbabwean Dollars. They had 14 zeros on the front and back. 7 c) They were issued in Morocco in 1944, and worth 50 centimes. 8 b) Diner's Club issued 200 cards in 1951 and their customers were able to use them in 27 restaurants in New York City. 9 c) It was used by Barclay's Bank in Enfield Town, London. Twenty-five years previously an American bank had made a mechanical ATM, but later took it out of use as customers didn't like it. 10 a) for his role in the film *Where the Day Takes You* 11 c) The notes were made from deer skin, in 140 BC. 12 b) In 1782, it was decided that they would use the Spanish currency in the USA.

FOUR GUESSES

Materials: One card per group

Tell the students you are thinking of a common and successful item, for example, an iPod. Describe the item using relative clauses and tell Ss to guess what it is, e.g. *It's something which was first sold in 2001. It's something which is small and light.*

Divide the class into five teams of two or three and distribute the cards. First, tell Ss to think of another successful, common thing like an invention, food, a famous place or even sport. They write four clues using relative clauses like in the examples. Monitor closely to make sure that the relative clauses are used correctly and that the clues are not too difficult or too easy.

When Ss are ready, tell the first team to choose one of their items and to read the first clue. The other teams listen and guess what is being described. Tell the other teams not to call out their guess, but to write it on a piece of paper. When all the teams are ready, they hold up their answers. If any team or teams guess correctly, they win the number of points in brackets for that clue. If no team or teams guess correctly then the team reading the clues read the next one and the process continues. You can keep score on the board. The winners are the team with the most points.

LET'S CELEBRATE!

Materials: One copy of the worksheet per group

Start by asking Ss about any big parties they have been to or organised themselves. Tell Ss they are going to plan their own party. Arrange Ss into groups of three and distribute the party planner cards to each group. Tell Ss to fill in the card together. Help with any vocabulary.

When Ss have finished, tell Ss that there are four places they can have their party and they have to decide which is the most suitable for them. Give Ss the four party venues. Encourage Ss to discuss the venues using *too much/many, enough* and *very,* e.g. *The Moon River Boat is not big enough, we have 100 guests. The Plaza Hotel is too much money. The Plaza Hotel is very expensive.*

When each group has chosen a venue, ask Ss to explain to the other groups why they chose it and if they needed to make any changes to their plan.

CAN I HELP YOU?

Materials: One role card per student

Divide the class in half: shop assistants and customers. Give role cards 1, 2, 3 and 4 to the shop assistants and role cards 5, 6, 7 and 8 to the customers. Tell Ss to read their role cards. Customers have details about the items they need to buy (size, colour) and sales assistants have information about the items they are selling. The object is for Ss to mingle and for the shop assistants to sell some items on their cards and the customers to buy the items on theirs. Tell the customers that they have a budget and must try not to exceed it. In some cases, they can 'shop around' for a bargain and in others they can't, there's only one shop assistant who sells what they want. Customers must record how much they spend. Remind Ss of some of the language from unit 8.3, e.g. *Can I help you? I'm looking for a white shirt.*

If the customer can't find what they want, they can ask for another item or move to another shop assistant. If they do find what they want, they can tell the shop assistant they would like to buy it.

When the transaction is complete, the shop assistant ticks the item to show it is sold and the customer ticks the item to show they have bought what they want. Ss must change after every transaction and continue to mingle until they have sold or bought all they can.

When Ss have finished, ask how much money customers have spent, if they over or under budget, and how much the sales assistants sold.

Unit 9

IT'S A CHEETAH

Materials: One copy of worksheet A, worksheet B and worksheet C per group and one answer sheet per group

Arrange Ss in groups of three and distribute the worksheets and give one answer sheet to each group which they fill in as they do the activity. Ss decide on a team name and write it at the top. Preteach *spots*, *mammal* and *trunk* or encourage students to use dictionaries.

Explain the activity. Starting with Student A, Ss take turns to read their clues to each other. When all three have been read, Ss have to agree what they think the animal is and write its name in the boxes on the answer sheet. This continues until the sheet is complete. You should remind Ss not to look at each other's worksheet.

When Ss have finished, swop answers sheets between groups for marking and go through the answers. The winners are the group with the most correct answers.

Answers: 1 dolphin 2 butterfly 3 shark 4 bear 5 ostrich 6 whale 7 crocodile 8 penguin 9 cheetah 10 mosquito 11 tortoise 12 chimpanzee 13 elephant 14 eagle 15 camel 16 pigeon

COMPARE IT!

Materials: One copy of the board and a dice per group and a counter per student

Arrange Ss into groups of four and give each group a board (A3 size if possible), a dice and a counter or small object each. Tell Ss to put their counters at the start and to take it in turns to move around the board. If you don't have a dice, use a coin. If it is heads they move their counter forward two spaces and if it's tails they move one. If Ss land on a dark square, they make a superlative sentence from the three things given. If Ss land on a white square, they make a comparative sentence by comparing the two things given. Ss must use the adjective at the top of the box and can use any other language that is appropriate for the comparison, e.g. *Cheetahs are faster animals than horses but horses can run for a long time. Cheetahs can't. Cities are more exciting places than the countryside because you can do many things like …* . Some of the boxes require students to state facts, others opinions. Ss can challenge anything they disagree with and if a student does not know an answer to something factual, it does not matter: they can say *I think …* or *In my opinion …* . The activity finishes when all the Ss have reached the end.

RACE TO THE SOUTH POLE

Materials: One copy of the worksheet per group

For the introduction, elicit *explorer* and discuss the kinds of places they go and what kind of person they have to be. Introduce the text and asks the class: *Was Scott a successful explorer?* Ss read the text quickly to answer the question.

> **Answer:** Partially, he got to the South Pole but lost the race and died on the way back.

Arrange Ss into groups of two or three. Tell Ss that each line of the text has one mistake relating to articles, including missing articles. Ss have to identify the mistakes to win points. Ask Ss to look at the first line and to discuss it quickly. Invite each group in turn to identify the mistakes. Reveal the answers once all groups have responded. If they identify it correctly they win one point and record this at the box at the end of the line. This continues for all the lines.

> **Answers:** 1 *the* race (*a* race) 2 *the* Great Britain (Great Britain) 3 *a* Norwegian (*the* Norwegian) 4 *the* horses (horses) 5 *the* dogs (dogs) 6 journey (*the* journey) 7 in *an* end (in *the* end) 8 *a* four men (four men) 9 South Pole (*the* South Pole) 10 *the* five weeks (five weeks) 11 *a* race (*the* race) 12 coast (*the* coast) 13 weather (*the* weather) 14 at *the* night (at night) 15 *an* eight months (eight months) 16 *a* story (*the* story)

IT MIGHT BE …

Materials: One copy of the worksheet per group

Arrange Ss into groups of three or four and distribute one worksheet to each group. Tell the group to speculate about what the close-up pictures are showing. Encourage Ss to use speculative language as well as the 'Give yourself time to think' language from unit 9.3. They should also give reasons for their ideas whenever they can, e.g. *What do you think A is? Well, it must be a machine. It could be a car. Perhaps it's a motorbike …* . Monitor the activity and remind Ss to use the appropriate language and avoid *It's a car! No, it's not! Yes, it is!*, etc.

When Ss have reached decisions about all the objects, do open class feedback to see if the different groups' ideas are the same. Then tell Ss the answers.

> **Answers:** A car B camera C clock D boot/shoe E bicycle F chair G helicopter H washing machine

Unit 10

CRIME CROSSWORD

Materials: One worksheet A and B and a crossword per pair of students

Arrange Ss into pairs and distribute the worksheets and give each pair a blank crossword grid. Sit Ss face-to-face and tell them not to show their worksheets to each other. Tell Ss that they will work together to complete the crossword. Student A has the clues for words going across and Student B for those going down. Ss take turns to read the clues and describe the word for their partner. If the student guesses the word correctly, they can write it in the correct place in the crossword. If the student does not know the answer, he/she can try another one.

WHAT'S IT LIKE?

Materials: One copy of the board and a dice per group and a counter per student

Arrange Ss into groups of four and distribute the board (enlarged to A3 if possible) and a dice to each group and a counter to each student. Quickly review the difference between *what something is like*, which you use to describe things, and *what do you like/dislike about something* to talk about something's good and bad points.

Tell Ss to take it in turns to move around the board and speak about the subject in the box they land on. After they have spoken about the topic, they should also ask another student one question about the topic, e.g. *mobile phone, My mobile is a Nokia. It's silver and has a big screen. I like it because it looks very modern. Pablo what's your mobile phone like? What do you like about it?* The other Ss can ask additional questions, e.g. *Where did you buy it?* If Ss don't own a particular object, for example a car, they can describe the car of someone they know instead.

If Ss land at the foot of a ladder, they go up it and if they land on the head of a snake they go down it. If you don't have any dice, Ss can use a coin and move one space for heads and two spaces for tails. The winner is the first student to reach the finish. You should monitor and help Ss if there are communication problems as well as note any errors related to the uses of *like*.

I DON'T BELIEVE IT!

Materials: One copy of worksheet A, worksheet B and worksheet C per group

Arrange Ss into pairs so there are two Student As, two Student Bs and two Student Cs working together. Give Ss the appropriate worksheet. Preteach *colouring* and *shell* and any other new vocabulary.

Tell Ss to complete the sentences by putting the verbs in brackets into the correct passive form. Some are present and some are past. Monitor and check any incorrect tense form use and irregular past participle errors.

When Ss have finished, regroup the Ss into threes with an A, B and C in each group. With one student keeping score, the Ss take it turns to read each other their facts and decide if they are true or not. They win a point for every correct guess and the winner is the student with the most points.

Answers: A 1 is made 2 was bought 3 was given (*by France*) 4 was seen 5 was built 6 were not grown 7 is spelt 8 was written

B 1 is found (*China only*) 2 is chosen 3 was taken (*the French, 1820*) 4 is drunk 5 was stolen 6 is sung 7 are not sold 8 are ridden

C 1 was shown 2 were driven 3 was known 4 is eaten (*Swiss*) 5 are worn (*kilts are usually only worn in Scotland*) 6 was bitten 7 are not taught (*3–5 years*) 8 were hidden (*were never buried*)

EXCUSE ME ...

Materials: One copy of the worksheet per pair of students

Arrange Ss into pairs and distribute the worksheets. Tell Ss to identify the problems in each picture. Help Ss with any vocabulary they need, e.g. *bug/cockroach, delay*, etc.

Answers: A animal in food B faulty product C bad haircut D delayed flight E overcharged customer/incorrect bill F sold a holiday at a hotel not finished/noisy construction work next to the hotel

Tell Ss to then discuss what the people complaining want from each situation, e.g. *a refund, to replace the TV,* etc. Again, help Ss with any vocabulary.

Remind Ss of some of the language from unit 10.3 and to be polite, but firm when complaining. Tell Ss to role-play the situations and to take turns to be the person complaining and the person dealing with the complaint. You should encourage Ss to reach an agreement about what to do in each situation.

Unit 11

DOMINOES

Materials: One set of cards per group

Arrange Ss into groups of four and distribute the cards. Explain the activity and demonstrate. One student deals the cards and each player places them face up in front of them. One student starts by putting down a card in the middle. Ss take it in turns to add a card to either side. If they place a card to the left, it needs to be the correct adjective. If they place a card to the right, it needs to be a situation which matches the adjective. If they can't go, they miss a turn. The winner is the first player to put down all their cards.

When Ss have finished, tell Ss to discuss in groups the last time they felt the different feelings. Preteach the question form *When did you last feel ... ?*

Answers: see the worksheet (in two columns)

WHO AM I?

Materials: One copy of worksheet A and worksheet B per pair of students

Arrange Ss into pairs and distribute the same worksheet to each student in the pair. Each worksheet contains information about five men or women who the Ss will describe to their partner. There are also pictures of five other people who they will identify.

In the first stage, tell Ss to make sentences with the prompts using the present perfect and *just, yet* and *already*. These sentences will be used in a guessing game, e.g. *Emma has just visited the hairdresser's. She hasn't finished university yet ...* , etc.

Regroup the Ss into new pairs of Student A and Student B. Sit Ss face-to-face and tell Ss not to look at each other's worksheets. Tell Ss to take turns to read out their sentences. The other student listens and tries to identify who the sentences are about and writes the name of the person they think it is by the picture. Tell Ss not to reveal the answers until the end because they will make guesses by eliminating people using the information they are told.

When Ss have finished, tell Ss to look at each other's worksheets and to check their answers are correct.

CONDITIONAL WHEELS

Materials: One copy of the worksheet per pair of students

Arrange Ss into pairs and give each pair a wheel. You can cut out the wheels, but it is not essential. Explain the activity and demonstrate. Start at number 1 and elicit a first conditional sentence using the prompts: *If I get a new job, I'll have more money.* Tell Ss to rotate the wheel clockwise and to take it in turns to make a conditional sentence using the prompts that link with the previous one (see answers). Ss take it in turns and do this until they reach the start again. Encourage Ss to do this without writing. They then repeat the whole chain but more quickly.

Answers:

1 If I get a new job, I'll have more money.

2 If I have more money, I'll go shopping.

3 If I go shopping, I'll buy a new computer.

4 If I buy a new computer, I'll play more online games.

5 If I play more online games, I'll be tired.

6 If I'm tired, I'll do less work.

7 If I do less work, my boss will be angry.

8 If my boss is angry, he'll shout at me.

9 If he shouts at me, I won't feel happy.

10 If I don't feel happy, I'll look for a new job.

11 If I look for a new job, I'll have some interviews.

12 If I have some interviews, I'll get a new job.

Tell Ss to work in the same pairs and to write their own conditional sentence chains in the blank wheel. These should also come full circle but Ss don't have to use all twelve stages. If Ss find it difficult to link the start and finish, suggest ideas. Ss can write prompts or full sentences. When Ss have finished, tell them to practise orally until they can do it without the wheel. Remind Ss to take it in turns.

When Ss have finished, you can invite Ss to exchange wheels with other groups.

GADGETS

Materials: One copy of the worksheet per pair of students

Arrange Ss into pairs and distribute the worksheets. Tell Ss to discuss what the gadgets do, who could use them and in what situations. Provide any vocabulary they need related to the gadgets, but also language like: *It won't/might work. It's really useful/not useful.*

Rearrange Ss into groups of four. Tell them they are the bosses of a company called *Go Gadgets* and they must choose just three of the gadgets for future development. Encourage Ss to use the language of giving opinions and disagreeing from unit 11.3.

When groups have reached agreement, ask a representative from each group to tell the class why they chose certain gadgets. You can write the three ideas from each group on the board. Then encourage the class as a whole to agree on the three gadgets *Go Gadgets* will develop.

Unit 12

NOUGHTS AND CROSSES

Materials: One copy of the worksheet per group

Arrange Ss in groups of three. Two Ss are players and one student is the referee. Give the players the larger grid and give the referee the answers. The object is to make a line of four squares either horizontally, vertically or diagonally by choosing a definition and giving the correct word.

Explain the rules. One student starts and chooses a square. They read the definition and try to identify the word, e.g. *A film which is about real life. A documentary!* This is checked by the referee. If the answer is correct, the student wins that square and can draw either a O or an X. If they give an incorrect answer, the referee must not tell them the correct answer. The square can still be won by the other player or the same player if they chose it again.

When Ss have finished, ask Ss to think of examples of the words where they can or to say what their favourite one is.

STAR INTERVIEW

Materials: One worksheet per student

Tell Ss to imagine themselves as a film star and create a star persona. It can be based on reality, but encourage the class to be imaginative and inventive if they want. Tell Ss to work individually and complete the star card. Help with vocabulary and ensure Ss complete the cards before the next stage.

Arrange Ss into pairs and tell them to take turns being the star and journalist. The journalist interviews the star by using the questions on the interview card and making notes of their answers.

Then tell Ss they are all now journalists and regroup them with new partners – this can be in pairs or larger groups. Tell Ss that they are looking for the best stories to use in their newspaper. Ss tell their new partners who they interviewed and report the most interesting things the star said to them, e.g. *Leon Fox told me he was filming a new action film.* Tell Ss to use *say* and *tell* when they are reporting and to correct each other's use of these two words as well as any back-shifting errors.

When Ss have finished, you can take the role of Editor of a newspaper and ask your journalists for their stories. Remind Ss that you want interesting, even scandalous stories because this sells newspapers. The Ss report their stories and the class decides which stories the newspaper will write about.

THREE IN A ROW

Materials: One worksheet per pair of students

Review the meaning and form of second conditional sentences with the class using a sentence from the activity. Write the structure *If + past simple, would + infinitive* on the board.

Arrange Ss into groups of four and give each group one board, enlarged to A3 if possible. The object of the activity is to win boxes by making second conditional sentences and to make lines of three. The lines can be horizontal, vertical or diagonal.

Explain the rules and demonstrate. Point to the spider icon and elicit a second conditional sentence about the picture, e.g. *if I saw a spider, I would be scared.* Tell Ss to take turns to make sentences using the pictures as prompts. If their partner agrees that the sentence is meaningful and correct, they win that box and initial it. When a student has won three boxes in a row they can draw a line through them and win one point. Ss can make lines from boxes that they have already won and Ss may want to stop each other from making lines by blocking. The winner is the student who has made the most lines at the end of the activity. Monitor the activity to ensure that the sentences, although imaginary, are meaningful and that Ss try to contract *would*. You may wish to give Ss dictionaries or help them with vocabulary.

When Ss have finished, elicit Ss' ideas for each picture.

ALL IN A DAY'S WORK

Materials: One copy for worksheet A and worksheet B per pair of students

Start by eliciting *tour* as a noun and verb and the phrase *go on tour/be on tour.* Ask Ss what problems a tour manager might have. Preteach/check *chauffeur*, *gym equipment* and *VIP suite.*

You may want to revise the functional phrases from unit 12.3 before instructing the role-play.

Arrange Ss into pairs and distribute the worksheets. Explain the role-play situation. One student is the tour manager of the band Hot Lava and the other is the receptionist. For the second role-play, the receptionist then becomes the tour manager of the band Head Space.

Give Ss a few minutes to read through the flowchart and think about what language they are going to use. In the case of the tour manager, they need to think of another couple of requests. Go round and help with vocabulary and ideas.

When both are ready, Hot Lava's tour manager can start the conversation. Monitor to ensure that the Ss make polite requests and offers. After the first role-play, Ss change roles.

At the end of the activity, ask what other requests were made and give feedback on the use of the functional phrases.

TESTS INDEX

LISTENING

1 ▶ 37 **Listen and circle the correct answer,**
a), b) or c).

1 Freddie's new salary will be ____.

  a) €40,000   b) €18,000   (c) €80,000)

2 Caroline thinks Freddie's new job will be in ____.

  a) England   b) Rome   c) Cambridge

3 Freddie has to move to Rome because ____.

  a) he'll travel all over the world

  b) the European sales office is there

  c) the schools are better there

4 Caroline is worried about the children going to school in
Rome because ____.

  a) they don't have any friends there

  b) there aren't any good schools in Rome

  c) they don't speak Italian

5 Freddie thinks their parents will come to visit them in
Rome because ____.

  a) they can drive there

  b) it's very easy to fly from England

  c) they like Italian food

6 When Caroline goes to Rome, she can ____.

  a) learn Italian

  b) get a new job

  c) work online

        | 5 |

2 ▶ 38 **Listen to the phone call and complete the notes.**

Apollo Travel

Name of customer:	¹ _Robert Travis_
Destination:	Corfu
Dates:	15th to ² _____ September
Breakfast included:	³ Yes/No (circle correct answer)
Total price:	€ ⁴ _____
Fly from:	⁵ _____ airport
Flight leaves at:	⁶ _____ p.m.

        | 5 |

PRONUNCIATION

3 ▶ 39 **Listen and pay attention to the underlined**
sounds. Circle the word with a different sound.

1 wife science (business) exercise

2 lettuce plumber brother cousin

3 keen cricket peas niece

4 broccoli cough onion squash

5 salary map fashion staff

6 daughter caught audience aunt

        | 5 |

VOCABULARY AND GRAMMAR

4 **Rearrange the letters and write the last word**
in each group.

1 consultant/trainer/courier/tplio ___*pilot*___

2 artist/sculpture/exhibition/apignitn _____

3 chemistry/science/languages/tyihsor _____

4 tram/underground/balloon/pihs _____

5 backache/flu/antibiotics/slipl _____

6 rugby/judo/snorkelling/oflg _____

        | 5 |

5 **Complete the sentences with the correct form of the**
word in CAPITALS.

1 He's always late. He isn't a very good _employee_.
EMPLOY

2 It's never too late to learn a _____ instrument.
MUSIC

3 Your daughter gave a very good _____ in the school
play. PERFORM

4 He wants a personal _____ because he doesn't have
time to go to the gym. TRAIN

5 You're so keen on computers, you should be an IT
_____. CONSULT

6 I always wanted to be a _____ when I grew up.
SCIENCE

        | 5 |

6 Circle the correct answer, a), b) or c).

1 You ____ hang out with those boys.
 a) might not   (b) shouldn't   c) should

2 What time ____ he getting the train tonight?
 a) did   b) is   c) are

3 She's never been keen on ____.
 a) fly   b) to fly   c) flying

4 I heard that they ____ got back together.
 a) have   b) has   c) didn't

5 He wants ____ something more interesting with his life.
 a) to make   b) doing   c) to do

6 You must stop ____ your health in that stressful job.
 a) to risk   b) risking   c) to risking

7 ____ he collect stamps at primary school?
 a) Did   b) Have   c) Were

8 Mark lost his job because he ____ too much time off.
 a) has   b) was having   c) was spending

9 Don't look up every new word in that book or you ____ enjoy reading it.
 a) won't   b) may   c) will

10 She spent all day ____ the most delicious meal.
 a) to do   b) to cook   c) cooking

11 Carl has to work late tonight so I ____ see him.
 a) am going to   b) might not   c) mustn't

`10`

7 Complete the sentences using the words in CAPITALS.

1 You can't make mistakes in the exam. MUST
 You _mustn't make mistakes in the exam_

2 She hates making decisions. STAND
 She _____.

3 I quite like working under pressure. MIND
 I don't _____.

4 We haven't eaten out since July. WEEKS
 We _____.

5 Matt's going to phone me later. PROMISE
 Matt _____.

6 My grandparents were eating when I arrived. LUNCH
 My grandparents _____.

`5`

8 Find and correct the mistakes in the questions below. Then write short answers.

1 Did you ~~saw~~ /see the Monet exhibition in Paris last year?
 No, I ___didn't___.

2 Is he going to made a speech at the conference?
 Yes, he _____.

3 Do we have to wearing a school uniform?
 Yes, you _____.

4 Have they written to you since recently?
 No, they _____.

5 Was she working as a fashion designer when you've seen her in Paris?
 Yes, she _____.

6 Will I to deal with customers in this job?
 No, you _____.

`5`

9 Make questions with the prompts. Then match questions 1–6 to answers a)–f).

1 Which director / make / the film ET?
 Which director made the film ET?   e

2 Where / they / get / know /each other?
 _____

3 Who / give / her / that watch?
 _____

4 What time / he / arrive / tomorrow?
 _____

5 Whose book / win / the Man Booker prize / in 2008?
 _____

6 Which subject / study / when you / be /at university?
 _____

a) Aravind Adiga's The White Tiger.
b) At about six in the evening.
c) I did Computer Technology.
d) Her boyfriend did.
e) Steven Spielberg.
f) I think they worked in the same office.

`5`

10 Complete the travel advice with ONE word in each gap.

First, don't forget ¹___to___ check your passport one month before you travel. Only ²_____ week, a friend of mine missed her plane to Rome because her ³_____ was out of date. It took two days to get a new one ⁴_____ she had to buy another flight to meet up with her friends in Rome. They ⁵_____ having a great time while she was standing in a passport office queue!

Secondly, it's a ⁶_____ idea to get to the airport early. Passengers usually have to check in at least two ⁷_____ before their flight. The last time I travelled, I got to the airport three hours early. There ⁸_____ no queue and I got the best seat on the plane.

Thirdly, the aeroplane meals might not ⁹_____ very tasty so take your favourite sandwiches in case you get ¹⁰_____.

Finally, avoid sitting by the window. Then you ¹¹_____ need to climb over the other passengers during the night to go to the bathroom.

[10]

READING

11 Read the article and circle the correct answer, a), b) or c).

Exercise your brain

EXERCISE IS ESSENTIAL FOR GOOD HEALTH. It keeps the body young and helps the brain to grow. However, physical exercise is no longer enough. Scientists have discovered new ways of increasing our brain power. Take their advice – you'll think faster and you'll be more intelligent.

WATCH LESS TV. When you watch television, your brain usually switches off. If you must do it, try to watch interesting, informative programmes to keep your brain active.

DON'T MISS BREAKFAST. It's the most important meal of the day. Children who have fizzy drinks and sugary cereals before they go to school get lower marks on tests of memory and attention. Eat baked beans for the best results!

INCREASE YOUR VOCABULARY. This will help to make a good impression on those around you. Try to learn five new words every day. Write the words on cards and look at them three or four times during the day. By the end of the year, you will know over 1,500 more words.

LAUGH. Scientists have proved that people think more creatively after they've watched a comedy show. They feel more active and interested in life around them.

LEARN SOMETHING NEW. Study a new language or join a drama club. Doing new activities will stimulate your brain and make it more powerful. If you don't have time for this, try doing crosswords – or brushing your teeth with your other hand!

1 Scientists have discovered that we ___ increase our brain power

(a) can   b) can't   c) mustn't

2 Watching cartoons on TV ___ help to keep your brain active.

a) will   b) might   c) won't

3 Children will get better marks in tests if they have ___ for breakfast.

a) cereals   b) baked beans   c) fizzy drinks

4 It's possible to learn five new words ___.

a) every week   b) every day   c) every year

5 You'll be more creative if you ___.

a) laugh   b) think   c) watch TV

6 Your brain power will improve if you ___.

a) brush your teeth
b) go to the theatre
c) learn new things.

[5]

12 Read the poster and the message. Then complete the notes.

Memorial Theatre
North Street
The Magnus Quartet
20 June   **7.00p.m.**
Book early. Call 01647 639403
Admission: £10 and £15

Hi Mack,
Just going to the airport to catch the flight to Shanghai. I'll be back on the 19th. Can you do me a favour? I forgot to buy tickets for the jazz concert yesterday – I had so much to do. Please get two tickets for the 20th – the more expensive ones. I hope you'll come with me! The phone number is on the fridge in the kitchen. I'll pay you when I get back – promise!
Sally xxx

Name of theatre:	¹ Memorial	
Type of music:	² _____	
Time:	³ _____	
Number of tickets:	⁴ _____	
Price of each ticket:	⁵ _____	
Date wanted:	⁶ _____	June.

[5]

COMMUNICATION

13 Match sentences 1–6 with a)–f).

1 Where exactly do you come from? __c__

2 I've got this marvellous new running machine. ____

3 Why don't we go and see the Cézanne exhibition? ____

4 How much time do people spend eating in their lives? ____

5 So it's straight on and second right? ____

6 How long have you had a sore back? ____

a) No, straight on and second left.

b) No, thanks. I can't stand Impressionist paintings!

c) Antalya. It's on the south coast of Turkey.

d) Really? So how does it work?

e) Since I played tennis last week.

f) About 70,000 hours!

☐ 5

14 Complete with conversation with the words in the box.

don't look	getting on	back together	welcome
can't stand	seeing her	to her	started	known you
month ago	thinks		

A: Hi, Jim. You ¹____ *don't look* ____ very happy. What's wrong?

B: Oh, hi, Marcia. Nothing.

A: Come on, Jim. I've ²_____ since we were six. I can see there's something wrong.

B: Yeah, well … it's Lindsay. I'm not ³_____ anymore.

A: What? I thought you two were ⁴_____ so well.

B: We were. But then we ⁵_____ arguing about a ⁶_____.

A: About what?

B: I don't know – little things really. And my rugby. She ⁷_____ it.

A: How often do you play?

B: Every Saturday – and we train three nights a week.

A: Ah, now I understand! She ⁸_____ that rugby's more important than she is.

B: I suppose so.

A: Do you want to get ⁹_____?

B: Yes! I really miss her. What should I do?

A: You should talk ¹⁰_____. Tell her that rugby is very important to you – but that she's more important.

B: You're right, Marcia. Thanks.

A: You're ¹¹_____, Jim. Good luck!

☐ 10

WRITING

15 Join the sentences using the linking word in brackets.

1 I want to live a healthy life. I do regular exercise. (so)
   I want to live a healthy life so I do regular exercise.

2 I'm careful about what I eat. I don't eat junk food. I don't eat fatty food. (so/or)
   _____
   _____

3 I try to eat oily fish twice a week. I eat vegetables every day. (and/also)
   _____
   _____

4 I do yoga. I may start playing tennis soon. (and)
   _____
   _____

☐ 5

16 Write a story about a memorable journey/holiday that went very well or very badly. Use the questions in the box to help you. Write 75–100 words.

When?   Who with?   Where was it?   What happened?   Why was it good/bad?   Why do you remember it?

I'll never forget … _____
_____
_____
_____
_____
_____
_____
_____
_____
_____
_____
_____
_____
_____
_____
_____
_____

☐ 10

Total: ☐ 100

LISTENING

1 ▶ 37 **Listen and circle the correct answer, a), b) or c).**

1 Freddie's new salary job will be ____.
 a) €40,000   b) €18,000   **c) €80,000** *(circled)*

2 Caroline doesn't want to live in ____.
 a) England   b) Rome   c) Oxford

3 The European sales manager has to live in Rome because ____.
 a) he can visit other European countries more easily
 b) he travels around Italy all the time
 c) the schools are better there

4 Freddie thinks the children ____.
 a) are too young to change schools
 b) won't make new friends in Rome
 c) will learn Italian easily

5 Caroline and Freddie's parents can visit them in Rome because ____.
 a) it's only a short trip from England
 b) they can drive there
 c) they like Italian food

6 When Caroline goes to Rome, she can ____.
 a) get a new job
 b) learn Italian
 c) work online

☐ 5

2 ▶ 38 **Listen to the phone call and complete the notes.**

Apollo Travel

Name of customer:	1 Robert Travis
Destination:	Corfu
Dates:	2 _____ to 30th September
Name of hotel:	3 _____
Dinner included:	4 Yes/No (circle correct answer)
Deposit:	€ 5 _____
Flight arrives at:	6 _____ p.m.

☐ 5

PRONUNCIATION

3 ▶ 39 **Listen and pay attention to the underlined sounds. Circle the word with a different sound.**

1 w<u>i</u>fe   sc<u>i</u>ence   **b<u>u</u>siness** *(circled)*   exerc<u>i</u>se
2 lett<u>u</u>ce   pl<u>u</u>mber   br<u>o</u>ther   c<u>ou</u>sin
3 k<u>ee</u>n   cr<u>i</u>cket   p<u>ea</u>s   n<u>ie</u>ce
4 br<u>o</u>ccoli   c<u>ou</u>gh   <u>o</u>nion   squ<u>a</u>sh
5 s<u>a</u>lary   m<u>a</u>p   f<u>a</u>shion   st<u>a</u>ff
6 d<u>au</u>ghter   c<u>au</u>ght   <u>au</u>dience   <u>au</u>nt

☐ 5

VOCABULARY AND GRAMMAR

4 **Rearrange the letters and write the last word in each group.**

1 consultant/trainer/courier/tplio   ___pilot___
2 backache/flu/pills/adaehhec   _____
3 jogging/judo/golf/enistn   _____
4 painting/exhibition/sculpture/trsiat   _____
5 science/physics/history/ogolbiy   _____
6 underground/ferry/ship/ohcac   _____

☐ 5

5 **Complete the sentences with the correct form of the word in CAPITALS.**

1 He's always late. He isn't a very good _employee_. EMPLOY

2 Every child should have the chance to learn a _____ instrument. MUSIC

3 He so keen on computers, he should be an IT _____. CONSULT

4 When I was a student, I had a holiday job as a sales _____. ASSIST

5 Their son gave a very good _____ in the school concert. PERFORM

6 I'd like to be a personal _____ because the salary is better. TRAIN

☐ 5

6 Circle the correct answer, a), b) or c).

1 You ____ hang out with those boys.
a) might not   (b) shouldn't   c) should

2 ____ you collect stamps when you were a child?
a) Did   b) Have   c) Were

3 Her brother lost his job because he ____ too much time off.
a) has   b) was having   c) was spending

4 Don't try to understand every word when you listen or you ____ understand anything.
a) won't   b) may   c) will

5 He wanted ____ a Chinese meal for us.
a) make   b) to cook   c) cooking

6 Emma has to go to a meeting tonight so you ____ see her.
a) am going to   b) might not   c) mustn't

7 What time ____ his train arriving tonight?
a) do   b) is   c) are

8 He's never been keen on ____ golf.
a) play   b) to play   c) playing

9 Joe and Ann ____ got back together.
a) have   b) has   c) didn't

10 She should ____ something more interesting with her life.
a) to do   b) making   c) do

11 You must stop ____. It's dangerous.
a) to smoke   b) smoking   c) to smoking

⬜ **10**

7 Complete the sentences using the words in CAPITALS.

1 You can't make mistakes in the exam. MUST
You *mustn't make mistakes in the exam*

2 Their father's got a new wife but they don't like their new stepmother. MARRY
Their father _____.

3 I hate working in an office. STAND
I _____.

4 Alan's going to take me out for dinner. (PROMISE)
Alan _____.

5 She quite likes meeting new people. (MIND)
She doesn't _____.

6 We haven't been to the theatre for months. (SINCE)
We _____ October.

⬜ **5**

8 Find and correct the mistakes in the questions below. Then write short answers.

1 Did you s̶a̶w̶ see the Monet exhibition in Paris last year?
No, I ___*didn't*___.

2 Was he working as a sales rep when you've met him?
Yes, he _____.

3 Will you spend long holidays in your new job?
No, I _____.

4 Is she going to made a cake for your birthday?
Yes, she _____.

5 Do children have to wearing a school uniform in your country?
Yes, they _____.

6 Have they seen you since the last week?
No, they _____.

⬜ **5**

9 Make questions with the prompts. Then match questions 1–6 to answers a)–f).

1 Which director / make / the film ET?
Which director made the film ET?   *c*

2 Whose book / win / the Orange Prize / in 2008?
_____

3 Which subject / study / at university / next year?
_____

4 Where / they / get / know / each other?
_____

5 Who / buy / him / that car?
_____

6 What time / we / leave / tomorrow?
_____

a) I'd like to do Modern Languages.
b) His father did.
c) Steven Spielberg.
d) They met on holiday in Thailand.
e) After breakfast I think.
f) Rose Tremain's The Road Home.

⬜ **5**

10 Complete the travel advice with ONE word in each gap.

First, don't forget ¹___*to*___ check your passport one month before you travel. Only last week, a friend of mine ²_____ her plane to Rome because ³_____ passport was out of date. It took two days to get a ⁴_____ one and she had to buy another flight to Rome. Her friends were ⁵_____ a great time there while she was standing in a passport office queue!

Secondly, it's ⁶_____ good idea to get to the airport early. Passengers ⁷_____ have to check in at least two hours before their flight. The last ⁸_____ I travelled, I went to the airport three hours early. There was no queue and I got the best seat on ⁹_____ plane.

Thirdly, aeroplane meals aren't usually very tasty so ¹⁰_____ your favourite sandwiches in case you get hungry.

Finally, avoid ¹¹_____ by the window. Then you won't need to climb over the other passengers during the night to go to the bathroom.

	10

READING

11 Read the article and circle the correct answer, a), b) or c).

Exercise your brain

EXERCISE IS ESSENTIAL FOR GOOD HEALTH. It keeps the body young and helps the brain to grow. However, physical exercise is no longer enough. Scientists have discovered new ways of increasing our brain power. Take their advice – you'll think faster.

WATCH LESS TV. When you watch television, your brain usually switches off. If you must do it, watch interesting programmes to keep your brain active.

DON'T MISS BREAKFAST. It's the most important meal of the day. Children who have fizzy drinks and sugary cereals before they go to school get lower marks on tests of memory and attention. Give them baked beans for the best results!

INCREASE YOUR VOCABULARY. This will help to make a good impression on those around you. Try to learn five new words every day. Write the words on cards and look at them three or four times during the day. By the end of the year, you will know over 1,500 more words.

GET LOTS OF VITAMINS. The brain can't store energy so you must feed it every day. Eat a good variety of food to provide what you need: nuts, vegetables, fruit and fish.

LAUGH. Scientists have proved that people think more creatively after they've watched a comedy show.

LEARN SOMETHING NEW. Study a new language or join a drama club. Doing new activities will stimulate your brain and make it more powerful. If you don't have time for this, try doing crosswords – or brushing your teeth with your other hand!

1 Scientists have discovered that we ____ increase our brain power
   a) can   b) can't   c) mustn't

2 It's a good idea to avoid ____ boring programmes on TV.
   a) watch   b) to watch   c) watching

3 Children will get better marks in tests if they don't have ____ for breakfast.
   a) cereals   b) fizzy drinks   c) baked beans

4 You ____ learn five new words every day if you write them on cards.
   a) have to   b) can   c) might not

5 To give our brains energy, we should eat ____.
   a) food   b) chocolate   c) apples

6 You will improve your brain power if you ____.
   a) go to the theatre
   b) learn new things
   c) brush your teeth

	5

12 Read the poster and the message. Then complete the notes.

Memorial Theatre
North Street

Magic Sounds

9–11 June   **8.00p.m.**

Book early. Call 01647 639403

Admission: £8 and £12

Hi Nicky,

Just going to the station to catch my train to Edinburgh. I'll be back on the 11th. Can you do me a favour? I forgot to buy tickets for the reggae concert - I had so much to do. Please get four tickets for the 11th - the more expensive ones. I'm going with Ellie and Jack - hope you'll come too! The phone number is on my desk in the study. I'll give you the money when I see you - promise!

Shaun x

Name of theatre:	¹	*Memorial*
Name of band:	²	
Time:	³	
Number of tickets:	⁴	
Price of each ticket:	⁵	
Date wanted:	⁶	June.

	5

COMMUNICATION

13 Match sentences 1–6 with a)–f).

1 Where exactly do you come from? __c__

2 So it's first right and straight on? ____

3 How long have you had a sore throat? ____

4 I've got this marvellous new exercise machine. ____

5 Why don't we go and see the Damian Hirst exhibition? ____

6 How much time do we spend watching TV in our lives? ____

a) No, straight on and second right.

b) No, thanks. I can't stand modern art!

c) Athens. It's the capital of Greece.

d) About 80,000 hours!

e) Since I went jogging in the rain last week.

f) Really? So how does it work?

`5`

14 Complete with conversation with the words in the box.

| ~~don't look~~   since   I understand   should I   important than   were getting   suppose so   'm not   started arguing   to get   stand it |

A: Hi, Jim. You ¹___don't look___ very happy. What's wrong?

B: Oh, hi Marcia. Nothing.

A: Come on, Jim. I've known you ²_____ we were six. I can see there's something wrong.

B: Yeah, well …it's Lindsay. I ³_____ seeing her any more.

A: What? I thought you two ⁴_____ on so well?

B: We were. But then we ⁵_____ about a month ago.

A: About what?

B: I don't know – little things really. And my rugby. She can't ⁶_____.

A: How often do you play?

B: Every Saturday – and we train three nights a week.

A: Ah, now ⁷_____! She thinks that rugby's more important than she is.

B: I ⁸_____.

A: Do you want ⁹_____ back together?

B: Yes! I really miss her. What ¹⁰_____ do?

A: You should talk to her. Tell her that she's more ¹¹_____ rugby.

B: You're right, Marcia. Thanks.

A: That's OK, Jim. Good luck!

`10`

WRITING

15 Join the sentences using the linking word in brackets.

1 I want to live a healthy life. I do regular exercise. (so)
I want to live a healthy life so I do regular exercise.

2 I do yoga. I'm thinking of playing tennis. (and/also)
_____
_____

3 I'm careful about what I eat. I don't eat junk food. I don't eat fatty food. (so/or)
_____
_____

4 I try to eat oily fish twice a week. I eat vegetables every day. (and)
_____
_____

`5`

16 Write a story about a memorable journey/holiday that went very well or very badly. Use the questions in the box to help you. Write 75–100 words.

| When/Where was it?   Who with?   What happened? Why was it good/bad?   Why do you remember it? |

I'll never forget … _____
_____

`10`

Total: `100`

LISTENING

1 ▶ 40 **Listen and circle the correct answer, a), b) or c).**

I Mary thinks the thief should go to prison for ___.
   a) three months   (b) five years)   c) 10 years

2 The woman thinks the new tennis teacher could be ___.
   a) English   b) Spanish   c) Scottish

3 The woman has just bought some ___.
   a) milk   b) food   c) books

4 The woman is buying a sweater for her ___.
   a) brother   b) boyfriend   c) father

5 The Globe Theatre is in ___.
   a) Queen's Street   b) Queen's Road   c) Prince Road

6 The man went to the doctor because he was ___.
   a) sick   b) sleepy   c) tired

| | 5 |

2 ▶ 41 **Listen to the phone calls and complete the notes.**

Hotel Complaints Book

Date: *15/04/09*

1) Name: *Major* [1] *Brown*

   Room Number: [2] _____

   Problem: *Breakfast eggs were*
   [3] _____ *and* [4] _____
   were cooked too much.

   Action: *Talk to the* [5] _____

- - - - - - - - - - - - - - - -

2) Name: *Mrs* [6] _____ *Peters*

   Room Number: [7] _____

   Problem: *Man in room* [8] _____
   [9] _____ *loudly in the*
   [10] _____.

   Action: *Talk to the* [11] _____.

| | 5 |

PRONUNCIATION

3 ▶ 42 **Listen and tick (✓) the words in each group that have a different stress pattern.**

1 Oo	2 oO	3 Ooo
history	extinct	geography
delayed ✓	divorced	confused
arrest ✓	business	audience
chocolate	sculpture	souvenirs
4 oOo	**5 ooOo**	**6 oOoo**
decision	technology	ability
dictionary	education	investigate
recommend	politician	electrician
director	celebrity	performance

| | 5 |

VOCABULARY AND GRAMMAR

4 Cross out the word that does not fit in each group.

1 company   employee   salary   ~~tram~~
2 racket   painting   gallery   exhibition
3 drama   languages   ocean   homework
4 grapes   jogging   pineapple   mango
5 badminton   rugby   whale   cricket
6 technology   search engine   peas   software
7 lend   fax   cash   earn
8 waterfall   spam   volcano   rain forest
9 wild   domestic   farm   insect
10 suitcase   audience   band   performance
11 moped   staff   ship   speedboat

| | 5 |

5 Complete the sentences with the correct form of the words in CAPITALS.

1 John's parents have got two children and five *grandchildren*. GRAND

2 I had a terrible headache so I took two strong _____. PAIN

3 Mark has wanted to be a fashion _____ since he was six years old. DESIGN

4 She hated history exams because she had to _____ lists of dates. MEMORY

5 You must make a _____ soon or he'll find someone else for the job. DECIDE

6 If you want to go to Paris, I'll make the _____. RESERVE

| | 5 |

6 Circle the correct option to complete the sentences.

1 We've been to India (on)/ for holiday three times.

2 He's never been keen *on* / *of* eating meat.

3 They used to smoke forty cigarettes a day but they've just given *out* / *up*.

4 Why don't we go to Luigi's restaurant? We haven't eaten *in* / *out* for ages.

5 If she was better at dealing *with* / *for* people she'd be an excellent boss.

6 Last night, thieves broke *in* / *out* and stole £50,000 worth of paintings.

```
                                          5
```

7 Complete the sentences with the correct form of the verbs in the box.

```
go (x2)   make (x2)   take (x2)   do
have   play   work   earn
```

1 He won't want tickets for that play. He ___went___ to see it last weekend.

2 This CD player doesn't work so I'm going _____ it back to the shop tomorrow.

3 We _____ a delicious picnic by the river when it started raining.

4 His business _____ so well now, he might take on more staff soon.

5 When she passes her exams, she _____ a much better salary.

6 We _____ (not) skiing yet this winter.

7 You have to practise for at least six hours every day _____ an instrument well.

8 Over fifty television sets _____ back to the shop because they were faulty.

9 Tom won't find it easy _____ friends if he talks to them so rudely.

10 She'd soon get promoted in that job if she _____ well under pressure.

11 You'll never learn a foreign language if you _____ (not) mistakes.

```
                                         10
```

8 Match 1–6 with a) to f).

1 They didn't have enough customers __c__

2 I don't often go dancing ___

3 Which films have ___

4 She said she didn't mind ___

5 Will you be able ___

6 If you didn't go to bed so late, ___

a) lending you her car.

b) you'd sleep better.

c) so they had to close the shop.

d) but I enjoy doing it once in a while.

e) to go out with me this weekend?

f) won an award recently?

```
                                          5
```

9 Circle the correct alternative, a), b) or c).

1 He's the man ___ helped me get the job.
  a) which   (b) that)   c) whose

2 People eat too ___ junk food these days.
  a) many   b) enough   c) much

3 He's ___ asked her to go with him.
  a) already   b) yet   c) ever

4 We walked around ___ garden of his house while we talked.
  a) a   b) the   c) –

5 The schoolchildren ___ home early because of the bad weather.
  a) are sent   b) sent   c) were sent

6 Sorry I'm late. It was ___ than I thought.
  a) further   b) far   c) more far

7 When I go to university, I ___ have my own flat.
  a) –   b) 'll   c) don't

8 I can't imagine ___ in that hotel – it's so expensive.
  a) staying   b) to stay   c) stay

9 What ___ their new house like?
  a) does   b) 's   c) are

10 They told us they ___ at nine.
  a) 'd come   b) comes   c) come

11 I don't know ___ keys they are.
  a) who   b) that   c) whose

```
                                          5
```

10 Complete the article with ONE word in each gap.

New mobile ¹ *phone* technology continues to influence and change our lives. People can now sign up to a new service ² _____ will find their family and friends on a computer map ³ _____ their mobiles. However, many people are unhappy about this technology and have made complaints about ⁴ _____ protection of their privacy. The phone companies have replied, saying that users would have ⁵ _____ sign up and agree to be located. They don't have to sign up to the service if they don't ⁶ _____ to. And if they do, they can switch ⁷ _____ the service whenever they want. The service will ⁸ _____ popular with parents but their children may ⁹ _____ feel the same. One thing is certain: it's ¹⁰ _____ easy and convenient way to answer the ¹¹ _____ frequently asked question on a mobile: 'Where are you?'

	10

READING

11 Read the article and circle the correct answer, a), b) or c).

Grandmother fails test again

A SIXTY-EIGHT-YEAR-OLD grandmother from the South Korean city of Jeonju has just failed her written driving test for the 771st time. The woman's name, which was given only as Cha, first took the written part of the exam in April 2005. At the time, she thought it would help if she had a car for her job.

In the beginning, Cha went to the licence office almost every day. Now, she no longer works but still goes to the office once a week. The office said she's spent more than £1,600 on exam fees.

'You have to get at least sixty points to pass the written part,' said Kim Rahn, who wrote about Cha in the Korea Times, an English-language daily newspaper. 'She usually gets under fifty.'

Bloggers have already responded to the news about Mrs Cha's misfortunes with comments that range from sympathy to anger. One wrote, 'There's a time in every person's life when, if they fail something over 700 times, they should stop.'

Other bloggers complained about a system that allows people to take a driving test so many times. One man commented: 'It's not a very good system if you can take the test as often as you want. I mean, she might be a danger to other people even if she passes the test after the 1,001st try.'

Mrs Cha seems to be ignoring the bloggers. She said that she'd be back for another attempt. If she passes, then she can begin to prepare for the practical test.

1 Cha has taken the written test more than ___.
   a) 700 times   b) 800 times   c) 750 times
2 She wanted to learn to drive because ___.
   a) she didn't have a car
   b) it would be useful for her work
   c) it was her dream
3 Cha usually takes the written test ___.
   a) four times a month   b) every day   c) occasionally
4 Bloggers have written ___ things about Cha.
   a) positive   b) negative
   c) both positive and negative
5 One blogger thinks that Cha ___ drive a car if she passes the test.
   a) should   b) can   c) shouldn't
6 Mrs Cha ___ planning to give up trying to pass the written test.
   a) isn't   b) is   c) will

	5

12 Read the poster and the message. Then complete the notes.

Island Tour
Take a boat trip around ten beautiful islands.
Mon–Fri: 10.00 a.m. to 1.00p.m
Sat and Sun: 10.00a.m. to 4.30p.m
Leaves from the boat tour office in the port.
Tickets:
£10 *(Mon–Fri with coffee/cold drink)*
£25 *(Sat/Sun with lunch and drinks)*

George,
I'm just going shopping for the afternoon. Hope your game of golf was good. I've just seen an ad for a boat trip round the islands. We can't go tomorrow because we have the coach trip to the old Greek ruins. How about Saturday? We can have a lovely day sailing around the islands with lunch included! Do you think you could get the tickets? I'm sure you'll love it.
Jx

Notes		
Name of tour:	¹ *Island Tour*	
Day:	² _____	
Time:	³ _____	to 5.00p.m.
Number of tickets:	⁴ _____	
Price per ticket:	⁵ _____	
Leaves from:	⁶ _____	tour office

	5

COMMUNICATION

13 Match sentences 1–11 with responses a)–k).

1 I hope to see you again soon. _a_

2 Can I speak to the manager please? ___

3 I get really nervous when I have to speak in public. ___

4 Can you show me where it hurts? ___

5 Do you know where the study centre is? ___

6 Is the theatre open in the mornings? ___

7 Do you sell that stuff for deleting mistakes in your writing? ___

8 Everyone should go to the gym at least three times a week. ___

9 Go straight on until you reach the corner. ___

10 I'm afraid I have a complaint. The shower in my room doesn't work. ___

11 Would you be able to recommend a good clothes shop? ___

a) Yes, let's keep in touch.

b) Why don't you do a course to help you?

c) The corner. Thanks.

d) Yes, it's next to the library over there.

e) Correction fluid? Yes, we do.

f) I'm sorry, I don't know any. I don't live here.

g) Of course. Can I ask who's calling?

h) It might be, but maybe you should phone and check.

i) I'm sorry, there's nothing we can do at the moment. The water's been cut off.

j) Here, on my right foot.

k) I'm afraid I don't agree. Not everybody likes exercise.

| 10 |

14 Complete the conversation with ONE word in each gap.

A: Would you ¹___like___ to be famous?

B: I don't ²_____. Why?

A: I watched the news earlier. They ³_____ talking about the paparazzi.

B: What – those people ⁴_____ follow celebrities around all the time?

A: Exactly. I ⁵_____ they should stop it.

B: How can they do that?

A: They could arrest them, and give them large fines. Or put them ⁶_____ prison!

B: Maybe, but it's not their fault. It's ⁷_____ newspapers that pay a lot of ⁸_____ for the photos.

A: Yes, I suppose you're ⁹_____.

B: But I agree with you. I ¹⁰_____ stand those photos of celebrities having fun with their friends or children.

A: Right. If I was famous, I ¹¹_____ hate it.

B Me too.

| 5 |

WRITING

15 Match the underlined words in the email to formal phrases a)–f).

> ¹Hi, Mr White
>
> ²Just a quick note about the plans for the new airport in Bigsby. I think it's ³a great idea. I travel to Paris a lot and the airport will make my life much easier. ⁴Also, it'll bring foreign tourists to our town.
>
> ⁵Write back soon,
>
> ⁶Bye,
>
> Sally Evans

a) In addition ___

b) Yours sincerely ___

c) Dear _1_

d) I look forward to hearing from you ___

e) I'm writing about ___

f) an excellent ___

| 5 |

16 Write an answer to the question below in 75–100 words. Include at least two positive and two negative points in your answer.

'How do you think technology will change our lives in the next twenty years?'

It seems to me that/in my opinion, … _____

_____

_____

_____

_____

_____

_____

_____

_____

_____

_____

_____

_____

_____

_____

_____

_____

_____

_____

_____

| 10 |

| **Total:** | 100 |

LISTENING

1 ▶ 40 Listen and circle the correct answer, a), b) or c).

1 Mary thinks the thief should go to prison for ___.
   a) three months   (b) five years   c) 10 years

2 The man says the tennis teacher has a ___ name.
   a) English   b) Italian   c) Scottish

3 The books the woman bought were reduced to ___.
   a) £3.50   b) £5.99   c) £7.99

4 The woman buys a ___ size sweater.
   a) small   b) medium   c) large

5 The Globe Theatre is on the ___ in Queen's Street.
   a) left   b) right   c) corner

6 The doctor advised the man to ___.
   a) walk   b) sleep   c) have lunch

| 5 |

2 ▶ 41 Listen to the phone calls and complete the notes.

Hotel Complaints Book

Date: 15/04/09

1) Name: Major ¹__Brown__

   Room Number: ²_____

   Problem: The ³_____ were cold and the sausages were ⁴_____ too much.

   Action: ⁵_____ to the chef.

- - - - - - - - - - - - - - - - - - - -

2) Name: Mrs Julia ⁶_____

   Room Number: ⁷_____

   Problem: The ⁸_____ in room 308 sings too ⁹_____ in the bath.

   Action: Talk ¹⁰_____ the ¹¹_____.

| 5 |

PRONUNCIATION

3 ▶ 42 Listen and tick (✓) the words in each group that have a different stress pattern.

1 Oo	2 oO	3 Ooo
history	extinct	geography
delayed ✓	divorced	confused
arrest ✓	business	audience
chocolate	sculpture	souvenirs

4 oOo	5 ooOo	6 oOoo
decision	technology	ability
dictionary	education	investigate
recommend	politician	electrician
director	celebrity	performance

| 5 |

VOCABULARY AND GRAMMAR

4 Cross out the word that does not fit in each group.

1 office customer boss ~~ship~~
2 coach ferry mango lorry
3 insects tiger lion elephant
4 painting gallery racket exhibition
5 primary science secondary college
6 audience band chicken performance
7 borrow onion cabbage lettuce
8 cricket drama squash tennis
9 software technology fax earn
10 cheque wild coins notes
11 map desert ocean lake

| 5 |

5 Complete the sentences with the correct form of the words in CAPITALS.

1 John's parents have got two children and five _grandchildren_. GRAND

2 She was employed as a _____ in their new office in the city. RECEPTION

3 Her _____ as a writer grows every year. POPULAR

4 He had a terrible toothache so he took two _____. PAIN

5 If you want to go to that new restaurant, I'll make the _____. RESERVE

6 They should make a _____ soon or he'll find another house to buy. DECIDE

| 5 |

6 Circle the correct option to complete the sentences.

1 We've been there (on)/ for holiday three times.

2 If he was better at working *with / of* people, he'd be an excellent employee.

3 The man was sentenced *to / of* three years in prison for fraud.

4 If you want to get *off / on* well with him, you have to be friendlier.

5 I've never liked the people he hangs out *with / of*.

6 Children would behave better if parents didn't give *up / in* to them so easily.

☐ **5**

7 Complete the sentences with the correct form of the verbs in the box.

> go (x2)   take (x2)   make (x2)   do
> have   get   be   work

1 He won't want tickets for that play. He ____*went*____ to see it last weekend.

2 Over fifty CD players _____ back to the shop because they were faulty.

3 She'd soon get promoted in that job if she _____ well under pressure.

4 They'll never learn anything if they don't take risks and _____ mistakes.

5 My car's not going well so I'm going _____ it to the garage tomorrow.

6 When he passes his driving test, he _____ a car from his parents.

7 We _____ (not) jogging yet. Let's go now.

8 You have to study hard _____ a good architect.

9 They _____ a beach party when it started raining.

10 The company _____ very well now so they might employ more people.

11 Emily won't find it easy _____ friends if she's so unfriendly.

☐ **10**

8 Match 1–6 with a)–f).

1 They didn't have enough customers __*d*__

2 You mustn't drop litter on the street ___

3 Whose car is the blue one ___

4 She said she wasn't keen ___

5 If you didn't go to bed so late, ___

6 What time are we ___

a) meeting tonight?

b) on lending you her car.

c) you'd be able to get up earlier.

d) so they had to close the shop.

e) that's parked outside?

f) or you'll get an £80 fine.

☐ **5**

9 Circle the correct alternative, a), b) or c).

1 He's the man ___ helped me get the job.
   a) which   (b) that)   c) whose

2 I hate ___ up early on Monday morning.
   a) get   b) going   c) getting

3 What ___ her new boyfriend like?
   a) do   b) 's   c) are

4 They told ___ they were coming early.
   a) –   b) to us   c) us

5 I don't know ___ keys they are.
   a) whose   b) who   c) that

6 Kids eat too ___ chocolates and not enough fruit.
   a) many   b) enough   c) much

7 He hasn't asked her to go with him ___.
   a) already   b) yet   c) ever

8 She told the children to play in ___ garden.
   a) a   b) the   c) –

9 I can't imagine ___ there – it's so boring.
   a) living   b) to live   c) live

10 ___ tigers are very beautiful animals.
   a) The   b) A   c) –

11 It ___ be him. He was with us when it happened.
   a) can't   b) mustn't   c) might not

☐ **10**

10 Complete the article with ONE word in each gap.

New mobile [1] _phone_ phone technology continues to influence and change our lives. People [2]_____ now sign up to a new service that will find their [3]_____ and friends on a computer map on their mobiles. However, many people [4]_____ happy about this technology and [5]_____ complained about the protection of their privacy. The phone companies have replied, saying that users would have [6]_____ sign up and agree to be located. They don't have to [7]_____ up to the service if they [8]_____ want to. And if they do, they can switch off [9]_____ service whenever they want. The service should be popular with parents [10]_____ their children may not feel the same. One thing is certain: it's an easy and convenient way to answer [11]_____ most frequently asked question on a mobile: 'Where are you?'

```
10
```

READING

11 Read the article and circle the correct answer, a), b) or c).

Grandmother fails test again

A SIXTY-EIGHT-YEAR-OLD grandmother from the South Korean city of Jeonju has just failed her written driving test for the 771st time. The woman's name, which was given only as Cha, first took the written part of the exam in April 2005. At the time, she thought it would help if she had a car for her job.

In the beginning, Cha went to the licence office almost every day. Now, she no longer works but still goes to the office once a week. The office said she's spent more than £1,600 on exam fees.

'You have to get at least sixty points to pass the written part,' said Kim Rahn, who wrote about Cha in the Korea Times, an English-language daily newspaper. 'She usually gets under fifty.'

Bloggers have already responded to the news about Mrs Cha's misfortunes with comments that range from sympathy to anger. One wrote, 'There's a time in every person's life when, if they fail something over 700 times, they should stop.'

Other bloggers complained about a system that allows people to take a driving test so many times. One man commented: 'It's not a very good system if you can take the test as often as you want. I mean, she might be a danger to other people even if she passes the test after the 1,001st try.'

Mrs Cha seems to be ignoring the bloggers. She said that she'd be back for another attempt. If she passes, then she can begin to prepare for the practical test.

1 Cha has taken the written test more than ___.
a) 700 times   b) 800 times   c) 750 times ⃝
2 Cha started taking the test ___.
a) last year   b) in April   c) in 2005
3 She wanted to learn to drive because ___.
a) she had a car   b) it would be useful for her work
c) it was her dream
4 Cha needs to get ___ points to pass the test.
a) 600   b) 50   c) 60
5 One blogger thinks that Cha ___ give up trying to pass the test.
a) should   b) can't   c) shouldn't
6 Another blogger said that Mrs Cha ___ be a safe driver even if she passed the driving test.
a) might   b) might not   c) could

```
5
```

12 Read the poster and the message. Then complete the notes.

Island Tour
Take a boat trip around ten beautiful islands.
Mon–Fri: 9.30 a.m. to 1.00p.m
Sat and Sun: 10.00a.m. to 5.00p.m
Leaves from the boat tour office in the port.
Tickets:
£12 *(Mon–Fri with coffee/cold drink)*
£22 *(Sat/Sun with lunch and drinks)*

George,
I'm just going shopping for the afternoon. Hope your game of golf was good. I've just seen an ad for a boat trip round the islands. We can't go tomorrow because we have the coach trip to the old Greek ruins, so how about Sunday? We'll have a lovely day sailing around the islands with lunch included! Do you think you could get the tickets? I'm sure you'll love it.
J x

Notes
Name of tour: [1] _Island Tour_
Day: [2] _____
Time: [3] _____ to 5.00p.m.
Number of tickets: [4] _____
Price per ticket: [5] _____
Leaves from: boat [6] _____ office

```
5
```

COMMUNICATION

13 Match sentences 1–11 with responses a)–k).

1 I hope to see you again soon. _a_

2 People should do exercise three times a week. ___

3 Keep going and then turn left. ___

4 I'm afraid I have a complaint. The internet in my room doesn't work. ___

5 Can I speak to Mrs Thomas, please? ___

6 He gets really nervous when he has to make a speech. ___

7 Can you tell me where it hurts most? ___

8 Do you know where the library is? ___

9 Is the theatre open in the mornings? ___

10 Do you sell that stuff for cleaning glass? ___

11 Excuse me. Would you be able to recommend a good bookshop here? ___

a) Yes, let's keep in touch.

b) Why doesn't he do a course to help him?

c) Yes, the library's over there.

d) Do you mean window cleaner?

e) I'm afraid I don't agree. Not everybody likes exercise.

f) I'm sorry, I can't. I don't live here.

g) Straight on, turn left. Thanks.

h) Of course. Can I ask who's calling?

i) I'm not sure. Perhaps you should phone them and check.

j) I'm sorry, there's nothing we can do at the moment. The system's faulty.

k) Here, on my right shoulder.

| | 10 |

14 Complete the conversation with ONE word in each gap.

A: Would you ¹___like___ to be famous?

B: I ²_____ know. Why?

A: I watched the news earlier. They were complaining ³_____ the paparazzi.

B: What – those people who follow celebrities around all ⁴_____ time?

A: Exactly. I think they should stop it.

B: How can ⁵_____ do that?

A: They could arrest them, and give ⁶_____ large fines. Or put them in prison!

B: Maybe, but it ⁷_____ their fault. It's the newspaper bosses ⁸_____ pay a lot of money for the photos.

A: Yes, I suppose ⁹_____ right.

B: But I agree ¹⁰_____ you. I can't stand those photos of celebrities out with their friends or children.

A: Right. If I ¹¹_____ famous, I'd hate it.

B: Me too.

| | 10 |

WRITING

15 Match the underlined words in the email to formal phrases a)–f).

> ¹Hi Mr White,
>
> ²Just a quick note about the plans for the new library in Bigsby, I think it's a ³great idea. I love books and hope that more children will start reading if there's a library in our town. ⁴Also, we'll be able to rent DVDs and audiobooks.
>
> ⁵Write back to me soon,
>
> ⁶Goodbye,
>
> William Hunt

a) Best regards ___

b) Dear _1_

c) I look forward to hearing from you ___

d) Regarding ___

e) wonderful ___

f) In addition ___

| | 5 |

16 Write an answer to the question below in 75–100 words. Include at least two positive and two negative points in your answer.

'How do you think technology will change our lives in the next twenty years?'

It seems to me that/in my opinion, … _____

_____

_____

_____

_____

_____

_____

_____

_____

_____

_____

_____

_____

| | 10 |

| Total: | 100 |

Mid-course Test A

LISTENING

1

Audioscript

A=Freddie   B=Caroline

A: Caroline! I've got some great news! I've had a promotion!

B: A promotion?!

A: Yes, I'm going to be the new European sales manager – and my salary will double. I'll get €80,000 instead of €40,000 a year!

B: Oh, Freddie, that's fantastic! We can buy a lovely house with a big garden for the children. That one we saw near Oxford the other day would be perfect!

A: Umm ... er ... sorry Caroline – but the new job's not in England. It's in Rome.

B: Rome! What?! We have to move – and live in a foreign country?!

A: Well, yes. I'm afraid we must if I'm going to take this job. The European sales office is there – it's easier to travel to other European countries from Italy ...

B: But what about the children's school? They love it there.

A: They're still very young, Caroline. Jeremy's seven and Kristen's only five. There are some great international schools in Rome – they'll love it. And the company will pay.

B: But they don't speak Italian! How will they make friends?

A: They can go to an international school where they speak English as the first language. And it'll be so easy for them to learn Italian while they're so young. They'll probably become bilingual – and speak English and Italian.

B: Yes, I suppose you're right ... But what about our parents? They'll miss us.

A: Yes, and we'll miss them too. But it only takes two hours to fly to Rome. I'm sure they'll love coming to stay with us.

B: Yes, we'll probably have visitors all the time! Rome is a wonderful city – and I've always loved Italian food. Oh, I've just remembered. What about my job?

A: Well, you didn't like it anyway, did you? And you won't have to work when we're in Rome.

B: Great!

A: So you can study Italian – and do that online computing course you've always wanted to do.

B: You're right. It's going to be fantastic. Let's tell the kids!

A: Good idea. Kirsten! Jeremy!

  2 a 3 b 4 c 5 b 6 a

2

Audioscript

A=Travel agent   B=Mr Travis

A: Good morning. Apollo Travel. Brian speaking.

B: Oh, hello. I'm calling to confirm my holiday booking.

A: Right, sir. Can I have your name, please?

B: Travis – Robert Travis.

A: Thank you, Mr Travis. I'll just get the details up on my computer. Let me see ... Yes, here it is – destination, Corfu in Greece.

B: That's right – Corfu.

A: The holiday's from the 15th to the 30th of September.

B: Yes, it's a double room in the Hotel Athens.

A: A double room – yes – with bathroom.

B: That's right. Is breakfast included?

A: Yes, it is. You can have dinner included for £50 extra each if you like?

B: No thanks. Room and breakfast is fine. We like to go out in the evening and try different restaurants.

A: I understand, sir. OK, that's confirmed then. You can pay a deposit of €200 and the rest in June – or the full amount now. You decide.

B: What was the total price again?

A: €870 for two – that's €435 each.

B: €870. OK, I'll just pay the €200 deposit now if that's all right.

A: That's fine, sir.

B: And can you tell me the flight times, please?

A: Of course. You leave from Bristol airport at 4.30 in the afternoon and arrive in Corfu at 9.15.

B: Leave Bristol at 4.30 and arrive at 10. Thank you very much.

A: You're welcome, sir. We'll send the tickets to you once you've paid the full amount.

B: Great. Thank you. Bye, then.

A: Bye, Mr Travis.

2 thirtieth (30th) 3 Yes 4 870 5 Bristol
6 four thirty (4.30)

PRONUNCIATION

3

2 lettuce 3 cricket 4 onion 5 staff
6 aunt

VOCABULARY AND GRAMMAR

4

2 painting 3 history 4 ship 5 pills
6 golf

5

2 b 3 c 4 a 5 c 6 b 7 a 8 b
9 a 10 c 11 b

6

2 musical 3 performance 4 trainer
5 consultant 6 scientist

7

2 can't stand making decisions
3 mind working under pressure
4 haven't eaten out for weeks
5 ('s) promised to phone me later
6 were having lunch when I arrived

8

2 made make, is 3 wearing wear, do
4 since, haven't 5 've seen saw, was
6 to, won't

9

2 Where did they get to know each other? f
3 Who gave her that watch? d
4 What time's he arriving tomorrow? b
5 Whose book won the Man Booker Prize in 2008? a
6 Which subject did you study when you were at university? c

10

2 last 3 passport 4 and/so 5 were
6 good 7 hours 8 was 9 be
10 hungry 11 won't

READING

11

2 c 3 b 4 b 5 a 6 c

12

2 jazz 3 7.00p.m 4 two 5 £15
6 20th

COMMUNICATION

13

2 d 3 b 4 f 5 a 6 e

14

2 known you 3 seeing her 4 getting on
5 started 6 month ago 7 can't stand
8 thinks 9 back together 10 to her
11 welcome

WRITING

15

2 I'm careful about what I eat so I don't eat junk food or eat fatty food.

3 I (also) try to eat oily fish twice a week and I (also) eat vegetables every day.

4 I do yoga and I may start playing tennis soon.

16 (sample answer)

I'll never forget the first time I went on holiday with three of my friends. We went camping because we didn't have much money. We were all in the same class at school and we were seventeen. We loved surfing so we went to Cornwall because the beaches there are famous for it. It was August and the weather was fantastic. We stayed there for ten days and it didn't rain once. We made lots of new friends and had great parties on the beach at night. I'll always remember it because I met Sara there. Now she's my wife. (100 words)

Mid-course Test B

LISTENING

1
Audioscript
See test A.
2 b 3 a 4 c 5 a 6 b

2
Audioscript
See test A.
2 (fifteenth) 15th 3 Athens 4 No
5 200 6 (nine fifteen) 9.15

PRONUNCIATION

3
2 lettuce 3 cricket 4 onion 5 staff
6 aunt

VOCABULARY AND GRAMMAR

4
2 headache 3 tennis 4 artist
5 biology 6 coach

5
2 a 3 b 4 a 5 b 6 b 7 b 8 c
9 a 10 c 11 b

6
2 musical 3 consultant 4 assistant
5 performance 6 trainer

7
2 has married again but they don't like their new stepmother
3 I can't stand working in an office
4 (has) promised to take me out to dinner
5 mind meeting new people
6 haven't been to the theatre since October

8
2 you've you, was
3 spend have/get, won't
4 made make, is 5 wearing wear, do
6 the, haven't

9
2 Whose book won the Orange Prize in 2008? f
3 Which subject are you going to study at university next year? a
4 Where did they get to know each other? d
5 Who bought him that car? b
6 What time are we leaving tomorrow? e

10
2 missed 3 her 4 new 5 having 6 a
7 usually 8 time 9 the 10 take/pack
11 sitting

READING

11
2 c 3 b 4 b 5 c 6 b

12
2 Magic Sounds 3 8.00p.m. 4 four
5 £12 6 (eleventh) 11th

COMMUNICATION

13
2 a 3 e 4 f 5 b 6 d

14
2 since 3 'm not 4 were getting
5 started arguing 6 stand it
7 I understand 8 suppose so 9 to get
10 should I 11 important than

WRITING

15
2 I do yoga and I'm also thinking of playing tennis.
3 I'm careful about what I eat so I don't eat junk food or fatty food.
4 I try to eat oily fish twice a week and I eat vegetables every day.

16
See sample answer in Test A.

End of Course Test A

LISTENING

1
Audioscript

1
A: Did you see the news, Mary?
B: No I didn't, Agnes. Why?
A: It was about that man who robbed an old lady in our street. He was only given three months' community service!
B: What? He should go to prison.
A: Yes, for ten years!
B: Well, I'm not sure about that ... but five years at least.

2
A: Have you seen the new tennis teacher at the club?
B: Yes, he looks very nice.
A: Do you know where he's from? He could be Italian or Spanish with that lovely dark hair.
B: Yes, but his name's Stuart McDonald. That's not an Italian or Spanish name, is it?
A: No, he must be from Scotland!

3
A: Would you like me to carry your bag, gran? It looks a bit heavy.
B: Yes, it is a bit. Thank you very much.
A: Oh, it is heavy, isn't it? What have you got in it? Tins of food? Bottles of milk?
B: No, I've just been to the bookshop in town. They're having a sale and all the books are reduced.
A: Really? How much are they selling them for?
B: The ones I bought were reduced from £7.99 to £3.50. So I bought six!
A: I think I'll go there later and buy some myself!

4
A: Excuse me. Do you have one of these green sweaters in a smaller size?
B: I think so. Just a moment ...Yes, here you are. I've got a medium and a small.
A: Oh, great. I think the medium will fit.
B: Would you like to try it on? The fitting room's over there.
A: Oh no, it's not for me.
B: Is it for your father?
A: No, it's for my boyfriend – for his birthday. I'll take the medium, please. How much is it?

5
A: Excuse me. Is this the right way to the Globe Theatre?
A: Not really, no. Go back down this road and turn right into Prince Road.
A: Turn right?
A: Yes. Keep going until you get to Queen Street. Turn left into Queen Street and you'll see the theatre on the right.
A: Queen Street, turn left, on the right. That's very kind of you, thank you.
A: You're welcome.

6
A: Why do I feel so tired all the time, Doctor?
B: How long have you felt like this?
A: Well, since I started my new job, I suppose.
B: Do you sit in an office all day?
A: Yes, I do actually – in front of a computer!
B: That must be it then. Why don't you go for a walk at lunchtime, get some fresh air?
A: That's a good idea – I think I'll do that. Thank you, doctor.

2 b 3 c 4 b 5 a 6 c

2
Audioscript

1

A=Hotel receptionist B=Major Brown

A: Good morning. Hotel reception. Stewart speaking.
B: Good morning. This is Major Brown, room 308.
A: Hello, Major. How can I help you?
B: I'm afraid I have a complaint.
A: What's the problem, Major Barnes?
B: I ordered a full English breakfast in my room this morning, with English tea.
A: Was it late, sir?
B: No, no, it was on time. But the eggs were cold and the sausages were cooked too much – they were almost black. I could hardly cut them!
A: I'm really sorry about this, sir. We have a new breakfast chef – that might be the reason. Shall I send up another breakfast?

B: No, no. That won't be necessary. But please make sure it doesn't happen tomorrow.

A: Of course, Major. I'll go and talk to the chef immediately. Don't worry, it won't happen again.

B: I hope not. This is totally unacceptable...

2

A=Hotel receptionist   B=Mrs Peters

A: Good...

B: Good morning. This is Mrs Julia Peters, room 309. I'd like to speak to the manager, please – at once!

A: Ah, good morning, Mrs Peters. This is Stuart in reception. I'm sorry but the manager isn't here at the moment. Can I help?

B: I hope so! I was woken up at 7 o'clock this morning by a terrible noise from room 308.

A: A noise, madam? Was the TV too loud?

B: Well, I thought that it must be the TV – but then I went to the bathroom and I could hear it more clearly. I realised it was a man having a bath next door – and singing at the top of his voice. The worst part was that he couldn't sing at all – it was ghastly!

A: I'm sorry … [interrupted]

B: You really must do something about it – or I'll have to move to another hotel!

A: Don't worry, Mrs Peters. I'll speak to the manager as soon as he comes back. I'm sure he'll look into it immediately.

B: I'd like to talk to him myself … when is he expected back?

2 three-oh-eight (308)   3 cold
4 sausages 5 chef 6 Julia
7 three-oh-nine (309)
8 three-oh-eight (308)   9 sings   10 bath
11 manager

PRONUNCIATION

3

2 business (Oo), sculpture (Oo)
3 confused (oO), souvenirs (ooO)
4 dictionary (Ooo), recommend (ooO)
5 technology (oOoo), celebrity (oOoo)
6 electrician (ooOo), performance (oOo)

VOCABULARY AND GRAMMAR

4

2 racket 3 ocean 4 jogging 5 whale
6 peas 7 fax 8 spam 9 insect
10 suitcase 11 staff

5

2 painkillers 3 designer 4 memorise
5 decision 6 reservation

6

2 on 3 up 4 out 5 with 6 in

7

2 to take 3 were having 4 is doing
5 'll earn 6 haven't gone 7 to play
8 were taken 9 to make 10 worked
11 don't make

8

2 d 3 f 4 a 5 e 6 b

9

2 c 3 a 4 b 5 c 6 a 7 b 8 a
9 b 10 a 11 c

10

2 that/which 3 on 4 the 5 to
6 want 7 off 8 be 9 not 10 an
11 most

READING

11

2 b 3 a 4 c 5 c 6 a

12

2 Saturday 3 10.00a.m. 4 two 5 £25
6 boat

COMMUNICATION

13

2 g 3 b 4 j 5 d 6 h 7 e 8 k
9 c 10 i 11 f

14

2 know 3 were 4 who/that 5 think
6 in 7 the 8 money 9 right
10 can't 11 'd/would

WRITING

15

2 e 3 f 4 a 5 d 6 b

16 (sample answer)

In my opinion, technology will continue to bring both positive and negative changes to our lives. Most people will be connected to the Internet at home so more of them will be able to work from home. They won't have to travel to their offices every day. This will reduce the amount of traffic on the roads, which will reduce pollution. On the negative side, life will also get faster and people will get even more stressed. I hope that we'll find a way of dealing with this stress and be able to live with technology in a healthier way.

End of Course Test B

LISTENING

1

Audioscript

See test A.

2 c 3 a 4 b 5 b 6 a

2

Audioscript

See test A.

2 three-oh-eight (308) 3 eggs 4 cooked
5 Talk 6 Peters 7 three-oh-nine (309)
8 man 9 loudly 10 to 11 manager

3

2 business (Oo), sculpture (Oo)
3 confused (oO), souvenirs (ooO)
4 dictionary (Ooo), recommend (ooO)
5 technology (oOoo), celebrity (oOoo)
6 electrician (ooOo), performance (oOo)

VOCABULARY AND GRAMMAR

4

2 mango 3 insects 4 racket 5 science
6 chicken 7 borrow 8 drama 9 earn
10 wild 11 map

5

2 receptionist 3 popularity 4 painkillers
5 reservation 6 decision

6

2 with 3 to 4 on 5 with 6 in

7

2 were taken 3 worked 4 make
5 to take 6 'll get 7 haven't gone
8 to be 9 were having 10 is doing
11 to make

8

2 f 3 e 4 b 5 c 6 a

9

2 c 3 b 4 c 5 a 6 a 7 b 8 b
9 a 10 c 11 a

10

2 can 3 family 4 aren't 5 have 6 to
7 sign 8 don't 9 the 10 but 11 the

READING

11

2 c 3 b 4 c 5 a 6 b

12

2 Sunday 3 10.00a.m. 4 two 5 £22
6 tour

COMMUNICATION

13

2 e 3 g 4 j 5 h 6 b 7 k 8 c
9 i 10 d 11 f

14

2 don't 3 about 4 the 5 they
6 them 7 isn't 8 who/that 9 you're
10 with 11 was/were

WRITING

15

2 d 3 e 4 f 5 c 6 a

16

See sample answer in Test A.

Pearson Education Limited
Edinburgh Gate
Harlow
Essex CM20 2JE
England
and Associated Companies throughout the world.

www.pearsonelt.com

First published 2011
Fifth impression 2013

ISBN: 978-1-4082-1-6804

Set in Gill Sans Book 9.75/11.5

Printed in Malaysia, CTP-PJB

Illustrated by Eric Smith

All other images © Pearson Education